B   Donaldson, Frances
WODE
HOUSE P. G. Wodehouse

DATE			

3404

© THE BAKER & TAYLOR CO.

Also by Frances Donaldson

FREDDIE LONSDALE

THE MARCONI SCANDAL

EVELYN WAUGH:
PORTRAIT OF A COUNTRY NEIGHBOUR

EDWARD VIII

P. G. Wodehouse

A BIOGRAPHY

P. G. Wodehouse

A BIOGRAPHY

by

Frances Donaldson

ALFRED A. KNOPF

New York   1982

THIS IS A BORZOI BOOK
PUBLISHED BY ALFRED A. KNOPF, INC.

Library of Congress Cataloging in Publication Data

Donaldson, Frances Lonsdale, Lady.
P. G. Wodehouse, a biography.

"The works of P. G. Wodehouse": p.
Includes bibliographical references and index.
1. Wodehouse, P. G. (Pelham Grenville), 1881–1975.
2. Authors, English—20th century—Biography.
I. Title.
PR6045.053Z63   823'.912   81-48111
ISBN 0-394-50580-8   AACR2

Manufactured in the United States of America
First Edition

To inhabit the same world as Mr. Wodehouse is a high privilege; to inhabit the same volume, even as a doorkeeper, is perilous.

Ogden Nash

Contents

PART III

AMERICA

APPENDICES

Illustrations

Following page 140

Preface

In a little-known introduction to a book by Charles Graves—so little known indeed that I hope by the mere mention of it to confound the pundits from the start—P. G. Wodehouse wrote: "It is always best for an author who writes an introduction to another author's book to disarm the critics by explaining his qualifications to do so." And he added: "Mine, in the present case, are unexceptionable."[1] Reading this, I wished that the question of my own qualifications for the more presumptuous task I am about to undertake could be so felicitously disposed of.

P. G. Wodehouse was unique in the history of literature. He lived to the age of ninety-three and throughout his adult life worked almost every day that he was not physically prevented. No one knows the exact extent of his output, because he wrote a good deal when young under other people's names or noms de plume, but he appears to have written ninety-six books, written or collaborated in the writing of sixteen plays, written the lyrics, or some of the lyrics, of twenty-eight musical plays, while collaborating in the books of eighteen of these. Herbert Warren Wind estimated that he wrote more than three hundred short stories (many of which are in the twenty collections counted in the number of books given above), much humorous verse, and the scenarios for half a dozen films.[2] Again, nobody knows how many copies of his books have been sold, although the figure runs into millions, and he has consistently been translated into other languages. At the present day, new hardback editions continually appear, and Penguin attempts to keep all the more important titles in paperback. No writer with a greater output, no more popular writer, ever lived. One may quote Alistair Cooke, who spoke of "Psmith and Jeeves and Lord Emsworth and Bertie Wooster, who don't exist anymore except in the puzzled and fascinated imaginations of eighty or ninety nations."[3]

Yet this is only one side of it, for Wodehouse has become a national cult. There may be nothing remarkable about this, because from time to time this happens to other people, not all of them worthy, many quickly forgotten. What is unique about Wodehouse in the world of popular art is the ever-increasing strength of the admiration accorded him, and the places where his devotees are to be found. They recognize each other by casual quotations in the junior and senior common rooms of our most eminent universities, in the Cabinet offices, and the offices of the leader writers of our national newspapers, in the homes of our most distinguished poets, playwrights, novelists, and literary critics, and at Clarence House. Wodehouse is an idol in intellectual society as well as a household word.

However, on turning once more to Wodehouse's introduction to Charles Graves's book to see what qualifications so modest a man thought unexceptionable, I discovered that he merely knew Charles Graves, his brother, and his father. By this criterion I too could pass the test, since I first met the Wodehouses—P. G., who was called Plum or Plummie, his wife, Ethel, and his daughter, Leonora—when I was about fourteen, and Leonora became one of my closest friends. (This relationship should be clarified from the start. Leonora was not Wodehouse's daughter; in fact, she was nine years old when he first met her. But she was his adopted daughter as well as his stepdaughter, and she took the name Wodehouse. Her children, Edward Cazalet and his sister, Sheran [now Hornby], are not therefore related by blood to Plum, but they are Ethel Wodehouse's grandchildren, and it is as much for the spirit of the thing as for convenience that they are spoken of here, as they are everywhere else, as his grandchildren too.)

In 1921, when we first met the Wodehouses, my parents were disturbed by the precocity of my two sisters and myself and had decided to send us to boarding school. Taking the (extremely bad) advice of the Wodehouses, they sent us to the Old Palace at Bromley, where Leonora also passed the years during which she should have been educated. Her future husband, Peter Cazalet, bore in his youth the same sort of relationship to my husband, Jack Donaldson, since they messed together at Eton. I first met Jack in the Cazalets' house, and we built our own house on Peter's land. But before this, Plummie and Jack had met, and they used to play golf together every Monday at Addington (a golf club near Croydon). Jack visited the Wodehouses at Le Touquet just before they were captured by the Germans in 1941, and he went to see them in Paris in 1944, soon after it was liberated.

I do not suggest that these things by themselves would constitute qualifications to write about one of the simplest yet most idiosyncratic writers who ever graced the literary scene, were it not for the fact that they led directly to the generosity of Edward Cazalet in making available to me many private papers—including the diary Wodehouse kept while interned in camp in Germany, and his letters to his wife and other members of his family—while his encouragement has persuaded other people to do the same.

There are other reasons for attempting a new biography. In *Wodehouse at Work* and in many essays, Richard Usborne has written a definitive analysis of the whole of Wodehouse's fiction, a feat of scholarship I could never attempt. Other writers (Geoffrey Jaggard and R. B. D. French, for example) have examined particular aspects of Wodehouse's work, while in magazines and newspaper articles and in a distinguished volume called *Homage to P. G. Wodehouse* some of our most eminent writers have paid tribute to him.

However, the only full-length biography—by David Jasen—was written while Wodehouse was still alive, and the author did not have access to many of the most important papers. Jasen does not, and in the circumstances probably could not, attempt any very serious study of Wodehouse's work or of the sensitive areas of his life. Nevertheless, one cannot record too soon the debt which everyone interested in Wodehouse owes to David Jasen. With incredible persistence and patience, he elicited from Wodehouse all the main facts of his childhood and his career, and he has undertaken the colossal task of cataloguing, as far as possible, the whole of the Wodehouse oeuvre—plays, musical comedies, and films as well as novels and collections of short stories. Both Jasen's biography and his bibliography will have permanence as an archive for people interested in Wodehouse, and it is not too much to say that without them it would hardly have been possible for any other biography to have been written. I take the earliest opportunity of acknowledging my debt to him.

I believe, however, that with the passing of the years there is room for a more complete portrayal of the man, a more serious estimate of his work.

But the reason which weighs heaviest with me is the need to establish the truth of the old, sad episode of his broadcasts from Germany during the war. When Wodehouse was first free to do so, he wished to tell it himself, and for several years he worked anxiously at different versions for publication (that is, versions for different media), while he was concerned at that time that the text of the broadcasts should be known. He was dissuaded from publication not merely by family and friends, but by his legal advisers and publishers. The whole of this advice was based not on the belief that his story would not bear telling, but on "the less said the better," or the idea that time should be given for the public hostility, so violently whipped up, to die down.

Looking back, one can see that this advice was probably mistaken. Wodehouse did not wittingly betray his country; he spoke no word of propaganda, he did no deal. But he did commit a technical offence of a kind a certain number of people have found difficult to understand. When he fully realized this—and it took him some years to do so—his self-disgust made him determine never to publish anything on the subject. He wished to hear no more about it. In 1951 *Encounter* published the text of the broadcasts, but even then, for reasons which I shall explain, in a version that was not identical with the originals. Otherwise he would allow no word in excuse or explanation. In a radio interview at the end of his life, referring to the fact that it was at first believed he had broadcast propaganda for the Germans, he said: "I don't think you'd ever get rid of a thing like that. If people get an idea like that in their heads, I don't think they'd ever let go."

In fact, opinion has divided into two extremes, and it is usual to believe either that he was innocent of any offence and badly treated by his country or that he wittingly, however trivially, betrayed her. As long ago as 1961, Evelyn Waugh, in a broadcast now part of the Wodehouse canon, publicly asked his forgiveness for everyone who had ever spoken ill of him. Yet others continued to regard him as a traitor. On 19 January 1978 Miss Mary Greaves, who, severely disabled by polio in childhood, had nevertheless made a successful career as a civil servant, discussed with Sue MacGregor in a BBC radio interview her reasons for returning the OBE.

> I was really rather ashamed of it because I think the honours system has got a little out of hand in this country. I dared not refuse it, because I didn't know who'd recommended it, and I didn't want to hurt their feelings. It was meant well. It was great fun going to the Palace, of course, and getting it. I loved that, but then I returned it to the Prime Minister because I felt very, very strongly that Wodehouse shouldn't have been given a knighthood as he had collaborated with the Nazis. It wasn't a case of just an enemy, but the Nazis to me . . . was something one really couldn't countenance and I didn't wish Mr. Wodehouse any harm, but I felt it was very inappropriate to give him an honour.

Wodehouse made a very stupid mistake, but one that surprised no one who knew him well. He was not a very complex character, but he was a very peculiar one, and only those who knew him well enough to recognize and respect his peculiarities can understand (if not entirely explain) the reasons for this mistake. Here, after all, I have a special qualification, and it is because of it that Edward Cazalet has approved of the suggestion that I should write a biography and has put so many previously unpublished letters at my disposal.

For many years the only available account of these years was a letter Wodehouse himself wrote to the Dulwich College magazine, the *Alleynian*, in answer to criticism of his conduct; but after his death a typescript was found entitled "Now That I've Turned Both Cheeks," which seems never to have been published and which is much fuller. The story he told in both documents was a fairly simple one, and the more important points in it have been confirmed by Werner Plack, who was attached to the German Foreign Office at that time and whose job was to look after the American press and radio correspondents in Berlin. Herr Plack was in charge of the Wodehouses while they were in Germany, and he was responsible for the broadcasts.

In 1980 a far more important source of information was released. The Wodehouses were living in Paris at the time of the liberation in 1944, and at the request of the Home Office they were interrogated by Major Cussen of M.I.5 SHAEF, who also interrogated some other witnesses and who wrote the report (known as the Cussen Report) on which all official opinions and actions were based. On several occasions in the past attempts were made to persuade the Home Office to release this report, but the reply was invariably that, because it was in the files of "Security," in a category of document closed for public inspection by an order under section 5(1) of the Public Records Act of 1958, no one but the Home Secretary of the day (and presumably the Prime Minister) would be allowed to see it before a hundred years had passed. Then in June 1980 it was unexpectedly released.

In his report Major Cussen (later His Honour Judge Cussen) constantly speaks of an intention to interview the Germans concerned with the Wodehouses, but although it is known that he did later see Werner Plack, he left no report of this interrogation. The chief witness, therefore, in this document, as in both the others, is Wodehouse himself, the difference being that before he was interrogated by Cussen he was cautioned that, although he was not obliged to say anything, what he did say would be written down and might be given in evidence.

Wodehouse's three accounts are substantially the same, and, while the Cussen Report is more explicit on some points, it is less so on others. All three are therefore quoted in my account, the source of the quotations being indicated in footnotes. Where the accounts differ, the Cussen Report will, with or without explanation, be preferred to the others.

Hardly less than to Edward Cazalet, I am indebted to Richard Usborne. The foremost authority on Wodehouse's work, Mr. Usborne has for many years also had an interest in his life. I think he never intended to write a biography, but he has the insatiable curiosity of the scholar, and he collected material partly for its own sake, partly for a book of a different kind. He became particularly well informed on the whole question of the German broadcasts, and it was only when he generously agreed to make his collection available to me that I finally decided to write this book. My debt to him in the chapters about the broadcasts—11, 12, and 13—is obvious, and indeed these chapters could not have been written without his original research. Starting when he was writing his book *Wodehouse at Work*, as long ago as 1958, he sought out and interviewed people who have since died, and he assembled most of the facts which make it possible to tell the story in so much detail. He must not be held responsible for anything I say. Indeed, it will be seen that I sometimes disagree with him, so it is not to be expected that he will always agree with me. The area of my disagreement is very small, however, smaller than it may appear to the reader of this book, where I cannot continually record all the points Mr. Usborne has illuminated for me.

Next I would like to thank George Rylands, who has been enormously helpful to me. He and I spent much time on holiday in Corfu discussing the question of rhythm in style, and later he read the manuscript of the book and was kind enough to give me his criticisms. Some of his views appear with acknowledgement in the text.

Wodehouse's sister-in-law, Nella (Mrs. Armine) Wodehouse, and her son made many invaluable family papers available to me and gave me permission to use the notes Edward Cazalet made of his conversations with them.

Mary Ryde and Anne Yorke did me an invaluable kindness in allowing me to see all Wodehouse's letters to their father, Denis Mackail, as well as Ethel Wodehouse's account of the years 1939 to 1945 and Leonora Wodehouse's letter to Denis Mackail at the time of the German broadcasts. I sometimes wonder how I would have written the book without these letters.

James Heineman has been extraordinarily kind in letting me make use of the letters in his collection, which include all Wodehouse's letters to Guy Bolton and the files of his correspondence with his American publishers, Simon & Schuster, as well as the Wodehouse–von Bodenhausen papers quoted in Chapter 13. He also gave me much help in tracing letters in American universities.

Barry Phelps gave much help in collecting a set of Wodehouse's books and lent me his unique collection of press cuttings and other papers about him.

I must most particularly thank Patrick Wilkinson, Public Orator of the University of Cambridge from 1958 to 1974, for the learned and elegant translation of the speeches made by the Public Orator and Vice-Chancellor of Oxford University when Wodehouse received the degree of honorary Doctor of Letters, and for sending me the story of A. E. Housman. Trevor Daintith drew my attention to the very amusing account of Monk Eastman, and Aidan Evans generously allowed me to see his work on Wodehouse's similarities to W. S. Gilbert. Thanks also to Sir Victor Pritchett for the letter quoted on page 263.

Sir Robert Birley very kindly gave me permission to publish certain papers relating to the Gutenberg Bible; Professor Barbara Bowen of Illinois University sent me her essay "Rabelais and P. G. Wodehouse"; and John Douglas Forbes sent me letters and book reviews. Ormonde de Kay, Jr., sent me the quotation from Ogden Nash which appears as an epigraph. Alex Faulkner and Charles and Oliver Bovill have all allowed me to talk to them and have given me information and papers, and a letter from F. E. Puxon is quoted in the text. Mrs. Alistair MacLeod gave me invaluable information about her uncle Baldwin King-Hall, at whose school at Emsworth Wodehouse stayed as a young man, and she is also quoted in the text, while Mrs. Le Geyt wrote to me about Ethel Wodehouse's early life and Hugo Irwin about Wodehouse, his wife, and his daughter. Mrs. Grillo also gave me letters and much information. Peter Schwed and Scott Meredith gave me advice and permission to quote from their letters.

Last, but only because their contributions came last in time, I have to thank Robert Connor and Ralph Champion. The former is the son of William Connor, the author of the "Cassandra" column in the *Daily Mirror* and of the famous BBC broadcast following Wodehouse's own broadcasts from Berlin. Mr. Connor not merely agreed to my quoting the whole of the text of this broadcast, but gave me, with permission to use it, his father's correspondence with Duff Cooper, the then Minister of Information, as also his later correspondence with Wodehouse himself. He further introduced me to Mr. Champion, whom I have to thank for an account of the luncheon in New York at which William Connor and Wodehouse met. These things throw much light on what is the strangest event in Wodehouse's whole career.

In the same context, I am most grateful to Viscount Norwich for generously giving me permission to use his father's letters to "Cassandra."

I have had letters from so many people who knew or corresponded with Wodehouse that it is impossible to thank them individually here, although I wish to express my gratitude to all of them. Herbert Studdis, Anthony Powell, Richard Ingrams, Anthony Lejeune, and Michael Holroyd sent me letters of particular interest.

The titles, authors, and publishers of books and articles quoted will be found in the Notes section at the end of the book, as will the details of Wodehouse's letters previously published in *Performing Flea*. The originals of the unpublished letters to William Townend disappeared for some years, but before that Townend lent them to Richard Usborne, who took copies of parts of them and to whom I am indebted for allowing me to quote them. In 1981 the originals came to light once more when Mr. Grimsdick gave them to Dulwich College. Unfortunately, my book had reached proof stage by then, and although I made an attempt to find and check all the letters quoted, I failed in the case of the letter on page 112, which may therefore have minor mistakes. The letter quoted in the first paragraph on page 255 from Wodehouse to Marie Meloney is from the Paul R. Reynolds Papers, Rare Book and Manuscript Library, Columbia University, and I am grateful to Columbia Libraries for permission to use it. The recipient of all other letters and the approximate date on which they were written will be obvious from the text.

I would also like to thank Peter Schwed for permission to quote his description of his first meeting with Wodehouse; Dulwich College for allowing me to do research in their library; the BBC Written Archives at Caversham for the information about the BBC on pages 220–21; and Syndication International for permission to quote from the "Cassandra" article in the *Daily Mirror* of 28 June 1941.

Finally, I have to thank Mrs. Crisp for typing and retyping the manuscript and for devising methods of keeping it in some order.

P. G. Wodehouse

A BIOGRAPHY

INTRODUCTION

The Master

Hilaire Belloc is usually given the credit for being the first person to draw attention to the excellencies of P. G. Wodehouse's fiction, and he did it in extreme terms. In a broadcast to America in the middle thirties he said that Wodehouse was "the best living writer of English," and at "the head of my profession." Belloc's habit was to express his opinions with provocative strength, but his example has been followed by almost everyone who has praised Wodehouse, not merely in critical but also in academic circles, particularly at Oxford. He has been compared to Swift, to Rabelais, to the Restoration dramatists, even to Shakespeare, and, among his contemporaries, to Max Beerbohm.

The extravagance of the praise given to Wodehouse has tended to baffle the general reader. In 1939 Belloc wrote in an introduction to *Week-end Wodehouse* that he had received many letters from people who, puzzled by what he had said in his broadcast, wished to know exactly what he meant; and, in spite of all that has been written since, this bewilderment is still widely felt. Occasionally it provokes a small rebellion. Someone sitting next to me at dinner put it in the following way: He said that he had been at Oxford as an undergraduate at the time when that university made Wodehouse a Doctor of Letters, and he regarded the whole thing as simply a game played by the dons. "They enjoyed reading Wodehouse," he said, "and it allowed them to do so without loss of face." I put this point of view to two distinguished Oxford dons of my acquaintance. "It is true that it is half affectation," the first replied, adding on reflection, "but only half." The second, whom I already knew to be an admirer of Wodehouse, agreed to some extent with this opinion and said that knowledge and appreciation of Wodehouse's novels had the further advantage of allowing the dons to appear human in conversation with undergraduates. But neither had any doubt that their attitude, if affected, was securely based.*

*As an illustration of this, I quote from a letter I received from Patrick Wilkinson: "Sir Frank Adcock used to tell how once at a Faculty Board meeting here he quoted anonymously

3

One must therefore ask what it is about Wodehouse, as opposed to any other writer, that allows the dons to put on these airs. The answer has been most neatly put by Bernard Levin, who wrote: "It is difficult to find comparisons which do not jar, because his matter was so utterly unlike that of his true peers of manner, and none of those whose matter was recognizably similar to his could write like him."[1]

In all modesty, the general reader believes himself to be a judge of fine writing, while he would not set up to judge painting or musical composition. And there is often justice on his side. It is not derogatory to Henry James to say that it must be apparent to everyone that he wrote well, and yet the qualities that have been praised in Wodehouse's work are in many respects the opposite of those we most admire in James. Indeed, it may be that the simplicity of Wodehouse's style and the natural felicity of his choice of words and phrases—which so delight his profession—are the very qualities which lull the reader who reads for pleasure into a mood where he takes it all for granted.

Wodehouse did not develop in the way many writers do, and his books can be divided into two periods only—that of the school stories and that of the rest. Evelyn Waugh has told us that it is possible to mark precisely the transition from one period to the other:

> One can date exactly the first moment when he was touched by the sacred flame. It occurs half-way through *Mike*, written in 1910. Collectors prize as bibliographical rarities such early works as *William Tell Told Again* and *Swoop*, but it is impossible to discern in them any promise of what was to come. Then in Chapter XXXI of *Mike*, which was then being serialised in the *Captain*, and had run an easy course of agreeable, conventional schoolboy fiction, Psmith appears and the light is kindled which has burned with growing brilliance for half a century.[2]

It is convenient to mark the beginning of the great period with the entry of Psmith; but John Hayward, writing in 1941, hit upon the truth when he said that there was no question of Wodehouse going from strength to strength; on the contrary, "he maintained a remarkably uniform steady level of achievement, his most distinguished work appearing concurrently with sound but undistinguished work."[3] Once he had found his true form, Wodehouse never changed; and, except perhaps in a geographical sense, one cannot relate different aspects of his work to different periods of his life.

---

from Wodehouse. A. E. Housman passed him a note: 'Will you please tell me the name of the man you were quoting?' And the notes continued: 'P. G. Wodehouse.' 'Will you please lend me something by him?' A book was sent and returned next day with a note, 'Will you please lend me another?'; and so it went on."

To a very exceptional extent, Wodehouse's life was his work. As a young man he wrote almost every hour of every day, often for weeks at a time, and for the last thirty years of his life he wrote every morning and walked every afternoon, either alone or with Guy Bolton (who lived near him), and thought or talked about his work.* The extent of his output must surely be unsurpassed in the history of literature. In his middle years the demands of his profession and those of his wife (Ethel Wodehouse was very gregarious and a natural party giver), as well, I think, as some belief in the necessity to appear more as other men, forced him to take account of the rest of the world. But he never cared for it. In his old age he said to Alistair Cooke: "You know, I've always been a recluse. I got it all from the newspapers."⁴ And in a broadcast interview: "I haven't any violent feelings about anything. I just love writing. What really makes me happy is to get a really good plot for a novel and then sit back and write it." When asked by someone if he was lonely, he replied that he had his wife and Guy Bolton. "You only need one friend."

His fear of contact with the human race was so great that he could not overcome it, and one cannot establish too early that he was really a freak in this respect. Sitting in a room in New York with Guy Bolton on an occasion when his wife, Ethel, was going out to look for a flat, he called to her: "Get one on the ground floor." "Why?" she asked, and he replied: "I never know what to say to the lift boy." The world in which he felt at home was the world he created, and but for an intense sweetness of disposition, which made him beloved by all who knew him, he might have seemed a dull dog. His career, with the exception of one sensational period and a few years working in the theatre, was so entirely without incident that unless one approaches it through his work, one cannot reach any level of involvement. By a reversal of the natural order, it is the man who throws light on the child, and the sparse facts available to us about his early life can be illumined only by knowledge of what he became.

In his introduction to *Week-end Wodehouse*, Hilaire Belloc replied to those people who had been puzzled by the remarks he had made in his broadcast, and in this short essay he said so nearly all there is to be said about Wodehouse that, except by expansion and illustration, he left very little for anyone else to say. Like many other writers, he laid the greatest emphasis on the excellence of Wodehouse's prose:

> The end of writing is the production in the reader's mind of a certain image and a certain emotion. And the means towards that end are the use

---

*Guy Bolton, the playwright, died in 1979 at the age of ninety-five; immensely successful in the early part of the century, he is best known for the musical comedies in which he collaborated with Wodehouse and Jerome Kern.

---

of words in any particular language; and the complete use of that medium is the choosing of the right words and the putting of them into the right order. It is *this* which Mr. Wodehouse does better, in the English language, than anyone else alive; or at any rate than anyone else whom I have read for many years past.

And he also said:

It is a test of power in this craft of writing that its object shall be obtained by some method which the reader cannot directly perceive. . . . In all the various departments of his skill Mr. Wodehouse is unique for simplicity and exactitude, which is as much as to say that he is unique for an avoidance of all frills. He gets the full effect, bang.

Every writer about Wodehouse has his favourite passage and wishes to press on his readers illustrations of some point. Here is a passage in illustration of what Belloc has said there. Bingo Little, forever in love, is in love again:

"You'd better come along and meet her at lunch," he said, looking at his watch.

"A ripe suggestion," I said. "Where are you meeting her? At the Ritz?"

"Near the Ritz."

He was geographically accurate. About fifty yards east of the Ritz there is one of those blighted tea-and-bun shops you see dotted about all over London, and into this, if you'll believe me, young Bingo dived like a homing rabbit; and before I had time to say a word we were wedged in at a table, on the brink of a silent pool of coffee left there by an early luncher. (*The Inimitable Jeeves*, Chapter 3)

If we had never met these two young men before, we should know almost all there is to know about them, and also of the girl who is about to enter the scene. Then there is the magic word *silent*. Wodehouse has been praised (by Belloc) for his sparing use of adjectives and adverbs, but when he does use them they are pivotal. Here Bertie Wooster is speaking to his Aunt Dahlia: "I could see that she was looking for something to break as a relief to her surging emotions—what Jeeves would have called a palliative— and courteously drew her attention to a terra-cotta figure of the Infant Samuel at Prayer." (*The Code of the Woosters*, Chapter 5)

Prose may be simple merely because it is impoverished, but Wodehouse had the most flexible, fresh, and imaginative style. He sometimes wrote colloquially, usually in short sentences, often for pages at a time in dialogue, but he was not in the least afraid of the long sentence which depends on balance, on what Bernard Levin has called "firm, delicate, and unmistakeable rhythmic form."[5] The balance of a sentence determines whether or not it is easy to read aloud. A reader who is in firm control of a tendency to laugh too soon will find Wodehouse easy to read aloud. Here is an example.

> In his bearing, as he hurried along the path that skirted the kitchen garden—in the oily smirk beneath his repellent moustache, in the jaunty tilt of his snub nose, even in the terraced sweep of the brilliantine swamps of his corrugated hair—there was the look of a man who is congratulating himself on a neat bit of work. Brains, reflected Percy Pilbeam—that was what you needed in this life. Brains and the ability to seize your opportunity when it was offered to you. (*Heavy Weather*, Chapter 12)

In that passage there is also a good example of what Belloc called parallelism. (I have already recorded that when I asked Evelyn Waugh why he so much admired Wodehouse, he replied: "One has to regard a man as a Master who can produce on average three uniquely brilliant and entirely original similes to every page."[6] Here one is in a realm where everyone has his own favourites, and one can either take a short cut by reading one of the devotees—for example, Richard Usborne or one of the writers contributing to *Homage to Wodehouse*—or one can read with attention any of the works of the Master himself. Belloc gives "quaking like a jelly in a high wind," and of a lady's laugh, "it was like cavalry over a tin bridge," while Evelyn Waugh characteristically chose "the acrid smell of burnt poetry." I am very fond of the whole of the following passage (about a golfer):

> The lunches of fifty-seven years had caused his chest to slip down into the mezzanine floor, but he was still a powerful man, and had in his youth been a hammer-thrower of some repute. He differed from his colleagues . . . in that, while they were content to peck cautiously at the ball, he never spared himself in his efforts to do it a violent injury. (*The Heart of a Goof*, "Chester Forgets Himself")

At the risk of being struck by lightning, I must nevertheless confess that it is not in the use of direct analogy that I find Wodehouse supreme. His images are usually external, and I can think of many other writers who, with no less imagination, go more to the heart of the matter. Rather it is in the totally unexpected image, the odd metaphorical word, the use by association of a word which has not the meaning it conveys, that he so excels. What could tell us more about Bertie Wooster than "the tall thin one with a face like a motor mascot"? Yet what is a motor mascot? (This is hotly followed by the remarks about Lord Bittlesham: "What has he ever done except eat four square meals a day. If you opened that man now you would find enough lunch to support ten working-class families for a week." [*The Inimitable Jeeves*, Chapter 11]). Wodehouse has a language of his own, and he uses it as a poet does to convey meaning as much by sound as by sense. In the following passage which illustrates this quality, Archie, for reasons which will not need explanation to any regular reader of Wodehouse, is in a New York apartment awaiting the arrival of his host, and dressed in a lemon-coloured bathing suit. Becoming impatient, he fidgets out onto the passage in a useless attempt to find out what has happened. Then he turns to re-enter the flat.

> His progress was stayed by a solid, forbidding slab of oak. Somehow or other, since he had left the room, the door had managed to get itself shut.
>
> "Oh, dash it!" said Archie.
>
> The mildness of the expletive was proof that the full horror of the situation had not immediately come home to him. His mind in the first few moments was occupied with the problem of how the door had got that way. He could not remember shutting it. Probably he had done it unconsciously. As a child, he had been taught by sedulous elders that the little gentleman always closed doors behind him, and presumably his subconscious self was still under the influence. And then suddenly he realised that this infernal, officious ass of a subconscious self had deposited him right in the gumbo. Behind that closed door, unattainable as youthful ambition, lay his gent's heather mixture with the green twill, and here was he, out in the world alone, in a lemon-coloured bathing suit. (*Indiscretions of Archie*, Chapter 5)

Belloc's next two points are interrelated. On construction, he says:

> Properly this does not concern the excellence of the writer as such. It is the art of the playwright more than of the prose-writer pure and simple. But observe how admirably it is used in these hands! The situation, the climax, general and particular, the interplay of character and circumstance, are as exact as such arrangements can be. They produce the full effect and are always complete.

I do not myself quite understand Belloc's remarks as applied to the average prose writer, but in the context of Wodehouse there is no doubt he hit the nail on the head when he compared his work to that of a playwright. When Wodehouse's letters to William Townend appeared in *Performing Flea*, it was a matter for surprise and amusement to many people who had been reading him for years for his inimitable style and his hilarious jokes, to find how much store he himself put on the construction of his plots, which, however important as a vehicle, are in no other sense important at all. He was completely preoccupied by construction, and the only times he ever seemed to suffer from discouragement or dissatisfaction with his work ("My art is not going too well at the moment") were when he was short of a plot, or in difficulties in working one out, or when he was asked to write something not within his range. However, his letters to Townend show how perceptive Belloc's remarks are.

I wrote an elaborate scenario of the first third of my novel yesterday. I've got a new system now, as it worked so well with *Bill the Conqueror:* that is to write a 30,000 word scenario before starting the novel. . . . By this means you avoid those ghastly moments when you suddenly come on a hole in the plot and are tied up for three days while you invent a situation. I found that the knowledge that I had a clear path ahead of me helped my grip on the thing. Also, writing a scenario of this length gives you ideas for dialogue scenes and you can jam them down in skeleton and there they are, ready for use later. . . .[7]

When you're doing a long story you have got to be most infernally careful of the values of your characters. I believe I told you once before that I classed all my characters as if they were living salaried actors, and I'm convinced that this is a rough but very good way of looking at them.

The one thing actors—important actors, I mean—won't stand is being brought on to play a scene which is of no value to them in order that they may feed some less important character, and I believe this isn't vanity but is based on an instinctive knowledge of stage craft. They kick because they know the balance isn't right. . . .[8]

In writing a novel, I always imagine I am writing for a cast of actors. Some actors are natural minor actors and some are natural major ones. It is a matter of personality. Same in a book. Psmith, for instance, is a major character. If I am going to have Psmith in a story, he must be in the big situations.[9]

The letters in *Performing Flea* entirely dispose of the idea that Wodehouse was a literary simpleton, a man who, although supremely talented, remained fixed forever in his schooldays. He was rather callow in other ways, which I shall try to explain, and remarkably unresponsive to many aspects of the world around him. But he was consciously professional, and *Performing Flea* is the work of a craftsman, a manual like that of a master carpenter.

Following his remarks on construction, Belloc praises Wodehouse for his repeated use of one set of characters—the inhabitants of the English country house, the young ladies and gentlemen with too much or too little money, the New York scene with its own special characters. He does not directly relate these remarks to his earlier statement that Wodehouse's art is that of the playwright rather than the prose writer pure and simple, but they are related, and Ernest Newman wrote most interestingly on this point. He said:

> We have only to read Mr. Wodehouse *en masse* to realise the full force of Goethe's dictum that it is in limitation that the master reveals himself. . . . Mr. Wodehouse's strength is not in invention but in treatment. . . .
>
> Mr. Wodehouse, in truth, is the last perfect representative of a once great race of artists—the practitioners of the commedia dell'arte. These people did not trouble about anything so easy as inventing new forms, new settings, new characters. They took the standardised characters of Pulcinella, Scaramouche, Harlequin, the Captain, the Doctor, the Notary, and so on and re-created them afresh each time out of the abundance of their own genius. This was really a much harder thing to do than to invent quasi-new beings with names and place them in new situations. To do that is to play a game the rules of which you make yourself as you go along. But in the other case the rules of the game are already agreed upon between the actors and their audiences, so that the former had either to play the game with a new brilliance each time or be frankly given the bird by a disappointed audience.[10]

Wodehouse was a man of the theatre. It is often said that his world no longer exists, but it never did exist except in musical comedy. I have been told on the very highest authority that Lord Emsworth is a true picture of a certain type of aristocrat, and he may be an exception to the rule. Nevertheless, English peers have for so long taken advantage of their privileges to indulge their eccentricities that they have entered the cast of stock figures. My father, Frederick Lonsdale, with a totally different treatment, also made good use of them, and I think it is often forgotten how close Wodehouse (and, for that matter, my father) was working to the world of the stock company, the English equivalent of commedia dell'arte. In the nineteenth century the provincial theatres of England had resident stock companies who played all the supporting parts, while the leads were played by visiting stars. These stock companies consisted of actors engaged to play stereotyped parts—the Juvenile Lead and the Leading Lady, the Low Comedian, the Heavy Father, the Chambermaid (later known as a soubrette), and Walking Ladies and Gentlemen, later to be known as supers. Playwrights of the nineteenth century had to write plays which included parts for the salaried stock company, and the playwrights of the early twentieth century were their immediate descendants. Here is Wodehouse himself on the same or an associated theme, in a passage which, as it happens, is about my father:

> What *is* plagiarism? Did you ever see a play by Freddie Lonsdale called *The Last of Mrs. Cheyney*? It was about a Society woman who was one of a band of crooks, and this is revealed to the audience at the end of Act

I. An exactly similar situation was in an American play called *Cheating Cheaters*. And the big scene in Act II was where the hero gets Mrs. Cheyney into his room at night and holds her up for something by saying he is going to keep her there till they are found in the morning, which is exactly the same as Pinero's *Gay Lord Quex*. And yet nobody has ever breathed a word against Freddie for plagiarizing. Quite rightly. The treatment is everything.[11]

I think writers on Wodehouse have sometimes been misled because they did not give sufficient weight to the fact that almost all his life he pursued two parallel careers (as well as several subsidiary ones), as novelist and as librettist and lyricist. His heyday in the theatre was from about 1914 until the Second World War; but all through the period when he lived at Remsenburg (roughly the last thirty years of his life), he and Guy Bolton worked on plays together, even though few of these were produced. Wodehouse constantly turned novels into musical plays and back again into novels without the slightest difficulty, because his plots and the majority of his characters were basically suited to both.

The idea is sometimes put forward that some of Wodehouse's characters are drawn from real life. In particular, it is suggested that Aunt Agatha and Aunt Dahlia were suggested to him by two of his own aunts—Aunt Mary and Aunt Louisa. Richard Usborne believes that these aunts, who occur so often in the novels, to be derided and in the long run outwitted, are symbols of revenge against the disciplinary influences of his youth. He says that Wodehouse spent much of his childhood with aunts, and he goes on to argue: "Whereas other writers dispossessed too early of their parents looked back in anger and indulged in revenge fantasies, Wodehouse blew out the perilous stuff in profitable, plot-fertile mockery." Now, with all deference to Mr. Usborne, I simply cannot see this. However individual the treatment, Aunt Agatha and Aunt Dahlia are stock characters in a long line of British humour. We believe that Aunt Dahlia is much nicer than Aunt Agatha because Bertie keeps telling us so, but she is a relentless blackmailer, completely unconcerned by the discomfort and indignity she causes him in order to attain some objective of her own. In the long run he suffers far more at her hands than he does at Aunt Agatha's. Wodehouse wrote to Townend:

I've spoken of this before and I want to emphasize it again—you *must not* take any risk of humanizing your villains in a story of action. And by humanizing I mean treating them subjectively instead of objectively.

Taking Moriarty as the pattern villain, don't you see how much stronger he is by being an inscrutable figure and how much he would have been weakened if Conan Doyle had switched off to a chapter showing his thoughts? A villain ought to be a sort of malevolent force, not an intelligible person at all.[12]

Neither Aunt Agatha nor Aunt Dahlia is a villain, but they are monsters in human shape and the inheritors of a long tradition of British comedy, usually played by a female impersonator. The author leaves no doubt that this is how he regarded his characters. "I believe there are only two ways of writing a novel," he wrote to Townend. "One is mine, making the thing a sort of musical comedy without music, and ignoring real life altogether; the other is going right down deep into life and not caring a damn."

There are also dozens of suggestions in his novels that his characters start life in musical comedy. He is addicted to the word *heavy*, which comes straight from the old stock companies. In *Much Obliged, Jeeves* L. P. Runkle, speaking to Bertie, says, "The odd thing is that you haven't a criminal face. It's a silly fatuous face, but not criminal. You remind me of one of those fellows who do dances with the soubrette in musical comedy." (Chapter 16) While in the same book Bertie remarks: "Aunt Dahlia is as jovial and bonhomous as a pantomime dame in a Christmas pantomime." (Chapter 6)

I would not myself regard the question of whether Aunt Agatha and Aunt Dahlia were drawn from life worth considering were it not that in questioning it one runs up against not only Mr. Usborne, but two other authorities as well. The first of these is David Jasen, who writes:

Of the many Deane children [Plum's mother was one of them] the oldest was Louisa, who practically brought up the rest of them. She was to become one of young Pelham Grenville's favourite aunts, and would later be the blueprint for Bertie Wooster's kind-hearted Aunt Dahlia. One of her sisters, Mary, was also destined to be the basis for a fictional aunt— but not quite so happily. A professional writer, Mary was something of a tyrant; and her demeanour made an indelible impression on her young nephew that was to manifest itself in Bertie Wooster's unsympathetic Aunt Agatha.[13]

Now, this seems so patently absurd (any Wodehouse reader must know that no human being could possibly be a "blueprint" for Aunt Dahlia) that again one would not waste time on it except for the fact that the third authority happens to be P. G. Wodehouse. It is known that when Mr. Jasen was writing his biography he saw a great deal of Wodehouse, and that the latter read his book and approved it. Even more conclusive, one might think, is that, in a letter to Richard Usborne, Wodehouse agreed that his Aunt Mary was the model for Aunt Agatha.

The truth is that Plum would agree to almost anything. (Writing to a fellow novelist, Denis Mackail, he derides the idea.) This was partly, I assume, from an understandable laziness, since he personally dealt with what must have been one of the largest posts ever received by anyone from people unknown to him, but it was also because of an inherent dislike of dispute. In a letter written after Plum's death, Guy Bolton said: "Plum was so determined never to be contentious that he said: 'Let's agree that if someone says an unkind thing about the other, don't argue, just agree— adding details.' "

The last two words of that sentence (which I find a trifle exaggerated) bring me to one of the main difficulties confronting any biographer of Wodehouse. Plum and Guy were both extraordinarily sweet men, honour-able, kind, and reliable. On all important matters one could have trusted them absolutely, while both had the traditional values of English gentle-men. Yet in relation to the difference between fact and fiction in their published works, neither had the slightest regard for the truth. All the autobiographical works, all letters, all verbal statements, insofar as they concern their publications, have to be subjected to the gravest scrutiny, checked, and rechecked; traps for the biographer abound. Both men had the perfectionism of the dedicated professional and they put the business of entertainment first, while Plum at least had the undivided motivation of the artist. There was the slight difference between them that, whereas Plum seemed to retain some recollection of what had happened and what had been imagined, Guy, having once invented an anecdote, told it so often that it was impossible to know whether in the end he believed it or not.

A remark in some notes made by Plum for Guy's use both illustrates these things and brings us back to the subject under discussion. During the course of his life Plum gave several different answers to the question "Who was the model for Jeeves?" But when writing to Guy, he said: "When we did *Bring On the Girls*, if you remember, I said that I drew Jeeves from a butler I had called Robinson. Untrue, of course. At the start I had no model for him except the conventional stage butler."*

One further point still remains. When Mr. Usborne alludes to "the perilous stuff that weighs upon the heart," presumably he speaks not of a conscious design on Wodehouse's part, but of the workings of the subcon-scious. Plum himself seems to have interpreted the remark in this way. In an interview with Alistair Cooke (quoted with much modesty and candour by Mr. Usborne himself), he spoke of "a certain learned Usborne," and went on to say: "It's a rather frightening thing, you know. I'm sure it's very conscientious and impressive to have someone go into one's stuff like

*See also *Performing Flea*, p. 105: "You're absolutely right about Freddie Rooke. Just a stage dude—as Bertie Wooster was when I started writing about him. If you look at the early Jeeves stories, you'll find Bertie quite a different character now."

that, but it's rather unsettling. I mean you turn the stuff out and then public orators begin to declaim and critics analyse . . . well, it's rather unsettling."[14]

And it is not difficult to see that, sliding into the chair in front of your typewriter, with all the ease of an amphibian taking to water, and with a new idea for an old character, it would be unsettling to recall that all you were really doing was having another slap at Aunt Mary.

The view that in his novels Wodehouse drew nothing from real life or real people was given definitive expression by Evelyn Waugh.

> Mr. Wodehouse's characters are not, as has been fatuously suggested, survivals of the Edwardian age. They are creations of pure fancy—and I use pure in both its senses. . . . Mr. Wodehouse was an early member of Buck's Club. He knew exactly how young men talked; the language of the Drones was never heard on human lips. It is all Mr. Wodehouse's invention, or rather inspiration. They fall in love impetuously and ar- dently, these figures of Mr. Wodehouse's imagination. Their sole failure of chivalry is the occasional mercenary pursuit of an heiress. Seduction and adultery are unknown among them. But they are capable of most other moral lapses. They fall into rages. They get drunk. They smuggle. They rob. They commit arson. They kidnap. They blackmail. They even resort to violence—quite a number of innocent and guilty alike, even the police, get knocked on the head. Professional criminals abound, but they are not the brutes of recent fiction, still less of real life. There are horrific aunts in plenty, but they are not the aunts of "Saki" Munro. All, whatever the deliquencies attributed to them, exist in a world of pristine paradisal innocence.
>
> For Mr. Wodehouse there has been no fall of Man; no "aboriginal calamity." His characters have never tasted the forbidden fruit. They are still in Eden. The gardens of Blandings Castle are that original garden from which we are all exiled.[15]

Yet Wodehouse's is a world of purely masculine fantasy. The chief ingredient of musical comedy—the sentimental love story, treated roman- tically and played by two superhuman beings—is left out. In musical com- edy proper—the musical comedy of the Gaiety and Daly's Theatres in London and of Ziegfeld in New York—the jokes and the girls (who sup- plied sex, not romance) were there for the men; but they were built round the central theme of the love story, which was attractive in some degree to both sexes, but especially to women—hence the term matinée idol. In his novels Wodehouse usually manages what passes for love interest, but it is not of the romantic sort, and his early attempts at romance were disastrous. His girls are "young prunes," and his other characters can seldom compre- hend the attraction they find in the man of their choice—who is often not

merely half-witted but can reasonably be described as "that young Fish"—
a far cry from those magnetic beings with whose fate every woman in any
audience identifies herself. This departure from musical comedy practice
makes it more or less certain that out of every ten Wodehouse addicts only
one will be a woman.

Women as a whole do not care for masculine fantasy. They have more
imagination than men but a different sense of humour. One should perhaps
explain what one means by a sense of humour. It is quite usual for someone
to say of someone else that he has none, the inescapable corollary being
that the speaker believes himself a judge of the matter. Yet a sense of
humour may take many forms and differs from person to person, and it is
not always those with the finest taste who make these remarks. Here,
however, it is possible to say exactly what one means. Because of their
greater imagination, women do not care for music-hall jokes, farcical comedy, or any humour that relies on total disregard for the sufferings of
innocent characters, while, because of their need to involve themselves,
situations of mistaken identity or serious misunderstanding merely arouse
their anxiety. They are incapable of isolating the element of humour from
all the other aspects of a situation, possibly because traditionally their range
of experience has been so circumscribed. Rebecca West reminds us that the
word *idiot* comes from a Greek root meaning "private person." "Idiocy,"
she says, "is the female defect."[16] (She goes on to say some fairly harsh
things about the male obsession with public affairs.)

Women appreciate wit, which is usually much more sharply focussed,
and they have no objection to malice, but they are too subjective to be
amused by the indiscriminate heartlessness of knockabout farce. Wodehouse puts all his literary grace, his talent for dialogue, and his inspired
humour entirely at the service of knockabout plots. This is his claim to be
unique, and it accounts for his appeal to a wide (and intellectually distinguished) male readership; but—with many exceptions to the rule—it puts
him out of reach of the female sex.

It may have become obvious that I am not myself naturally an aficio-
nado—and indeed Mr. Usborne gave the game away some time ago: "Frances
Donaldson," he wrote, "who knew the Wodehouses, but is not quite a
devotee of Wodehouse's writings . . ."[17] * And indeed in my youth, when
I saw something of Wodehouse himself and a great deal more of his stepdaughter, Leonora, it was a source of embarrassment to me that, like so
many other women, I could not read his novels with any pleasure. I read
then for pleasure only, and I was too ignorant and too much bored by
Wodehouse plots and characters to notice the felicities of his style or to

*One cannot but admire the courtesy with which Mr. Usborne makes the hideous charge.

enjoy his jokes. For fifty years or more I made no attempt to remedy this state of affairs, and it was only when (for reasons I have explained) I began to read him with a professional interest that I understood what all the fuss was about. "What an enormous, uncovenanted blessing," Evelyn Waugh wrote, "to have kept Henry James for middle age."[18] What luck, then, to have found Wodehouse at the age of seventy. And, in case there should be any doubt of my sincerity, I must say that during the last two years (the task made easier by three months' convalescence from illness) I have read almost every book he ever wrote, many articles and lyrics, hundreds of letters, and much that has been written about him. No one has the stamina to do that except for pleasure.

However, although I have acquired the detachment to enjoy as well as to admire his work, I still retain elements of the feminine point of view. I prefer, for instance, Psmith to Jeeves, although I believe the latter to be in some respects a development of the former. Both Psmith and Jeeves are clever talkers, masterminds, defenders of the simple; both employ certain well-known Wodehouse tricks. The difference is that Psmith was conceived when his creator still had the romantic, even sentimental, attitudes of youth, while Jeeves is an altogether more sophisticated article. Psmith is generous, chivalrous, and kind, confessing to a crime he has not committed because he believes Mike is guilty; rescuing Mike from his dreadful lodgings and installing him in his own flat; finally persuading his father to pay for Mike's education at Cambridge in order later to employ him as agent. The great Jeeves, on the other hand, who seems almost certain of a place in the vocabulary of the nation as well as in its literary history, often seems to me merely a man with a dictionary of quotations where his heart ought to be. He thinks nothing of leaving Bertie roaming about all night with a blacked-up face, or quite unnecessarily bicycling for miles on a perishingly cold evening, and this kind of thing is often as much in the interests of ridding himself of some article of clothing of which he disapproves as of saving Bertie from some threatened fate. I am not unaware that he is a vehicle for much that is most characteristic of Wodehouse's humour and a necessary part of the scene, and I shall have more appreciative things to say about him later. Nevertheless, in those aspects which I have spoken of here, he represents masculine humour at its most unsympathetic from a woman's point of view.

However, enough of the woman's point of view. It needs explaining, but it should not be overemphasized, because to do so is rather discourteous. For Wodehouse, unaware that he gives women so little pleasure, delights in us when we are young and lively.

Here I come into conflict with one of our most distinguished contemporaries, and I cannot continue the theme before examining his views.

Anthony Powell is a great admirer of Wodehouse, but in a review of *Ice in the Bedroom* he took the trouble to analyze the reason why he personally finds his work not wholly sympathetic. He enjoys, he says, what he calls "the journeyman Wodehouse books"—that is, the school stories with improbable plots—and he goes on to say: "At the other end of the scale, I enormously admire Mr. Wodehouse as a creator of phrases that bring an individual or a situation dazzlingly to life. It would hardly be going too far to speak of this as Wodehouse the poet." And yet he finds that Wodehouse cannot consistently hold his attention:

> This is, of course, purely a matter of taste, reflecting, I like to think, adverse criticism on neither Mr. Wodehouse nor myself. Mr. Wodehouse himself insists on the necessity in his books of his own particular sort of unreality. Awareness of this need is, in itself, a mark of his self-assurance as an artist. . . .
>
> Trying to analyse what I find amiss in some of the Wodehouse *mystique,* I came to the conclusion that it is the constantly reiterated doctrines that nice men are ill at ease with the opposite sex. It is an interesting question when this teaching—later to spread through the country like wildfire—arose in the 19th century. An equally brilliant comic writer like Surtees—with whom Mr. Wodehouse might reasonably be compared—would have found it preposterous. Kipling, of course, played a malign part in the game.
>
> In saying this, I do not, of course, mean that the embarrassments of love and sex are not admirable subjects for comedy, or that every Englishman is a Don Juan. It is just the fact that this point of view became in late Victorian writers, and in Edwardian ones like Ian Hay, almost a matter of social propaganda.[19]

This is an interesting point of view, and, as far as it goes, undeniable. It seems to me the masculine equivalent of the feminine objection that there is no romantic love affair. In all his early novels Wodehouse tried hard to supply what is known as "love interest," but he never reached a level of performance higher than that of most popular novel writers. When he decided, quite rightly, to abandon the attempt to involve his readers in the emotions of his characters, he began to use the tongue-tied lover as a device to keep the plot going, although it may also be true that it is a projection of his own personality. In musical comedy the lovers are played by the stars, and everyone knows that they will fall into each other's arms at the end. But for three acts they have to be kept apart by plot and subplot, and to do this Wodehouse used intervention from some person in a powerful situation (because of the "aunt" theory already discussed, it is usually assumed that this will be a woman—but what about Baxter, Bassett, Glossop, and Spode?) and the inability of the man to speak his love.

Yet all other men, from Uncle Gally to Bertie himself, have a charming relationship with young women: "Uncles occasionally find their nephews trying and are inclined to compare them to their disadvantage with the young men they knew when they were young men, but it is a very rare uncle who is unable to fraternize with his nieces."[20]

This comes from *Sunset at Blandings*, the last book he wrote, but before that Uncle Gally had proved it in novel after novel. In my opinion, Wodehouse departs from his own rule when writing of young women. His antiheroines, such as Honoria Glossop, are part of the stock company, but his real heroines have none of the pallor and woodenness of the heroines of other popular novels. He is not, of course, at his happiest when describing their physical appearance, but when they speak for themselves, they are bright, humorous, and sufficiently determined. They seem to me to be a work of love. Here is Bertie Wooster talking at dinner to a young prune called Cynthia:

"Ah, there he is," I said. "There's the old egg."

"There's who?"

"Young Bingo Little. Great pal of mine. He's tutoring your brother, you know."

"Good gracious! Is he a friend of yours?"

"Rather! Known him all my life."

"Then tell me, Bertie, is he at all weak in the head?"

"Weak in the head?"

"I don't mean simply because he's a friend of yours. But he's so strange in his manner."

"How do you mean?"

"Well, he keeps looking at me so oddly."

"Oddly? How? Give an imitation."

"I can't in front of all these people."

"Yes, you can. I'll hold my napkin up."

"All right, then. Quick. There!"

Considering that she had only about a second and a half to do it in, I must say it was a jolly fine exhibition. She opened her mouth and eyes pretty wide and let her jaw drop sideways, and managed to look so like a dyspeptic calf that I recognised the symptoms immediately.

"Oh, that's all right," I said. "No need to be alarmed. He's simply in love with you."

"In love with me. Don't be absurd."

"My dear old thing. You don't know young Bingo. He can fall in love with *anybody*."

"Thank you!"

"Oh, I didn't mean it that way you know. I don't wonder at his taking to you. Why, I was in love with you myself once."

"Once? Ah! And all that remains now are the cold ashes. This isn't one of your tactful evenings, Bertie."

"Well, my dear sweet thing, dash it all, considering that you gave me the bird and nearly laughed yourself into a permanent state of hiccoughs when I asked you—"

"Oh, I'm not reproaching you. No doubt there were faults on both sides. He's very good-looking, isn't he?"

"Good-looking? Bingo? Bingo good-looking? No, I say, come now, really!"

"I mean, compared with some people," said Cynthia. (*The Inimitable Jeeves*, Chapter 13)

Finally, Lord Emsworth's Girl Friend is one of the most loveable young ladies in humorous fiction.

However, the real question, perhaps sometimes given too little weight by serious scholars of Wodehouse, is: Does he make you laugh? Can you read the long interlocking passages without a smile on your face from what Richard Ingrams has described as "an acute sense of satisfaction at the humorous aptness of his phrasing,"[21] or, as Bernard Levin puts it, "a wit which comes out of the shape of the sentence"?[22] Can you sit upright in a subway train, casually reading one of his books, without risk of becoming what he might have called a cynosure for all eyes?

There has been a certain diffidence among writers, even leading critics, about discussing Wodehouse's humour. Comic masterpieces, David Cecil says, are composed to make us laugh, "so that the critic who writes of them with an unsmiling face reveals himself as comically unable to appreciate the primary intention of these writers."[23] Philip Toynbee expresses the same thing with the Wodehousian apostrophe "to break a butterfly on the wheel."[24]

This is in marked contradiction to Wodehouse's own attitude to his work, which has all the glamour of a storekeeper considering the best way to set out his wares. The difference is that Wodehouse is thinking of the technique of his craft, while the others are speaking of his comic and literary genius. *Performing Flea* has the subtitle "A Self-Portrait in Letters," but it is of interest primarily because Wodehouse continually advises his friend Townend on the business of writing novels or short stories. He writes almost entirely about those parts of his own technique which were valuable to Townend, and we can be sure that, modest and professional as he was, he understood and made use of all the tricks of the trade.

A few are easily recognized, and of these the most obvious is the trick of repetition. This is as old as the hills and consists of repeating a name or catch phrase that, though often not intrinsically funny, becomes so through familiarity. From Leo Maxse in the *National Review* to the writers in

Private Eye, from George Robey to the Crazy Gang, this trick has always worked. In its more subtle manifestation, remarks given to one character in an early scene are repeated by a different character in another. Possibly the best example of this in all literature is Gussie Fink-Nottle's speech at the prize giving at Market Snodbury Grammar School (*Right Ho, Jeeves*). This consists very largely of a hazily remembered and mixed-up version of suggestions made to him earlier by Wooster and Jeeves. Wodehouse is always extremely difficult to quote except at some length, because he is not epigrammatical or often witty in the sense of the punchline, but relies on a benevolently humorous and skilfully interlocking prose.

But if one looks for it, one can often find the first scene on which the second and major scene is based. The artist as opposed to the technician makes the first scene stand on its own. In *Something Fresh* (the first of the Blandings novels) it is essential at a certain point in the story that the reader should already know that Lord Emsworth is so absentminded that, finding a scarab of immense value in his hand, it would be natural to him, after looking at it in bewilderment, to put it in his pocket. In the first scene, which ensures this understanding, Lord Emsworth is talking to the steward in his club:

> "Tell me, Adams, have I eaten my cheese?"
> "Not yet, Your Lordship. I was about to send the waiter for it."
> "Never mind. Tell him to bring the bill instead. I remember that I have an appointment. I must not be late."
> "Shall I take the fork, Your Lordship?"
> "The fork?"
> "Your Lordship has inadvertently put a fork in your coat-pocket."
> Lord Emsworth felt in the pocket indicated, and, with the air of an inexpert conjurer whose trick has succeeded contrary to his expectations, produced a silver-plated fork. (*Something Fresh,* Chapter 3)

And here is what he does with repetition in a single scene. Gussie Fink-Nottle is talking to Bertie Wooster:

> "And you can't get away from it that, fundamentally, Jeeves's idea is sound. In a striking costume like Mephistopheles, I might quite easily pull off something impressive. Colour does make a difference. Look at newts. During the courting season the male newt is brilliantly coloured. It helps him a lot."
> "But you aren't a male newt."
> "I wish I were. Do you know how a male newt proposes, Bertie? He just stands in front of the female newt vibrating his tail and bending his body in a semi-circle. I could do that on my head. No, you wouldn't find me grousing if I were a male newt."

"But if you were a male newt Madeline Bassett wouldn't look at you. Not with the eye of love, I mean."

"She would, if she were a female newt."

"But she isn't a female newt."

"No, but suppose she was."

"Well, if she was, you wouldn't be in love with her."

"Yes, I would, if I were a male newt."

A slight throbbing about the temples told me that this discussion had reached saturation point. (*Right Ho, Jeeves,* Chapter 2)

Wodehouse is also adept at the throwaway line, the joke inserted so casually that its impact is felt a second late. Freddy Threepwood's future father-in-law is telling Lord Emsworth that he is a millionaire, the owner of Donaldson's Dog Biscuits, and that he proposes to offer Freddy a steady and lucrative job in his firm: "Lord Emsworth could conceive of no way in which Freddie could be of value to a dog-biscuit firm, except possibly as a taster." (*Blandings Castle,* Chapter 1)

He may use many other tricks recognizable by the comedian or comic writer, but Wodehouse's unique contribution to literature consists of mastering the cliché. While this form of speech is a trap for every other writer and exerts a tyranny which constant vigilance can minimize but never overcome, Wodehouse simply conscripts it into service. Examples of his use of it abound on every page, and here once more everyone has his favourites:

"You can tell him that I am going to break his neck."

"Break his neck?"

"Yes. Are you deaf? Break his neck."

I nodded pacifically.

"I see. Break his neck. And if he asks why?"

"He knows why. Because he is a butterfly who toys with women's hearts and throws them away like soiled gloves." (*The Code of the Woosters,* Chapter 6)

An extension of this is his use of all the best-known tags of English literature. Shakespeare is his favourite, and "sicklied o'er with the pale cast of thought" among his favourite Shakespeare, but he plundered the whole field of well-known quotations. He employed this joke even in his earliest books: in *Mike* the cricket professional speaks of the "alpha and omugger" of the game.

Yet these things are all matters of technique. No amount of discussion of them throws any light on the nature of comic genius, of which Wodehouse himself said: "To be a humorist one must see the world out of focus. You must, in other words, be slightly cock-eyed." Nor does it tell us very much about the perfection of his prose style. The question that has interested and amused his admirers is whether he understood very much about this himself. Evelyn Waugh thought not:

> Most of us who rejoice in his work do so primarily for the exquisite felicity of the language. That, it seems, is a minor consideration to the author. Either it comes to him unsought, an inexplicable gift like Nijinsky's famous levitations, or it is a matter on which he is so confident in his own judgment that he does not trouble to mention any hesitations he may experience. From his letters he seems to write, as the Norwegians read, for the plots. . . .
>
> I should say that his exquisite diction, as natural as birdsong, is a case of genuine poetic inspiration. I don't believe Mr. Wodehouse knows where it comes from or how; wherever he is, in luxury or in prison, he is able to sequester himself and, as it were, take dictation from his daemon.[25]

However, it must be understood that in this passage Evelyn Waugh is referring specifically to the fictional style. He was, as far as I know, the only commentator to recognize and point out that in, for instance, *Performing Flea,* Wodehouse's style was completely different. Wodehouse was a natural parodist, but quite apart from this, he had at least four main prose styles of his own. The first was the fictional; the second was used in articles and autobiographical essays such as *Bring On the Girls* and *Over Seventy;* the third was a letter-writing style used when writing for publication or answering fan letters, or indeed in any letters except to close intimates; the fourth was the letter-writing style he used when writing, without thought of publication, to Townend, to Guy Bolton, to Denis Mackail, and, at its best, to his daughter, Leonora. Only in the first and sometimes in the fourth do the birds sing.

The style that Wodehouse used for articles and autobiographical books is seldom in the least like that of his best fiction and gives the impression of being the result of hard work. Often contrived, it is not as a rule very funny.* *Bring On the Girls* is not easily distinguishable from nine out of ten theatrical memoirs and consists largely of strings of anecdotes, many of which are inventions. The same may be said of *Over Seventy.* Both these books owe something to his *Punch* articles, which have the same faults. The third style, that of all letters except those to his intimates, is plain and rather hearty. The heartiness appears to spring from the desire of this kindly, but shy and uncommunicative man to appear at ease with his

---

*Wodehouse seems to have agreed with this view himself. In a broadcast interview given in his old age, he said: "I've done a lot of articles and things. They never strike me as very funny—though some of the books do."

fellows. The fourth style is natural to him and has much in common with the first.

Wodehouse always claimed to work extremely hard and to write and rewrite, and this has led some authorities to believe that in his best books he polished his prose to its ultimate perfection. He says in *Over Seventy* that he rewrote some sentences as much as ten times. Possibly by then he did, but this was not the period of his best work. Until he reached that age where his novels were to some extent pastiche of his earlier work and he needed to make sure he was not too obviously repeating himself, I think the claim he made to work over and over his books was justified only in relation to the extreme care he took over the plots. After he had perfected this part of the work, he took "dictation from his daemon," and the difference in his autobiographical style suggests that it was when he consciously interfered with the flow of his prose that he lost inspiration and his humour became contrived. In the novels, I believe one can detect a loss of inspiration when there is a heavy reliance on technique. Thus, if Bertie asks Jeeves several times in the first few pages to supply or finish some tag, or when there is much use of the joke of using initials—"I could see at a g."—I take it as a sure sign that the old Master is labouring a bit, and turn to better things. What one might term the physical evidence supports this view. Writing to Townend, he said:

> As I rule, I find a week long enough for a short story, if I have the plot well thought out. On a novel I generally do eight pages a day, i.e. about 2,500 words. . . .
> I have written sixty-four pages of *Thank You, Jeeves*, in seventeen days and would have done more but I went off the rails and had to re-write three times. That is the curse of my type of story.
> Unless I get the construction absolutely smooth, it bores the reader. . . .
> I then sat down to finish *Leave It to Psmith* for *The Saturday Evening Post*. I wrote 40,000 words in three weeks.[26]

For years he worked at a similar speed, and these feats, astonishing in themselves, were often performed while he kept the deadline on articles or wrote musical comedy lyrics. It is surely unnecessary to underline the fact that this could not be done unless the prose style was left to look after itself; and this could only occur when the intricacies of the plot had been solved. Anthony Powell writes:

> One of Hugh Kingsmill's categories (adapted from Horace Walpole) was the "inspired imbecile," the writer whose books do not stand up to "serious" examination, perhaps are not even intended to do so, but remain alive, readable, even poetic. Kingsmill put the Sherlock Holmes stories in this class, a useful one, critically speaking.[27]

I am not sure what is meant by "serious" examination, but I have already shown that Wodehouse's books have received a good deal. With reservation, therefore, on this score, the category fits him so aptly that it might have been specially invented for him.

Because of his constant allusions to the classics, it is often assumed that Wodehouse was a man of wide learning and culture, but, as Richard Usborne has already pointed out, the knowledge he exhibited in his books is not greater than that easily available to someone with a public school education. He was certainly brought up on the Bible, and as a boy at school he read very widely. In later life he acquired a very extensive knowledge of Shakespeare, although we have his own authority for saying that this occurred after the age of fifty-eight. In the first of the Berlin broadcasts, speaking of packing to go to an internment camp, he says:

> I would like my biographers to make careful note of the fact that the very first thought that occurred to me was that here was my big chance to buckle down and read the Complete Works of William Shakespeare. Reading the Complete Works of William Shakespeare was a thing I had been meaning to do any time these last forty years, and about three years previously I had bought the Oxford edition for that purpose. But you know how it is. Just as you have got *Hamlet* and *Macbeth* under your belt, and are preparing to read the stuffing out of *Henry the Sixth, Parts One, Two, and Three*, something of Agatha Christie's catches your eye and you weaken.
>
> I did not know what internment implied—it might be for years, or it might be a mere matter of weeks—but the whole situation seemed to point to the Complete Works of William Shakespeare, so in they went.
>
> I am happy to say that I am now crammed with Shakespeare to the brim, so whatever else internment has done for me, I am, at any rate, that much ahead of the game.[28]

And in *Over Seventy,* speaking of his youth in New York, he says with his usual simplicity:

> Bubbling over with hope and ambition, I took a room at the Hotel Duke down in Greenwich Village and settled in with a secondhand typewriter, paper, pencils, envelopes and Bartlett's book of *Familiar Quotations,* that indispensable adjunct to literary success.
>
> I wonder if Bartlett has been as good a friend to other authors as he has to me. I don't know where I would have been all these years without him. It so happens that I am not very bright and find it hard to think up anything really clever off my own bat, but give me Bartlett and I will slay you.[29]

It might be argued that both these two passages were written to amuse, were simply jokes. But he always wrote to amuse, and there is plenty of evidence that he embroidered the truth with a humorous style. More important, it is essential that the quotations and allusions in his books should be of a kind that will be recognized by the ordinary reader, otherwise the point will be lost. He got immense joy out of these quotations, and there seems no doubt he used them as much to amuse himself as his reader. Possibly no one who has not, as I have, read almost all the novels in the space of about two years, would notice that his store of quotations is comparatively small and that he uses the same ones again and again. He knew them all by heart and clearly he did not bother to check them, because he is not always entirely accurate. Among his favourites are the lines—partly quoted by Richard Usborne—in which Macbeth asks the doctor to "cleanse the stuff'd bosom of that perilous stuff which weighs upon the heart." Sometimes he uses the whole quotation, sometimes a few words. Thus: "He contented himself with bounding into the garden, his bosom seething with that perilous stuff which weighs upon the heart." (He complains somewhere that Shakespeare should have known better than to use *stuff'd* and *stuff* in the same sentence. This has apparently also worried some scholars, who have had to accept it because it is in the First Folio; they suggest that Shakespeare may really have written *slough*.) The reasons for his choice are not always the same. In "like quills upon the fretful porpentine," it seems to be the actual word *porpentine* that he cannot resist, but more often than not the lines he loves express the human plight: "Of all sad words of tongue or pen, the saddest / are these: it might have been" (Bret Harte) or "The toad beneath the harrow knows / Exactly where each tooth-point goes; / The butterfly upon the road / Preaches contentment to that toad" (Kipling). Nor can he resist a certain kind of high-toned morality. Thus Lord Ickenham, after some very successful blackmail based entirely on planted evidence:

> He linked his arm in Sir Aylmer's and led him out. As they started down the hall Major Plank could hear him urging his companion in the kindest way to pull himself together, turn over a new leaf and start life afresh with a genuine determination to go straight in the future. It only needed a little will-power, said Lord Ickenham, adding that he held it truth with him who sings to one clear harp in divers tones that men may rise on stepping stones of their dead selves to higher things. (*Uncle Dynamite*, Chapter 14)

Owen Edwards tells us that Philip Toynbee called Wodehouse a philistine.[30] This may be true, but in reply to a letter asking where he said it, Philip Toynbee wrote: "If I ever did write that Wodehouse was a philistine, it must have been a tiny island of reproof in an ocean of praise. I have always been a tremendous fan." Nevertheless, if *philistine* is too harsh a word to apply to a writer of Wodehouse's subtlety and taste, there is no doubt that—in a figure of speech much used in his own day—he was a lowbrow.

This was not uncommon at a time when—to adapt Anthony Powell's words—it was the constantly reiterated doctrine that intellectual prowess was actually to be feared as standing in the way of good, or even stable, character. It is an interesting question how this teaching, which was prevalent in the late nineteenth and early twentieth centuries, arose. Spreading like wildfire through the middle classes, it also had much support in the upper. It was the rich Oppidans at Eton who labelled the scholars "tugs," and believed that they did not wash, while it was not unusual for the owners of the great houses of England to be grossly ignorant about the large art collections bequeathed them by their ancestors. Writers, and particularly humorous ones, certainly reflected this attitude.

> "After all, I don't see much point in economy, do you, Mr. Carter?"
> "Economy," I remarked, putting my hands in my pockets, "is going without something you do want in case you should, some day, want something which you probably won't want."
> "Isn't that clever?" asked Dolly in an apprehensive tone.[31]

Cleverness was particularly to be avoided in women, who were forced to do their best to disguise it.

I do not propose to spend much time in proving that Wodehouse was naturally a lowbrow, because readers of this book will find that in the most delightful way he proves this again and again himself. I will merely refer any fan to the index of *Performing Flea*, where he will find a fairly good indication of what Wodehouse read in his spare time (and, if he wishes to follow this up in the text, what he thought about it), and, in illustration of his artistic tastes, point out that he thought *Pagliacci* a reasonable answer to the crossword puzzle clue "an Italian composer in nine letters" (*Summer Moonshine*), while at the same time believing that the clown who laughed to hide a broken heart was called Figaro (Fore in *Week-end Wodehouse*). What must be underlined is that the division between the highbrow and the lowbrow, which today becomes indistinct somewhere along the line of the National Theatre and Italian opera (and cannot be observed at all in the audiences on ballet nights at Covent Garden), was in Wodehouse's youth quite hard and fast. On each side of this line there existed a good deal of genuine hostility towards the other side.

Leonard Woolf in an essay called "Hunting the Highbrow" gave consideration to the term *highbrow* as he understood it to be used by certain best-selling writers and journalists. He thought that he could detect five main varieties of the species. Of these only two concern us here: "*altifrons altifrontissimus,* the original, primitive and real highbrow or intellectual who . . . prefers the appeal to his intellect rather than that solely to his senses"[32] and "*pseudaltifrons intellectualis,* the man who only likes what nobody else can understand."[33] Woolf later defines the second of these species as something between a snob and a bore who attaches himself to intellectual things and to *altifrons altifrontissimus.*

The distinguishing mark of the true early–twentieth-century lowbrow is that he did not believe in the existence of *altifrons altifrontissimus,* only in that of *pseudaltifrons intellectualis*—that is to say, he believed that anyone who said he liked something he did not himself understand was activated more by affectation than anything else, affectation and a desire to console himself for being unable to sell his own wares. Wodehouse invariably takes this view. All his heroes are golfers, cricket players, or the mentally unendowed. Antiheroes (of both sexes) read or write poetry, run poetry societies, and publish slim volumes. Occasionally a writer is found among the heroes, but he is almost invariably a playwright and usually on his way to Hollywood—e.g., Boko in *Joy in the Morning* or Joe in *Summer Moonshine.* Often an undisguised hostility is generated, as in *The Clicking of Cuthbert,* and there is much of that rather boneless satire often to be found in novels where serious but financially unsuccessful writers are derided. "My work is on somewhat different lines. The reviewers usually describe the sort of thing I do as Pastels in Prose. My best liked book, I believe, is *Grey Myrtles*" ("Ukridge Sees Her Through"). Florence Cray is the supreme example of *pseudaltifrons intellectualis,* but the type occurs again and again.

I speak of the professional lowbrow with a good deal of confidence, because I was brought up by one. My father wrote a play called *Canaries Sometimes Sing* in which one of the characters is called Mrs. Lymes. At any time that Mrs. Smethurst (*The Clicking of Cuthbert*) or the President of the Pen and Ink Club ("Ukridge Sees Her Through") or Mrs. Pett (*Piccadilly Jim*) had fallen ill on the day of a literary gathering, Mrs. Lymes could have stood in for her.

One must not necessarily assume that the lowbrow is a person without taste. He is more often a person without intellectual curiosity—and this (in rare cases of which Wodehouse was undoubtedly one) may be a necessary protection against dissipation of resources. Richard Usborne quotes a sentence about Wodehouse from *Bring On the Girls*: "As Charles Lamb said of Godwin, he read more books not worth reading than any man in England"—a sentence he attributes to Bolton but which Wodehouse almost certainly wrote himself. "Do you know," he wrote to Townend, "I think the greatest gift one can have is enjoying trash. I can take the rottenest mystery story out of the library and enjoy it. So I can always have something to read. But what bilge they are producing now. I couldn't get beyond the first page of *Lolita*."[34]

In his essay Leonard Woolf argues that it is not true to say that a book, play, or picture which appeals to ninety-nine people out of a hundred cannot possibly have artistic merit; but he adds that some very severe aesthetic highbrows would maintain that the qualities which make a book or picture a great work of art are never those which appeal to ninety-nine people out of a hundred. And later he says: "It is probably true that when a book is both a work of art and popular, the qualities which gave it aesthetic merit are not those which have most to do with its popularity."[35] Wodehouse, almost alone among writers of genuine literary talent, seemed to be unaware of the qualities which gave his work aesthetic merit until these were pointed out to him, although he understood exactly what made them popular. He wrote, as he read, for entertainment, and he expected to be sneered at by *pseudaltifrons intellectualis*.

I am aware that in much that I have said I am crossing swords with Richard Usborne, who wrote that *Joy in the Morning* is Wodehouse's best book and tells us that he believes this was because, writing it in wartime without a deadline, Wodehouse was able to polish and repolish it as he never could in peacetime. Yet surely Mr. Usborne is basing a false conclusion on false premises. *Joy in the Morning* is not Wodehouse's best book, and I find it just as surprising that Mr. Usborne should think it is as that Wodehouse should think *Quick Service* his best. Both are good books, although I find *Quick Service* more inspired than *Joy in the Morning* (which does show signs of having been reworked). But surely, if in the days to come Wodehouse's oeuvre does not survive as a whole and but one or two books live on to represent this great twentieth-century humorist, nobody can think that either of these will be preferred to *Right Ho, Jeeves* or *The Mating Season*, or to the best of Blandings, Psmith, or Uncle Fred, or even to *The Small Bachelor*. Then again, I do not know what Mr. Usborne's evidence is for saying that Wodehouse polished *Joy in the Morning*. He was writing it in Le Touquet before he was interned, and he finished it in Germany between July and November 1941.

There is very little in his own statement to suggest much preoccupation with the actual writing of his books. In all the hundreds of letters I have read, I might quote one written to his agents in 1934 in which, speaking of *Right Ho, Jeeves*, he said he liked it better than *Thank You, Jeeves*, because it was more carefully written: "In *Right Ho, Jeeves*, I was conscious all the time that the plot was not too strong, so I developed every possible chance there was for bright dialogue." And he wrote in much the same terms to Townend about *The Mating Season*. Over a lifetime of discussion of his work, however, his general attitude is more nearly expressed in the following sentence in a letter to Denis Mackail (1944): "The actual writing of a story always gives me a guilty feeling, as if I were wasting my time. The only thing that matters is thinking the stuff out." And he wrote to Henry Slessar (author of the television series *The Edge of Night*, to which he was addicted): "Do you do much revising? I don't as a rule." Such manuscripts as remain are very much more heavily corrected than I would have expected, but they are all of late work.

Wodehouse drew what he needed from his surroundings and his vast knowledge of all the clichés of thought were valuable to him. It is usual to say that his is a world of pure fantasy and that he was of too kindly a humour to be a satirist. This is true, but no humour is consistently funny which is not related to human experience. Wodehouse was not interested in the higher planes of intellect or feeling; and the humour, which is so instinctive that it emerges from the shape of his prose, is derived from an affection for the more ordinary foibles of the ordinary man.

Here are three examples of his work taken from different periods:

Mr. Shepperd's manner was inclined to bleakness.

"This is most unfortunate," he said. "Most unfortunate. I have my daughter's happiness to consider. It is my duty as a father." He paused. "You say you have no prospects. I should have supposed that your uncle . . . ? Surely with his influence . . . ?"

"My uncle shot his bolt when he got me into the bank. That finished him, as far as I'm concerned. I'm not his only nephew, you know. There are about a hundred others, all trailing him like bloodhounds."

Mr. Shepperd coughed the small cough of disapproval. He was feeling more than a little aggrieved.

He had met Owen for the first time at the house of his uncle Henry, a man of unquestioned substance, whose habit it was to invite each of his eleven nephews to dinner once a year. But Mr. Shepperd did not know this. For all he knew, Owen was in the habit of hobnobbing with the great man every night. He could not say exactly that it was sharp practise on Owen's part to accept his invitation to call, and having called, to continue calling long enough to make the present deplorable situation possible; but he felt it would have been in better taste for the young man to have effaced himself and behaved more like a bank-clerk and less like an heir.[36]

And though the theme is not original, will there ever be a generation of English men who do not laugh at this?

Into the face of the young man who sat on the terrace of the Hotel Magnifique at Cannes there had crept a look of furtive shame, the shifty, hangdog look which announces that an Englishman is about to talk French. One of the things which Gertrude Butterwick had impressed upon Monty

Bodkin when he left for his holiday on the Riviera was that he must be sure to practise his French, and Gertrude's word was law. So now, though he knew that it was going to make his nose tickle, he said:

"Er, garçon."

"M'sieur?"

"Er, garçon, esker-vous avez un spot de l'encre et une piece de papier—note-papier, vous savez—et une envelope et une plume."

The strain was too great. Monty relapsed into his native tongue.

"I want to write a letter," he said. And having, like all lovers, rather a tendency to share his romance with the world, he would probably have added "to the sweetest girl on earth" had not the waiter already bounded off like a retriever, to return a few moments later with the fixings.

"V'la, sir! Zere you are, sir," said the waiter. He was engaged to a girl in Paris who had told him that when on the Riviera he must be sure to practise his English. "Eenk—pin—pipper—enveloppe—and a liddle bit of bloddin-pipper."

"Oh, merci," said Monty, well pleased at this efficiency. "Thanks. Right-ho."

"Right-ho, m'sieur," said the waiter. (*The Luck of the Bodkins*, Chapter 1)

The third example is from *Ice in the Bedroom*, first published in 1961, one of his best books outside the great sagas and one which upsets the theory that all his best work was done in the period before 1939. Leila Yorke is a writer of "slush" novels and Sally is her secretary (Leila is not the character one has come to expect a Wodehouse woman novelist to be).

The function at which Leila Yorke had committed herself to speak was the bi-monthly lunch of the women's branch of the Pen and Ink Club, and she had completely forgotten the engagement till Sally reminded her of it. On learning that the curse had come upon her, she uttered one of those crisp expletives which were too sadly often on her lips and said that that was what you got for letting your guard down for a single moment with these darned organising secretaries. Iron unremitting firmness was what you needed if you were not to be a puppet in their hands.

"They're cunning. That's the trouble. They write to you in December asking you to do your stuff in the following June, and you, knowing that June will never arrive, say you will, and blister my internal organs if June doesn't come round after all."

"Suddenly it's Spring."

"Exactly. And you wake up one morning and realise you're for it."

(*Ice in the Bedroom*, Chapter 10)

One should not make too much of all this. He does not go very wide or very deep; but he has great sensibility, and he succeeds admirably in his own intention—that is, in the gentle art of poking fun.

When one comes at last to the inevitable question "Will he live?" the first answer must be that he *does* live. Auberon Waugh tells us that when he found his daughter spluttering in a corner over a Wodehouse novel, she was the fourth generation of this highly critical literary family to do so, while Wodehouse has already been widely praised by six or seven decades of contemporary writers. He must be admired for his narrative power (a necessary if not a sufficient characteristic of the great novelist), for his exquisite style, for his ability to make one both laugh out loud and take pleasure from page after page of benign humour, for the elegance and wit with which he keeps his fantasies aloft. Some writers have gone outside these boundaries. Hilaire Belloc, it has already been observed, achieved his effects by deliberately outrageous statements; so too does Bernard Levin, who once compared the phrase "in my heliotrope pyjamas with the old gold stripe"[37] to one of the more thunderous passages of *Macbeth*. But, although in fact more than one other writer has compared Wodehouse to Shakespeare, it is not a claim that should be taken seriously; and it merely adds to the confusion Wodehouse himself has created by the idiosyncratic conjunction of his matter and his manner.

One may with some confidence expect for him a lasting place among the great British humorists, and one, too, among our minor classics (when the currency is debased in the manner of Belloc and Levin, such vast compliments lose their force). There is no need to worry that he does not, as he might have put it, widen our horizons or deepen our understanding of human nature. He keeps company with such artists as Lewis Carroll or Charlie Chaplin, whose imaginative fancies continue to give pleasure to the most fastidious among us long after more profound thinkers have become mere names.

And if it adds to the bewilderment to set his claims too high, it must in the long run damage his reputation to pretend that the quality of his work was all the same. His critics have been too grateful for the hours of pleasure he has given them ever to wish to complain; but no man can turn out books, articles, and short stories at the rate he did and remain at his best throughout. Wodehouse wrote any number of novels of the highest quality and more than one comic masterpiece; but all of his work is not of the same standard. When he was young, he was very modest and also too willing to write what he believed the public wanted; and when he was old, although skill and experience carried him through, his inspiration sometimes failed. It is too much to expect that his executors will be persuaded to discriminate very closely in any selection for publication, not merely because of his exceeding popularity, but also because if, as he himself once put it, it needs a cockeyed vision to create humour, there is also an angle of distortion in our appreciation of it which differs considerably from person to person, so much so that what I think contrived another may find side-splitting. But one would wish, nevertheless, to warn the youth of the future not to mistake *Ring for Jeeves* or even *Much Obliged, Jeeves* for *Right Ho, Jeeves*, or, if picking indiscriminately, to avoid *The Coming of Bill* (1919) or *The Girl in Blue* (1970).*

Enough, however, of fault finding. If the task had not been so much neglected by my predecessors, I need not have embarked upon it. For no man had so large an output, and none sustained his standard better. Such set pieces as the prize giving at Market Snodbury (*Right Ho, Jeeves*), of which there are many examples, most of the golf stories, the short story "Lord Emsworth and the Girl Friend," which Kipling thought one of the best humorous short stories in the English language, and dozens and dozens of others, will be found in anthologies of humour for years to come.

Lastly, he succeeded in the greatest of all a novelist's ambitions, because (to quote once more from Belloc) he created "one more figure in that long gallery of living figures which makes up the glory of English fiction." Belloc refers to Jeeves, but there is reason to believe that Bertie Wooster and Lord Emsworth share the honours, while even figures such as Ukridge are sometimes referred to without explanation. In October 1977 Callaghan (then Prime Minister) was applauded through the hall at the Labour Conference when he compared the then Shadow Secretary for Education and Science, St. John Stevas, to Bertie Wooster. Immediately Ferdinand Mount, the political correspondent of the *Spectator*, complained of the comparison:

> "I am inclined to think that there must be some mistake, and that this bird who has been calling here is some different variety of Fink-Nottle. The chap I know wears horn-rimmed spectacles and has a face like a fish. How does that check up with your data?"
> "The gentleman who came to the flat wears horn-rimmed spectacles, sir?"
> "And looked like something on a slab?"
> "Possibly there is a certain suggestion of the piscine, sir."
> "Then it must be Gussie."[38]

And in the Christmas number of the same paper, no less than three writers individually made reference to Wodehouse.

I have, for reasons not all connected with its difficulty, been a long time writing this book. I therefore intended to replace these references with some which were more up-to-date before it went to the printers. I have not done so, because I have found it hardly exaggerating to say that no week

---

*"If you ask me frankly whether I consider *Sam the Sudden* or *The Man with Two Left Feet* any good today, I must tell you no. Are people still reading the stuff?" Wodehouse, on his seventieth birthday, to William Foster, quoted in *The Sunday Times*, 14 October 1956.

passes without some quotation from Wodehouse or some reference to his name appearing in the national press. One can confidently predict that, nearly eighty years after he wrote his first novel, any reader interested in doing so may continue to find substitutes for himself.

As an appendix to what I have written, I think I should try to do justice to some of the things which have been said to me while I have been writing this book, since certain points are made again and again.

Many people believe that Jeeves and Bertie Wooster could not have been conceived without Sherlock Holmes and Dr. Watson, and, as a subclause, that Mike and Psmith are forerunners of Bertie and Jeeves. The debt to Conan Doyle is obvious, although I personally think in this form exaggerated. I hope to show that Jeeves is derived more directly from the American humorous writer Harry Leon Wilson. As to Mike and Psmith, I can only concede that like Bertie and Jeeves, they are a pair. Mike is a schoolboy hero, and a fairly stolid one at that, bearing no resemblance to Bertie; and it was not until Wodehouse became interested in musical comedy librettos that he struck a lasting vein. In the same way, Jeeves may owe some of his qualities to Psmith; but, as I shall again endeavour to show in the appropriate place, Psmith exhibits qualities never again to be found in a Wodehouse character.

Wodehouse is sometimes compared to Ivy Compton-Burnett, and the likenesses which exist are obvious. One difference is that where her admirers are the most esoteric of all literary groups, Wodehouse's are to be found in every class and almost every country in the world.

Then he is said to derive much from W. S. Gilbert. Mr. Aidan Evans has written a paper on the subject, which he generously allowed me to see. I do not know Gilbert well enough to speak with any authority, but I can only say that, although there is no doubt that he was one of Wodehouse's youthful heroes, there are only a certain number of ways in which anything can be said, and I cannot see that the similarities reflect much more than that.

He is thought to have been influenced by Dickens. To this one can only reply in words he adapted from Rudyard Kipling (whom he did read all his life): "Not so, but far otherwise"—a statement which he will be allowed to prove for himself.

Finally, he is so often spoken of as an Edwardian, because of the misconception that in that golden age people like his characters really existed. Yet if one thinks of Edwardian humorous writers—Saki, E. F. Benson, Anthony Hope—Wodehouse seems so genially free from superciliousness and from their essentially upper-class tone.

I

ALMOST A LIFETIME

1

Childhood and Youth

P. G. Wodehouse was born on 15 October 1881, at 1 Vale Place, Epsom
Road, Guildford. His father, Henry Ernest Wodehouse, always known as
Ernest, was a magistrate in Hong Kong, but his mother, Eleanor, was
staying with her sister in England when her third son was born.

Ernest Wodehouse was the grandson (through a younger son) of Sir
Armine Wodehouse (fifth Baronet), whose elder son was created first Baron
Wodehouse in 1797, and who was descended from the Lady Mary Boleyn,
a sister of the more famous Anne. The heredity of this otherwise fairly
uninteresting man has been seen by at least one commentator on the work
of the famous novelist as having some direct influence on it. In a review of
Wodehouse at Work, Anthony Powell takes Richard Usborne to task for
an omission he regards as important. Mr. Usborne does not tell the reader
that P. G. Wodehouse himself belonged to the cadet branch of an unusually
ancient family, holding one of the oldest baronetcies extant (of which he
could, in theory, be the heir), later submerged in an earldom.* "In other
words the nostalgia for an aristocratic world of fantasy has some obvious
base in circumstances to encourage that personal myth. It seems to me as
interesting to know this as to know that Mr. Wodehouse's brother fell in
with Mrs. Besant and became a key figure among the theosophists of
India."[1]

Yet it is possible, I think, to hold the view that these words tell us more
about Anthony Powell than they do about P. G. Wodehouse. This is no
base charge of snobbery. Mr. Powell's close interest in the tribal customs
of society is well known to all his readers, while everyone who knew
Wodehouse would deny that he had the remotest interest of a personal
kind either in class or in his antecedents.† The spread of heredity being
what it is, members of middle-class families are often able to claim descent,

---

*The third Baron Wodehouse was created Earl of Kimberley in 1866.
†Anthony Powell once astonished Evelyn Waugh, who had taken him to see a house that
was for sale, by remarking to the owner as he entered the hall: "Ah! A gunner, I see."

if fairly distant, from some noble family, and this is commonly a source of pride. Yet in all the letters and other papers I have examined in the course of my researches for this book, I have come across only one reference by Plum to his ancestors. This is in a letter to his daughter, Leonora, and concerns what he describes as a "laughable imbroglio" with Jerome Kern:

> I got a furious cable from Jerry . . . ending "You have offended me for the last time!" Upon which the manly spirit of the Wodehouses (descended from the sister of Anne Boleyn) boiled in my veins—when you get back I'll show you the very veins they boiled in—and I cabled over "Cancel permission to use lyrics."

More serious evidence that Wodehouse had no interest in his antecedents, conscious or subconscious, is that when David Jasen was writing his biography (which he did in consultation, it may be remembered, with Wodehouse himself), Wodehouse appears to have entirely forgotten to tell him certain interesting facts about his mother's family. Plum's mother was born Eleanor Deane, and Jasen writes: "What Eleanor Deane's family may have lacked in distinctive lineage in the Wodehouse tradition it more than made up for in size."[2] Yet the truth is that in the matter of lineage the Deanes yield nothing to the Wodehouses. Eleanor's father was a Reverend John Bathurst Deane, whose parents had bought for him the parish of St. Helen's, Bishopsgate. He hired a curate to look after the parish, and except for visiting it once a month to preach a sermon, lived himself in a house called Chyne Court in Bath. He received a stipend of £1,000 a year from his parish and during the last fifteen years of his life did even less than before to earn it, since by that time he was completely blind. His lifetime's work was research into the genealogy of his family. The result of this labour was not published during his lifetime, but appeared in 1899 as *The Book of Dene, Deane, Adeane: A Genealogical History* by Mary Deane (one of John Bathurst Deane's daughters and none other than Aunt Mary herself). From this book we learn the history of the many different branches of Deanes or Adeanes, who are indeed one of England's well-known families and who, we are told, descend from Roberto de Dena, one of the Norman nobles at the court of Edward the Confessor. Among the subscribers to the publication of the Book of Denes are members of almost all the different branches of the family.

Of equal if not greater interest (although not apparently to Plum) is the fact that his maternal grandmother, born a Miss Fourdrinier, was a sister of Cardinal Newman's mother. In a letter written by Guy Bolton to Richard Usborne soon after Plum's death, Guy says: "I am up to my neck in work but I must pause to tell you an astounding thing. I was talking to

Plum after 1916 in closest intimacy. He never told me that Cardinal Newman was his great-uncle. A man who wrote English like that."

If one wishes to look for the sources of Wodehouse's talent, the evidence
suggests that it came from his mother's rather than his father's family. His
paternal grandfather was a soldier who fought at Waterloo and married an
heiress named Lydia Lee. His father, Ernest Wodehouse, was a quiet,
although apparently humorous, man, with no great claim to our interest,
from whom Plum inherited his physical build and his kindly temperament.
He served all his working life in the Civil Service in Hong Kong, but at the
age of forty-five he made and won a bet that he could walk right round the
island in a given time, and as a result suffered from a sunstroke so severe
that his health was permanently affected. For something like forty years he
drew a government pension, a fact that was a perpetual source of interest
and sardonic admiration to his future daughter-in-law, Ethel.

Eleanor Wodehouse, Plum's mother, was the tenth of thirteen children—four boys and nine girls. She had a small gift for drawing and
painting and a romantic taste in Christian names (she is given the credit for
the choice of her children's names). Her eldest son, Philip Peveril (he was
born on the Peak in Hong Kong), was known as Peveril; her second,
Ernest Armine, was called Armine; her third, Pelham Grenville, quickly
became known as Plum or Plummie; her fourth, Richard Lancelot, was
called Dick. Armine was a Wodehouse family name, and Plum's godfather
was a Colonel Pelham Grenville von Donop. There is no other evidence
that Eleanor was a very imaginative person. When her husband died in his
eighties, she went to live with her son Armine and his wife, Nella (Helen),
and after Armine died she stayed on with Nella (like her third son, she
lived to be over ninety). Armine and Nella referred to her as the "Memsahib" and called her this quite openly to her face. Talking about her, Nella
said: "Memsahib was not an intelligent person. She used to look at pictures
in the papers and only read the odd book. . . . If you look at the picture
of Cardinal Newman in the National Gallery and a picture of Memsahib,
you will see that there is a likeness. They have absolutely identical fea-
tures."

However, if Memsahib was not an intelligent person, there is evidence
of both intelligence and imagination in two of her sisters. Mary Deane,
who was a professional writer, was a strong, bossy woman, and the rather
simple notion that she was the model for Aunt Agatha has tended to
obscure the possibility, both more interesting and more likely, that she was
the source of Plum's open hostility to the pretensions of literary ladies and
even contributed to his aversion to the "highbrow."

A second sister, Emmaline, has some real claim to talent, because it is
her portrait of Cardinal Newman which is referred to in Nella's notes. This

belongs to the National Portrait Gallery, but at present hangs in the gallery of the House of Commons.*

One may look to Wodehouse's heredity for the sources of his talent, but if one is to understand his personality and character, one must look to his childhood environment. The biographer, although in many ways so handicapped and so dependent on the records of those who knew the subject of his studies in life, has one inestimable advantage: He has access to the whole span of the life and need not wait on the passage of time to observe development or to relate cause and effect, and he may share his overall view with his readers. From the point at which we stand, it is easy to see that while the circumstances of Wodehouse's childhood constitute an almost classic example of an environment likely to inflict emotional damage, he himself exhibited to an unusual degree exactly those eccentricities of personality which might be expected to result from such a childhood.

At the time of his birth it was common practice for middle- or upper-class parents to hand the care of their children over to servants, and this was almost invariably done in the colonies, where one of the attractions was the cheapness and excellence of labour, and where a nanny was regarded not so much as a symbol of status as a part of normal life. One may assume with great confidence, therefore, that Plum would have had an *amah* or Chinese nurse, who may well have been more important to him than his own mother.† Psychologists are agreed that this kind of mother substitute, providing she is both loving and stable, can fulfill the needs of the growing child.

However, a second practice, almost equally common in families established in the colonies, was that of sending very young children home to England to be educated. This was regarded as a supreme but necessary sacrifice, and it is very curious how much the fashion in society at any moment can increase or diminish such an apparently basic emotion as maternal love. Probably it was necessary in the interests of their education and of their health to send children to England in the long run; but when the time came to send her eldest child home, Eleanor Wodehouse made something in the nature of a clean sweep and sent not merely Peveril, aged six, and Armine, aged four, but the baby Plum, aged two. Years passed before she saw any of these children again, and she would never establish any close relationship with them.

*In 1979, when St. John Stevas became Leader of the House of Commons, he provoked a small controversy by removing this picture to his room.
†I asked Nella Wodehouse whether during the course of her married life Armine had ever spoken of any particular person, and she said not. But she added that there must have been one, because Memsahib would have been quite incapable of looking after her children herself.

She travelled to England herself and rented a house in Bath, where she engaged a Miss Roper, a complete stranger, to look after the children. Then she returned to Hong Kong. Memsahib was a stupid woman, and her actions continually suggest that her emotions were as undeveloped as her intellect; but in leaving her children to be brought up by strangers, she did no more than conform to the established pattern of the day. Rudyard Kipling's mother was extremely bright and emotionally responsive, and yet although, like Eleanor Wodehouse, she had plenty of relations in England, she condemned him to years of misery with "Aunt" Rosa Holloway, about whom she knew no more than Eleanor Wodehouse knew about Miss Roper. (Given Plum's addiction to aunts, it may be worth pointing out that the word was often used as a courtesy title for women who for reasons not of blood but of friendship or convenience were in some relationship to children. These were often more disapproving than real aunts, having no ties of blood to prejudice them.) Nothing in the history of children's suffering is more desolate than Kipling's sister's account of the house in which they were left when their parents brought them home from India, and one must accept that there was nothing unusual in Eleanor Wodehouse's wholesale abandonment of her children, however abnormal it may seem today.

Miss Roper's regime lasted until Plum was five. Then in 1886, on a visit to England, his father and mother moved the three boys to a Dame school in Croydon, run by two sisters named Prince. For the next three years the boys were based at this school, in the holidays as well as in the term. In the holidays they visited their many Deane uncles and aunts, and they went occasionally to their paternal grandmother at Ham Hill, Powick, and to their maternal grandfather, John Bathurst Deane, at Chyne Court, with whom lived the redoubtable Aunt Mary. I do not believe that any of these relations played a large enough part to be regarded as highly significant in the development of the future novelist.

After three years with the Prince sisters, Peveril developed a weak chest, and the boys were moved once more, this time to a small public school in Guernsey. Two years later Armine was sent to Dulwich and Plum to a school called Malvern House, a preparatory school for the navy. His eyesight would have precluded his serving in the navy, and after a visit to Armine at Dulwich, he implored his father to send him there too. When he achieved this ambition, he acquired, for the first time, a degree of permanence and stability.

Few people today would dispute the fact that the early years of a child are of paramount importance to his general development. (In discussing the findings of psychology, one must not allow the fact that Wodehouse himself regarded it with much of the jeering hostility he felt for modern novels, literary ladies, and Socialist politics, to deter one from using it to throw light on his own personality. In fact, one suspects that his hostility may itself be a sign of the disturbance which results from some awareness of the complexity of repressed emotions.) Nor is it necessary today to stress the fact that the relationship of a baby with his mother (or mother substitute) is of vital significance to his future. What may not be so generally recognized is the strength of despair that may be felt by very young children who are deprived of a warm and intimate relationship of this kind, or, perhaps even worse, where this has been formed and then early or continually disrupted. When this happens, the capacity to form relationships with other people may be permanently impaired.

We do not know whether Plum had a warm relationship with an *amah* which was broken when at the age of two he was sent to England (it seems unlikely that he had such a relationship with his mother). But there is no doubt that henceforth his life for many years was only a little short of the extreme deprivation of children in institutions.

The reaction of a child to the absence or disruption of a loving relationship is sometimes one of aggressive independence—Kipling is an obvious example—but some children reach a state of apathy where they no longer seem to mind. This absence of reaction, which sadly often seems reassuring, may be either "because he has never experienced a continuous loving relationship or, more frequently, this has been disrupted so severely that he has not only reached but remained in a state of detachment. As a result he remains detached and so incapable of experiencing either separation, anxiety or grief. . . . Analysis shows the springs of love are frozen."[3]

Both Plum and his elder brother Armine remember their childhoods as passed under the supervision of people who were strict and remote. Plum remembered Miss Roper as very severe in her manner and most particular about cleanliness, while the Prince sisters felt truth so important that they were unable to pretend to such fables as that of Father Christmas. Plum's known recollections of his childhood are few, but they are most important, with their suggestion of an apathy which was almost certainly construed as contentment.

> Looking back I can see that I was just passed from hand to hand. It was an odd life with no home to go to, but I have always accepted everything that happens to me in a philosophical spirit; and I can't remember ever having been unhappy in those days. My feeling now is that it was very decent of those aunts to put up three small boys for all those years. We can't have added very much entertainment to their lives. The only thing you could say for us is that we never gave any trouble.[4]

And he also said, speaking of the Prince period:

> Croydon in those days was almost in the country, and I remember getting
> into bad trouble for stealing a turnip out of a field. . . . I suppose it was a
> good bringing up, but it certainly did not tend to make one adventurous.
> I can't remember having done any other naughty thing the whole of the
> three years I was there. One other thing I remember is how fond I was of
> the various maids who went through the Prince home. It may have given
> me my liking for the domestic-servant class.[5]

There is no suggestion in any of this of the real severity experienced by
H. H. Munro (Saki), whose childhood was in many ways so similar, or of
the hardship and terrible unhappiness endured by Rudyard Kipling when
he was separated from his parents for the same reasons. Nor is there any
hint in Plum's account of his childhood of the bitterness felt by Edgar
Wallace against his mother, who gave him to foster parents and to whom,
when he was rich and famous, he refused entry into his house; or of the
maudlin self-pity felt by Somerset Maugham until the end of his life because
of the early death of his mother and his consequent transplantation into the
alien and unwelcoming atmosphere of his uncle's house at Whitstable—
nothing except the unnaturally good behaviour which seems suspicious
only in the light of modern psychology. All these four children grew up to
be storytellers, but Plum's response to the rejection of his early demand
for love was unusually direct. He simply detached himself from the cold
and unrewarding world and retreated into fantasy. From the earliest age he
was happiest alone with his own company, and in the absence of any family
life or stimulus to the emotions, he cultivated his imagination in solitude.
He said he could remember no time when he did not intend to be a writer,
and he started to make up stories even before he could write. The first,
written down in 1888 when he was seven, read as follows:

> About five years ago in a wood there was a Thrush, who built her nest in
> a Poplar tree. and sang so beautifully that all the worms came up from
> their holes and the ants laid down their burdens. and the crickets stopped
> their mirth. and moths settled all in a row to hear her. she sang a song as
> if she were in heaven—going up higher and higher as she sang.
>   at last the song was done and the bird came down panting.
>   Thank you said all the creatures.
>   Now my story is ended.
> Pelham G. Wodehouse.[6]

I have written this in the same way as Mr. Jasen, who, I assume, took it
from the original. If one inserted punctuation and capital letters, this little
story, which is obviously rather remarkable for the observation and the

neatness of the words chosen to describe the behaviour of the creatures, would seem so also for the rhythmic balance of the long sentence. It is clear that Plum was already interested in and well informed about animals. When I showed the story to George Rylands, he made the following more interesting comments: The long sentence, he said, owes much to knowledge of the words and cadences of the Bible, while the sentence beginning "she sang a song as if she were in heaven" is blank verse, two lines of decasyllables. He said, in addition, that whereas most children would have put simply "The End," by writing "Now my story is ended. Pelham G. Wodehouse" this child had made even his name part of the rhythmic whole. We have no evidence that the Misses Prince introduced their charges thus early to the words and cadences of the Bible, but one would expect that they did. So here is the impeccable ear—like perfect pitch in a musician—showing itself at the age of seven.

The Wodehouses seem to have been singularly lacking in parental affection. When Ernest's retirement in 1896 brought them back to England and to the sons they hardly knew, they at first took a house in Dulwich, where Armine and Plum were by now at school, but very soon they moved away to Shropshire, and the two boys became boarders once more. Plum became attached to the silent man who was his father, but he never achieved a relationship with his mother. He was fifteen when she re-entered his life, and to him she seemed a stranger.

Speaking of Memsahib, Nella said:

Plum always said she was "guvvy." Apparently she could never keep a servant. Plum always said that he could not think of anything to say to her. He told me once that a captain who was a friend of theirs gave him £5. Memsahib immediately took the money from Plum and only allowed him to keep a few shillings.

Nella also told me that during all the years that her mother-in-law lived with her, Plum visited her only once. His feeling for her was not hostile, however, and he was always anxious that Leonora should go to see her.

He seems to have been reasonably happy while at school at Guernsey, which he described later as a delightful place full of lovely bays. His life seems to have been free from tiresome restrictions, and he enjoyed roaming about the island. But it was not until he was sent to Dulwich that he knew real stability or any settled happiness.

Dulwich College is an old foundation with an interesting history, since it was built and endowed by a famous seventeenth-century actor named Edward Alleyn. It is in one of the most beautiful of London's suburbs; and if one could take away everything built since the 1890s, when Plum first saw it, it would consist chiefly of very good seventeenth- and eighteenth-century houses, the beautiful picture gallery designed by Sir John Soane, and the well-kept acreage of grounds and playing fields in which the college stands. The buildings of the school are imposing rather than beautiful. In 1858 it was divided into two schools—the Upper School, or Dulwich College, and the Lower, or Alleyn's School. The main buildings, designed by Sir Charles Barrie, are therefore Victorian. Not an enchanted place like Eton or Westminster, it is spacious, peaceful, and well kept. Plum, and before him his father, fell in love with it on sight. On one of his visits to England, Ernest had happened to see Dulwich from a train, and he so much admired the grounds and buildings that he immediately decided to send Armine there.

Class distinctions in England in the late nineteenth century were so intricate and so numerous that they were not merely incomprehensible to foreigners, but understood only by Englishmen of a high enough social status to view their ramifications with a knowledge of upper-class taboos, and they were nowhere more prevalent than in the public school system. The exactitude of Plum's description of Dulwich is therefore most interesting.

> It was what you would call a middle-class school. We were all the sons of reasonably solvent but certainly not wealthy parents, and we all had to earn our living later on. Compared with Eton, Dulwich would be something like an American State University compared with Harvard or Princeton. Bertie Wooster's parents would never have sent him to Dulwich, but Ukridge could very well have been there.[7]

For his first term at Dulwich Plum was a day boy, lodged at the house of an assistant master. Then he boarded at one of the school houses, named Ivyholme, and later, after his parents left for Shropshire, at a house called Elm Lawn. He had a combination of qualities that enabled him to adapt easily to the life of a public school. The Wodehouse family were unusually able, both at work and at games. Armine and Plum were in the school teams for cricket and for football, although Armine was a better cricketer than Plum. (Neither of them was of the class of their cousin N. A. Wodehouse—Uncle Fred's son—who captained the England rugger team.)

> I was in the school cricket team two years and in the school football team one. I was a forward—what corresponds to the line in American football—and was very heavy for a school footballer, weighing around a hundred and seventy pounds. At cricket I was a fast bowler—the equivalent of a baseball pitcher. We had a great team my year, not losing a school match.[8]

One may pause here to remark that it was important to Plum's later career that he was above average at games. In the school stories both games and boxing are described with a practical knowledge, and an enthusiasm, which only personal participation and enjoyment could give. And although he took up golf too late in life to excel, his theoretical knowledge is immense, culled, one imagines, more from books than from braving the horrors of personal contact with a professional. But he must have had some lessons to begin with, and he would have regarded professional games players with less apprehension than other forms of humanity.

The two brothers were also above average intellectually. Armine won a scholarship to Oxford, and Plum might have done so if Ernest could have afforded the additional fees for both sons. Armine won the Newdigate prize and the Chancellor's essay prize, and he got a first-class honours degree in Classics. (Plum's younger brother, Dick, who scarcely comes into this story, was a German scholar and, at school at Cheltenham College, won the Schacht German prize. He also had the curious distinction of being the child croquet champion of Gloucestershire.)

No boy who is good at games ever has a bad time at school. He is assured of the admiration of his fellows; and to those who are physically well co-ordinated, there is nothing in the world more exhilarating than regular games. In addition, Plum had the great good fortune to be at Dulwich in Gilkes's time. A. H. Gilkes, a famous headmaster, was a brilliant classical scholar, and his teaching must have been an important influence on Plum. J. T. Sheppard, who became Provost of King's, Cambridge, and is remembered as a most distinguished classical scholar and as a producer of plays, was also a pupil of his. He once said that no one who had the fortune to learn Latin prose and Greek verse from Gilkes could fail to acquire a mastery of language. While Gilkes was at Dulwich, work was taken as seriously as games.

At Dulwich Plum lived in a community and took part in all its activities as he was to do only once more in the whole of his life. In his early years there, he worked very hard in order to try for a scholarship at Oxford. "In my day, to the ordinary parent, education meant Classics. I went automatically on the Classical side and, as it turned out, it was the best form of education I could have had as a writer." But after he learned that he would not in any case go to Oxford, he ceased to make any special effort. Instead he took a prominent part in all the activities of the school. He shared a study with William Townend, who wrote to Jasen:

> Plum was an established figure in the school, a noted athlete, a fine footballer and cricketer, a boxer: he was a school prefect, in the Classical Sixth, he had a fine voice and sang at the school concerts, he edited the *Alleynian:* he was, in fact, one of the most important boys in the school.[9]

This picture of Plum as a schoolboy is completely unexpected to those who knew him only later in life, and important to an understanding of his qualities as a man. He was not one of those who simply find security and protection in male society, as is not uncommon with middle-class Englishmen (possibly as a result of their early segregation in public schools). When he grew up, he disliked clubs as much as he disliked parties. Writing to Richard Usborne in 1956, he said:

I was at one time a member of Garrick, Beefsteak, Constitutional and over here Coffee House and the Lotos of New York. At a very early stage I was a member of a ghastly little bohemian club called the Yorick, and later, of course, the Dramatists Club. But I hated them all and I never went into them. I loathe clubs. The trouble is, it's so difficult to resign. I think I hated the Garrick more than any of them. I did resign from the Garrick.

And again to Richard Usborne, in 1964, he wrote:

Poor old Malcolm [Muggeridge]! He's always getting into hot water. I wonder why he doesn't leave the royal family alone. Still, I do think he has a case against the Garrick. I can't see that a club has any right to censor the doings of members outside the club. Of course, personally I think the Garrick is doing a member a favour when it gives him a legitimate excuse for resigning.

Clearly, his fear of society was never confined to fear of female society. He was a genuine recluse and socially incompetent. He could converse, if necessary, with one person at a time—an interviewer, for instance—but he disliked and feared it beyond anything his companion could be aware of. It seems likely that his happiness at Dulwich was at least in part because in the atmosphere of a public school he was submerged in a group, while he had opportunities for the expression of his considerably varied talents. "Dulwich was like an American College," he said to David Jasen, "in that if you're playing football you mix with people in the football side, and so on. I was pretty friendly with everybody, but I had no very intimate friends."[10]

At Dulwich he was taken for granted—his nickname was "Podge," which suggests a degree of familiarity and tolerance—and boys do not expect or require intimacy except from a very close friend. The conversation in any closed community is a kind of "shop" in which it is easy for the initiated to take part even with people whose background and character are basically dissimilar. At Dulwich Plum could participate without being drawn in.

When he said to David Jasen that he had no very intimate friends at

Dulwich, I think he had forgotten William Townend. One of the great happinesses of Dulwich may have been that he did have a friend. Townend has left this picture of him:

> We were together in one of the four boarding houses, Elm Lawn, [which is] still standing with its war damage repaired and [is] now the residence of the Master of Dulwich, the headmaster. Plum and I shared a study at the back of the house: a small room with a sloping roof; though we preferred to work downstairs in what was known as the Senior Common Room—or Senior Study—which had a large table and was unoccupied during the two hours sacred to prep—preparation—each evening. We were supposed to prepare our lessons for the next day. I don't remember that Plum ever did. He worked, if he worked at all, supremely fast, writing Latin and Greek verses as rapidly as he wrote English. This is my recollection. But certainly the two hours were not filled entirely with work: we talked incessantly, about books and writing.[11]

Townend said Plum was such an omnivorous reader that it was impossible to say who were his favourite writers, and he gave a short list—Barry Pain and James Payne, Kipling and W. S. Gilbert. Probably at this time Plum also read some of the classics, Dickens in particular. Townend adds: "And from the first time I met him, he had decided to write. He never swerved."

There are other memories of him. In 1939 the *Daily Mail* quoted the whole of his report for the summer term 1899:

Classical VI Form.

Place in form 23	No in form 25
Latin Prose	V. Fair
Greek Prose	Poor
Latin Verse	Often good
Greek Verse	Fair only
Latin Unseen	V. fair
Greek Unseen	Good
Prepared Authors	Just satisfactory
General Paper	Fair
Critical Paper	Bad
Ancient History	Weak
English Essay	Not very strong

General remarks

He has done just fairly in the Summer examinations, but no more. I fear he has spent too much thought upon his cricket and the winning of colours.

He is a most impractical boy—continually he does badly in examinations from lack of the proper books; he is often forgetful; he finds difficulties in the most simple things and asks absurd questions, whereas he can understand the more difficult things.

He has the most distorted ideas about wit and humour; he draws over his books and examination papers in the most distressing way and writes foolish rhymes in other people's books. Notwithstanding, he has a genuine interest in literature and can often talk with much enthusiasm and good sense about it. He does some things at times astonishingly well, and writes good Latin verses.

He is a very useful boy in the school and in the VI form, and one is obliged to like him in spite of his vagaries. We wish him all success, and if he perseveres he will certainly succeed.

William Townend told Richard Usborne that Plum had a habit of decorating his textbooks with tiny matchstick figures.One day in class Gilkes asked Plum to lend him his Euripides. "Gilkes handed this book back, saying with a shudder: 'No thanks. This book has got a man in it!' This, William Townend told me, made Wodehouse laugh for about a year."[12]

Also in illustration of the headmaster's remarks, A. H. Smith, the famous Warden of New College, who was at Dulwich with Plum, told the following story to Lord Robbins, who told it to me.

Plum had to read aloud some poetry containing the line "Think not that I am unfaithful to thee, O King." He read: "Think not that I am unfaithful to thee, Old Horse." When asked why he had read the line in that way, he replied that he did not know; it had seemed appropriate. (I am aware that this story would be much improved if I had succeeded in tracing the source of the line that seems to be inaccurately quoted; but I give it because the point has so inimitably the Wodehouse flavour that one may be sure the narrator's memory has not failed here.)

Plum never fell out of love with Dulwich; indeed, the intensity of his feeling needs explanation. "Except for Alec Waugh," he said to David Jasen, "I seem to be the only author who enjoyed his schooldays." And he added: "To me, the years between 1894 and 1900 were like heaven."[13] Until the war, when he left England forever, he always visited Dulwich; and, however busy he was he always found time to report the school football matches for the *Alleynian*. In later life he followed these matches with as much personal involvement as if he had still been a member of the team. None of this may strike one as very peculiar (although the strength of his interest in the matches forty or fifty years after he had left the school is surely unusual), but the degree of emotion described in the following passage from Richard Usborne's *Wodehouse at Work* certainly needs explanation.

"Billy" Griffith, who captained the Dulwich Rugger side through a season without defeat, told me that he had a letter from Wodehouse (whom he had not met) after the last desperate school match. Wodehouse, writing from Dorchester, said he had tried to see the match through from the touchline, but couldn't bear the tension and had to go and walk round the outside of the school grounds, waiting for the whistle and the final cheer to make sure that Dulwich had held their slight lead to the end. When he deduced the good news, he walked home to his hotel and found he remembered absolutely nothing of the seven-mile footslog through the streets, as he was thinking only about the match.[14]

There is an intensity of emotion and a passionate involvement in that passage which cannot be attributed merely to the immaturity of a man who had never outgrown the successes of his schooldays. Plum did not require identification with some early glory of his own (surely he had no need to). Instead there is the quite unusual attachment to what is basically an abstraction—even though one solidly built in bricks and mortar—which is quite outside general experience.

Before Plum went to Dulwich, he was moved from one base to another, and in the holidays from one household to another, and he would have found even small details of behaviour learned in one place subject to correction in the next. There is no suggestion that (with the possible exception of his favourite aunt, Louisa) anyone felt any particular affection for him or that he regarded anywhere as home. In later life he often said that he believed his affection for servants was a result of spending so much time with them as a child. At Dulwich he entered for the first time a stable society, whose manners, habits, and philosophy were unchanging and whose discipline imposed intelligible limits.

Above all he joined a group of boys with whom he lived on comparatively easy terms. Several studies have been made of the adult personalities of children brought up in groups without parents or parent substitutes; and although the findings relate to groups who came together at a much younger age, they describe some of Plum's characteristics in a manner too striking to be ignored. They suggest that although the ability to make relationships is impaired by lack of experience of love, the emotions normally aroused by single persons are not lacking but concentrated instead on the group. "There is a flatness of emotion between single people, a physical and psychical distance . . . intimacy, comradely friendship is praised in theory and dreaded in practice . . . [yet] group-centred feelings are very strong indeed, and rewarding. They [the members of the group] dwell lovingly on the things they have done together when young, on the shared joys and adventures."[15]

Plum cannot be categorized as a psychological type, since he was full of contradictions as well as highly idiosyncratic. He dreaded individual contacts, and, having no strong feeling for other people, often aped what he believed to be the proper response (as in his praise of the books of acquaintances, which was almost always excessive). But he was genuinely affectionate to a few people, and his personality was not cold. His contradictions are revealed in the many letters and the diary which will be quoted here. The purpose of these remarks is merely to attempt to throw light on the intensity of his feeling for his school.

One further event of his childhood was important. After Ernest and Eleanor Wodehouse left the house in Dulwich where they had stayed so short a time, Plum spent his holidays in Shropshire. Here he had his first dog. All his life he would lavish on animals the stores of affection he could not bestow on man.

Plum continued to visit his family until his father died in 1929. After that his closest tie was with his brother Armine. He occasionally saw Peveril, but Dick, so much younger than himself, he hardly knew. Even his relationship with Armine was disrupted, because the latter, with the exception of the war years, when he was severely wounded while serving with the Scots Guards, spent almost the whole of his life in the Indian Educational Service, holding professorships at several different colleges. In 1911, when Professor of English at the Central Hindu College at Benares, he joined Mrs. Besant and the Theosophists, becoming President of the Theosophical College at Benares. For a time he edited the Theosophist newspaper *Herald of the Star*, and for a time he acted as tutor to Krishnamurti and his brother, Nityananda. Like his more famous brother, he wrote verses, and these appeared regularly under the name "Senex" in the *Times of India*. Plum kept in touch with him until the end of his life and grew fond of his wife, Nella, and their son.*

---

*A street in South Bombay is named Wodehouse after Armine, and one in Hunstanton, Norfolk, after Plum.

2

The Early Years

In *Psmith in the City*, Mike, the schoolboy cricketer, is unable to go to a university because his father has suffered a severe and unexpected financial loss. To his dismay, chivalrously hidden, he is sent instead to London to earn his living in the New Asiatic Bank. On his first night in London he goes to Acacia Road in Dulwich to find a room to live in.

> There is probably no more depressing experience in the world than the process of engaging furnished apartments. . . . In answer to Mike's knock, a female person opened the door. In appearance she resembled a pantomime "dame," inclining towards the restrained melancholy of Mr. Wilkie Bard rather than the joyous abandon of Mr. George Robey. Her voice she modelled on the gramophone. Her most recent occupation seemed to have been something with a good deal of yellow soap in it. (*Psmith in the City*, Chapter 3)

In answer to his question about a bed-sitting-room, the pantomime dame tells Mike to walk upstairs, and at the top of a dark flight of stairs she opens a door.

> It was a repulsive room. One of those characterless rooms which are only found in furnished apartments. To Mike, used to the comforts of his bedroom at home and the cheerful simplicity of a school dormitory, it seemed about the most dismal spot he had ever struck. A sort of Sargasso Sea among bedrooms. (*Psmith in the City*, Chapter 3)

On this first evening Mike goes out after engaging his room and walks to the Dulwich College cricket field, where he sits down.

> Up till now the excitement of a strange adventure had borne him up; but the cricket-field and the pavilion reminded him so sharply of Wrykin. They brought home to him with a cutting distinctness, the absolute finality of his break with the old order of things. . . .
> The clock on the tower over the senior block chimed quarter after quarter, but Mike sat on, thinking. It was quite late when he got up and

began to walk back to Acacia Road. He felt cold and stiff and very miserable. (*Psmith in the City,* Chapter 3)

The following day Mike goes to St. Paul's by tube and follows "the human stream" till he finds himself outside the massive building of the New Asiatic Bank.

> Inside, the bank seemed to be in a state of some confusion. Men were moving about in an apparently irresolute manner. Nobody seemed actually to be working. As a matter of fact, the business of a bank does not start very early in the morning. Mike had arrived before things had really begun to move. As he stood near the doorway, one or two panting figures rushed up the steps, and flung themselves at a large book which stood on the counter near the door. Mike was to come to know this book well. In it, if you were an employee of the New Asiatic Bank, you had to inscribe your name every morning. It was removed at ten sharp to the accountant's room, and if you reached the bank a certain number of times in the year too late to sign, bang went your bonus. (*Psmith in the City,* Chapter 4)

Mike is taken to the postage department, where the work is "not intricate." "There was nothing much to do except enter and stamp letters, and, at intervals, take them down to the post office at the end of the street."

The interest in all this is that it is the first and by far the best account of P. G. Wodehouse's own period in the Hong Kong and Shanghai Bank. It will be remembered that his father, while sending Plum's elder brother Armine to Oxford, was unable to afford the fees for two. In September 1900, at the age of nineteen, Plum was therefore sent to London to earn his living. The details of the book in which one had to sign one's name, and of the "not intricate" work in the postage department, appear again and again in his accounts of this time; so too does the image of squalor in his lodgings. He told David Jasen that he lived alone in a small bed-sitting-room off Markham Square, which he described as "horrible lodgings off the King's Road." (Today Markham Square is regarded as one of the nicest squares of small houses in London, while Acacia Road has been rejuvenated and, though not central, is also very pleasant.)*

When Mike arrives in the postage department, he has a conversation with his predecessor which again follows the experience of P. G. Wodehouse:

> Men are always leaving for the East, and then you get shunted on into another department, and the next new man gets the postage. That's the best of this place. It's not like one of those London banks where you stay in London all your life. You only have three years here, and then you get

---

*There is no Acacia Road, but Plum was probably thinking, as I was, of Acacia Grove.

your orders, and go to one of the branches in the East, where you're a
dickens of a big pot straight away, with a big screw and a dozen native
Johnnies under you. (*Psmith in the City*, Chapter 4)

In *Over Seventy* Wodehouse wrote:

> At the end of two years . . . [the bank trainees] were sent out East to
> Bombay, Bangkok, Batavia and suchlike places. This was called getting
> one's orders, and the thought of getting mine scared the pants off me. As
> far as I could make out, when you were sent East you immediately became
> a branch manager or something of the sort, and the picture of myself
> managing a branch was one I preferred not to examine too closely. I
> couldn't have managed a whelk-stall.[1]

Mike was luckier than Plum, for during his first day in the bank who
should arrive, to solace his friend and confuse the authorities, but Psmith.
Later Plum used his period in the Hong Kong Bank, like everything else
that happened to him, as material for humour; but one gets the impression
that it was the most boring and unhappy time of his life, saved only by his
confidence in his ability to escape. He waited all day for his return to his
"horrible lodgings" in the evenings.

"I wrote everything in those days," he said, "verses, short stories, articles for the lowest type of weekly paper, only a very small portion of them
ever reaching print." According to Jasen, he had a total of eighty items
published during his two years at the bank. Among the newspapers for
which he wrote then and in subsequent years were *The Captain* and the
Public School Magazine, *Titbits*, *Fun*, *Weekly Telegraph*, *Sandow's Physical
Culture Magazine*, *Answers*, *St. James's Gazette*, and *Today*.

The first two of these were most important to his development. He read
a serial in *The Captain* and realized this was something he could do: "I
first started writing public school stories because it was the only atmosphere I knew at all." In the short term the most important event was not
the school stories, however, but his association with the *Globe* newspaper.
Plum learned that William Beach-Thomas, whom he had known as a master
at Dulwich, was working as assistant editor of a column called "By the
Way." He went to see him and asked him to help him get work; and
Beach-Thomas, who remembered his articles in the *Alleynian*, arranged
that when either he or Harold Begbie, the editor of the column, wished to
take a day off, Plum should fill in for him. This he did several times,
apparently giving satisfaction, because one day he was suddenly asked
whether he would do the work for five weeks while Beach-Thomas took a
holiday.

In *Over Seventy* Wodehouse seems to suggest that he was sacked from
the Hong Kong Bank for writing a piece called "The Formal Opening of a

New Ledger" on the front page of one. In fact he was not sacked, but, again like Mike (who was suddenly asked to play cricket for his county and, finding the offer irresistible, left the Asiatic Bank on the spur of the moment), he was forced suddenly to decide between the security of a job, even one he hated, and what might be the chance of a lifetime. "On September 9, 1902," he wrote in his diary, "having to choose between the *Globe* and the Bank, I chucked the latter and started out on my wild lone as a freelance. This month starts my journalistic career."²

Almost a year later William Beach-Thomas resigned from the *Globe*, and Plum inherited his position. The "By the Way" column consisted of humorous comments in short paragraphs or verses on the topics of the day. Every morning the newspapers were scanned for the main topics, and the material had to be ready by midday. Today it seems an execrable mixture of puns and facetious comment, of which the following examples are no worse than the rest.*

Today's Great Thought

To be chicken-hearted is the worst defect from which a man or an egg can suffer.—Mr. Keir Hardie (addressing a meeting in South Africa).

Today's Greater Thought

Sea-sickness is a universal scourge. We read in Keats that "Stout Cortez stared with eagle eyes at the Pacific." In those days they leaned over the side.—Sir Thomas Lipton.³

Plum himself seems to have been well aware in later life that the column did him no great credit. "The column itself was an extraordinary affair in England," he told Jasen. "You would quote something from the morning paper and then you'd make some comment on it. It was always the same type of joke. Nobody had altered that formula in all the fifty years of its existence."⁴ And he said of *The By the Way Book*—a collection which is now exceedingly scarce—that it was an "awful production," while in 1955, in answer to some questions about his early work from Richard Usborne, he wrote:

When you come over here I will give you the book in which I kept a record of all the money I earned from writing from the time I started till 1908. . . . It's very interesting, though I find it slightly depressing as it shows the depths I used to descend to in order to get an occasional ten-and-six. Gosh, what a lot of slush I wrote! . . . But I hope you aren't planning to republish any of the stuff I wrote then. What a curse one's early work is. It keeps popping up. I got a nasty shock a month or so ago

*This example has been chosen as quite certainly by Wodehouse. Stout Cortez is one of his great favourites, appearing again and again in his books.

when I picked up the magazine Charteris . . . publishes over here and
found in it a detective story—yes, a detective story and a perfectly lousy
one—which I sold to *Pearson's Magazine* somewhere around 1910.

And yet some of his work in those days shows extraordinary verbal ease
and felicity. The following is an example of his work for *Punch* in the year
1902:

'Tis Folly to Be Wise

(An American scientist has come to the conclusion that the tendency of too
much education or intellectual development in women is to make them lose
their beauty.)

> O PHYLLIS, once no task to me was sweeter
>   Than, grasping my enthusiastic quill,
> To hymn your charms; erratic though the metre,
>   It gained in fervour what it lacked in skill.
> But now, alas, those charms are like to vanish.
>   Without preamble duty bids me speak.
> The rumour runs that you are learning Spanish,
>   And also—simultaneously—Greek.
>
> Those eyes, to which I loved to dash off stanzas,
>   No longer gaze, as erstwhile, into mine;
> They're fixed on *Quixote's* deeds, or *Sancho Panza's*
>   Or rest upon some Aeschylean line.
> Or, as you spell THUCYDIDES his speeches,
>   Your face assumes a look of care and pain.
> O PHYLLIS, heed the moral that it teaches,
>   And cease to run the risk of growing plain.
>
> Shun, I implore, the vampire Education.
>   Be guided by my excellent advice.
> You owe a solemn duty to the nation—
>   Simply to give your mind to looking nice.
> Learning may be acquired, but beauty never:
>   Dry books, believe me, were not meant for you.
> Be fair, sweet maid, and let who will be clever.
>   If brains are wanted, I've enough for two.

Wodehouse had two articles published in *Punch* in 1902. One, entitled
"Under M.V.C. Rules," combines to a remarkable degree the style of
Punch in the early years with the style we are now able to recognize as that
of Wodehouse. It is a comment on a newspaper article about a new game
called Vigoro, which is said to have the characteristics of both cricket and

tennis, to be played with a soft rubber ball, and to be playable all the year round by both sexes. Beginning "And so ended the first of the five Test matches . . . ," the article goes on to say that England did well to win in spite of bad luck:

> During the majority of the three days snow fell heavily, and it is common knowledge that Larwood is never at his best on a snowy wicket. Indeed we seriously question the wisdom of the selection committee in playing him. . . .
> In fielding we still have much to learn from our visitors. The performance of the New Zealanders in England's first innings, and indeed throughout the match, was a treat to behold. Anything finer than the catch by which Miss Slogginson dismissed Gilbert Jessop it has never been our lot to witness. At first sight the hit appeared perfectly safe. The ball had all the known force of Mr. Jessop's racquet behind it, and, as so often happens with soft india-rubber balls, was swerving nastily. Miss Slogginson, however, although fully thirty yards away, and up to her waist in a deep drift, nevertheless contrived to extricate herself and arrest the ball on her racquet just as it was about to clear the ropes. A wonderful effort, which brought down the house, together with a small avalanche from the roof of the pavilion.[5]

(None of his work for *Punch* is signed, but *Punch* keeps an index of their contributors so that even today it is possible to identify the authors of the various pieces.)

Some of the best and most amusing of Wodehouse's early verses appeared not in *Punch,* however, but in the *Daily Express* at the end of 1903. Because these were unsigned, and because it seems likely he classed them with the rest of the "slush" of that time, he seems not to have mentioned these to Jasen or to anyone else, and they have until now been lost.

The great political issue of the time was Free Trade. Joseph Chamberlain, who believed the Empire could be held together only by material ties, was in favour of a measure of Imperial Preference which would involve a tariff barrier against other countries. He was supported by a majority of the Unionist Party, although opposed by a minority. Being unable to persuade the Prime Minister to accept his policy at that time, he resigned from the Government in order to hold meetings all over the country to put forward his ideas. "If you are to give preference to the colonies," he told the House of Commons, "you must put a tax on food." The Liberal Party would eventually come to power on this issue, and one of the main planks of their programme was that Imperial Preference would mean that the cost of food would rise.

On 30 September 1903 there appeared on the front page of the *Daily Express*—a Unionist and protectionist paper—the following set of verses:

The Parrot

Where the Cobden Club relaxes into grief at "stomach taxes"
A parrot perches daily just above the entrance door.
He doesn't mind what's said to him, or sung to him or read to him
For he can answer nothing but: "Your food will cost you more."

He's a bird of solid tissue and he meets each fiscal issue
With the tiring repetition of a venerable bore.
He never says "Explain to me," or "Just repeat the same to me,"
He simply ends discussion with: "Your food will cost you more."

When you show him that a duty is a thing of perfect beauty,
That it sets the mills a-buzzing with an ever-growing roar,
That our wages will be rising to an altitude surprising,
He offers the suggestion that: "Your food will cost you more."

To the promise "Joe" is giving—that the cost of daily living
No farthing will be higher than it ever was before
He replies by calmly closing both his eyes as if in dozing
And repeating quite distinctly that: "Your food will cost you more."

When you prove that separation would destroy the Empire's station,
That the Colonies are asking what their Mother can't ignore,
That they'll buy the things we're making while their crops at home we're taking,
He remarks without a tremor that: "Your food will cost you more."

With a parrot thus repeating an invariable greeting
The arguments are wasted that upon his head you pour
When you cry "Oh! Free Food mummy!—can't you once forget your tummy?"
He's safe to say in answer that: "Your food will cost your more."

Under these verses there appeared the legend: "This wonderful parrot will give his views on fiscal matters tomorrow."

In fact this wonderful parrot gave his opinions six days a week right through October and until 15 November, after which he continued intermittently, when particularly provoked, until the middle of December. His efforts were always on the front page and always headed "The Parrot." When some particular political issue arose he commented on that; otherwise he took for his theme various topics of the day, or merely his own thoughts.

Of those with no particular application, among the best is the following.

In the usual Fleet-street garret
Sat a poet; and the Parrot,
Full of quaint misinformation,
Fluttering idly through the door,
Found him dashing off a sonnet.
He was gently musing on it,
When the Parrot broke the silence
With "Your food will cost you more!"

Said the bard, "Ah, pray be quiet!
What have I to do with diet
When the myst'ries of Parnassus
I am trying to explore?
With this aim my soul obsessing
I consider it depressing,
This degrading, fleshly question
Whether food will cost us more.

"I consume not steak nor chop. I
Take a lily or a poppy,
And I gaze on it, enraptured,
Every day from one to four.
Insignificant my bill is
For a day's supply of lilies.
Now I hope you understand why
Food can never cost me more."

And while I risk excessive length, I cannot close this topic without mention
of the cassowary.*

Having lunched on missionary,
A voracious cassowary
Had composed himself for slumber,
He had just begun to snore—
When he saw a Parrot flutter
To the ground and heard him utter
His inevitable dictum
That "Your food will cost you more."

---

*If I were a cassowary
On the plains of Timbuctoo
I would eat a missionary
Cassock, band, and hymn-book too.

Bishop Samuel Wilberforce (1805–73)

"Though I'm mostly somewhat chary,"
Said the courteous cassowary,
"Of attending to a stranger
Whom I've never seen before,
On the subject that you mention
I can give you my attention,
For I dote on fiscal questions,
Why 'Your food will cost you more.'

"In the past my 'Little Mary' "*
(Said the blushing cassowary)
"I have filled with men and hymn-books,
A cuisine which I adore.
May I ask your grounds for saying
That the bill I'll soon be paying
Will be longer?" Sighed the parrot
"Ah, Your Food Will Cost You More."

"Come now, hang it, I declare I"
(Said the outraged cassowary)
"Never met with such a person.
Fancy putting in your oar!
This debate you'd best abandon.
Why, you've not a leg to stand on."
And the Parrot found no answer
But "Your food will cost you more."

This is only a small sample of the verses, which, for the speed and skill with which they were produced, can be compared to the work of Osbert Lancaster.

On 9 November the Parrot verses, which had continued to appear on the front page, were supplemented by an article on page 5. Mr. Dan Leno, it was said, had two parrots and was endeavouring to teach them to say "Your food will cost you more." On 11 November it was announced that the *Daily Express* offered a prize of £25 to anyone who succeeded in teaching the sentence to a parrot. On 12 November it was reported that many people had already begun to teach their pets and that dealers were offering parrots who could say the sentence. Then in December it was announced that so many parrots had been entered for the £25 prize that a competition would be held in the French Saloon of the St. James's Restaurant on 17 December. Further announcements connected with this competition became a regular feature, and these might have been written by anyone on the *Daily Express* staff, but there is no doubt about who wrote

*"Tummy."

the report of the competition which appeared on 18 December. Occupying two columns, this was headed "Screech Day," and it opened with the following sentence: "If the tail-feathers of all the parrots present in the French Saloon of the St. James's Restaurant yesterday afternoon could be placed end to end they would reach part of the way to the North Pole."

The difficulty was that although the parrots present had learned to say the required words in the privacy of their own homes they refused to do so in public.

> Some of them looked very shamefaced, as though burdened with the memory of past recklessness. One bird, after repeated coaxing, plaintively started out on the absurdity and delivered himself of "Your food will cost you"—when reason got the better of him, and he hid his head under one wing, refusing to commit himself to any degree of comparison. . . .

> There was one parrot which . . . should have walked away with the prize. In private life, it appeared, the talented fowl could not only say "Your food will cost you more," but make long speeches and sing snatches of song. Yet in the hour of need not one syllable proceeded from its beak.

> "Pretty Polly," shouted its owner, hitting it on the nose to quicken its wits. "Marie Louise, I love thee. My name is Polly Sceptre Cwibel. Fiscal policy! Fiscal pol-icy! (irritably). I'll twist your neck! Shut up!" An unnecessary exhortation this last one . . .

> One owner struck a sinister note. "You can bet your life your food will cost you more," said he grimly to his speechless pet, as he took it back to the ante-room.

And so on.

Wodehouse's early work remains quotable because of his humour and his great verbal dexterity. His ear was that of a parodist, and he could fall into almost any style required with ease.* What is astonishing, too, is that he should be able to carry out that most difficult of all assignments, a regular daily feature which has to be composed on the day it goes to press—not once but twice every day.

During the whole of this period he was also engaged on the school stories. In 1902 his first book, *The Pothunters*, which had run as a serial in the *Public School Magazine*, was published as a novel by Messrs. A. & C. Black. The same publishers brought out his second book, *A Prefect's Uncle*, in 1903; and while *Tales of St. Austin's*, a collection which formed his third book, had all been written earlier and published in *The Captain* and the *Public School Magazine*, *The Gold Bat* was actually run as a serial in *The Captain* at the same time as the *Daily Express* published the Parrot verses.

*Two more of his poems published in *Punch* in 1902 appear in *The New Oxford Book of Light Verse*, chosen by Kingsley Amis (Oxford University Press, 1978), pp. 211–14.

There are several accounts of how he came to write the school stories. Probably the most complete and the best was given to Richard Usborne in a letter written in 1955:

> When was the first number of *Chums?* Was it 1892? Anyway, it contained—in addition to Max Pemberton's "Iron Pirate"—a school story by Barry Pain called "Two" (published in book form as *Graeme and Cyril*). It made an enormous impression on me. It had practically no plot but the atmosphere was wonderful. I was re-reading it only the other day and it's great stuff.
>
> Then—in 1900—*The Captain* appeared, and in the first number was a serial by Fred Swainson called *Acton's Feud.* It began, I remember, "Shannon, the old international, had brought down a hot side to play the school . . . ," and if there has ever been a better opening line than that, I have never come across it. It was something entirely new in school stories—the real thing—and it inflamed me to do something in that line myself. If it hadn't been for *Acton's Feud,* I doubt if I would ever have written a school story.
>
> As a child, of course, I read *Eric* and *St. Winifred's* and the Talbot Baines Reed stories in the BOP [*Boy's Own Paper*] I loved them all. I think it is only later that one grows critical of *Eric* and *St. W's. . . . Tom Brown,* fine. Also *Vice Versa.* But *Acton's Feud* was the best of the lot.

The Wodehouse school stories are extraordinarily good. It is common and quite justified to regard them as a preliminary canter for what was to come, but although they are completely ingenuous and entirely about boys under eighteen, for this very reason they reveal his great gifts as a storyteller as nothing more sophisticated could do. My neighbour T. R. Fyvel tells me he has lately been reading *The White Feather* to his grandson, with equal pleasure to both of them, while in my seventy-second year I have read all the school stories, obviously not at a sitting, but at a gallop, and have found myself going in early from the garden to find out what happened at Aldershot or whether Sedleigh beat Wrykin. The great talent of the storyteller is to make you itch to reach the solution even though you are aware that, in the ethics of the popular story, only one is possible. After more than seventy years, the Wodehouse school books can still do that.

Humour breaks through only occasionally, but there are most of the other hallmarks of a Wodehouse novel—the carefully worked out plot and subplots, the affectionate treatment of clichés, and, although sometimes rather clumsily introduced, a roving delight in quotation. The accounts of boxing, football, and cricket gain immensely, as the golf stories would later, from an all-round knowledge of the sports, while one may recognize, in hindsight, many a well-known character in the embryonic stage. There is, in particular, a boy called Clowes, who might be said to have developed in several directions:

> Clowes became quite animated at the prospect of a real row.
> "We shall be able to see the skeletons in their cupboards," he observed. "Every man has a skeleton in his cupboard, which follows him about wherever he goes. Which study shall we go to first?"
> "We?" said Trevor.
> "We," repeated Clowes firmly. "I am not going to be left out of this jaunt. I need bracing up—I'm not strong, you know—and this is just the thing to do it. Besides, you'll want a bodyguard of some sort, in case the infuriated occupant turns and rends you."
> "I don't see what there is to enjoy in the business," said Trevor, gloomily. "Personally, I bar this kind of thing. By the time we've finished, there won't be a chap in the house I'm on speaking terms with."
> "Except me, dearest," said Clowes. "I will never desert you. It's of no use asking me, for I will never do it. Mr. Micawber has his faults, but I will *never* desert Mr. Micawber." (*The Gold Bat*, Chapter 20)

It has been said that the Wodehouse school stories were unusual in their period because they were free from moralizing. This is an interesting point, and particularly so in relation to Wodehouse's known addiction to Kipling. In *The Strange Ride of Rudyard Kipling*, Angus Wilson says:

> [Kipling's] is a code that seeks to give the fullest rein to individual skills, energies and cunning for the evasion of minor rules and the outwitting of lesser authorities, while always upholding a strong sense of the overall need for a higher law or social cohesion to which the individual must submit himself in total self-discipline and responsibility. In *Stalky & Co.* he conveniently brought home the lesson, by constantly overriding the prevailing English public-school ethics, which derived ultimately from the great influence of Thomas Arnold's reforms at Rugby School in the early years of Victoria's reign. A mature boy . . . will not accept the ruling of his life by repeated rotes, whether "pijaws" from the padre, or talks about house honour from the housemaster, or pep talks on the team spirit from the prefects.[6]

And he says later:

> For instance when a housemaster tries to make a scapegoat of a boy, by declaring him "a moral leper," not to be spoken to by other boys, he may learn with surprise that his supposed victim is taking every advantage of the seclusion of his moral leperhood to live his own life without regard for the school's conventions.[7]

In Wodehouse there are no " 'pijaws' from the padre, talks about house honour from the housemaster, or pep talks on the team spirit from the prefects," because none of these things is necessary. All Wodehouse school heroes accept and live by the Arnold code of honour, morality, and team spirit, as, it is fairly obvious, their creator does. Loyalty, to one's friends, house, school (probably in that order), is the essential virtue, while physical courage is (as Evelyn Waugh once put it) not a virtue but a necessary quality.

> "And what are you going to do about Rand-Brown?"
> "Fight him, of course. What else could I do?"
> "But you're no match for him."
> "We'll see."
> "But you *aren't*," persisted Clowes. "He can give you a stone easily, and he's not a bad boxer either. Moriarty didn't beat him so very cheaply in the middleweight this year. You wouldn't have a chance."
> Trevor flared up.
> "Heavens, man," he cried, "do you think I don't know all that myself? But what on earth would you have me do? Besides, he may be a good boxer, but he's got no pluck at all. I might outstay him."
> "Hope so," said Clowes.
> But his tone was not hopeful. (*The Gold Bat,* Chapter 21)

In *The White Feather,* Sheen (an unpopular and lonely boy) is accompanying Drummond (one of the bloods) when they come across some of their school fellows in a fight with the boys of the town. Drummond plunges joyfully in, but Sheen, muttering "The old man might not like— sixth form you see—oughtn't we to . . . ?" turns away. Later he calls on Drummond in his study:

> "Drummond, I . . ."
> Drummond lowered the book.
> "Get out," he said. He spoke without heat, calmly, as if he were making some conventional remark by way of starting a conversation.
> "I only came to ask . . ."
> "Get out," said Drummond again.
> There was another pause. Drummond raised his book and went on reading.

Sheen's and Drummond's house is Seymour's; Sheen has been seen running away by members of rival houses:

> So the thing was out. Linton had not counted on Stanning having seen what he and Dunstable had seen. It was impossible to hush it up now. The scutcheon of Seymour's was definitely blotted. The name of the house was being held up to scorn in Appleby's, probably everywhere else as well . . .

Seymour's was furious. The senior day-room to a man condemned Sheen. The junior day-room was crimson in the face and incoherent. The demeanour of a junior in moments of excitement generally lacks that repose which marks the philosopher.

"He ought to be kicked," shrilled Renford.

"We shall get rotted by those kids in Dexter's," moaned Harvey.

"Disgracing the house," thundered Watson. (*The White Feather*, Chapter 5)

Sheen is treated to a period of "moral leperhood," not because of any intervention from a housemaster, but as a natural consequence of his failure. His reaction is not to take advantage of the seclusion thus afforded him "to live his own life without regard for the school conventions," but to take boxing lessons in order to be able to redeem himself (incidentally, from a boxing instructor who, when acting as his second in the ring, advises him to "Bear't that the opposed may beware of thee").

Nor does the typical Wodehouse schoolboy regard authority with much hostility. The prefects and heads of houses are usually good at games and therefore heroes, and the masters are quite decent people, although they live on the other side of a high fence and by a totally different set of rules. If, by an accident, one finds the silver cups that have been stolen, one cannot simply go to the headmaster and tell him, because it would also involve a confession that one had been out of bounds. This is necessary to the exigencies of the plot, in that too early a solution would be fatal, but it is also convincing and quite clear that the master is not so much an enemy as a person with an indiscriminate rigidity which prevents him from distinguishing between what is important and what is not. Wodehouse's code and Kipling's (as Angus Wilson interprets it) are both essentially romantic and about equally dated; but the quiet and modest Wodehouse hero, who will win in the end but may suffer on the way, is more in tune with the mood of today than is Stalky with his too easy victories and his horrible war cries.

In 1904 Plum was commissioned to write the text to accompany some pictures with captions in verse for a children's book called *William Tell Told Again*. This book has not survived, having been reprinted soon after it first appeared, but not again. The pictures are not inspiring, and the verses serve only to show how much better Wodehouse himself did this sort of thing. His text is sympathetic, not very easy to quote, but with the pleasantness and balance of his other work: "The Lord High Executioner entered the presence. He was a kind-looking old gentleman with white hair, and he wore a beautiful black robe, tastefully decorated with death's-heads." (*William Tell Told Again*, Chapter 1) The only book of the early period in which it is difficult to find much merit is *The Swoop,* and this again has become a collector's piece and one almost impossible to find.*

When Plum was a very old man, Edward Cazalet asked him whether he had ever thought of writing a detective story. He replied that he had often been tempted and would have loved to do so, but he had refrained because he did not want to let himself down. He did not refer to his reputation, but to a feeling that it was better to stick to one's last. It is interesting, therefore, to note that certainly *The Pothunters* and arguably *The Gold Bat* have plots that are based on a theft and the subsequent detection of the thief.

**The Swoop was not in fact published until 1909, but it falls into the early period. So rare is it today that at the time of his death Wodehouse himself had only a photostat copy made from a library copy.*

3

Ukridge

During the first three years of his life in London Plum seems neither to have had nor to have desired to have any personal friendships or any leisure. In *Psmith in the City,* he describes Mike's life in the bank in words which recall those used in an earlier chapter to explain his own attitude to his school friends.

> Mike, as day succeeded day, began to grow accustomed to the life of the bank, and to find that it had its pleasant side after all. Whenever a number of people are working at the same thing, even though that thing is not perhaps what they would have chosen as an object in life, if left to themselves, there is bound to exist an atmosphere of good-fellowship; something akin to, though a hundred times weaker than, the public school spirit. Such a community lacks the main motive of the public school spirit, which is pride in the school and its achievements. Nobody can be proud of the achievements of a bank. (*Psmith in the City,* Chapter 13)

This friendly tolerance towards colleagues who make no great personal appeal, but with whom a natural reluctance to superficial contacts has been dulled by familiarity, is clearly a description of his own feelings for the men he met in the Hong Kong Bank. His parents had now moved from Shropshire, which he loved, to Cheltenham, which he thought "beastly," and no outside claims interfered with his total absorption in writing. His output at this time was prodigious. He must have gone occasionally to the theatre, because he early exhibited knowledge of the current productions, and I learn in a letter from Mr. F. E. Puxon that he attended a school of dramatic art run by a Mrs. Marie Tickell, Mr. Puxon's great-aunt. Mr. Puxon writes: "She had had a stage career, and was the sister of Frederick Mouillet, fairly well-known actor/manager/dramatist and author of *What the Butler Saw. . . .* My impression now is that the school was not a great success, and that my great-aunt was rather proud of the fact that P.G.W. was one of her pupils!" The theatre would soon become so much a part of Plum's professional activities that this can hardly be regarded as a leisure pursuit, but it is curiously characteristic that, so professional himself, he should have chosen a school which was "not a great success" and run by a woman.

Soon, however, a new life opened out as a result of a visit from a man named Herbert Westbrook. Plum had by now installed himself in a large bed-sitter in 23 Walpole Street, Chelsea, and Westbrook, who wished to make a career as a writer, called there to ask his advice on how best to establish himself. The two men became friends, and as a result, Westbrook took Plum down to Emsworth House, a small preparatory school in a village of the same name on the borders of Hampshire and Sussex at which he was an assistant master.

Emsworth House was run by Baldwin King-Hall, known to his intimates as "Baldie," and that Plum should have found himself there is a happy example of the ease with which even the most idiosyncratic of men fall among friends. The school itself is described as a "rather eccentric, but efficient and happy establishment," and an account of its conduct by Baldie written by his nephew Stephen King-Hall brings to mind that other eccentric John Christie of Glyndebourne, who as a master at Eton is reputed to have taken Early School in his pyjamas.

> After a few curious months spent at a small preparatory school at Emsworth, conducted by a lovable genius (another uncle called Baldwin King-Hall, who had failed to become the third brother in the navy because of bad eyesight), I was deposited at La Villa. All I can remember about Emsworth is that we sat round my uncle's bed at ten every morning whilst he ate his breakfast and conducted what I suppose one might call a seminar on life in general, and that Mr. P. G. Wodehouse was a member of the staff.[1]

A further (unpublished) description of Emsworth House, written by Mrs. Alistair MacLeod (a sister of Stephen King-Hall and a niece to Baldwin), whose husband taught there in the 1920s, is as follows: "When my husband went there . . . he found no clocks going, Uncle Baldie in bed most mornings—but everyone *happy* & a devoted domestic staff! and boys passing out quite well too! Which just proves—what?" And of the incidents described by her brother, Mrs. MacLeod writes:

> Two young men came to teach at Emsworth House. . . . P. G. Wodehouse and Herbert Westbrook. I remember PG helping my Aunt, Ella King-Hall, to produce "musicals" for the boys. My Aunt was extremely musical (she composed for Adeline Genée, the ballerina, & Melba sang one or two of my Aunt's compositions). PG was fun—we youngsters thought, but my Mamma disapproved of Emsworth House as a school, especially a frivolous young master called Wodehouse. So when my Father (then a Captain) was away in China, my Mother descended in a cab

& removed my brother Stephen. . . . PG helped her—as it was a real family row—with Stephen's trunk & tried to explain things to my Uncle.[2]

At no time in his life could Plum have been justly described as "frivolous," although the distinction may well have been too difficult for Mrs. King-Hall to make. The view that he was actually a master has support from several other people who have written to me, but it seems not to be true. (This was a long time ago, and memories for detail are apt to be faulty.) He told David Jasen that he went there because it was a good place to write, and in more than one letter he stated categorically that he was never a master, "although I used to stay there." There is no conceivable reason to disbelieve him; he was earning enough to live on, and the size of his published output would not have disgraced three writers. It left no time for teaching. The mistake probably arises because he used to play cricket with Baldie and the boys, and to help Baldwin King-Hall's sister, Ella, put on plays. It was in character, nevertheless, that quite unconscious of being thought frivolous, or even a master, he should have helped Mrs. King-Hall to get Stephen away. He was very happy now, and mildly in love with Ella King-Hall, who, although eighteen years older, was talented, affectionate, and charming. She was much loved by everyone. Her niece, Mrs. Mac-Leod, says that Ella recognized from the first that Plum was a quite exceptional young man, "who lived in his own (marvellous) world and fled from harsh reality." She goes on: "[My aunt] added something I'm a bit vague about. It was to the effect that when someone called at Emsworth House (had he a brother or a nephew?) he didn't want to see, P.G.W. locked himself into the bathroom for *hours*."

But of all the odd characters at Emsworth, not even Plum was odder than Westbrook. As a young man he must have had a persuasive charm, because, although his eccentricities had none of the innocent and benign character of the lay-abed Baldie's, he seems to have been generally liked. He was born with the egotistical temperament of the artist, but unfortunately without the compensating gifts; and, extraordinarily idle, he spent such talent as he had on optimistic schemes for his future. He expected unwavering support from his friends for all ideas touching his own advancement, and was full of heartfelt reproaches if it was not immediately forthcoming. He borrowed money he did not repay, and an attractive and spontaneous generosity when he had money (his own or other people's) too often came to grief through some initial miscalculation. David Jasen tells the story of how on one of the few occasions that Plum went out to dinner, he was forced to wear a dinner jacket belonging to an uncle who was much taller and bigger than he was, because he found at the last minute that Westbrook had already sauntered out in his own.* Westbrook, in short, was Ukridge, or, more accurately, Ukridge was very largely Westbrook.

Curiously enough, although Ukridge is a rather squalid character, there have been several candidates for the part of the original from which he was drawn. The honour must be divided between Westbrook and a man called Carrington Craxton. William Townend gave Wodehouse the idea for *Love among the Chickens,* in which Ukridge first appeared, when he described to him the character and real-life adventures of Craxton. Wodehouse undoubtedly saw similarities in the character of Westbrook and embroidered on the basis given him by Townend. In 1952, in reply to a fan letter, he volunteered the following information: "Ukridge is a real character. He was drawn from a man with whom I used to run about London from 1903 onwards." The exigencies of *Love among the Chickens* required Ukridge to have a wife, but Plum had a short way with unwanted characters, and in later stories he did away with her.

Of all the main Wodehouse characters, Ukridge is generally regarded as the least satisfactory. Evelyn Waugh spoke of him as being "contrived" ("I do not believe that in his work he distinguished between a contrived character like Ukridge and an inspired one like Bertie Wooster"),[3] and while it does not in the least invalidate the criticism, it is curious that it should have been made about one of the few characters who are consciously taken from life. It is surprising that Ukridge appeared so soon, for he lacks the innocence of most Wodehouse characters and might well be the creation of a writer whose inspiration was on the wane. Wodehouse himself loved him and thought him very funny. "I'm glad you've come round to Ukridge," he wrote to Leonora in 1935. And if Ukridge himself is not thought entirely successful, surely the narrator of these stories is one of the best in literature. He has none of the flatness and lifelessness of most narrators, but is tolerant, humorous, and kind, and it is easy to see through his eyes.

> Except that he was quite well-dressed and plainly prosperous, the man a yard or two ahead of me as I walked along Piccadilly looked exactly like my old friend Stanley Featherstonehaugh Ukridge, and I was musing on these odd resemblances and speculating idly as to what my little world would be like if there were two of him in it, when he stopped to peer into a tobacconist's window and I saw that it was Ukridge. It was months since I had seen that battered man of wrath, and, though my guardian angel whispered to me that it would mean parting with a loan of five or even ten shillings if I made my presence known, I tapped him on the shoulder. Usually if you tap Ukridge on the shoulder, he leaps at least six

*See "First Aid for Dora," Chapter 4 in the collection *Ukridge;* and "Ukridge and the Old Stepper" in *Eggs, Beans and Crumpets.*

inches into the air, a guilty conscience making him feel that the worst has happened and his sins have found him out, but now he merely beamed, as if being tapped by me had made his day.

Ukridge is in funds and, generous as ever, he takes his friend to lunch at the Ritz. Over lunch he tells the diverting but not very edifying story of how he comes to be in a position to entertain in such style. Then, sixteen pages later, a man comes up to their table.

> His eyes, as they bored into Ukridge, were bleak.
>
> "I've been looking for you for a long time and hoping to meet you again. I'll trouble you for sixty pounds."
>
> "I haven't got sixty pounds."
>
> "Spent some of it, eh? Then let's see what you *have* got," said the man, turning the contents of the wallet out on the table-cloth and counting it in an efficient manner. "Fifty-eight pounds, six and threepence. That's near enough."
>
> "But who's going to pay for my lunch?"
>
> "Ah, that we shall never know," said the man.
>
> But I knew, and it was with a heavy heart that I reached in my hip pocket for the thin little bundle of pound notes which I had been hoping would last me for another week. (*Plum Pie*, Chapter 4)

But if Plum loved Ukridge, his feeling for Westbrook was ambivalent. Between 1903 and 1914 he spent a good deal of his time at Emsworth. When he first went there he lived in lodgings; but in January 1904 he rented a house called Threepwood, and in 1910 he bought this house, for £200. Westbrook stayed with him there a good deal, and until 1909 the two men shared a flat in London. When Plum became assistant editor of the *Globe* "By the Way" column, he gave Westbrook his old job of filling in on days off, and when, in August 1904, he was promoted to editor, he made Westbrook his assistant. There is something affectionate, too, in the dedication to *The Gold Bat*: "To that Prince of Slackers, Herbert West-brook." However, there is also evidence that he was not always as tolerant of Westbrook as his narrator is of Ukridge. William Townend tells us in *Performing Flea* that he and Plum corresponded regularly after they left school, but that all letters before 1920 were lost. A few survived, however, and the following clearly refers to the plot for *Love among the Chickens*. (It has the added interest of being the first known letter written by P. G. Wodehouse.)

March 3, 1905   22 Walpole St.
                                                             S.W.

Dear Willyum,

This is great about our Westy. Damn his eyes. What gory right has he got to the story any more than me? Tell him so with my love. As for me, a regiment of Westbrooks, each slacker than the last, won't stop me. I have the thing mapped out into chapters, and shall go at it steadily. At present it isn't coming out quite so funny as I want. Chapter One is good, but as far as I have done of Chapter Two, introducing Ukridge, doesn't satisfy me. It is flat. I hope, however, to amend this. . . .

Do send along more Craxton stories (not improper ones). I am going to pad the book out with them, making Ukridge an anecdotal sort of man. If they are *mildly* improper, it's all right.

Do come up on the 10th. You needn't bring Westy, though. I am very much fed up with him just now, as he has been promising all sort of things in my name without my knowledge to some damned cousins of his, the Goulds, which might have made a lot of worry for me. . . .

R.S.V.P. I have locked up your MS in case of a raid by Westy. Don't give him all the information you've given me. Not that he would ever get beyond Chapter 2 though. His intention of rushing through *his* book doesn't worry me much!

Yrs.
PGW

In 1907 Plum published a book called *Not George Washington* written in collaboration with Herbert Westbrook. All his life he collaborated with other people, because his insatiable appetite for writing could be appeased only by a stream of plots beyond the inventive capacity of one mind. It is characteristic of his habit of using his own experiences in his fiction that the plot of *Not George Washington* turns on the point that the hero writes under many different names and in collaboration with others. The novel itself, written in three parts, has three different narrators. The first part is set in Guernsey and its hero is a young man named James:

> It seemed that a guardian—an impersonal sort of business man with a small but impossible family—was the most commanding figure in his private life. As for his finances, five-and-forty sovereigns, the remnant of a larger sum which had paid for his education at Cambridge, stood between him and the necessity of offering for hire a sketchy acquaintance with general literature and a third class in the classical tripos.[4]

James wishes to become a journalist, and he discusses this with the heroine, Margie, who is also the narrator of the first part:

> "Of course I mean," he said, "I suppose it would be a bit of a struggle at first, if you see what I mean. What I mean to say is, rejected manuscripts and so on. But still, after a bit, once get a footing, you know—I should like to have a dash at it. I mean, I think I could do something, you know."
>
> "Of course, you could," I said.
>
> "I mean, lots of men have, don't you know."

"There's plenty of room at the top," I said.
He seemed struck with this remark. It encouraged him.[5]

Margie's mother is a philosopher, and she is reading *The Deipnosophists of Athenaeus* when Margie goes nervously to her to ask her permission to marry James. "My mother likes James. 'Margie,' she once said to me, 'there is good in Mr. Cloyster. He is not for ever offering to pass me things.' "[6]

The author of the first part is clearly recognizable, but the novel goes slightly to pieces after that. It has rather a silly plot and will probably never be thought worth a reprint.

In 1909 Westbrook married Ella King-Hall, although, like Plum, he was considerably younger than she was. Westbrook and his wife continued to play a part in Plum's life, but it soon ceased to be a very close one. Westbrook failed as a writer, and Ella's family never approved of him. At the end of his life he became a much embittered man. In 1912 Ella Westbrook set up as a literary agent, and after serving in the 1914 war, Westbrook joined her in this undertaking. Their agency never became very extensive, but its survival was made certain because it received the commission for the publication in England of the work of a single author—P. G. Wodehouse.

To give an adequate description of Plum's prodigious output and varied undertakings during the ten years after 1902 when, at the age of twenty-one, he decided to leave the bank, is exceedingly difficult. In 1904, having a five-week holiday from the *Globe*, he spent his accumulated savings on the first of many trips to America. All his life he would feel at home there, and in *Over Seventy* he wrote:

> Why America? I have often wondered about that. Why, I mean, from my earliest years . . . was it America that was always to me the land of romance? It is not as though I had been intoxicated by visions of cowboys and Red Indians. Even as a child I never became really cowboy conscious, and to Red Indians I was definitely allergic. I wanted no piece of them.
>
> And I had no affiliations with the country. My father had spent most of his life in Hong Kong. So had my Uncle Hugh. And two other uncles had been for years in Calcutta and Singapore. You would have expected it to be the Orient that would have called me. . . .
>
> This yearning I had to visit America . . . was due principally, I think, to the fact that I was an enthusiastic boxer in those days and had a boyish reverence for America's pugilists—James J. Corbett, James J. Jeffries, Tom Sharkey, Kid McCoy and the rest of them.[7]

Plum's autobiographical reminiscences are invariably written more to amuse than to inform, but they usually have a basis in fact, and it may be true that his passionate interest in boxing was one of the reasons for this particular visit. He did meet Kid McCoy, who later reached print as Kid Brady. Yet it may be supposed that, like other Englishmen who have difficulty in communicating with their fellows, he felt an exhilaration in the company of the Americans which he had never known in his own country. From bootblack to tycoon, the American is not merely friendlier than the ordinary Englishman but is unconcernedly prepared to lead the conversation. From the beginning Plum clearly recognized there was something here for him, and we can surely believe that on this first visit to New York he spent most of his time listening, some of it in one of the innumerable bars. In any case he was soon writing dialogue like this:

> "Well?" said Billy, looking up. "Hello, what have you got there?"
> Master Maloney eyed the cat as if he were seeing it for the first time.
> "It's a kitty what I got in de street," he said.
> "Don't hurt the poor brute. Put her down."
> Master Maloney obediently dropped the cat, which sprang nimbly on to an upper shelf of the book-case.
> "I wasn't hoitin' her," he said, without emotion. "Dere was two fellers in de street sickin' a dawg on to her. An' I comes up an' says, 'G'wan! What do youse t'ink you're doin', fussin' de poor dumb animal?' An' one of the guys, he says, 'G'wan! Who do youse t'ink youse is?' An' I says, 'I'm de guy what's goin' to swat youse one on de coco if youse don't quit fussin' de poor dumb animal.' So wit dat he makes a break at swattin' me one, but I swats him one an I swats de odder feller one, an' den I swats dem bote some more, an' I gets de kitty, an' I brings her in here, cos I t'inks maybe youse'll look after her." (*Psmith, Journalist*, Chapter 2)

Soon, too, he acquired a sound working knowledge of New York's underworld. In *A Gentleman of Leisure* (1910) the Captain of Police has made a huge fortune through corruption, but he had been led into this (not unwillingly) because he was forced to pay for his promotion. And *Psmith, Journalist* (1915) must be one of the earliest novels to have as a theme the warfare between the New York gangs, which, with protection money, was to bring about, there and in Chicago, an era of illegal harassment and violence unequalled in peacetime in any other country. J. B. Priestley remarked in an article on Wodehouse, "In the matter of wildly metaphorical slang he has beaten the Americans at their own game. Meet a New York crook of Mr. Wodehouse's invention and you find he talks not as such crooks actually do talk, but as they would like to talk." This may be so, but the kitty in the above passage (taken from *Psmith, Journalist*) belongs to a New York gang leader named Bat Jarvis, the owner of twenty-three cats, who, in return for the services done to this one, protects Psmith in times of greatest need, and he clearly had a real-life counterpart. In

Playboy's Illustrated History of Organized Crime, the following passage occurs:

> Born Edward Osterman in Brooklyn's emerging Jewish ghetto about 1873, where his immigrant father had set up shop as a kosher restaurateur, Monk Eastman . . . soon proved himself adept in the violent, hectic criminal streets of that borough. About the only gentle aspect of this squat, massive, muscular, bullet-headed, cauliflower-eared thug was his love of cats and pigeons. At one time he owned 100 cats and 500 pigeons and he usually travelled with a cat under each arm, several more tagging at his heels and a great blue pigeon that he had tamed perched on his shoulder. . . . "I like the kits and the boids," he said often, "and I'll beat up any guy dat gets gay wit' a kit or a boid in my neck of the woods."[8]

A second event of 1904 of importance equal to Wodehouse's trip to America was his first entry into the London theatre. He was asked by an actor-manager named Owen Hall to write an extra lyric for a musical comedy called *Sergeant Brue*. Edwardian musical comedies were designed to attract an audience who found the rigours of classical music too great for them. They were a watered-down version of light opera, very often adapted from Viennese operetta (*The Merry Widow* was the most famous), and consisted of spoken dialogue interspersed with song. Their success depended to a very large extent on the music; the book and lyrics—usually written by two different people—were as a rule simple if workmanlike, while nothing much was required of the performers except to look beautiful, wear clothes well, and sing in tune, although the leading actors usually had what is known as star quality. These productions were superseded in the 1920s by the American-style musical comedy, technically more athletic and more accomplished, which introduced jazz.

Plum had a good ear for music, and Guy Bolton told me that, although he was not a trained musician or an instrumentalist, he could whistle accurately any tune he had once heard. He preferred to write lyrics to music already composed, which is unusual. His first lyric for *Sergeant Brue* was a success; (called "Put Me in My Little Cell") it was a comedy number about the comforts of gaol: "There are pleasant little spots my heart is fixed on, / Down at Parkhurst or at Portland on the Sea, / And some put up at Holloway and Brixton, / But Pentonville is good enough for me." As a result he was sent for by Seymour Hicks (possibly forgotten, but an actor with a great name in the theatre in his day) who offered him a job at the Aldwych as part of the resident staff who wrote or adapted musical comedies, sometimes as ghosts for Hicks, sometimes under their own names. In his diary on the day he was engaged, Plum wrote: "Regular job at £2 a week, starting with the run of *The Beauty of Bath* (March 19th), to do

topical verses etc." But Westbrook, who was with him when he was offered a job, recorded: "On leaving the stage door, Plum was so stunned
with joy and excitement that we walked a mile along the Strand without
him knowing where he was or whether he was coming or going."[9]

The name of the composer of the music for *The Beauty of Bath* was
Jerome Kern, and ten years later this early meeting would lead to the
famous collaboration between Wodehouse, Kern, and Guy Bolton.

4

Psmith

Plum became a friend of Seymour Hicks and his wife, whose stage name was Ellaline Terriss. In her published memoirs she recalls that he used to stay with them in the country: "We called him 'the Hermit' because he would go and hide himself away for hours in a little plantation of trees while he did his writing."[1] She also says that he was "like a rather large boy, with an open and happy nature," a description which, as far as it goes, is true.

One very curious incident occurred as a result of this friendship which throws light on Plum's attitude toward money. We know from a letter he wrote to Richard Usborne that when he left the Hong Kong Bank he had fifty pounds saved, and he makes the interesting comment that fifty pounds meant that you could live on your capital for about eighteen weeks. In 1903, the first year of his literary career, he made £215 18s. 1d., in 1904, £411 18s. 1d., in 1905, £500; in 1906, £505; and in 1907, £527 17s. 1d. In 1905 he also sold both the book and serial rights of *Love among the Chickens* in America for a thousand dollars, but owing to his choice of literary agent, he either did not receive this or received it only over the years and after much trouble. It is therefore astonishing to find that he paid £450 to Seymour Hicks for a secondhand Darracq motorcar.

In *Mike* a boy called Spiller complains because Psmith has moved into his study.

> "It's beastly cheek," he repeated. "You can't go about the place bagging studies."
>
> "But we do," said Psmith. "In this life, Comrade Spiller, we must be prepared for every emergency. We must distinguish between the unusual and the impossible. It is unusual for people to go about the place bagging studies, so you have rashly ordered your life on the assumption that it is impossible. Error! Ah, Spiller, Spiller, let this be a lesson to you."
>
> "Look here, I tell you what it—"
>
> "I was in a car with a man once. I said to him: 'What would happen if

you trod on that pedal thing instead of that other pedal thing?' He said, 'I couldn't. One's the foot brake, and the other's the accelerator.' 'But suppose you did?' I said. 'I wouldn't,' he said. 'Now we'll let her rip.' So he stamped on the accelerator. Only it turned out to be the foot brake after all, and we stopped dead, and skidded into a ditch. The advice I give to every young man starting in life is: 'Never confuse the unusual and the impossible.' " (*Mike*, Chapter 33)

For a master of the analogy, this is a very surprising one, long-winded, clumsy, and unrelated to the matter in hand. But we need to know that this is a description of a recent event in Plum's own life. According to his own account in *Over Seventy*, he smashed the Darracq car up in the first week, and he gave David Jasen a fuller account. After one rather sketchy driving lesson from Seymour Hicks, he set off by himself to Emsworth. He got nearly there in safety, but just outside the village he drove the car into a ditch. He clambered out of it, walked to the local railway station, and took a train to London. He left the car where it was and never drove again. This story, so difficult to believe if one compares the cost of the car with his earnings, becomes more credible if one imagines the situation in 1905, without garages or any obvious means of pulling a car out of a hedge. Taking into account Plum's exceeding dislike of contacts with the human race, one can believe it happened as he said. In any case, he lost for the first time—but not, I think, the last—the whole of his accumulated savings.

Another friend of Plum's early years was Charles Bovill, a writer of some repute in the theatre and of short stories for the *Strand*. I find it impossible to establish the chronology of this friendship. The first evidence of their association is in 1907, when they both wrote lyrics for *The Gay Gordons,* and they collaborated later in a series of stories for the *Strand* called "A Man of Means" (Plum stated that they worked out the plots together, but that he did the actual writing, and the latter part of this statement is fairly obvious). Yet Bovill's sons, who have been good enough to help me with their recollections, believe that he was influential in getting Plum started both in the theatre and on the *Strand,* in which case they must have known each other much earlier, because by 1907 Plum needed no help. At any rate, at some period Plum used to stay at the Bovills' flat when he was in London (this seems most likely to have been after Westbrook married), and he also stayed with them in their country house. The Bovills were fond of Plum, but they remembered him as very mean. A story was told me of how, when the two men were travelling down to the country together, Plum merely fumbled while Bovill bought his ticket until finally the latter said, "And a third single for my man." Although Plum could be exceptionally generous to friends and collaborators, he was sometimes very mean in small matters. Yet, if his visits to the Bovills coincided with his purchase of Hicks's car, it may have been that he had no money.

During this period there occurred one of the major events of his whole career. In 1907 he wrote a two-part serial for *The Captain*, the first part being called *Junior Jackson*, the second *The Lost Lambs*, afterwards published in book form as *Mike*. (Today they are once more available in two parts, *Mike at Wrykin* and *Mike and Psmith*.) Now, although Psmith is generally considered to be one of the most original and most inspired of Wodehouse's characters, he spans, unlike Ukridge, who persisted for many years, only a very short period of his creator's output. For this reason he deserves, and indeed requires, a good deal of attention.

It is not by chance that Evelyn Waugh dates the beginning of the great period with complete precision as coinciding with the entry of Psmith (he is wrong, though, in giving the publication date as 1910); clearly he was brought up on him. In 1935, his father, Arthur Waugh, then Chairman of Chapman and Hall, wrote to Wodehouse:

> There was a time, in Alec's schooldays, when we used to read your books together with enormous enjoyment; and, though we are never long enough together nowadays—to read more than a telegram—we have still preserved a sort of freemason's code of Psmithisms, which continually crop up in our letters. Indeed, I can truly say, in emulation of Wolfe, that I would far rather have created Psmith than have stormed Quebec.[2]

Admirers of Evelyn Waugh will be interested to know that he inherited his tastes from his father, because Psmith is the only Wodehouse character possessed of the aristocratic virtues. Evelyn adored the aristocratic virtues, which for him were the only thing (apart from piety) which separated mankind from the lower forms of life, and in consequence he was considered a snob. Yet it is dull to confuse people who like the qualities which, because of their upbringing, background, and circumstances, are more likely to be found in dukes than in those less materially fortunate, with those who simply like dukes. All the aristocratic virtues are based on self-confidence, an equipment which makes for quick-wittedness, moral fearlessness, unconformity, and lack of envy, although sometimes for less attractive qualities.

Psmith, as is well known, sprang fully formed into the mind of his creator as the result of a chance phrase. Wodehouse has described more than once how this happened. This is from the introduction to the 1969 edition of *Something Fresh*:

> People are always asking me . . . well, someone did the other day . . . if I draw my characters from living figures. I don't. I never have, except in the case of Psmith.* He was based more or less faithfully on Rupert

*Not true, as we have seen already in the cases of Ukridge and Bat Jarvis.

D'Oyly Carte, son of the Savoy theatre man. He was at school with a cousin of mine, and my cousin happened to tell me about his monocle, his immaculate clothes and his habit, when asked by a master how he was, of replying: "Sir, I grow thinnah and thinnah." I instantly realised that I had been handed a piece of cake and bunged him down on paper, circa 1908.

In a letter written to me when it was announced that I would write this biography, Dame Bridget D'Oyly Carte writes:

> It was not until after Mr. Wodehouse's death that I came across a copy of the collected Psmith stories and read the introduction he had written for it.
>
> He makes the point, as of course you know, that Psmith was a favourite character of his and almost the only one he had based on a real person, described to him by a friend as Rupert D'Oyly Carte, my father.
>
> I have unfortunately no evidence of any kind that this story is incorrect, but I am of the opinion that my father was in no sense such a character and that on the contrary his elder brother, who was also at Winchester, Lucas D'Oyly Carte, might well have been just such a person and in fact I think he was. As Lucas D'Oyly Carte died as a relatively young man it is probably not generally known that my grandfather (Richard D'Oyly Carte, of Gilbert and Sullivan fame) had two sons.

Psmith (the *P* is silent: "Like the tomb. Compare such words as *ptarmigan, psalm* and *phthisis*.") is elegant in appearance, imperturbable by nature, a magniloquent tease. He enters recklessly into situations which may turn out awkwardly (some of his qualities reappear in Uncle Gally and Uncle Fred), and he is loyal to his friends. In *Mike* he arrives at Sedleigh, having been removed from Eton by his father for doing no work, and meets Mike, who has been taken away from Wrykin for the same reason. By unorthodox means he immediately secures a study and various other privileges, and his methods would amount to insolence if it were not for his courtesy and personal charm. Like Stalky, he leads a little band to victories, but by far other means.

Psmith in the City, the second in the series, begins with a cricket match at the country house of Psmith's father, where a Mr. John Bickersdyke perpetrates the crime of walking across the screen behind the bowler's arm just as Mike is about to make his century. He is rebuked furiously by Mike and characteristically by Psmith. On Mike's first day in the New Asiatic Bank, he goes to the manager's office to be told what he is to do. He finds him talking on the telephone: "Mike waited till he had finished. Then he coughed. The man turned round. Mike had thought, as he looked at his back and heard his voice, that something about his appearance or his way of speaking was familiar. He was right. The man in the chair was Mr. Bickersdyke, the cross-screen pedestrian." (*Psmith in the City*, Chapter 4)

Later in the day another new recruit to the bank appears—Psmith. The two go out to a tea shop together:

"When I last saw you," resumed Psmith . . . "you may remember that a serious crisis in my affairs had arrived. My father inflamed with the idea of Commerce had invited Comrade Bickersdyke—

"When did you know he was a manager here?" asked Mike.

"At an early date. I have my spies everywhere. However, my pater invited Comrade Bickersdyke to our house for the week-end. Things turned out rather unfortunately. Comrade B. resented my purely altruistic efforts to improve him mentally and morally. Indeed, on one occasion he went so far as to call me an impudent young cub, and to add that he wished he had me under him in his bank, where, he asserted, he would knock some of the nonsense out of me. (*Psmith in the City*, Chapter 6)

In the chapter that follows, Psmith is seen to be haunting Mr. Bickersdyke in his private life. He has previously persuaded his father to make him a member of the Senior Conservative Club, to which his employer belongs. One day, coming down the main staircase of the club, Mr. Bickersdyke passes a tall young man in "faultless evening dress," who smiles and nods faintly but patronizingly and passes on. Mr. Bickersdyke immediately sends a waiter to question him, and he returns with the information that the young man is a member. On the following day Mr. Bickersdyke meets Psmith in the club three times, and on the day after that, seven. Each time the latter's smile is friendly but patronizing. Mr. Bickersdyke begins to grow restless. On the fourth day Psmith sits down in a chair beside him:

"The rain keeps off," said Psmith.

Mr. Bickersdyke looked as if he wished his employee would imitate the rain, but he made no reply.

Psmith called a waiter.

"Would you mind bringing me a small cup of coffee?" he said. "And for you?" he added to Mr. Bickersdyke.

"Nothing," growled the manager.

"And nothing for Mr. Bickersdyke." (*Psmith in the City*, Chapter 9)

Finally, Psmith appears at a political meeting at which Mr. Bickersdyke is speaking as a prospective candidate, and successfully heckles him. The next day the manager sends for Psmith, and in the course of a longer conversation the following exchange occurs:

"That is enough, Mr. Smith. I confess that I am absolutely at a loss to understand you—"

"It is too true, sir," sighed Psmith.

"You seem," continued Mr. Bickersdyke, warming to his subject, and turning gradually a richer shade of purple, "you seem to be determined to endeavour to annoy me." ("No, no," from Psmith.) "I can only suppose that you are not in your right senses. You follow me about in my club—"

"Our club, sir," murmured Psmith.

"Be good enough not to interrupt me, Mr. Smith. You dog my footsteps in my club—"

"Purely accidental, sir. We happen to meet—that is all."

"You attend meetings at which I am speaking, and behave in a perfectly imbecile manner."

Psmith moaned slightly.

"It may seem humorous to you, but I can assure you it is extremely bad policy on your part. The New Asiatic Bank is no place for humour, and I think—"

"Excuse me, sir," said Psmith.

The manager started at the familiar phrase. The plum-colour of his complexion deepened.

"I entirely agree with you, sir," said Psmith, "that this bank is no place for humour."

"Very well, then. You—"

"And I am never humorous in it. I arrive punctually in the morning, and I work steadily and earnestly till my labours are completed. I think you will find, on enquiry, that Mr. Rossiter is satisfied with my work."

"That is neither here nor—"

"Surely, sir," said Psmith, "you are wrong? Surely your jurisdiction ceases after office hours? Any little misunderstanding we may have at the close of the day's work cannot affect you officially. You could not, for instance, dismiss me from the service of the bank if we were partners at bridge at the club and I happened to revoke."

"I can dismiss you, let me tell you, Mr. Smith, for studied insolence, whether in the office or not."

"I bow to superior knowledge," said Psmith politely, "but I confess I doubt it. And," he added, "there is another point. May I continue to some extent?"

"If you have anything to say, say it."

Psmith flung one leg over the other, and settled his collar.

"It is perhaps a delicate matter," he said, "but it is best to be frank. We should have no secrets. To put my point quite clearly, I must go back a little, to the time when you paid us that very welcome week-end visit at our house in August."

"If you hope to make capital out of the fact that I have been a guest of your father—"

"Not at all," said Psmith deprecatingly. "Not at all. You do not take

me. My point is this. I do not wish to revive painful memories, but it
cannot be denied that there was, here and there, some slight bickering
between us on that occasion. The fault," said Psmith magnanimously,
"was possibly mine. I may have been too exacting, too capricious. Perhaps
so. However, the fact remains that you conceived the happy notion of
getting me into this bank, under the impression that, once I was in, you
would be able to—if I may use the expression—give me beans. You said
as much to me, if I remember. I hate to say it, but don't you think that if
you give me the sack, although my work is satisfactory to the head of my
department, you will be by way of admitting that you bit off rather more
than you could chew? I merely make the suggestion."

Mr. Bickersdyke half rose from his chair.

"You—"

"Just so, just so, but—to return to the main point—don't you? The
whole painful affair reminds me of the story of Agesilaus and the Petulant
Pterodactyl, which as you have never heard, I will now proceed to relate.
Agesilaus—"

Mr. Bickersdyke made a curious clucking noise in his throat.

"I am boring you," said Psmith, with ready tact. "Suffice it to say that
Comrade Agesilaus interfered with the pterodactyl, which was doing him
no harm; and the intelligent creature, whose motto was '*Nemo me impune
lacessit*,' turned and bit him. Bit him good and hard, so that Agesilaus ever
afterwards had a distaste for pterodactyls. His reluctance to disturb them
became quite a byword. The Society papers of the period frequently
commented upon it. Let us draw the parallel."

The scene ends with Psmith saying: "Personally, . . . I should advise you
to stick it out. You never know what may happen. At any moment I may
fall from my present high standard of industry and excellence; and then
you have me, so to speak, where the hair is crisp." (*Psmith in the City*,
Chapter 12)

Although the scenes between Psmith and Mr. Bickersdyke are among
the best things Wodehouse ever wrote, they are not characteristic of his
work as a whole. Psmith is a rich and idle young gentleman, but he is not
an Egg, a Bean, or a Crumpet. In fact, quite apart from his intellect, there
is an un-Wodehousian toughness about him, a kind of ferocity when roused,
which is quite unlike anything to be found in the later books. There are
elements in the scene just quoted—" 'Our club, sir,' murmured Psmith,"—
which remind one of Evelyn Waugh himself.

In the next Psmith book—*Psmith, Journalist*—he is in America. He
arrives just as the editor of a paper called *Cosy Moments* is about to take a
ten-week holiday, and he persuades the deputy editor to depart from the
usual policy of the paper (which can easily be imagined by anyone familiar

with Wodehouse), partly in order to promote a boxer called Kid Brady, but chiefly to make things hot for the owner of a tenement building, the conditions in which have aroused his chivalrous wrath. He comes into opposition with the gangs of New York, but through his usual mixture of mental and physical agility (he has a useful uppercut) easily defeats them. The real difficulty arises when the editor of *Cosy Moments* returns from his holiday to find his paper, as he sees it, in ruins.

> "It is abominable," burst forth Mr. Wilberfloss. "It is disgraceful. I never heard of such a thing. The paper is ruined."
> "You keep reverting to that statement, Comrade Wilberfloss. Can nothing reassure you? The returns are excellent. Prosperity beams on us like a sun. The proprietor is more than satisfied."
> "The proprietor?" gasped Mr. Wilberfloss. "Does *he* know how you have treated the paper?"
> "He is cognisant of our every move."
> "And he approves?"
> "He more than approves."
> Mr. Wilberfloss snorted.
> "I don't believe it."

About now, any reader with his wits about him will begin to have his suspicions. Sure enough, after some more of that sort of thing:

> Mr. Wilberfloss uttered a cry of triumph.
> "I knew it," he said, "I knew it. . . . Now, perhaps, you will admit that Mr. White has given no sanction for the alterations in the paper."
> A puzzled look crept into Psmith's face.
> "I think, Comrade Wilberfloss," he said, "we are talking at cross-purposes. You keep harping on Comrade White and his views and tastes. One would almost imagine that you fancied that Comrade White was the proprietor of this paper."
> Mr. Wilberfloss stared. . . .
> "Fancied that Mr. White . . . ? repeated Mr. Wilberfloss. "I don't follow you. Who is, if he isn't?"
> Psmith removed his monocle, polished it thoughtfully, and put it back in its place. "I am," he said. (*Psmith in the City*, Chapter 28)

From all of the above it can be seen that in Psmith, as in so many other people, the aristocratic virtues rest on the possession of money. Psmith extricates Mike from the horrors of his lodgings and takes him to his own luxurious flat, persuades his father to make him a member of Mr. Bickersdyke's club and to make Mike his agent; in another scene, when it is necessary to make a quick escape from an outer suburb of London, he merely calls a taxi; finally, he becomes the owner of the magazine with which he has successfully but recklessly amused himself while on a visit to

New York. Why then, one must ask, did Wodehouse in the final volume—
Leave It to Psmith—allow him to lose his money and force him to work
for his living? Psmith without money is a relative failure, not so much a
pale as an uninspired version of his old, patronizing self. His author apparently felt this, because at the end of the book he marries him off—fatal to
a Wodehouse hero—and gets rid of him forever.

The answer may be that by now (1915) Wodehouse knew where his real
talents lay. Psmith was a bridge, although an inspired, completely finished,
and most fortunate one, between the youthful period of the school stories
and the humorous books, with their established casts of characters and
unchanging format. When one considers the apparently innocent intentions
suggested by the title of the second part of *The Captain* serial—*The Lost
Lambs*—one cannot help wondering whether Psmith was not only a character who sprang instantly to life, but also one who ran away with his
author. It may be that, like Apthorpe in *Officers and Gentlemen*, another
splendid comic invention who had to be killed, Psmith had to be married
because he was beginning to obstruct his author's purpose—which is only
another way of saying that by the time of *Leave It to Psmith* Wodehouse
had outgrown the romantic notions of his youth and learned that his
strength lay in fantasy of a humorous kind.*

*In fact, Wodehouse wrote *Leave It to Psmith* only after much badgering from Leonora for
another Psmith book. He dedicated it "To my daughter Leonora, Queen of her Species."

5

Marriage

After 1909 Plum went regularly to America. Although the boat journey took a week, the fare was cheap, and he must have been one of the first people to commute across the Atlantic. He would have remained in New York altogether had it not been that, although he received very high payments for the stories sold to the American magazines, *Cosmopolitan* and *Collier's*, he could not find a source of regular income in the United States. So, although he had resigned from the *Globe* in 1909, he returned to London in 1910 and rejoined it. From now on he also wrote regularly for the *Strand*.

Apart from *Psmith in the City*, his most important book of these years was *A Gentleman of Leisure*. This was a clever attempt to cash in on the fashion for gentlemen burglars. ("It's a hit all right," someone says on the first page of the book. " 'These imitation "Raffles" plays always are,' grumbled Willett, who played bluff fathers in musical comedy.") The Wodehouse hero is not a real burglar, but one who undertakes to break and enter for a bet, and then becomes so circumstantially incriminated that nothing can get him out of trouble but the unexpected determination of the girl he loves to believe what he says, however improbable it sounds, and some gentle blackmailing of the heavy uncle of the piece.

A Gentleman of Leisure is not in the first rank of the novels, but it has several claims to attention. The first is that it was twice put on as a play, once in New York in 1911, when the gentleman burglar was played by Douglas Fairbanks, Sr., and again in Chicago (with the title changed to *A Thief in the Night*), when he was played by John Barrymore. The second is that, as David Jasen has already pointed out, for the first time part of the action, which takes place on both sides of the Atlantic, is set in a stately home in Shropshire, and a number of characters are introduced who, under one name or another, are to become standard to Wodehouse plots. The third matter of interest is the use of the word *jargoon*.

In the introduction to the 1969 edition of *Something Fresh*, Wodehouse states that he had rashly placed Blandings Castle in Shropshire because as a boy he had spent his happiest days there, and that when he had said that Lord Emsworth was at Eton in the sixties, he had not realized that this was not an end but a beginning. Stuck in the Blandings Castle saga, with a house in Shropshire and a peer who rapidly, or so it seemed, would become a centenarian, he quite reasonably made the best of things; and, unaware that the dissection of his work would presently become a pastime for scholars, he made light of such matters as the passing of time or the running of trains. For this reason and one has to admit, because at the speed at which he wrote, he was often unconscious of mistakes—not to mention his curious indifference to the proper flowering seasons of garden plants— he has acquired a reputation for inattention to detail. Yet in intention he was as particular about accuracy as Ian Fleming was said to be, and he took immense pains to be accurate in small things. In *A Gentleman of Leisure* Jimmy is able to extricate himself from trouble through his knowledge of stones. The great diamond necklace, with which, by a series of mistakes, he has been caught, and which was Sir Thomas's wedding present to Lady Julia, is a fake.

> "You trotted off to a jeweller and put the thing to him confidentially. I expect you suggested paste; but, being a wily person, he pointed out that paste has a habit of not wearing well. It is pretty enough when it's new, but quite a small amount of wear and tear destroys the polish of the surface and the sharpness of the cutting. It gets scratched easily. Having heard this, and reflected that Lady Julia was not likely to keep the necklace under a glass case, you rejected paste as too risky. The genial jeweller then suggested white jargoon, mentioning, as I have done, that after an application or so of the blow-pipe, its own mother wouldn't know it. If he was a bit of an antiquary, he probably added that in the eighteenth century jargoon stones were supposed to be actually an inferior sort of diamond. What could be more suitable? 'Make it jargoon, dear heart,' you cried joyfully, and all was well. Am I right? I notice that you have not corrected me so far." (*A Gentleman of Leisure*, Chapter 27)

Zircon is the name by which jargoon is known today, but although the circumstances in which it is introduced are purely fantastic, one can bet with absolute safety that Wodehouse's description will be confirmed in any decent dictionary. It is put in because, having taken the trouble to acquire the knowledge, Wodehouse thought it interesting. His use of "dear heart" is always enjoyable, too, partly because it comes a little unexpectedly from him.

In the summer of 1914, an invitation to write some articles about John Barrymore proved to be one of those small quirks of fate without which a whole lifetime might have been different. To fulfill the commission, Plum travelled with Barrymore on a German ship to New York and landed on 2 August, two days before war broke out between England and Germany. In addition, the long arm of coincidence ensured that staying in New York at that time was a young English widow born Ethel Newton.

From what is already known about Plum, one would not expect to find him capable of intense, passionate love. His relationships with women, including his wife, have been speculated upon in the idle, gossipy way in which people speculate on the intimate affairs of their friends and of public characters about whom a good deal is known. Wodehouse may or may not have been inhibited sexually as well as emotionally, and this inhibition may have been partial or complete. Not a matter on which one is ever likely to have exact evidence, it is in this case not one which is very important. Plum needed a woman in his life, and clearly this need arose chiefly from reasons other than physical. It is not, for instance, in the least surprising to find that he chose women who were either older than himself or at least mature and experienced, or that these women were invariably in a dominating relationship to him, since men who have been rejected or deprived in youth often continue in their adult lives to seek a maternal relationship. Plum was pathologically inhibited in his ordinary everyday contacts with other people, and it was essential to him to have someone to stand between him and the outside world.

Richard Usborne, in a sentence which is deservedly famous in the literature about Wodehouse, has already said almost everything there is to be said about the effect on his work of this lack of a strong sexual urge. "There is no suggestion that either clubman or girl would recognise a double bed except as so much extra sweat to make an apple-pie of."[1] I say *almost* everything, because one must remark in passing that there was a period in Wodehouse's life when he believed that love scenes were an indispensable part of a popular novel. In his youth he interpreted a remark of J. M. Barrie's, to the effect that one should endeavour to write to please editors, to mean that it was necessary to have a strong sentimental interest in his stories. "I started going in exclusively for the mushy sentiment which, judging from the magazines, was the thing most likely to bring a sparkle into an editor's eye." This led for a good many years to passages like the following:

> "Are you very happy, Elsa?"
> Elsa's eyes danced. She drew in her breath softly. Betty looked at her in silence for a moment. The wistful expression was back on her face.
> "Elsa," she said suddenly. "What is it like? How does it feel, knowing that there's someone who is fonder of you than anything . . . ?"
> Elsa closed her eyes.
> "It's like eating strawberries and cream in a new dress by moonlight,

on a summer night, while somebody plays the violin far away in the distance so that you can just hear it," she said. (*The Prince and Betty,* Chapter 1)

Plum was never at his happiest in love scenes, although he became very much more adept than that. He was, as I have said earlier, capable of creating attractive young women, but he still had to struggle with a tendency to mushiness when they were left alone with their lovers. When an artist becomes supreme in a certain style, his weaknesses will often be found to have contributed to his development almost as much as his strengths. If Plum could have written a respectable love scene, we might not have had Bertie Wooster.

Plum's first love was probably Ella King-Hall, who was fifteen years older than he was. In 1909, when she married Westbrook, he formed a relationship with a Mrs. Lilian Armstrong, who was a widow. According to Charles Bovill, he used sometimes to leave London to spend time with her. Mrs. Armstrong had a small daughter of whom Plum was very fond and to whom he wrote one of the earliest of the letters that have been kept. It was written by hand.

July 13, 1914   Emsworth
                                                                  Hants.

My darling Bubbles,

I am dreadfully sorry, but I cannot possibly come & see you before I sail. I shall be so busy packing and getting ready. I will come and see you directly I get back.

Mind you have learned to swim by then. I want you to be a really good swimmer, and then we will go away together to the sea-side and swim all day.

I am sending you a little present. It doesn't look very nice, but it means quite a lot of money. It will buy you all sorts of nice things. Give it to Mrs. Pennington and tell her what you specially want to buy, and she will get it for you. Let me know some of the things you buy. You might get another doll if you wanted one.

                                     Love and kisses
                                           from
                                           PG

Bubbles grew up and married and became Mrs. Grillo. When I wrote to her to ask if she thought Plum had been in love with her mother, she replied:

I feel he must have been in love with her as she told me on many occasions when I was older that he wanted to marry her—but she refused him. I know he was fond of her as he always enquired after her when he wrote to me earlier and when I saw him. One of my earliest recollections is of sitting in a box at a pantomime with them both. I was about two and after that he went to America. . . . I don't remember seeing him when he returned but I think by then he had met his wife, Ethel, but we always corresponded and later I met Leonora.

In New York, less than a month after he wrote the letter to Bubbles, Plum met his future wife, Ethel. She was born Ethel May Newton in 1885, and she had no lineage to compare with either the Wodehouses' or the Deanes'. She belonged to the lower middle rather than the working class, but as a child she hated her mother because (she told Nella Wodehouse) she made her play on the streets. She told Edward Cazalet that her mother was an alcoholic. "I remember her drowning a big cat and being so horrified that I hit her in the face. I really hated her. I loved my father. He was a gentleman farmer. I lived most of my childhood with my grandmother (my father's mother)."

Ethel was very young when she married Leonard Rowley and went with him to India. They had one daughter, Leonora, born in 1905. When Leonora was five, Leonard Rowley died through drinking contaminated water. Ethel then returned to England and, until after she married Plum, left Leonora in the charge of one of Leonard Rowley's sisters. Ethel was in New York on a visit in 1914 and was taken by another woman to make a fourth with two men. One of these men was Plum. They met on 3 August, and on 30 September they were married.

Ethel was never beautiful, although she had a good figure and very long, well-shaped legs, but she had an uninhibited zest which Plum seems to have found immediately attractive. They used to go to Long Beach, Long Island, together to swim, and Plum told over and over again the story of how he proposed to Ethel because, one day when he had a cold, she kept well away from him and did not talk. He was very much given to repetitious accounts of small details in his early life, but it seems likely that he did find in Ethel a sensitivity to his needs to which he was infinitely responsive. She took entire charge of his affairs, and she stood between him and the rest of the world in all things except those which most immediately concerned his work. No hidden hand was ever felt by agents or publishers, but in all other professional matters one should always read Ethel for Plum.

Her influence cannot be exaggerated. Richard Usborne told me that because Plum's parents had quarrelled over money, Plum believed that one or the other of the partners to a marriage should manage it, but never both. This may be true, but Ethel would have managed theirs in any case, and he would have wished it. She took charge of everything, and from the beginning she made him a small weekly allowance for his petty cash. It cannot, however, be said that she married him for his money, because at the time of their marriage he had just one hundred dollars in the bank.

She was a great gambler, very gregarious by nature, and she loved parties. For many years she forced Plum into a semblance of participation in social life, and this was probably a good thing, because without her he would probably have been a recluse too early. (In spite of all appearances to the contrary, many ideas and small incidents in his books were founded on life.) But she always understood that writing was an absolute necessity to him, and at the end of their lives when they lived at Remsenburg she made very great sacrifices to provide the isolation that he wanted.

The typical Wodehouse heroine changed after Plum got married: she put on more flesh and blood. She was no longer someone who believed that to be in love was to live on a perpetual diet of strawberries and cream, eaten to the sound of soft music; sometimes she even behaved in the manner of real life. In *Joy in the Morning* Boko has made an ass of himself again:

> Nobby, who since the initial spilling of the beans had been sitting bolt upright in her chair with gleaming eyes, making little gulping noises and chewing the lower lip with pearly teeth, endorsed this.
>
> "Fathead," she concurred, speaking in a strange, strangled voice, "is right. Of all . . ." Preoccupied though Boko was, there must have penetrated to his consciousness some inkling of what the harvest would be, were she permitted to get going and really start hauling up her slacks. He strove to head her off with a tortured gesture. (*Joy in the Morning*, Chapter 20)

Plum once said that he thought of Lord Emsworth as rather like himself, and certainly Lady Constance had some of the characteristics of Ethel.* Ethel made him wear tiresome clothes, and go to London when the sun was shining on the garden, to interview people about affairs she understood far better than he did; she made him accept unwelcome people into the house and converse with them when he wanted to be left alone. But she ran the house and left him free to write, and Plummie loved her then and thereafter, and called her Bunny. Greatest happiness of all, she brought with her Leonora.

Leonora died before she was forty, more than thirty years ago. Yet when it became known that I was going to write this book, people immediately started saying to me: "I am so glad, because now you will be able to say something about Leonora." Several strangers wrote to me to say that they could not help me with any information about Wodehouse himself, but they had once met his daughter, and remembered her as an exceptionally

---

*Edward Cazalet once said: "The things that Lord Emsworth hated are all the things Plum hated himself." And in an interview at the end of his life with Graham Lord of the *Sunday Express*, Plum said that of all his characters he felt closest to Lord Emsworth: "I have a longing for peace and quiet and I am rather bossed about by female relations."

charming girl. Again and again there are references to her in letters about other things. Thus Hugh Kingsmill wrote in a letter in 1927: "Met P. G. Wodehouse's daughter . . . delightful girl of nineteen [*sic*], very intelligent and most amusing."

Charm is notoriously indefinable, and in this case more than usually so, because, although it is true that Leonora was very intelligent and full of humour, she had no outstandingly original characteristics by which one might convey her personality. Her charm, like Plum's prose, consisted more in an exquisite balance of qualities than in any particular one. Physically she was not really beautiful, but she was humorous looking, fair, blue-eyed, with a turned-up nose and a short upper lip, and very long legs like her mother's. Every Wodehouse heroine looks like the photograph with Peter Cazalet (see insert). I once asked her sister-in-law, Thelma Cazalet, why she thought Leonora was so much loved, and, after thought, she replied: "Because of her humanity." She was the only person she had ever known, Thelma said, who treated all men as equal. She had no understanding or feeling for class barriers, and she was interested in everyone she met. This is true, and it is also true that she was very feminine in the sense of having the qualities commonly attributed to women. All over the world large, good-natured men can be seen soothing little, fussy women who are worrying about small things, but it is still believed that women, through a mixture of calmness, instinct, and maternal love, exert a hidden but benevolent despotism over the men they are attached to. Leonora really did conform to this pattern. Possibly because she was brought up by Plum, her attitude to men was, as near as I can describe it, not so much one of belonging to a superior creation as of belonging to an older one. She expected very little and was not easily disappointed. In *Joy in the Morning*, Nobby (that same Nobby) is explaining to Bertie that Uncle Percy does not approve of Boko, whom she wishes to marry.

> "How old do you have to be before you can marry without Uncle Percy's kayo?"
> "Twenty-one."
> "How old are you now?"
> "Twenty."
> "Well, there you are, then. I knew that if we looked close enough we should find that the sun was still shining. You've only got to wait another year, and there you are."
> "Yes. But Boko leaves for Hollywood next month. I don't know how you feel about this dream man of mine, but to me, and I have studied his character with loving care, he doesn't seem the sort of person to be allowed to go to Hollywood without a wife at his side to distract his attention from the local fauna." (*Joy in the Morning*, Chapter 6)

Leonora might have spoken with this tolerance about a man she loved, but I have never known any other woman who would. She was nine when Plum first saw her, and he is said to have adopted her. In reality, she adopted him. In spite of it all, she was a strong character—she must have had in addition to her other qualities much personal magnetism, because she was always the leader, always the most loved wherever she went—and by the time I first met her, when she was fourteen or fifteen, she was in full charge of Plum. To him, she was that infinitely precious thing, a dominant woman who was always affectionate and kind, a protector from the horrors of the rest of humanity, but one who exacted no penalties in return. He gave her all the affection he was capable of. Many of his letters to her have been preserved. They are loving and frank and funny, and without any of that spurious heartiness with which, when addressing other people, he attempted the good fellowship he could not feel.

Plum and Ethel seem to have forgotten many of the small events of their early lives, and they have both said that Leonora was sent to school at Bromley in England when they were first married. This is not correct. She did not go there until after the war, and for some years she was at school in America. At this school her name was corrupted, first to Nora, then to s'Nora, then to Snorky. This may not be thought a very felicitous adaptation of an originally rather beautiful name, but it instantly commended itself to the creator of Stiffy, Nobby, Boko, Bingo, Oofy, Pongo, Bimbo, Mugsy, and many another. He adopted it with the utmost cordiality and never called her anything else, except such variants as Snorks, Snorkles, and so on. Everyone who knew her before her marriage called her Snorky, but the Cazalets changed it back, and those who met her after it called her Leonora.

She took much colour from Plum as well as he from her, and by the time that I first met her, people had difficulty in believing she was not his daughter. If she ever had a fault, it was that when she was very young she believed, as he did, that humour was more important than anything else, and it was sometimes hard to get a hearing for any matter on which one felt seriously. She was inclined, too, to be undiscriminating in her friendships, but only in the sense of tolerating those who might be classed as bores, and it would not be possible to have her essential qualities of loyalty and kindliness and also a nice perception on matters of this kind.

She died more than thirty years ago. I still think of her and miss her.

6

Success

Plum, now thirty-three, had worked so hard for so long that success was overdue. Soon after his marriage this came in several directions. He wrote at the time for two editors, both of whom he admired very much. The first was Bob Davis, who edited *Munsey's Magazine*. Speaking in a radio interview in his old age, Plum said:

> We admired *The Saturday Evening Post* enormously. [By "we" I think he meant himself and other modest people who worked hard for a living.] We tried to get into *The Saturday Evening Post*. I did get into *Collier's* but not regularly. I really made a living writing for the pulps. That was more our form. There was an editor edited *Munsey's* and he was a great man because we used to go to his office and tell him we wanted a plot for a story. And he would take a turn up and down the room and come up with a plot, generally rather a ghastly plot, still it was a plot, and then you'd write it and he'd buy it for about fifty dollars or something. I just managed to get by in those days.

The second of the two editors was George Lorimer of *The Saturday Evening Post*. The following year, 1915, Plum appointed a new literary agent, Paul Reynolds, and Reynolds's first act was to sell the serial rights of *Something New* (in England *Something Fresh*) to *The Saturday Evening Post*. Lorimer was one of the most famous magazine editors of all time, and Plum was positively lyrical about him. In *Performing Flea* he wrote:

> I've always thought that his buying *Something Fresh* showed what a wonderful editor he was. Here was a story by an absolutely unknown man, and a story, what is more, about life in England, a country he didn't like, but it amused him, so he decided without any hesitation that the public of *The Saturday Evening Post* were jolly well going to be amused by it, too, and he didn't give a damn if they weren't.[1]

And he also wrote:

> My view is that the English magazine died of "names" and what is known over here as "slanting." The slanter, in case you don't know, is a bird

94

who studies what editors want. He reads the magazines carefully, and slings in a story as like the stories they are publishing as he can without actual plagiarism. And the editors—if they are fatheads—and they nearly always were in the days I'm thinking of—say "Fine!" and accept the things, with the result that after a while the public begin to find it a bit monotonous and stop buying. Names, though, were almost as deadly as poison. The *Strand* was better than most of them, but practically every English magazine would buy any sort of bilge, provided it was by somebody with a big name as a novelist. The reason *The Saturday Evening Post* was always so darned good was that Lorimer never fell into this trap. . . . The Boss was an autocrat, all right, but my God what an editor to work for. He kept you up on your toes. I had twenty-one serials in the *Post* but I never felt safe till I got the cable saying each had got over with Lorimer.[2]

Commenting on these remarks, Evelyn Waugh wrote:

Mr. Wodehouse's prestige has been founded on his readers rather than on his critics, but he is essentially a professional man who seeks to satisfy his clients and he takes as his clients those who sign the cheques, the editors and publishers. This is an American rather than a European attitude. We in Europe look on editors and publishers as necessary and often very agreeable middle-men between ourselves and our readers. We think of ourselves as the guardians of our own reputations. American editors regard themselves as employers, and many sharp misunderstandings arise when European writers publish their work in the New World.

Mr. Wodehouse has never expressed any annoyance, rather gratitude, at what in Europe would seem irksome presumption. Indeed he attributes the superiority of American magazines to this editorial interference.[3]

We, on the other hand, may well attribute the unevenness of Wodehouse's work, at least in some degree, to his tolerance of editors. In spite of the remarks quoted above, no one has ever been a greater slanter than Plum himself in his early days. He lived to write, and he wrote, as most writers do, for publication; but unlike most writers of talent, he was able as well as willing to adapt himself to almost anything the popular market required. One only has to compare his work for Davis with that for Lorimer to see that this is true. He wrote two novels at this time, *The Coming of Bill* and *Something Fresh*.* *The Coming of Bill* has a plot the editor of *Munsey's* dragged up after "taking a turn up and down the room," and which his obliging author then went home and worked on. *Something*

Something Fresh was published in September 1915 in both England and America. *The Coming of Bill* was published as *Their Mutual Child* in America in 1919 and under the former title in England in 1920, but it ran as a serial in *Munsey's Magazine* in 1914, and the two novels were therefore written about the same time.

Fresh was written to the dictates of his own imagination and accepted by the more exacting Lorimer.

The Coming of Bill is one of the worst books Wodehouse ever wrote. Any young man or woman who knew him by reputation only and read *The Coming of Bill* would be bound to wonder what the whole thing was about. It is a novel of a purely popular kind, with an insubstantial plot, almost no humour, and page after page of writing of which this is a fair sample.

> Kirk stood motionless at the rail, thinking. It was not what was past that occupied his thoughts, as the third officer had supposed; it was the future.
>
> The forlorn hope had failed; he was limping back to Ruth wounded and broken. He had sent her a wireless message. She would be at the dock to meet him. How could he face her? Fate had been against him, it was true, but he was in no mood to make excuses for himself. He had failed. That was the beginning and end of it. He had set out to bring back wealth and comfort to her, and he was returning empty-handed. That was what the immediate future held, the meeting with Ruth. And after? His imagination was not equal to the task of considering that. (*The Coming of Bill*, Book Two, Chapter 1)

There is also a good deal of babytalk, about which the less said the better. *The Coming of Bill* has only one merit, which is that in spite of it being the most intolerable tosh, one is driven on to the end. Even here the compelling storyteller keeps his grip. It seems incredible that it was written at the same time as *Something Fresh*, and that by now its author was reaching the period of his greatest inspiration.

Something Fresh was the first of the Blandings novels. Considered as part of the series, it is undeveloped. In spite of Lord Emsworth's sublime entrance onto the scene, quoted earlier, he is not yet the important literary figure he is to become, while there is no Empress of Blandings and no Lady Constance, only a pale and unimportant sister called Lady Julia. Beach, the butler, is a man destined to grow a little younger as the years go on. Yet as an example of the benignly humorous writing, the gentle teasing—so much less than satire—in which Wodehouse excels, it is hard to beat. Thus in the first pages we are told that the hero of the novel was "christened Ashe, after a wealthy uncle who subsequently double-crossed them by leaving his money to charities," and that "having managed to obtain a sort of a degree, enough to enable himself to call himself a Bachelor of Arts, and realizing that you can fool some of the people some of the time, he applied for and secured a series of private tutorships."

So much has been written about the Blandings Castle series that there would be little left to say were it not that the set of characters who inhabit the castle, unlike those who surround Jeeves, bear a slight, and in my view rather pleasant, resemblance to life. The grossly simplified theory of the aunts—roughly, that Wodehouse was conditioned by the aunts of his youth to regard all authority as an elderly female—has received so much credence that it seems pardonable to return to it. In a short book by R. B. D. French called *P. G. Wodehouse,* which has been justly admired, the author says: "A. P. Ryan has argued that every figure of authority in Wodehouse, if not actually an aunt, is an aunt disguised. The masters in the school stories are aunts in academicals. The aunt, he says, is the elder, and the elder always wins in the end."⁴

It is not quite clear whether Mr. French himself agrees with the aunt theory as such, although he shows conclusively that the aunt does not win in the end—"The essence of the books is successful rebellion by the young against their elders"—but, in any case, it seems to me not merely misleading but plainly untrue. For instance, anyone who takes the trouble to read the school stories will see that most of the masters are treated with sympathy—a different variety of the human species, but not necessarily one which provokes hostility. Nor is it true that all females except the youngest girls constitute the enemy; some of the jolliest figures are past their first youth—Bill in *The Old Reliable,* Leila Yorke in *Ice in the Bedroom*—and it really seems too much merely in order to sustain the theory to turn such figures as Sir Watkin Bassett, Sir Roderick Glossop and Roderick Spode, McAllister, and Baxter into aunts.* Wodehouse's only aggressions were against the highbrows—and surely it needs no labouring that, given his willingness to write anything for any publication, he might be on the defensive here—against professions such as psychiatry that he did not understand or believe in, and possibly feared, and against people with an intolerant moral attitude. The key to his character lies in his inability to feel strong emotions.

The important difference between the aunts Agatha and Dahlia and Lady Constance is that whereas the aunts bear no resemblance to life and act purely from stock motives such as stopping the hero from marrying the girl he loves (or plotting for him to marry one he does not love) until it is time for the third-act curtain, Lady Constance personifies certain everlasting characteristics of the female in every man's life. And if Lady Constance is based, to however small an extent, on Plum's own experiences, perhaps it is not too fanciful (if speculative and a trifle sentimental) to suggest that the following scene from "Lord Emsworth and the Girl Friend" also had a basis in life. Lord Emsworth's gardener, McAllister, of whom he is only a little less afraid than he is of Lady Constance, has discovered

---

*Why are there two Rodericks? Surely here is a splendid field for research.

Gladys, the little urchin from London, picking flowers with His Lordship's permission.

> Truth now compels us to admit that his [Lord Emsworth's] hardy attitude was largely due to the fact that he believed the head-gardener to be a safe quarter of a mile away among the swings and roundabouts of the Fete. The spectacle of the man charging vengefully down on him with gleaming eyes and bristling whiskers made him feel like a nervous English infantryman at the Battle of Bannockburn. His knees shook and the soul within him quivered.
> And then something happened, and the whole aspect of the situation changed.
> It was, in itself, quite a trivial thing, but it had an astoundingly stimulating effect on Lord Emsworth's morale. What happened was that Gladys, seeking further protection, slipped at this moment a small, hot hand into his.
> It was a mute vote of confidence, and Lord Emsworth intended to be worthy of it.

The next sentences describe Lord Emsworth's struggle with himself. And then:

> He removed his top hat and brushed it against his sleeve.
> "What is the matter, McAllister?"
> He replaced his top hat.
> "You appear agitated, McAllister."
> He jerked his head militantly. The hat fell off. He let it lie. Freed from its loathsome weight he felt more masterful than ever. It had needed just that to bring him to the top of his form.
> "This young lady," said Lord Emsworth, "has my full permission to pick all the flowers she wants, McAllister. If you do not see eye to eye with me in this matter, McAllister, say so and we will discuss what you are going to do about it, McAllister. These gardens, McAllister, belong to me, and if you do not—er—appreciate that fact, you will, no doubt be able to find another employer—ah—more in tune with your views. I value your services highly, McAllister, but I will not be dictated to in my own garden, McAllister. Er—dash it," added His Lordship, spoiling the whole effect. (*Blandings Castle*, "Lord Emsworth and the Girl Friend")

"Lord Emsworth and the Girl Friend" is noticeably different from any other Wodehouse story in that some real feeling enters into it. The "small, hot hand," I like to think, might have been Leonora's, the incident based on some unimportant family event with Ethel, rather than McAllister as the third person, and the moment the one when an unaccustomed emotion first stirred in Plum's heart.

In the autumn of 1915, Plum wrote a story for *The Saturday Evening Post* called "Extricating Young Gussie." The particular interest of this story was that it featured a drone and his manservant. "The drone was Bertie Wooster making his formal bow, not very forcefully assisted by Jeeves, whose potential was yet to be realised."[5] Since that day these two have become household words, and there can be few educated Englishmen who have not read at least one Jeeves story, while he and Wooster have been more written about than any other characters in modern fiction. What more is there to say? Something, at least about Jeeves. In the first place, one must comment on the fact that present-day writers keep trying to explain to themselves how Plum came to know so much about butlers. Yet he came from two families in each of which some members would have had a butler, while in his youth butlers were a customary feature even of middle-class households. Anyone born a gentleman and educated as Plum was would have accepted butlers as part of ordinary life. Certainly he knew all about them, enough to know—as apparently those who wonder about his acquaintance with them do not—that his own butlers were really only stage butlers. My father was born in a two-room cottage in Jersey, but he employed a butler for many years, and also a chauffeur, who acted as his valet when he visited grand houses (where I sometimes went with him). The truth is that butlers might have been found who behaved like Plum's butlers, but they were very often those who, not having been well trained when young, took their manners from the stage.

The same remarks can be made about his knowledge of the servants' hall. In those days the hierarchy of the housekeeper's room and the servants' hall was a matter for jokes in the upper part of the house, and no one who moved in the circles Plum did could have failed to know about it.

Jeeves, of course, was not a butler, but a valet—a gentleman's personal gentleman. (I have no idea of the antecedents of "a gentleman's personal gentleman," but it is certainly literary and not employed in real life.)

We have Plum's own word for the fact that Jeeves started as a stage butler, and in the introduction to *The World of Jeeves*, he says:

> I find it curious, now that I have written so much about him, to recall how softly and undramatically Jeeves first entered my little world. Characteristically, he did not thrust himself forward. On that occasion he spoke just two lines. The first was: "Mrs. Gregson to see you, sir." The second: "Very good, sir. Which suit will you wear?" That was a story in a volume entitled *The Man with Two Left Feet*. It was only some time later, when I was going into the strange affair of "The Artistic Career of Young Corky," that the man's qualities dawned upon me. I still blush to think of the off-hand way I treated him at our first encounter.[6]

Jeeves was a character who developed fairly swiftly and has no comparison in English literature, although, oddly enough, in American literature he has. In his old age Plum told an interviewer that he first thought of

Jeeves after reading *Ruggles of Red Gap*. He gave a good many different versions of how he came to think of Jeeves, and probably all of them were in some way contributory, but one cannot ignore this remark. *Ruggles of Red Gap*, by Harry Leon Wilson, is an accepted classic of American humour, but in spite of this it has been allowed to go out of print and is virtually unobtainable. So difficult is it to find that copies I read of *Ruggles* and of another book by Wilson called *Ma Pettigell* were Plum's own copies. Wilson is a very fine humorist whose elegance of thought and expression never fails, even though he often writes in dialect. His books are almost entirely about small-town or rural Americans, and he has a relish for snobbery. More sophisticated than Wodehouse, he writes more subtly of human character, but he has not the narrative power or the rigid self-discipline, and his books are slower and more discursive. This may account for the fact that they are not read today. The interest he has for us is that Ruggles, who preceded Jeeves in time, is a gentleman's personal gentleman of a most unusual kind, and the hero of the book, while in the copy I read of *Ma Pettigell* many passages have been marked by Plum. There is no particular pattern to these, and I can detect no evidence of direct plagiarism, but Harry Leon Wilson must be counted as an influence if nothing more.

Jeeves, as he developed, became the perfect vehicle for the exercise of Plum's addiction to the best-known tags of English literature. He is not the only character to speak in quotation, but he is the most beautifully constructed to do so. His name he got from a Warwickshire cricketer whom Plum saw play on a ground in Gloucestershire. Percy Jeeves was killed in the Second World War, but I am told he had been regarded as a potential England cricketer, "a fastish opening bowler and a good-hearted attacking no. 7 or so bat."[7]

As for Bertie, in the broadcast already referred to, Plum said:

> By the time I had written two or three books his character was all clear before me. He's very vivid to me now. Of course, he's altered tremendously. When he first began he was very much the sort of stage dude; he gradually became more and more individual. If you take the early stories written about 1916 or 1917, Bertie was a very different character from what he is today. He's picked up a lot of things from Jeeves.

And Richard Usborne, who is particularly good on both Wooster and Jeeves, says:

> Subliminally, I believe, Bertie Wooster was, and increasingly became, Wodehouse's main surrogate outlet for self-derogatory First Person singular mood. . . .
>
> Bertie is the only one of Wodehouse's heroes or protagonists for whom

the mere release from terror and pain is always a sufficiently happy ending. . . .

It is sufficient for the First-Personal Bertie that others get the jackpots and girls, and that he be simply released from bewilderment, indignity, bullying by aunts and other circumnambient menaces.[8]

But if in retrospect the first entrance of Lord Emsworth and that of Jeeves and Bertie Wooster seem to be the most important events of Wodehouse's career during those years, at the time everything else was overshadowed for him by his entry into the New York theatre. He had for some time been contributing articles to *Vanity Fair,* and he was given a job as its theatre critic in time to go in that capacity to the first night of a musical farce called *Very Good Eddie,* which opened at the Princess Theatre on 23 December 1915, with a book by Guy Bolton and music by Jerome Kern. *Very Good Eddie* is regarded as marking a turning point in the history of musical comedy in that, at the inspiration of Elizabeth (Bessie) Marbury, a very celebrated theatrical agent, it was decided to turn away from the grand-scale musical with expensive scenery and rows of beautiful girls, and to produce small and intimate shows which relied on a stronger book and musical score and on what was to become known as a situation comedy— that is, comedy arising out of the story rather than interpolated here and there in set-piece clowning or crosstalk acts.

On the first night of *Very Good Eddie* Plum bumped into Jerome Kern, with whom, it will be remembered, he had already worked in London, and Kern asked him to come to his flat the next day to meet Bolton. Both Bolton and Kern were dissatisfied with the lyrics of *Very Good Eddie,* and at this meeting, when the three men exchanged ideas on the future of musical comedy, it was suggested that Plum should collaborate with the other two in future. This began a collaboration which was to be responsible for *Miss Springtime* (New York, 1916), *Have a Heart* (New York, 1917), *Oh, Boy!* (New York, 1917, and, retitled *Oh, Joy!,* London, 1919), *Leave It to Jane* (New York, 1917), a flop called *The Riviera Girl* (New York, 1917), *Oh, Lady! Lady!* (New York, 1918), *Sally* (New York, 1920, and London, 1921), and *Sitting Pretty* (New York, 1924). Guy and Plum also collaborated in many other musical comedies, notably *Oh, Kay!,* for which they wrote the book together and George and Ira Gershwin wrote the music and lyrics, while Plum wrote the lyric "Bill," which appeared in *Show Boat,* and was credited with a share in the book of *Anything Goes.*

The meeting of Wodehouse and Bolton was important not only for their work in the theatre but because it began a friendship which lasted until Plum died in 1975. Guy was born in England, although of American parents. His father was an engineer who travelled a great deal between the two countries, and all his life, even when he was over ninety, Guy did the

same. He was an extremely sweet man, kind and courteous, talented within
the limits he set himself, and hard-working. Since he will appear in the
future at almost every stage of Plum's life, nothing more need be said about
him here. But, something must be said about the work they did together,
because, first of all, it earned both men an enormous fortune and a lasting
place in the history of musical comedy. In the encyclopaedic *American
Musical Theatre* Gerald Bordman raves about them both. Of *Have a Heart*
he says: "It had a good Guy Bolton–P. G. Wodehouse book, marvellous
Wodehouse lyrics, and ingratiating Kern music." He also says that the
Wodehouse lyrics were "literate" and "witty." Speaking of *Oh, Boy!* he
says:

> The book was fast moving, its characters well drawn and its humor . . .
> flowed logically from the characters and situations. Some assignments
> proved how stunningly Bolton and Wodehouse had advanced. The wryly
> comic "You Never Knew about Me" was given to the principal lovers,
> while the cosy "Nesting Time in Flatbush" was sung by the comic leads,
> and the show's top tune, "Till the Clouds Roll By," was sung by the hero
> and the comedienne. Wodehouse's lyrics were little short of miraculous.
> Again they were literate and natural, with a precisely right balance of wit
> and sentiment.[9]

These lyrics were praised quite as much when they first appeared. Dorothy Parker, who succeeded Plum as theatre critic for *Vanity Fair,* said that
you could get a seat for *Oh, Lady! Lady!* for just about the price of one
on the Stock Exchange, and went on:

> But then Bolton and Wodehouse and Kern are my favorite indoor sport,
> anyway. I like the way they go about a musical comedy. I like the way
> the action slides casually into the songs. I like the deft rhyming of the
> song that is always sung in the last act by two comedians and a comedi-
> enne. And oh, how I do like Jerome Kern's music.[10]

And an anonymous critic in *The New York Times* wrote the following
ditty:

> This is the trio of musical fame
> Bolton and Wodehouse and Kern;
> Better than anyone else you can name,
> Bolton and Wodehouse and Kern.
> Nobody knows what on earth they've been bitten by
> All I can say is that I mean to get lit an' buy
> Orchestra stalls for the next one that's written by
> Bolton and Wodehouse and Kern.[11]

Hardly a single Wodehouse lyric has lived, and none of the musical
comedies have survived to be performed in London or New York, while

most of Kern's music of that period is forgotten. For this reason, it is difficult to make any assessment of Wodehouse's lyrics today, for they are not of a kind which stand alone on the printed page. Noel Coward epitomized the self-accusatory, self-indulgent cynicism of the 1920s in "Dance, Dance, Dance Little Lady," and a whole century of British attitudes in "Mad Dogs and Englishmen"; Cole Porter caught in one or two songs the macabre humour immortalized by *The New Yorker;* while Ira Gershwin's songs have a natural vigour which makes them still bounce off the page. Without the music they were written for, Wodehouse's lyrics seem dexterous and neat but totally uninteresting. However, he was enormously admired by professionals. Guy Bolton insisted again and again in conversation with me that "Plum was the tops," and Benny Green, in a talk given to the PEN Club in London in July 1979, said more or less the same thing, adding that Ira Gershwin agreed with this estimate. Plum himself loved writing lyrics, and there is nowhere anything to suggest that he thought his work in the theatre inferior to the rest of his work. He had a good ear, but Leonora was probably correct in saying that his lyrics owed even more to his sense of rhythm.

> Jerry generally did the melody first [Plum told David Jasen] and I put the words to it. W. S. Gilbert always said that a lyricist can't do decent stuff that way, but I don't agree with him—not as far as I'm concerned, anyway. If I write a lyric without having to fit it to a tune, I always make it too much like a set of light verse, much too regular in metre. I think you get the best results by giving the composer his head and having the lyricist follow him. . . . Another thing . . . is that when you have the melody, you can see which are the musical high spots in it and can fit the high spots of the lyric to them. Anyway, that's how I like working, and to hell with anyone who says I oughtn't to.[12]

These remarks probably explain better than anything else Wodehouse's success in this field. His talent lay not in writing lyrics which can be read as light verse, but in fitting the words to the tune. Thus his most famous lyric, "Bill," which was sung for years after it was first written, and which I give as an example here, is sometimes heard today and still sounds wonderful with the music but does not stand alone.

> I used to dream that I would discover
> The perfect lover
> Some day
> I knew I'd recognize him if ever
> He came round my way.
> He'd have hair of gold
> And a noble head

> Like the heroes bold
> In the books I'd read
> Then along came Bill
> Who's not like that at all
> You'd pass him on the street and never notice him
> His form and face
> His manly grace
> Are not the sort that you
> Would find in a statue
> I can't explain
> It's surely not his brain
> That makes me thrill
> I love him because . . . oh, I don't know
> Because he's just my Bill.

The truth may also be that musical comedy was an ephemeral and unimportant art, which, starting in London with a debased form of light opera, advanced a stage with the Bolton–Wodehouse partnership, but was not of any real interest until, in America, Negro rhythms were introduced and talent and training required of the performers. The earlier musical comedies depended more on the composer and the actors than on the book or the lyrics, and if the reputations of Wodehouse, Bolton, and Kern rested on their work for the theatre, only Kern's name would survive.

As a dramatist Wodehouse has left even less reputation. He was responsible for the book of several musical comedies, and he wrote a few straight plays, mostly adaptations of European originals—notably *The Play's the Thing* from the Hungarian by Ferenc Molnar and *Her Cardboard Lover* from the French by Jacques Deval. He also collaborated with others on the dramatization of some of his own books—notably *A Damsel in Distress* and *Leave It to Psmith* with Ian Hay. Some of these were very successful at the time, although more so in New York than in London. *The Play's the Thing* ran for 326 performances in New York in 1926 and again for 244 in 1948, but in London, in spite of a cast headed by Gerald du Maurier, it was booed on the first night and received very bad notices. *Her Cardboard Lover*, again a moderate success in New York (1926), was a flop in London (1927), while *A Damsel in Distress*, although successful in London (1928), was not staged in New York.

Wodehouse continued to write plays and lyrics, because he enjoyed it and, incidentally, because he made a fortune out of it; but in hindsight the greatest importance of this work was the use he made of theatrical plots in his books. Thus a notice in *The Times* for a play called *Good Morning, Bill* (London, 1927 and 1934), which he adapted from the Hungarian by Ladislaus Fodor, makes it clear to the initiated that he lost no time in using Fodor's plot for a novel called *Doctor Sally.**

And, if he enjoyed the work in the theatre, Plum had as usual no illusions about himself. In a letter to Denis Mackail, written in 1950, he said:

> We finished the farce and it looks very good. As usual what happened was that I sweated my guts out writing acts 1 and 2 and handed them to Guy, and he wrote a completely different script, so practically all of it is now his. Guy's stuff is a hundred times better than mine. He has that knack of construction, which I can't get in a play, though I'm all right when it's a novel.

*The discussion of these plays is out of context, as none of them were produced until the 1920s and 1930s, but it has nevertheless seemed the appropriate place.

7

After the War

During all these years England was at war with Germany. Because of his eyesight, which as a child had been too bad for him to be accepted for the navy, there was no question of Plum being able to serve in any combatant force. The 1914 war, which caused the most tragic casualties in history, also produced propaganda of a rather poisonous kind, the white feather, reports of spies among the inhabitants of every village, and the enforced resignation of national personalities for the crime of possessing a German name. There was some criticism of Plum's conduct in not returning to England; and although in retrospect it may seem a minor offence not to have abandoned his extraordinary career in the theatre if he could not serve, there is a censorious streak in Englishmen which dwells with satisfaction on other people's failure in war. From time to time for many years, someone would mention that Plum had spent the period between 1914 and 1918 in America.

However, it is much easier to explain the fact that he did not make an enormous sacrifice which would have done no one any particular good than to understand the immaturity of his emotional response to the events of the time. His lack of belligerence was equalled only by his inability to feel any emotion which would have been adequate to the great tragic holocaust in Europe. He has been quoted as saying that one needs a cock-eyed vision to be a humorist. Perhaps one also needs an undeveloped capacity to respond to suffering, an emotional range too restricted to extend to concepts outside one's own experience.

I'll buck you up when I get home [he wrote to William Townend]—that's to say if I'm not arrested and shoved in chokey for not helping to slug Honble Kaiser. How *does* the law stand in that respect? I registered in the draft over here, aged 63, sole support of wife and nine children, totally blind, and all the rest of it, but ought I to have done anything as regards registering in England? I thought not as I was out of the country when the war started, and any way wouldn't have been a dam bit of good as my only pair of spectacles would have bust in the first charge.*

All these years after he wrote that letter, it is questionable which predominates: a mild if expostulatory amusement at this evidence of his failure to understand the ordinary proprieties, or a sense of shock that callous indifference to tragedy, even if part of the equipment of a humorist, should be carried so far. Allowance must be made for the obduracy of the written word, because in life it did not need much perspicacity to recognize that Plum was not as others, nor great sensibility to feel the kindly nature which gave warmth even to such complete detachment as his. He was not thrown into chokey, but, with Ethel and the irresistible Snorky, now approaching sixteen, welcomed with open arms. At least this was so in Birchington, a seaside village in Thanet, where I lived with my parents, and where the Wodehouses came in the summer of 1921.

Because of my father's presence there, Birchington enjoyed a short period as a summer resort immediately after the war. Various stars of the theatre came, and in their wake, the kind of mixed society which in more normal times might have gone to Le Touquet or Dieppe. Half the theatrical profession disported themselves on the tennis courts or lay about on the beach—it is always fine weather in one's childhood memories, but 1921 was an exceptional year—while I remember several legal lights, a composer of musical comedy songs, and at least two professional courtesans (a race which still existed). In the bushes behind the tennis courts, a troop led by a Cavalier called Daphne du Maurier lay in wait for any passing Roundheads.

This was not a very censorious society, but it was an unusually talented one, and perhaps more conscious than most of the beams in its own eyes. It says much for the sweetness of Plum's personality, however, that everyone who met him felt affection for him, since one cannot say too often that he was large and smiling but practically speechless and that he never made a joke. Sitting beside him watching the tennis, aged about fourteen, I asked him what he thought of Compton Mackenzie's new novel. "That is a terrifying girl," he told Snorky, and I forgave him the unkind remark long before, accepting me as her friend, he forgot this evidence of a highbrow tendency. These things need to be emphasized, because after this time people began to preserve his letters, and, as often happens, there is a marked difference in the personality which emerges from these and the one

---

*He almost certainly did register in America, but it seems very doubtful that, as he told David Jasen, he also registered in England before he left in 1914, as war had not then even been declared.

he presented in life. I think in his letters he tried to make up for his inability to behave with any normal sociability.

The Wodehouses first returned to England in 1918, and they rented a house in Walton Street in London, which they took again in 1919. In the latter year they came for the rehearsals of *Kissing Time* (*The Girl behind the Gun* in America), which ran for 430 performances at the Winter Garden. They returned to America for the summer, taking a house at Great Neck to be near Guy Bolton, but in 1920 they were in England again.

In the next ten years Plum travelled constantly backwards and forwards across the Atlantic, not because he was restless but in pursuit of his theatrical career. This still made the greatest demands on his attention and showed the largest financial return, although it never took first place in his affections or, in terms of actual working hours, first call on his energies. His output during this time was so great that, disbelieving in it, one goes over and over the dates of first performances or publications, but without being able to reduce it. In ten years he wrote the lyrics, and sometimes part of the book, for twelve musical comedies produced in London or New York, and for two others which were not performed. He also wrote or adapted four straight plays. Yet in spite of this he published twenty books, of which four were collections of short stories and the rest novels. But perhaps the most astonishing thing about these years is that at the height of his maximum output he usually found time when in England to visit Dulwich for the school matches and to report them at length for the school magazine the *Alleynian*. Thus a typical report, which is signed P.G.W. and runs to about one thousand words of a blow-by-blow description of a game, begins:

> As we were coming off the ground after this match, we overheard one Haileybury master discussing the game with another Haileybury master. The first Haileybury master said to the second Haileybury master: "If it had been a dry day, Dulwich would have won by twenty points." And, believe us, if ever a Haileybury master spoke a mouthful, this Haileybury master was that Haileybury master.

. . . and ends: "If it had been a dry day . . . !"

A list of the theatrical ventures in which he was involved and also of his books with the dates of performance or publication will be found in Appendix A. His output was so vast that any full description of it swiftly degenerates into a mere catalogue, which cannot reflect the excitement he felt for the theatre or increase our knowledge of him. Many of the books of these years have already been referred to in one context or another. The influence of his work in the theatre, and possibly of his marriage, began to be felt in some of the novels—notably in *Jill the Reckless* (1921) and *The*

Adventures of Sally (1922)—and it is noticeable that a Wodehouse chorus girl is almost always one who, without previous experience, takes to the stage because she needs money. *The Small Bachelor* (1927) is probably the best of all the nonseries books, and *Money for Nothing* (1928) introduced Chimp Twist and Soapy and Dolly Molloy, American crooks who bear testimony to a Wodehouse fondness for the financially amoral. This decade saw also *Indiscretions of Archie* (1921), a collection of inspired short stories which tends to be undervalued, three Jeeves books, *The Clicking of Cuthbert,* and two Mulliner collections—all these at the time when he appeared to spend most of his working life in the theatre.

The ten years of the twenties with the early years of the thirties are usually regarded as Wodehouse's best period. Certainly it was his most prolific, while it was also the period of his best short stories, although this may have been due not to any falling-off in his own talents but to the demise of the magazines in which short stories appeared. The twenties saw the best of the golf stories and the first two collections of the Mulliner stories, in both of which there is a narrator, the Oldest Member at the golf club, and Mr. Mulliner, whose tales of his nephews and nieces are told at the Angler's Rest. The technique of the short story is different from that of the novel, the length dictating the necessity for a single plot with no subplots and a simple approach. The comedy is therefore often chiefly in the plot—what Plum called situation comedy—while at other times a rather weak plot is redeemed by the humour in the writing. Many of those chosen both by Plum himself and by his admirers are of the first kind, e.g., "Honeysuckle Cottage" and "Cats Will Be Cats." I personally prefer the second kind, and would put among his very best "The Fiery Wooing of Mordred" (*Young Men in Spats*), where he achieves a hilarious effect almost entirely with the use of "subwords" like *tiddly-iddly-umpty-ay* and "The Knightly Quest of Mervyn" (*Mulliner Nights*), in which the following passage occurs:

> "Tell me, Clarice," he said, "why is it that you spurn a fellow's suit? I can't for the life of me see why you won't consent to marry a chap. It isn't as if I hadn't asked you often enough. Playing fast and loose with a good man's love is the way I look at it."
> And he gazed at her in a way that was partly melting and partly suggestive of the dominant male. And Clarice Mallaby gave one of those light, tinkling laughs and replied:
> "Well, if you really want to know, you're such an ass."
> Mervyn could make nothing of this.
> "An ass? How do you mean an ass? Do you mean a silly ass?"
> "I mean a goof," said the girl. "A gump. A poop. A nitwit and a returned empty. Your name came up the other day in the course of

conversation at home, and mother said you were a vapid and irreflective guffin, totally lacking in character and purpose."

"Oh?" said Mervyn. "She did, did she?"

"She did. And while it isn't often that I think along the same lines as mother, there—for once—I consider her to have hit the bull's-eye, rung the bell, and to be entitled to a cigar or coconut, according to choice. It seemed to me what they call the *mot juste*."

Sometimes he achieves both the humorous plot and humorous writing in one story, as, perhaps, with "Mulliner's Buck-U-Uppo."

Wodehouse is said to have immortalized the game of golf as Surtees immortalized fox hunting. He writes almost always from the point of view of the low-handicap man, but he is depicted with an accuracy which comes from an unusual degree of knowledge of how the game should be played. Plum himself played regularly at this time. The first collection of golf stories, *The Clicking of Cuthbert* (1922), contains a story of the same name which many people think his best golf story. I have a prejudice against it because it is an extreme example of the mocking of the highbrow, although the highbrows themselves find it funny. In the same volume there is a story called "Ordeal by Golf," which I think among the funniest he ever wrote.

Once back in England, Leonora spent much of the year at school in Bromley, and one can follow Plum's movements from his letters to her. On 7 August 1920 he wrote from an address in Felixstowe:

My darling Angel Snorkles,

At last I'm able to write to you! I finished the novel yesterday, and I wish you were here to read it, as I think it's the best comic one I've done. It's not meant to be in the same class as *The Little Warrior*, but as a farce I think it's pretty well all to the mustard. . . . Still, I'm going to keep it by me for at least two weeks before sending it off to America, so perhaps you'll be able to see it after all before it goes. If not you can read the original ms.*

I have now got three more Archie stories to do and then I shall have worked off all my present contracts. I haven't got a plot yet for the tenth Archie story, but they are using a golf story of mine in the Christmas *Strand*, which will give me a fair amount of time to think of one.†

Mummie went off to London yesterday, and I am all alone here and rather blue. I leave on Friday, and I hope we shall soon get a flat in town. . . .

Don't you think this is a good line in the book. Chap who's always thinking himself ill says to chap who is having a row with him "My face hurts!" Other chap says "You can't expect a face like that not to hurt!" I

*Almost certainly *The Girl on the Boat*.
†*Indiscretions of Archie*.

thought it was not only droll, but whimsical and bizarre, but Mummie said it was obvious! No human power, however, will induce me to cut it out.

I've got another good line. Chap is asked if he identifies the hero, with whom he has had a row. Hero has been found in the house late at night and they think he is a burglar. He says "I am Sam Marlowe." They turn to the other fellow and say "Do you identify him?" and the other fellow says "I suppose so. I can't imagine a man saying he was Samuel Marlowe unless he knew it could be proved against him." Somewhat humorous and not altogether free from espieglerie, I think, or am I wrong?

A man has just written to me asking if I will dramatize his new novel, which he says he wrote in imitation of my stuff. I had read a review of his novel, and had thought it was just the sort of thing to read and pinch situations from. And so we go on, each helping the other.

As a matter of fact, I really am becoming rather a blood these days. In a review of *Wedding Bells* at the Playhouse Theatre, the critic says "So-and-so is good as a sort of P. G. Wodehouse character." And in a review of a book in the *Times,* they say "The author at times reverts to the P. G. Wodehouse manner." This, I need scarcely point out to you, is jolly old Fame. Once they begin to refer to you in that casual way as if everybody must know who you are all is well. It does my old heart good.

My golf is terrific now. I seldom miss. Tom Irwin, one of your trustees for the money which I hope to find some way of pinching in the near future, was down here and has given me a new putter, which produces wonderful results. . . .

Well, pip pip and good-bye-ee and so forth

Your loving
Plummie

His next letter was dated 27 September 1920 and, written from the Constitutional Club in Northumberland Avenue, began, "My precious darling Snorky," and ended, "Well, cheerio, old bean. Lots of love." There then followed a postscript: "Oh, by the way you must stop pinching Mummie's clothes. It worries her frightfully and you know how nervous she is."

On 28 November 1920 he wrote again, this time from 16 Walton Street:

Darling Snorkles

We [Dulwich] beat Sherborne yesterday after a very hot game, so that we have wound up the season with five wins and one defeat. Pretty hot!

I forgot to tell you in my last letter the tale of the laughable imbroglio or mix-up—which has occurred with Jerry Kern. You remember I sent my lyrics over and then read in *Variety* that some other cove was doing the lyrics and wrote to everybody in New York to retrieve my lyrics. Then that cable came asking me if I would let them have "Joan of Arc" and "Church Round the Corner," which, after a family consultation, I answered in the affir. Well, just after I had cabled saying all right, I got a furious cable from Jerry—the sort of cable the Kaiser might have sent to an underling—saying my letter withdrawing the lyrics was "extremely offensive" and ending "You have offended me for the last time!" Upon which the manly spirit of the Wodehouses (descended from the sister of Anne Boleyn) boiled in my veins—when you get back I'll show you the very veins it boiled in—and I cabled over "Cancel permission to use lyrics." I now hear that Jerry is bringing an action against me for royalties on *Miss Springtime* and *Riviera Girl*, to which he contributed tunes. The loony seems to think that a lyricist is responsible for the composer's royalties. Of course, he hasn't an earthly . . . but doesn't it show how blighted some blighters can be when they decide to be blighters. . . .*

I have just heard from Reynolds that the editress of *The Woman's Home Companion* does not like *The Girl on the Boat*. Rather a jar, but she is going to pay for it, and Reynolds will try to sell it elsewhere. What on earth is wrong with that story? I thought it was the funniest I had ever done, and you yelled over it. The editors of *Pan*, who are publishing it serially here, think a lot of it. Yet quite a squad of editors have turned it down. It makes me feel a bit doubtful of my new story, which I start tomorrow.†

Well, cheerio.
Mummie sends her love. She is washing her hair or something this morning.

Your loving
Plummie

Plum also wrote regularly to William Townend. In 1921 he said, "I find that if I spend more than six months in this country I'm liable to pay income tax on everything I make in America as well as in England, in addition to paying American income tax. This is no good to Pelham, so I'm skipping." This letter heralds a theme which was to recur, but Plum must have been reassured at the time, because, although he and Ethel did go to America, it was for the purpose of selling their house at Great Neck, while during the next years they would twice become householders in England, first renting a house in Gilbert Street and then moving to one in Norfolk Street, both expensive and fashionable addresses in Mayfair. Ethel, who was an inveterate gambler as well as an inveterate party giver, also

---

*This imbroglio seems to have been settled, because the lyrics "Joan of Arc" and "Church around the Corner" appeared in *Sally*, which played for 570 performances at the New Amsterdam Theatre in New York (1920) and 383 at the Winter Garden Theatre in London (1921).
†*The Girl on the Boat* is one of the most unsatisfactory of all Wodehouse novels, with a slow-moving plot and not very much humour.

bought a steeplechaser called Front Line. On the 1921 trip to America
Plum wrote several times to Leonora, addressing her from the boat as
"Darling precious angel Snorklet," and from the Hotel Biltmore in New
York as "Prcious (or, rather, precious) angel Snork." From the boat he
was chiefly concerned about whether his stateroom table was steady enough
to write on, although he said, "I have already been interviewed by the
representative of the White Star Publicity for publication in N.Y. and
Mummie is running around in circles breathing smoke because I didn't lug
her into it. I tell her I will feature her when the reporters arrive at N.Y."
And he ended his letter: "Good-bye my Queen of all possible Snorkles."
From New York he told her he had had to pay seventeen dollars for a
bottle of whisky. "I suppose if you tried to get champagne you would have
to throw in your Sunday trousers as well."

All through 1921 he wrote to Leonora whenever she was not with him.
A letter on 1 May was written from Emsworth House (Baldwin King-
Hall's house):

> I hope this reaches you before you leave Felixstowe. I shall be up in time
> to see you before you biff off to school. Awful rot your having to go, is
> my verdict. I want you at my side as my confidential secretary and ad-
> viser. . . .
>
> I am now sweating away down here on the first act of the Adelphi
> show. I've done about half of it, but it has been an awful fag. I've now
> got to the point where Grossmith and Berry come on and I have to be
> frightfully funny. Unfortunately I feel very mirthless and my comedy will
> probably be blue round the edges.*
>
> I'm so sorry to hear you have had a cough again. You really must buck
> up and get fit. I wonder if Bromley will agree with you. If it doesn't, we
> shall have to shift you. We mustn't have our Snorky wasting away on
> us. . . .
>
> *Love among the Chickens* is out in the cheap edition. I'll send you a
> copy. Townend told me it was on sale at the Charing Cross bookstall, so
> I rolled round and found they had sold out. Thence to the Piccadilly
> bookstall. Sold out again. Pretty good in the first two days. Both men
> offered to sell me "other Wodehouse books," but I smiled gently on them
> and legged it.
>
> I have got four new freckles on the top of my head. Where will this
> end? I think I shall buy a parasol.

*George Grossmith and W. H. Berry, both noted comedians. George Grossmith was the
son of Weedon Grossmith (*The Diary of a Nobody*), and he deserves more space than he
gets in this book, since not only was he the first person to bring a Bolton-Wodehouse-Kern
musical to London (*Oh, Boy!*), but he also collaborated with Wodehouse on the book of
The Cabaret Girl and became a friend of the whole family. Information about this friendship
is rather scarce today.

On 20 May he wrote her a long letter beginning, "You will be thinking me a f.i.h.s. (fiend in human shape) for not having written to you before, but, gosh ding it, four separate jobs collided and I was sunk in the whirl-pool." He continues:

Old Savage arrived and I had to buckle to on the Lehar piece; Fred Thompson came back and I had to pop onto the Adelphi piece; Reynolds cabled and I had to revise the *Girl on the Boat;* and he also said that *Collier's* wanted the rest of *Sally.* My impulse in these circumstances was to go to bed with a hot-water bottle and a book, but I decided to have a dash at tackling the jobs, so I started by cutting twenty thousand words out of the *Girl on the Boat,* after which I wrote a scene of the Lehar piece and a scene of the Adelphi piece. I haven't touched *Sally* yet. They will have to wait a bit for that.

On Wednesday afternoon I had an interview with Savage, who read and liked my lyrics and then calmly told me that, for purposes of copy-right, he would have to have the remaining two lyrics by today (Friday) at four. I hadn't even got ideas for them. By great good luck I managed to get two good ideas, and now—at 2 o'clock—I have just finished them both. . . . He wants the book completed by two weeks from tomorrow. I think I can manage it all right, but it will be a sweat, and I would like to be out in this fine weather. Still, if I am so much in demand it can't be helped.

Mrs. Westbrook has written to say that the *Strand* have raised my price from one hundred and fifty quid to two hundred quid per short story, which, with the American rights, will make about a snappy six hundred quid per s.s.—which, as you will no doubt agree, is noticeably better than a dab in the eye with a burnt stick.

Mummie has biffed off to Lingfield, previously touching me for two pounds.

I am so glad that you like the jolly old school. It sounds ripping—or, as you would say now, *epatant* [*sic*]. How do you like talking French?

And at the end of the year he wrote:

The Wodehouse home is en fête and considerably above itself this p.m. Deep-throated cheers ring out in Flat 43, and every now and then I have to go out on the balcony to address the seething crowds in St. James's Street. And why? I'll tell you. (I'm glad you asked me.) This afternoon at Hurst Park dear jolly old Front Line romped home in the Hurdle Hand-icap in spite of having to carry about three tons weight. The handicappers crammed an extra ten pounds on him after his last win, so he had to carry thirteen stone three pounds, and it seemed so impossible that he could win that I went off and played golf instead of going to Hurst Park. . . .

We got four hundred quid in stakes—minus fifty quid which we have to cough up to the second horse and twenty-five to the third. Rot, I call it, having to pay them, and I am in favour of seeing if they won't be satisfied with seats for *The Golden Moth* or copies of my books, but apparently it can't be done. We also have to give the trainer a present of fifty quid, and a few extra tips to various varlets and lackeys, not omitting one or two scurvy knaves. Still, with what Mummie (the well-known gambler) got on at six to one, we clear five hundred quid on the afternoon, which, as you justly remark, is not so worse.

In addition to this, Mummie's judgment in buying the horse is boosted to the skies, and everybody looks on her now as the wisest guy in town. . . .

My first remark on hearing the news was "Snork will expect something out of this!" It seemed to me that the thing must infallibly bring on a severe attack of the gimmes in the little darling one. . . .

Well, that's that. So Mummie has started her career as the Curse of the Turf in great style. . . .

Cheerio, old cake
Oceans of love.
Plummie

In the only letter of interest in 1922, Plum asks for details of how schoolgirls behave.

I say, I've got out the plot of a Jeeves story where Bertie visits a girls' school and is very shy and snootered by the girls and the headmistress. Can you give me any useful details? What would be likely to happen to a chap who was seeing over a school? Do you remember—was it at Ely?— the girls used to sing a song of welcome. Can you give me the words of the song and when it would be sung? And anything else of that sort that would be likely to rattle Bertie.*

Soon after, he came himself to see Leonora, at the school at Bromley where I by now had joined her. I was standing at the window of one of the upper classrooms which looked out on the drive when a memorable apparition appeared.

"Snorky," I said, "come and look at this extraordinary old man."†

A bulky, red-faced man was bicycling down the drive, his (freckled) head adorned by a white handkerchief, tied in a knot at each corner, to shield it from the sun.

"That's Plummie," Snorky said, and, as she spoke, he got off his bicycle and wheeled it into the shrubbery on the side of the drive.

"What on earth's he doing?" I asked.

"He's frightened of Miss Starbuck, so he waits there and I go out and join him."

Miss Starbuck was the headmistress. She was tall, thin-faced, and shy;

---

*"Bertie Changes His Mind" from the collection *Carry On, Jeeves.*
†At this date Plum was just over forty.

she added to the severity of her appearance by wearing a boned collar; and I expect she was socially incompetent. But she was reasonably kind, and no less aware than any other head would have been of the desirability of having P. G. Wodehouse's daughter at her school. I never knew anyone but Plummie who was seriously afraid of her.

One event of the late twenties was important. This was Plum's meeting with Denis Mackail. Mackail was the son of J. W. Mackail OM, classical scholar, Professor of Poetry at Oxford, and the biographer of William Morris. Denis Mackail wrote many best-selling novels and the authorized biography of J. M. Barrie. He was a brother of Angela Thirkell and, consequently, an uncle of Colin MacInnes. Plum dedicated *Summer Lightning* to him with the words "To Denis Mackail, author of *Greenery Street, The Flower Show* and other books which I wish I had written."

Mackail has described his first meeting with Plum in an autobiographical book called *Life with Topsy*. In 1928 Plum wrote to him, he says, and congratulated him on his first novel, and a little later asked him to dinner at one of his clubs.

> As I need hardly tell anyone of his acquaintance, by the time I reached the Club in question he had already become disgusted with it, and rushed me off to the Savoy-Grill instead. There he provided a considerable banquet, and immediately started talking about writing, without a moment's delay.
>
> For this—apart from Pekes, which he, too, would presently own and adore, and cricket and football matches at his old school, with which he also seemed obsessed—was his own, great unending topic; and at all the evenings that we have spent together I can't remember his ever lingering, for more than a few seconds, on anything else.[1]

Mackail goes on to say that Plum soon started going to his house, where Plum and Ethel met Diana, Mackail's wife, and Rufus, his Peke, and both Mackails met Leonora.

> But every now and then Plum and I would have a quiet, literary evening together. . . .
> "I say, touching this matter of Pekes . . ."
> "I say, when you get absolutely stuck in a story . . ."
> "I say, what do you really make of old Somerset M?"
> These were all Plum's openings, as we smoked and sipped, and hammered each object with our mighty brains. Most enjoyable, I can tell you. At about half past ten—for we always dined early—we suddenly started rushing through the streets, at Plum's prodigious pace, until a point where, just as suddenly, he had vanished and gone. No lingering farewells from that quarter. I *might* hear him saying Good-night, from the middle of the traffic; I *might* catch a glimpse of his rain-coat swinging across the road.

But the general effect was that he had just switched himself off. It was the custom. And, in those days, of course—unless he were also dashing off to America—there would always be another of those evenings quite soon.[2]

Denis Mackail also describes staying with the Wodehouses some years later in the house at Rogate near Petersfield: "But Plum, with a butler and a country mansion, was exactly the same as ever. No better dressed. Just as determined to talk about nothing but ink. And just as adept at vanishing completely, whenever that sudden and mystical summons came."[3]

More than fifty years later Edward Cazalet described this vanishing act to a meeting of the PEN Club in London. Here one minute and gone the next—the trick was known in the family as "the Wodehouse glide."

Plum's letters to Mackail are an unparalleled source for an account of his daily doings and for an understanding of his character. Mackail, like Plum himself, liked receiving letters, and he always answered them. As a result the correspondence between the two men covers the whole of the rest of their lives until Mackail's death in the 1970s. Unfortunately, like so many other things, most of Mackail's letters to Plum have perished, lost either at Le Touquet during the war or in a great burning carried out by Ethel a few years before Plum died. He was, if less talented than Plum, better educated and more intellectual. His books are still worth reading, although they have the slow narrative form and discursive essayist's manner of so much Edwardian writing. He had a sharp and sometimes bitter wit, and one gets the impression that he was dominant in this friendship. Certainly Plum took pains to amuse him, and in these letters he occasionally exhibits a lighthearted malice which sometimes appears also in his letters to Guy Bolton, but was not often revealed. When Edward Cazalet first saw the letters to Mackail, he told me that they showed a side of Plum he had not known existed. It says much for these two men's appetite for writing that after the day's work was done, all the fan letters answered, after dealing with the accountant, the solicitor, and the agent, they sat down and wrote to each other.

The correspondence will be much quoted here, and certain explanations are necessary. Plum shared with Mackail an obsessive love of Pekes, which causes about one-fifth of every letter to be a Peke story. Some of these passages will be quoted to give the flavour, but where they are not quoted, they can safely be presumed to occur. The same may be said of Plum's letters to Leonora, Guy Bolton, and many other people. His feeling for Pekes, like his feeling for Dulwich, verged on the fatuous.

The second feature of his letters to Mackail is a constant, exaggerated, and almost fawning praise of the other's work. Again, only a few examples will be given, because these remarks are apt to be repetitive. Whether they represent a deep and sincerely felt appreciation of Mackail's work or are due to Plum's attempts to overcome his own difficulty in communication is not clear. There is no doubt that he did admire Mackail very much, but, like all extremely shy people, he had no natural standards of behaviour. Speaking of a novel called *The Flower Show*, he wrote:

> Honestly, the only books I have ever enjoyed and admired as much are *The Egoist* and *Vanity Fair*. It is simply a colossal performance, and, incidentally, it has had the most disturbing effect on my own work. I am in the middle of thinking out a plot, the big scene of which is a burglar trying to escape from a house, handicapped by having on his feet a pair of roller-skates, which a cheerful lunatic has put on him & which he can't get off. Somehow, after reading *The Flower Show*, I don't seem able to kid myself that is real literature.

And of *Greenery Street:* "What an amazingly good book that is. This makes my fifth reading of it and it seems just as good as ever. It fits conveniently into the pocket. I'm now going to re-read *The Flower Show* and as I've just read your story in *Pearson's*, what more do you want?"

One of the main issues of the twenties and early thirties was the one of where to live. For more than ten years the Wodehouses had a house in London, the one in Norfolk Street being very large. David Jasen writes:

> The rental was £450 a month, and the running of the establishment called for a retinue of servants such as the Wodehouses had never before required. There was a morning secretary to keep the household expenses books, an afternoon secretary to deal with Ethel's many business interests, a cook, a butler, a kitchen maid, a footman, two housemaids, one odd-job man, and a chauffeur for the new Rolls-Royce.[4]

Ethel's tastes were dominant at the moment, her business interests including a good deal of speculation on the Stock Exchange. She was rumoured to have lost an enormous fortune in the early twenties, but I can find no evidence of this. Usually she had one or two young men in attendance as well as Plum. A character referred to as Bobbie crops up from time to time in Plum's letters, and when I asked Guy Bolton who he was, he replied, "Bobbie Denby." "But who was Bobbie Denby?" I asked. "Oh! one of Ethel's young men." Plum seems to have taken this with unruffled calm. The postscript of a letter to Leonora reads: "Do write Bobbie a line, precious. He wrote you such a long letter and must be feeling blue all alone at Dinard." And later:

> Bobbie is at the Royalton. He doesn't seem to like New York much, but que voulez-vous? If he don't get an eddication he can't be a lawyer. In other words, if he doesn't stick around New York, how can he ever

become a millionaire? Also we think his complaints of the horrors of N.Y. are largely banana-oil, designed to get sympathy.

In London Ethel gave regular dinner parties, which Plum disliked, and occasional large parties, which he disliked even more. I once went to Norfolk Street with my father, and to our surprise the front door was opened not by the butler, but by Plum himself.

"Don't come in," he said hurriedly, seeing my father. "Don't come in. You'll hate it."

How is the cottage working out? [he wrote to Townend.] One thing about living in the country is that, even if the windows leak, you can get some work done. I find it's the hardest job to get at the stuff here. We have damned dinners and lunches which just eat up the time. I find that having lunch hanging over me kills my morning work, and dinner isn't much better. I'm at the stage now, if I drop my characters, they go cold.

Nevertheless, he was probably more sociable at this period of his life than at any other. He made many friends, most of them writers or in the theatre. He met A. A. Milne through Denis Mackail, and he collaborated with Ian Hay; he writes with friendliness about both my father and Michael Arlen; his relationships with George Grossmith, Heather Thatcher, and Dorothy Dickson were easy if not close; E. Phillips Oppenheim proposed him for the hated Garrick Club, and Max Pemberton seconded him; among those whose names are mentioned as his own guests were Walter Wanger and his wife, Justine Johnson, one of the girls in *Bring On the Girls* (the other being Marion Davies). And he too enjoyed a gamble. If Ethel was a natural operator, Plum was a natural punter. Writing to Denis Mackail about *Greenery Street*, he said:

The only possible criticism I would make is that it is not the sort of book which should be put into the hands of one who ought to be working on a short story. Ethel got skinned to the bone at Ascot yesterday—myself present, incidentally in a *grey* tophat and white spats—and I promised her I would work all day today at something that would put her square. So far I have done nothing but read *Greenery Street*.

In spite, or perhaps because, of all this, it was clear that London did not suit Plum, and other places were tried. Staying at Great Neck with Guy Bolton in November 1923, he wrote to Leonora (now grown up and in Paris with Ethel):

Well, ma belle, how goes it? You like the—how is it you Americans say?—the Gay City, hein?

Over here, figure to yourself how it is triste. One gets through the time somehow, but we miss the delicately nurtured. . . .

I am wondering if you and Mummie have decided that Paris is a good spot for the family to take up its headquarters. I must say I shouldn't mind trying it for a bit. I have got very tired of America. Great Neck seems quite different this year. Last winter, with the good old loved ones around me, I enjoyed it tremendously, but it makes me restless now. I suppose it is simply because I miss you and Mummie. This bachelor life is no good to me at all.

And a month later he wrote to her, dating his letter "Christmas Morning (or, putting it another way, Dec. 25, 1923)": "My precious angel Snorky, Your lovely letter (*billet le plus charmant*) arrived this morning while I was at breakfast (*dejeuner* [*sic*]) champing (*filling le visage avec*) about half a pound of sausages (*saussisons* [*sic*])." In this letter he wrote (after giving her news of two theatrical ventures):

When these two pieces are on, the scheme is to come over to Paris and settle down there for a bit. Mummie arrived quite in favour of the place, in spite of the gloom in some of her letters. I feel we should have a great time. I want to learn French and intend to pitch right into it. . . .

Oh, by the way. Mummie tells me you have taken to wine in your old age. I wish you wouldn't. I have always pointed with pride to you as the one female in the world who can subsist on water. I should preserve the record, if I were you.

In a letter written soon after Ethel returned to Great Neck he wrote:

We loved the photographs. You looked very beautiful. Though, while on the subject of looking beautiful, you ought to see the Light of the Home in her Paris dresses. A pip, believe me. She flashed the blue one with the white collar on me the other day and I keeled over. Nor is the beige to be despised.

Still from Great Neck, in the February of the following year (1924) he wrote to Leonora:

Well, say, listen, kid, lemme tell ya sum'fin. I sent the first 70,000 words of *Bill the Conqueror* off to the typist (*la stenographie*) yesterday, and believe me or believe me not, it's *good*. I'm taking a day off today and tomorrow plunge into the remaining 25,000, which ought to be pie. This is certainly one swell story, as good as the old man has ever done, and, thank God, I have been able to work in that line about "I know it's paraffin, but what have they put in it?" Judson has worked out immense, and Flick, the heroine, is so like you that the cognoscenti cannot help but be charmed.

The Wodehouses did not go to Paris, and in England less than a year later Plum was writing:

> Harrogate isn't such a bad old spot. I played golf today for the first time and feel fine. . . .
> I have just finished a short story. V. G. Mummie thoroughly approved of it. The central character may lead to further stories. . . .
> Mummie is the belle of the hotel; and dances like a breeze.

And six months later (30 March 1925) he wrote:

> Gallia Hotel
> Cannes
> (Famous Pleasure-Resort—Ha, ha!)
>
> I am now at last in a position to give you the low-down on the Riviera. . . .
> Of all the poisonous, foul, ghastly places, Cannes takes the biscuit with absurd ease. Until we came here, I was thinking Monte Carlo not all it might be, but now I look back to those dear old Monte Carlo days with an absolute pang.
> Mummie says in her letter that we have done nothing here but stay in the hotel and walk on the front, but this, with the exception of going to the Casino, is all there is to do. The only tolerable thing about Cannes is the hotel garden, which contains ornamental water with ducks, water-rats, etc., and forms an oasis in this bloodsome desert. Mummie and I have come to the conclusion that we loathe foreign countries. We hate their ways, their architecture, their looks, their language and their food. So we must simply buckle to and get a house for you in England somewhere. I am all for the Chippenham neighbourhood. We both want dogs and cats and cows and meadow-land. Directly you get out of England you get nothing but spiky palms and other beastly shrubs.

The following day, in a continuation of the same letter, he wrote: "I've been sitting in the garden all the afternoon, and, by Jove, Cannes doesn't seem so bad after all. I think the solution is never to go into it. I propose to spend all my time in the garden from now on." And in a postscript the following day: "Not a bad place, Cannes! We went to the Casino last night and I won 500 francs, which makes me feel a bit benevolent."

After this they tried English country houses. They stayed several times at a house in Norfolk called Hunstanton Hall, belonging to Charles Le Strange (it was later destroyed by fire). Plum wrote to Townend from there:

> The above address does not mean that I have bought a country estate. It is a joint belonging to a friend of mine, and I am putting in a week or

two here. It's one of those enormous houses, about two-thirds of which are derelict. There is a whole wing which has not been lived in for half a century. You know the sort of thing—it's happening all over the country now—thousands of acres, park, gardens, moat, etc., and priceless heir-looms, but precious little ready money. The income from farms and so on just about balances expenses.

I spend most of my time on the moat, which is really a sizeable lake. I'm writing this in a punt with my typewriter on a bed-table wobbling on one of the seats. There is a duck close by which utters occasional quacks that sound like a man with an unpleasant voice saying nasty things in an undertone. Beside me is a brick wall with the date 1623 on it. The only catch is that the water is full of weeds, so I can't swim in it as I would like to.[5]

In the summer of 1928 the Wodehouses rented a house called Rogate Lodge in Surrey, but in April 1929 Plum wrote to Townend from Hunstanton Hall once more:

It's so wonderful being back at Hunstanton again, though things aren't so frightfully bright at the moment, as host has had a row with butler, who has given notice. The butler is a cheery soul who used to be the life and soul of the party, joining in the conversation at meals and laughing appreciatively if one made a joke, but now he hovers like a spectre, very strong and silent. I'm hoping peace will be declared soon.

I think I like Hunstanton as well in winter as in summer, though, of course, I don't get the moat in the winter months. I laid the scene of *Money for Nothing* at Hunstanton Hall.[6]

All in all, one gets the impression that if Plum had not made an enor-mous fortune but, like Townend, had been forced to struggle to make enough money to live, or if Ethel had had less zest for life, they might have lived happily ever after with "dogs and cats and cows and meadow-land" in a small cottage in the English countryside. As it was, Plum went to Hollywood.

An Interlude

In January 1929 the *Strand* magazine published an article headed

P. G. WODEHOUSE AT HOME

By His Daughter

LEONORA WODEHOUSE

Beginning with a preamble to the effect that whereas the man in the street can get some idea of the personality of an actor, film star, or athlete, the personality of an author is not more than a blurred impression to him, it went on:

Plum, whose full name is Pelham Grenville Wodehouse—it's such a pomp-ous, frock-coated sort of name and has nothing to do with my breezy Plummy—started life as an artist at the age of three. It wasn't until he was six that he took to writing seriously. For two years he produced some rather complicated jungle tales, then after a silence of almost twenty years wrote school stories for The Captain and other magazines, and gradually evolved his world of cheerful, happy characters: Jeeves, Archie, Mr. Mulliner, and the others he writes of now.

He is really the hardest of hard workers, but sometimes I think that the literary life is altogether a delightful affair. Ian Hay is staying with us for three or four days, and shouts of laughter keep coming from the library where he and Plum are working on the second act of a play that they are writing together. And at lunch-time they will say what a hard morning it has been, and then go off and play golf, having finished work for the day. The funny part of it all is that in those three hours they really have done a very hard day's work.

When Plum is writing a novel or a short story, the procedure is very much the same. He writes in the morning and "broods" in the afternoon, when he must on no account be disturbed. It is understood that he is thinking deep thoughts and planning great novels, but when all the smoke has cleared away it really means that he is either asleep or eating an apple and reading Edgar Wallace. After tea, if we're in London, he usually goes for a long walk, or in the country plays golf.

His tastes are very simple; books, pipes, football matches—he adores them all. Nothing is a pleasure to him that involves pain to anything, so he doesn't enjoy shooting or fishing. A frosty November morning, a blazing fire and muffins on a January afternoon, old clothes—those are the things that he likes best. We are gradually smartening him up, and he is now occasionally to be seen in Bond Street whimpering nervously because his wardrobe is being re-stocked for him, which means that Mummie and the salesman decide what is best for him and order twelve of everything, paying no attention to the thin screams of my poor Plummy.

I think that you could say that he plays Bridge. When one has got up a table, Plum will come pottering around, giving advice, telling anecdotes, and offering to cut in; but when a fourth is needed he is nowhere to be found. Often I say to him: "But, my sweet, why didn't you lead your ace of spades sooner?" and he answers coldly: "I played it the second I found it." He believes that the fun of Bridge lies in finding kings and queens in one's hand just when things look blackest. The other night one of his partners, in a furious voice, said: "Had you any particular reason for your diamond discard, partner?" "Just a happy accident," said Plummy, pleased that his play had caused comment.

He has no real sense of money; a cheque for a thousand pounds means nothing to him except as a sort of good conduct mark. But if half a crown is missed in this house we all know who will stammer and turn pale when the hue and cry are raised. He would sell a cheque for fifty pounds to anyone at any time for seven-and-sixpence cash; as a matter of fact, that is how I keep my head above water. He has simply no idea of business or anything connected with it. Mummie looks after all his interests and is very clever about it. All Plum wants is an occasional pound to buy tobacco with and an account at a book shop. Mummie and I always arrange what our lives are to be, and where, because he hates making plans and is always perfectly happy whatever happens.

Sometimes I think of him as being amazingly faithful—I mean about places and things. An old pigsty, if he once knew the pig that lived there, is Heaven to him for always. And yet he never seems to like a steady diet of any one thing or person, so one can't make sense out of him either way.

He has an overwhelming horror of being bored, and an overpowering hatred of hurting people. You and I on being asked to lunch with someone we wanted to avoid would probably say how sorry we were, what a pity it was, and what a shame, but unfortunately we are sailing for Canada next week. Plum will do even better than that for you. Having said so, he immediately will sail for Canada; and to make quite certain will do it this week. I really have known him once in America go to Georgia because a lady reporter asked him to tea at four. He was profuse with apologies and mumbled about catching trains almost immediately. And having let himself in for it, he went South! Unfortunately they met again on his return, and this time my poor darling Plum, tired of train journeys, accepted. Then with great presence of mind he put four toothbrushes in his pocket and sailed for England the next day at three. Only the other day we found a note saying that he had "popped to Droitwich to brood"—but we didn't quite believe in that motive for escape, and the arrival of a very tedious caller in the afternoon justified us in our suspicions!

In two things, however, he is amazingly and amusingly steadfast—his devotion to an antique typewriter and his adoration of Pekes.

The typewriter he has had ever since he was twenty, and he adores it. The firm that made it is extinct, and it has been so much repaired that there isn't a single original part left. I think it manages to hang together somehow so as not to disappoint Plummy. If it is used too regularly it breaks down, and if it isn't used enough the keys stiffen. No one is allowed to touch it, and it goes everywhere with him. If necessary, it has a first-class seat in the train, and on no account is the porter allowed to carry it—they don't understand it, he says. We usually wire for a typewriter repairer to meet the train, since travelling always seems to make its insides slip. Plum has got five other typewriters that he has, at different times, in different countries, bought in despair when his darling has been pronounced dead; and the new ones are given to me or cast aside.

Then there is Susan.

Susan is our Pekingese, and Plum adores her. Just as we have planned glorious voyages to the Far East or lazy summers to be spent in Sicily, we remember that Susan would have to be left behind, so we stay in England to keep her amused, or see the world in relays. She is very pretty, small, with a chestnut coat and that dancing way of walking that Pekingese have. Plum will leave anyone in the middle of a conversation to ingratiate himself with Susan if she gives him the slightest smile; and a man may be without morals, money, or attractions, if the word goes round that he's "sound on Pekingese," Plum will probably somehow find excuses for his lack of morals, lend him money, and invent attractions for him.

She has three puppies which we had meant to give away, but they are so very adorable and have each got so much of Susan in them that we are keeping them all—moving into a larger house, I expect. In two years I suppose that they will have three puppies each, so like their grandmother that it will be impossible to give any away. And in two years after that . . .

But I promise to say something of how Plum works. He never seems to stop working: his idea of a holiday is to write a play instead of a novel, a short story instead of a musical comedy. I think his work is easy to read because he enjoys writing it so. I once read of a humorist who wrote that the little dots seen at intervals on the page "were not commas, they were drops of blood." Plum is so utterly different. Once he has got the plot more or less clearly fixed *in his mind he writes quickly and easily. It may be a scene which I beg him to tear up before a soul can see it, or five pages which eventually become a paragraph, but while he is writing it is effortless.*

He does take tremendous trouble with the construction of his work. No character of his ever does anything without a fairly plausible reason for it, farcical though it may be. For instance, in Bill the Conqueror, when the hero and heroine are to meet by chance, she answers in person a bogus begging letter from the enterprising, temporarily financially-embarrassed friend who shares the hero's flat. Bill opens the door and the romance begins.

I am so proud of him because he has never lowered his standard. You may prefer one story to another, definitely dislike some characters, but the same ingredients go to the making of them all. A plot and a sub-plot, a good scene or two, perhaps some surprises, and any amount of care and trouble. Last week he completely re-wrote a story. It is now told by Mr. Mulliner instead of by Bertie, the scene is laid in the Royal Enclosure instead of in a public-house, and he telegraphed me, saying: "Poor old Colonel got to go Mother now a Maiden Aunt."

A thing that has always amazed me about Plum is his ability to write lyrics, set them to music, and to carry a tune in his head that he had probably only heard three or four times. He's not a bit interested in music and can't play a note. Tosti's "Good-bye" and "Red-Hot Mamma" would sound exactly alike if hummed by Plummy, and neither of them could be recognized as Tosti's "Good-bye" or "Red-Hot Mamma." But in spite of this, at the back of his mind the tune is there; with no knowledge of music he recognizes the rhythm, the short beats and the long beats. I remember when he was writing a musical comedy in America, the composer would telephone Plum, probably a hundred miles away, put the telephone on the piano, and play the tune to him three or four times. And that night Plum would finish and send off a lyric which fitted the tune perfectly.

I can't imagine Plum as anything but a writer, a humorist, for humour seems to be so much a part of him. He laughs first and discovers the sob in his throat afterwards. That in a way is how he finds his plots and situations, I think. If his eye should skip over a paragraph dealing with the maintenance and salaries of Missionaries in the Far East, even as he is turning to the Sporting Page, something jumps up in his brain, saying: "All that explained at length to Bertie, driven into a corner by an elderly goofy aunt. Think of it!"

It is really difficult trying to explain someone you know very well; like writing history, I should think, whilst you are still living it. There is no perspective. I'm sure of this, though: that to both his great friends and casual acquaintances he is someone to be rather fond of. He has that quality that not many people seem to have, a quality of sweetness, I think it is, something that you can't help liking. For without one sign of sympathy from him you get a great impression of it; without one word of kindliness from him, kindliness is your first and last impression of him.

8

Hollywood

Plum went first to Hollywood for a short time in 1929, to look at the place and to discuss an offer to work there. According to David Jasen, Ethel, whom he rather unexpectedly describes as "an astute business woman," then went by herself to negotiate terms, and did indeed succeed in concluding a contract for six months, with an option for a further six months, at $2,000 a week. This is one of the few examples of Ethel extending her business activities to the working side of Plum's life, although, as the letters already quoted show, he consulted her in everything.

In the early part of 1930 he was in London, and then in April he left for New York and later Hollywood, his travelling companion being Leonora. Ethel, for some reason not now known, stayed on in London and did not join them until the following July.

We have a good deal of information about the period—a little more than a year—which Plum spent in Hollywood, because he wrote regularly from there both to Townend and to Denis Mackail. Many of the letters to Townend were published in *Performing Flea,* and where there is an alternative, the Mackail letters will be quoted here. The same ground is often covered, but the Mackail letters are usually the more amusing. The first, dated 2 June 1930, from the Metro-Goldwyn-Mayer studios, began:

> Frightfully sorry I haven't written before. I have been in a whirl of work. After three months absolute deadness my brain began to whirr like a dynamo. So you see one does recover from these blank periods. I hope yours has gone.
>
> I have written three short stories, an act of a play and the dialogue for a picture in three weeks, and have got six brand new plots for short stories!!! I believe our rotten brains have to go through these ghastly periods of inertness before getting a second wind.
>
> Susan [the Wodehouse Peke] is dead. Did Ethel tell you? Apparently she just toppled over quite quietly in the Park, and it was all over in a minute. She had no pain, thank goodness. It's just like losing part of oneself. The only thing is that everything is so unreal out here and I feel

so removed from ordinary life that I haven't yet quite realised it. . . .

This is the weirdest place. We have taken Elsie Janis's house. It has a small but very pretty garden with a big pool.* I have arranged with the studio to work at home, so I sometimes don't go out of the garden for three or four days on end. If you asked me, I would say I loved Holly-wood. Then I would reflect and have to admit that Hollywood is about the most loathsome place on the map but that, never going near it, I enjoy being out here.

My days follow each other in a regular procession. I get up, swim, breakfast, work till two, swim again, work till seven, swim for the third time, then dinner and the day is over. When I get a summons from the studio I motor over there, stay for a couple of hours and come back. Add incessant sunshine and it's really rather jolly. It is only occasionally that one feels one is serving a term on Devil's Island. We go out very little. Just an occasional dinner at the house of some other exile, e.g. some New York theatrical friend. Except for one party at Marion Davies's place, I've not met any movie stars.

He then described the practice at a dinner party in Hollywood which, he said, was to arrive at 7:15 and stand round drinking cocktails till 9:30.

By dinner time I was dying on my feet. Poor old Snorky had to talk to the same man from 7:15 till 9:30 and then found she was sitting next to him at dinner. Luckily it was such a big party that we were able to slip off without saying good-bye directly dinner was over.

The actual work is negligible. I altered all the characters to earls and butlers with such success that they called a conference and changed the entire plot, starring the earl and the butler. So I'm still working on it. So far I've had eight collaborators. The system is that A gets the original idea, B comes in to work with him on it, C makes the scenario, D does preliminary dialogue, and then they send for me to insert class and what not, then E and F, scenario writers, alter the plot and off we go again. I could have done all my part of it in a morning but they took it for granted that I should need six weeks.

The latest news is that they are going to start shooting quite soon. In fact there are ugly rumours that I'm to be set to work soon on something else. I resent this as it will cut into my short story writing. It is odd how soon one comes to look upon every minute as wasted that is given to earning one's salary. (Now don't go making a comic article out of this and queering me with the bosses.)

---

*I can offer no certain explanation of the fact that in a letter to Townend written three weeks later, he describes the house and garden in almost the same terms but says it was Norma Shearer's. But by now Norma Shearer was married to Irving Thalberg, of MGM, so it probably had been hers and now belonged to Elsie Janis.

On 18 August of the same year he wrote to Townend: "Ethel arrived a month ago, with Winks under her arm. Winks has settled down finely and seems to be very happy. We are devoted to her, and she seems to have taken on a lot of Susan's characteristics. She barks furiously at our Japanese gardener."[1] And on 28 October:

Well, laddie, it begins to look as if it would be some time before I return to England. The Metro people have taken up my option, and I am now with them for another six months and Ethel has just taken a new house for a year. Which means that I shall probably stay that long. . . .

I am still bathing vigorously three times a day, though in the early morning the water is pretty chilly. They tell me that with care you can bathe all through the winter.[2]

And on 14 March 1931: "I wish you were here for this weather. It is as warm as summer, and I am bathing regularly. The pool is a nice 62 degrees."[3] Then on 12 April he wrote to Denis Mackail:

April 12 1931   1005 Benedict Drive
                                          Beverly Hills

Talking of work, I'm so glad you liked *Big Money*. I feel about my stuff that it never contains what you might call surprises. . . . You are never likely to feel like Keats on first reading Chapman's Homer, but I do have the ambition to keep the old Wodehouse pemmican up to the level and I think *B.M.* fills the bill. . . .

We have at last got our beloved daughter home again, after a five months' absence in New York. She is sweeter than ever, and full of beans.

I don't know if she will want me to tell you before she does, but she wrote a short story and sent it to the *American* magazine without any name on it, so that it got no pull from the fact that I am writing for the *American,* and each of the four editors sent it on with enthusiastic comments, and they bought it for $300 and want lots more. She also sold an article for $150.

She really can write like blazes and thank goodness is now very keen on it. Her stuff has a terrific amount of charm and she has only got to stick to it to do awfully well.

Ethel has been entertaining largely lately. She starts by asking two people to lunch, then who can we get to meet them? This gets it up to four. Then come all the people who would be hurt at being left out, and eventually the thing becomes a Hollywood orgy. This afternoon we had fifty people to lunch! It's not as bad as it sounds, because in this lovely climate you feed out of doors. We had bridge tables spotted about the garden and patio, and a large table with cold food in the dining room, so that people simply helped themselves. As usual Ethel feels it was a frost, but it wasn't really. It went off splendidly. . . .

I suppose you have been working as hard as ever. Don't you feel that what you need is some really definite break between jobs of work? I do. I find there is nothing in this world I really want to do except read. From here it would be easy to go to Japan, for instance. But what would one do in Japan? Thank heaven I have three circulating libraries within easy walk. My only trouble is that so few writers ever do more than one decent book. Did you read *The Fool of the Family* and *Note in Music*—the second innings of the authors of *The Constant Nymph* and *Dusty Answer*?* Frightfully disappointing. The fact is that practically every author is a damned amateur. They have one good book in them and can't repeat it.

Miss Winks is flourishing. I wish we could see your Victoria. We've been putting up Maureen O'Sullivan's one-eyed Peke, Johnny (female). It was run over in the street and lost an eye and I thought I had at last found an ugly Peke. But as the days went by Johnny gradually turned beautiful, and now is an angel.

On 10 May 1931 he wrote again:

My contract with MGM ended yesterday and they have shown no sign whatever of wanting to renew it. . . .

I haven't been able to get much out of Hollywood so far, but then I have been restraining myself from satire out of love and loyalty for dear old MGM. Now that the pay envelope has ceased, maybe I shall be able to write some stuff knocking them good.

This place has certain definite advantages which make up for it being so far from home. I love breakfasting in the garden in a dressing gown after a swim in the pool. There's no doubt that perpetual sunshine has its points. I've never been able to stay more than a few months in one place before, let alone a year. And the people here are quite fun. I find I enjoy going out to dinner. . . .

A nasty jar the other day. A man prefacing his remark by saying he loved my stuff, wrote that he thought that I had over-written *Big Money*, and he sent me the book with his cuts!! The poor ass had cut out practically everything, including all the really funny bits which the critics had praised. And he obviously meant so well and was so genuinely trying to be friendly and helpful that I can't savage him. But the result has been to make me distrustful of my work.

Why is it that a single slam from even the most patent imbecile can undo all the praise of a hundred critics? If he had gushed about the story, I wouldn't have been a bit pleased. But just because this one man finds fault in it I find myself against all my reason becoming diffident.

The movies are getting hard up and the spirit of economy is rife. I was

*Margaret Kennedy and Rosamund Lehmann.

lucky to get mine while the going was good. It is rather like having tolerated some awful bounder for his good dinner, to go to his house and find the menu cut down to nothing and no drinks. The only thing that excused the existence of the Talkies was a sort of bounderish open-handedness.

Then, in June, he made the headlines of the national newspapers. On 7 June Alma Whitaker of the *Los Angeles Times* published an interview with P. G. Wodehouse and reported him as saying:

> It dazes me. They paid me $2,000 a week—and I cannot see what they engaged me for. They were extremely nice to me, but I feel as if I have cheated them. You see, I understood I was engaged to write stories for the screen. After all, I have twenty novels, a score of successful plays, and countless magazine stories to my credit. Yet apparently they had the greatest difficulty in finding anything for me to do. Twice during the year they brought me completed scenarios of other people's stories and asked me to do some dialogue. Fifteen or sixteen people had tinkered with those stories. The dialogue was really quite adequate. All I did was to touch it up here and there.
>
> Then they set me to work on a story called *Rosalie,* which was to have some musical numbers. It was a pleasant little thing, and I put in three months on it. When it was finished, they thanked me politely and remarked that as musicals didn't seem to be going so well they guessed they would not use it.
>
> That about sums up what I was called upon to do for my $104,000. Isn't it amazing?
>
> Personally I received the most courteous treatment, but see what happened to my friend Roland Pertwee at Warner Brothers. He did a story for Marilyn Miller, and they slapped him on the back and said it was great. He returned to the studio the next morning, and was informed by the policeman on the gate that he could not be let in as he was fired.
>
> It's so unbelievable, isn't it?

Two days later this interview was quoted in full in *The New York Times* and *New York Herald Tribune* and other newspapers all over the country. On 10 June the *New York Herald Tribune* published a leader under the title "All So Unbelievable" which began: "Mr. P. G. Wodehouse, that most engaging of authors, has rent the veil, if you know what we mean, laid bare the facts and told all." The final paragraph read as follows:

> The testimony has been uniform: but it has also been anonymous. Mr. Wodehouse must be among the first to bring it out into the open, to mention names and firms, and thus assure us of the truth in the astounding legends. He confirms the picture that has been steadily growing—the picture of Hollywood the golden, where "names" are bought to be scrapped,

talents are retained to be left unused, hiring (of distinguished authors) is without rhyme and firing without reason. It is indeed amazing. . . .

At the time it was widely believed (and it has since become part of the Hollywood legend) that this interview galvanized the bankers who supported the film industry into action to ensure reform—that single-handedly Plum rang the death knell of all those ludicrous practices which have been the subject of so many novels, plays, and films. This happened in the aftermath of the Wall Street crash of 1929, and it seems likely that reform of the film industry could not have been long delayed in any case, although, by the timing of the interview, Plum provided the bankers with a rod for the back of its directors.

If this is true—and there is no reason to doubt it—there is irony in the fact that the one form of the fictional art for which it is generally agreed Plum had little talent is the film scenario. Guy Bolton put it like this: "When a man leaves the stage in the theatre, you can't follow him. In a film you can, but Plum could never do that." This seems to have been fair criticism, and in a review of the film of *Summer Lightning* (for which Plum did the script and which starred Ralph Lynn) an English critic wrote: "It clings to the technique of the theatre and pays the inevitable price. . . . It lacks fluidity of movement and idea."

The Wodehouses did not leave Hollywood in a hurry, but returned to London in November, where, the Norfolk Street house being let, they took a flat for the winter. In the following March—1932—they rented a house in France at Domaine de la Fréyère, Aribeau, Alpes-Maritimes. On 8 April he wrote to Denis Mackail from there:

It's a Jeeves novel and ought to be easy to write but so far has proved a ghastly fag.* That first person stuff cuts both ways. It gives you speed, but you're up against the fact that nothing can happen except through the eyes of the hero. . . . I'm so glad you liked Snorky's story. I thought it was marvellous. It's such a pity that she writes with such difficulty. Have you ever seen a Snorky MS? She sits in bed with a very thin-paper pad and one of those pencils that make the faintest possible mark, and in about four hours produces a page. Then she writes another page next day and puts a ring round it and a hieroglyphic on page one—that is to show that a part of page two goes on page one. Then you read the rest of page one and go back to page two, in the meantime inserting a bit of page four. All in that filthy obscene handwriting of hers. Still, the results are good. Do egg her on to writing some more. I'm so afraid this beastly dress business of hers will absorb her.

*Probably *Thank You, Jeeves.*

In October 1932 the Wodehouses were still in France, but the address from which Plum wrote to Mackail was in Cannes. Speaking of a review of *Hot Water* he wrote:

Priestley, however, was the worst of all, because he analysed me, blast him, and called attention to the thing I try to hush up—viz. that I have only got one plot and produce it once a year with variations. I wish to goodness novelists wouldn't review novels. . . .

I always envy you being able to hold a reader with real life stuff. I have to have jewels, comic lovers and about a dozen American crooks before I can move. My great trouble is that I have to have rapid action for serial purposes, and how can one get rapid action without there being something at least half the characters want to steal.

I quite agree about there being too much plot in *Hot Water*. I modelled it on *Piccadilly Jim* which had so many ramifications that I couldn't follow the story myself.

According to present plans, Ethel and I dash over to London at the end of the month for a week or two. This, of course, involves leaving Miss Winks here and I doubt if when the time comes we shall be capable of it. What a curse that quarantine law is. It seems so damned silly to extend it to Pekes who couldn't possibly give rabies to anyone. . . .

Ethel wants to open Norfolk Street again, and I'm all for it but once more one comes up against the Winks problem. My latest scheme is to buy her a cat-skin and bring her in disguised as a cat.

Cannes is absolutely empty and we have let practically all our staff go. The chauffeur, a great pal of mine, left today. I do hate these partings and good-byes. The chef left last week and we are being cooked for by the gardener's English wife, and it is perfect luxury. Where anyone ever got the idea that French cooking is better than English, I can't imagine.

I expect your brain will start working away again soon. I have these blank periods. I had an awful one in 1924 when I really couldn't see how I could ever get another plot. And since then I have done about eight novels and fifty short stories. A month ago I got stuck, but have got out the plot such as it is of this *Summer Lightning* sequel in three weeks.

Incidentally did you read the story in this month's *S[trand]* by F. E. Baily called *Spare a Penny*? It gave me a nasty shock, being about twice as good as anything I've ever written. I hope he isn't going to go on in that vein. Thank goodness, most of the stuff he writes isn't funny. But *Spare a Penny* is great.

When Plum and Ethel returned to England in the autumn, it was for Leonora's wedding.* She married Peter Cazalet, the younger son and heir

---

*When Plum heard of Leonora's engagement to Peter Cazalet, he wrote to her: "I'm so happy about it that I want to tell everyone I meet. I want to stop French peasants on the road and say '*Figurez-vous, mon brave, ma fille est fiancée à Monsieur Pierre Cazalet, le*

to the estates of William Cazalet, a very rich man who owned the eighteenth-century house Fairlawne, near Tonbridge, and an estate of about one thousand acres. Peter inherited this house because Victor, the elder brother, who was an MP (as was his sister Thelma), did not want the duties of a country landlord and received instead an equivalent sum of money. For reasons connected with the payment of death duties, Peter and Leonora lived for the first six or seven years of their married life in a house on the estate called The Grange, at Shipbourne, moving into Fairlawne only just before the Second World War. The Grange itself was large enough to house a butler, housemaid, cook, and so on, and later a nanny and full nursery staff. I met my husband there, and after our marriage we lived in a house about half a mile away from The Grange, until the war broke up what had become a very close society.

I can never remember Ethel there, and certainly she did not come often, but Plum came several times.* I had a crib to his character through knowing Leonora, and I learned to understand him at least well enough never to be much surprised by anything he did. My husband, Jack Donaldson, also knew him, and between 1932 and 1935 used to play golf with him on Mondays at Addington.

William Cazalet had had racing stables at Fairlawne and during his lifetime ran horses on the flat. Peter rode for many years as an amateur in steeplechases, and began to train at Fairlawne soon after his father's death in 1933, continuing to do so, except for the war years, for the rest of his life. Later he had the honour to train for Her Majesty Queen Elizabeth, the Queen Mother. Anthony Mildmay, later Lord Mildmay, and known to the racing crowds as "Lordy," kept his horses with Peter from the start of his racing career. To ride often and seriously, even as an amateur, means riding your horses at work in the very early hours of the morning, and for this reason, as well as because of a great friendship with Peter, Anthony had to find somewhere to live in the district. It says much for Leonora's tolerance that he almost immediately moved into The Grange and remained a permanent member of the household even after the children were born, until this arrangement too was broken by the war. Plum was always most at ease with athletes (the Cazalets were a great games-playing family), and he accepted both Peter and Anthony without difficulty, loving Peter while Leonora was alive probably as much as he ever loved anyone except Leonora herself and Ethel.

---

jeune homme le plus admirable de l'Angleterre. . . .' Winks and Boo must be bridesmaids carrying your train in their mouths."

*Late in life, in an interview with Malcolm Muggeridge, he said he came to England only once in these years, but I can remember him there on at least three different occasions.

9

Income Tax

In December 1932, while staying at the Dorchester Hotel in London for Leonora's wedding, Plum wrote to Townend:

A very nasty wallop has recently hit the home. Denby wrote to us . . . saying that the [U.S.] income tax authorities had started to make enquiries and told us . . . to put everything in the hands of a firm who would manage things for us. Then we were told that the head of this firm must come over—at our expense!—to confer with our English man. . . . The first thing he did was to inform us that we owed the dear old Amer. Govt $187,000!!! After this shock, he rather gave us to hope that he could reduce this to about $70,000. Anyway . . . we have had to sell at an average of about 30 all those shares we bought for about $300. When the smoke has cleared away, I shall have lost around a hundred and fifty thousand quid since 1929. The position now seems to be that we shall have a capital of forty thousand quid, plus whatever we can save from the wreck in America. We have removed all our money from America, so that if there is any rot about them demanding huge sums we can sit tight over here and tell them to try and get it. Anyway, we always did have much too much money, and a nest egg of about fifty thousand quid in gilt edged securities is as much as anybody could want. . . .

I won a thousand quid gambling at Cannes. I am going to open an account for seven hundred quid at your bank and tell the manager that it is security for you to overdraw agst [sic] if you want to. . . .

. . . In some ways I am not sorry this income tax business has happened. . . . I now can spit on my hands and start sweating again, feeling that it really matters when I make a bit of money. . . .

In January 1933 he wrote from Domaine de la Fréyère:

The money has been transferred and is now in an English bank, where the American authorities can't touch it. It amounts to about seventy thousand quid. . . . The American income tax people . . . are demanding about fifty thousand. My scheme is to imitate dear old France . . . and sit tight. If they will settle at a reasonable figure, OK. If not, not a penny do they

touch. . . . I am hoping they will settle for about six thousand quid! . . .
I shall be glad to be settled in England. . . . This country is fine but we
are too far away. . . . And if one lives in Cannes there is the constant
temptation of the Casino.

And in November 1933 he wrote once more to Townend: "Meanwhile,
the jolly old Federal authorities are asking for $300,000 for income tax.
Most of this seems to be for penalties . . . we have taken counsel's opinion
and find that they have no possible way of collecting, as all my money is
in England where they can't touch it. . . ." And a week later: "I must say
the F. authorities seem loony to me. They want to charge 50 per cent
penalty for making a false return and 25 per cent penalty for not making a
return at all. . . . Also they charge me for profits on stock transactions,
but won't deduct losses."

Trouble came not singly but in pairs, and in December of the same year
he wrote to Townend: "Hell's foundations have been quivering again. Out
of a blue sky the English income tax authorities have just jumped on my
neck in re non-payment of income on my American earnings for the last
five years! This necessitated endless conferences with accountants etc."

For many years harassment by the tax authorities of Great Britain and
the United States of America would be a recurring theme in Plum's letters
and would play an influential part in his life. But for his difficulties over
tax, he would probably not have been living in France at the outbreak of
war in 1939; while the much publicized but inaccurate account of his
struggles with the authorities could not have been used as part of the
campaign to whip up resentment against him at the time of the Berlin
broadcasts.

Income tax is normally one of the dullest subjects, but luckily in Plum's
hands it takes on an unexpected freshness, not merely because even here he
retains his highly individual gift of expression, but also because of the
naivety of his approach to matters on which it is customary to preserve a
decent hypocrisy. Almost everyone avoids as much tax as he can, for the
large part legally, sometimes in small matters illegally, but it is unusual to
be so sturdily convinced of the righteousness of the cause.* In *Over Seventy* there is a chapter called "Crime, Does It Pay?" in which, after a

---

*On 22 October 1979 it was reported in the *Daily Telegraph* that 60 percent of those polled
by the Institution of Economic Affairs said "good luck" to people who ask for cash rather
than cheques so that they should not be taxed, while 69 percent felt that they should not
have to pay tax on spare-time earnings. These findings were reported in a booklet entitled
"Tax Avoision—A Study of the Economic, Legal and Moral Relationships Between Tax
Evasion and Avoidance."

humorous account of various methods of lifting money off the general public, he wrote: "But, while one respects practitioners like these and wishes them every success in their chosen careers, the world's worker one really admires is Robert Watson (45) of Hoboken, New Jersey, because he did down the income tax authorities—the dream of every redblooded man."[1]

There is no doubt that here, as in many other places, his humour reflects not merely a total lack of feeling for the duties of a citizen to the state, but also for the ordinary instinct of self-preservation which in most educated people prohibits such candid statements of views, since these, however widely held, are unethical. However, in case there should be any misunderstanding, it must be categorically stated that he never did file and never would have filed a false return. He did not do down the income tax authorities, and although at three different times he had cases to answer, he either won or achieved a compromise settlement in his favour in each. But he regarded it as an outrage that a man's proper earnings should be taken off him in this way, just as Ethel, who undoubtedly was responsible for the accountants they employed, until in grave difficulties would always have preferred people who told her what she wanted to hear to those who were concerned to keep them out of trouble. The Wodehouses did lose a very large part of their accumulated fortune at this time, but not, as Plum seems to suggest in the letter to Townend, because they sold shares in America and brought their assets to England in order to avoid unfair and unreasonable tax demands. This money had already gone in the Wall Street crash, and holding on to their shares could never have altered that.

"Women are funny," Plum said to my husband, playing golf at Addington. "We invested all our money at the top of the boom and lost the lot in the slump and Ethel was terribly worried"—a remark which brings one to the question of his own attitude to money. Everyone who knew him agrees that he had no interest in anything but the petty cash in his pocket, and in all his life never wanted much more than some pipe tobacco and a typewriter ribbon. Yet he had very strong objections to money being taken off him. He hated parting with small sums, and only Leonora, showing the most ruthless indifference to his feeling, could induce him to honour such ordinary obligations as presents to godchildren and so on. This was because Ethel kept him extremely short all his life, and also because he was naturally mean in small things.

Yet in all important ways he never thought about money at all. His English literary agent, Mr. Hilary Rubinstein, told me that while one can quickly detect which authors are interested in the financial side of contracts and which are not, Plum fell into the latter category and never concerned himself with this aspect of his work. Paul R. Reynolds, who succeeded his father as Plum's agent in America, was even more explicit, and wrote as follows:

> Wodehouse was one of the highest paid writers in the United States but he never understood the business side of his writing or the function of the agent. In 1939 *The Saturday Evening Post* offered $45,000 for a Wodehouse serial, the same price as they had previously paid. I went on to Philadelphia and told Wesley Stout, the editor of the *Post*, that if he could not pay $50,000 we would have to approach other magazines. Stout agreed to this price. When I told Wodehouse he was delighted at what he called the *Post*'s generosity. When I told him of my statement to Stout that it had to be $50,000 or we would go elsewhere, Wodehouse reproved me. He said he would not think of leaving such a generous magazine, and that my father would not have acted that way.[2]

Plum was also extremely generous to close friends. There is evidence that he constantly sent money to Townend, whose work he admired but who was unable to make a living as a writer. In October 1928 he wrote to him: "Just paid £64.2.0. to your account. Don't make any allusion to this in any letter. I still have about £40 in my Hong Kong account for you to use if required. So now you can go ahead and finish *Mother Jubilee*." And in December of the same year: "About three weeks ago I paid into your account English cheques for £49—that was the result of my winnings at Newmarket—and an American cheque for about £100."

Years later William Townend wrote to Richard Usborne:

> You will have discovered by now how often Plum has helped my wife and myself financially. He does not want this spread about, as it were, for a good many reasons. The fact is that although my 43rd novel is being published in a few weeks time, for years my books have failed to bring in more than a pittance, and I can count myself fortunate to have had them published. Without Plum's assistance I should have had to abandon the attempt to earn my living by my writing long since.

Plum's reason for the secrecy referred to in both letters was because he did not want Ethel to know of those bequests.

Other people bear witness to a lack of concern with money. Heather Thatcher, who knew the Wodehouses very well, told me that in the theatre they said that Plum could be happy with "a pound in his pocket, a pipe in his mouth, and a Peke." She also told me a story which shows, I think, not merely a complete detachment from money but also an admirable coolness in the face of any criticism of Ethel. She explained that Ethel often gambled in a very silly way. Most people run the bank at chemin de fer a few times when winning, but then respond to the cry of "Banco" and take away the "benefice." Ethel was inclined to persist until, predictably, she lost the lot. Someone watching her said to Plum, "It's terrible to watch Ethel losing so much money," to which Plum replied, "It's my money."

Although the U.S. Federal authorities had been the first in the fray, the case of the Inland Revenue was the first to be settled. On 19 January 1934, at a meeting of the Commissioners for the General Purposes of the Income Tax for the Division of St. Martin-in-the-Fields in the County of London, P. G. Wodehouse appealed against the assessments made upon him under Schedule D of the Income Tax Act 1918 for the years 1927 to 1934 in respect of literary earnings under contracts made by the Respondent in America and assigned by him to an American Company.

Plum was represented by a KC called Raymond Needham, and the case seems to have turned primarily on whether or not he was resident in England during those years and, in addition, on whether or not he could legally assign his contracts from dramatic and literary work to a company.

On the first point it was submitted that the house in Norfolk Street was purchased not for his own occupation, but for his stepdaughter, who had let it furnished for the past three years and recently again for the next three. The commissioners found that he had been resident in England in only two of the six years and also that he could legally assign his contracts to a company. (Without going too deeply into the matter, to form oneself into a company was a method adopted by many other writers and self-employed workers who earned comparatively large sums in some years and less in others. It was a loophole in the tax laws since closed.)

The income tax authorities initially decided to appeal, but finally they abandoned this decision, and in April 1935 Plum wrote to Townend: "Wonderful news. The income tax people have decided not to appeal against the decision which we won before the Commissioners in January. We might have had to cough up £14,000."*

Both Plum and Ethel were delighted. Plum wrote to Leonora:

Mummie says will you send Needham a telegram congratulating him— just a short line. . . . I know he would appreciate it, and he has been wonderful. Even now I can't see how he worked the thing. Looking back to that case on Jan. 19th, I see him proving us non-residents for years when—I should have said—we were out of England for about three days.

And Richard Usborne writes in *Vintage Wodehouse* that he was restrained only by Needham himself from dedicating *Right Ho, Jeeves* to him in terms of gratitude and congratulation which would have been injudicious in the extreme.

But although the English tax was settled, the argument with the Federal

*In *Vintage Wodehouse* Richard Usborne puts this figure at £25,000, but this probably refers to the original demand, which had been reduced before the case was heard.

authorities dragged on. In June 1934, Plum wrote to Townend: "I got an offer from Paramount to go to Hollywood at $1500 a week and had to refuse as I am Public Enemy No. 1 in America, and can't go there. But rather gratifying after Hollywood took a solemn vow three years ago never to mention my name again!" And in August:

> One's friends, as a class, are able to view one's misfortunes with forti-tude, if not indifference! . . . I have between £90,000 and £100,000 salted away in England, and I have always earned in England hitherto about £8,000 or £9,000 a year.
> It will be rather fun seeing if I can build up another name [in America].
> [U.S. income tax people] know that I shall have offers to go to Holly-wood . . . little knowing that I don't want to go to Hollywood at all. . . . So long as my English market holds out, I'm all right.

And in October of the same year, to Denis Mackail:

> I'm sorry I haven't written for so long. I have been much persecuted by scoundrels and also have been sweating my eyes out on a musical comedy which has just gone into rehearsal in New York. And what I am worrying about is, Will the U.S. Govt. pinch my royalties or Can the Manager get them through to me?
> I expect you saw in the news-sheet about the Amer. Govt. wanting fifty thousand quid for unpaid income tax. I am now offering them ten thousand down on the nail and shake hands and start a new deal. I hope they take it. They certainly aren't going to get any fifty thousand.

In the end they did take it, or something very like it, and it is possible to guess what happened.*

At that time writers and others were in constant trouble with the income tax authorities of America or England, because there was no agreement between the two governments. This meant that an Englishman living in England would have had to pay tax to the American authorities on any American earnings, and then pay again on what was left to the English. (Today there is an agreement by which tax is paid in one country or the other, but not in both.) Secondly, tax was not deducted from writers at source, so that, as Alec Waugh put it in a letter to Richard Usborne, "a foreigner could decline to fill in tax returns and not pay demands for tax . . . but just ignore these things until the policeman called. I think that was what P.G.W. did."

There is no evidence to support this view, but substituting the word *neglect* for the word *decline,* I would agree with it. Given all the circum-stances of the management, or lack of management, of Plum's affairs, and also of his free-and-easy attitude to income tax, it seems very likely, and would account for the enormous demands for penalties which were in the

*They were asking for $300,000 and settled for $88,000.

Plum's mother.   Plum's father.

Armine, Peverill, and 5-year old Plum, January 1887.

Plum, Peverill, and Armine.

Family group with Plum on left.

Plum as a young man.

Dulwich College, London.

Ethel and Plum in middle age.

Denis Mackail   Jerome Kern

With Guy Bolton.

Beatrice Lillie in *Oh, Joy!*, 1919.

LEARNING WITHOUT TEARS 17·9·27

Miss Gertrude Lawrence shows how the impossible may be achieved, by means of a smile and Mr. P. G. Wodehouse's comfortable shoulder, while reading over her part for *Oh Kay* during rehearsals. The popular comedienne, who has been seen at most of the recent first-nights since her return from America, will make her bow from the other side of the footlights next Wednesday, in *Oh Kay*, at His Majesty's

With Gertrude Lawrence during rehearsals for *Oh Kay*, 1927.

Leonora with her husband, Peter Cazalet.

Plum at the civil internment camp,
Tost bei Gleiwitz, December 1940.

Baroness Ange von Bodenhausen, in
whose house the Wodehouses spent
the greater part of their period in
Germany.

With Baron Plack in Berlin, 1942.

Plum with Baroness von Boden-hausen's daughter (right) and friend.

Plum

Ethel

The official founding of the Wodehouse shelter for stray dogs and cats.

Remsenburg

Ethel and Plum

Plum's gravestone, designed by his wife.

end waived. In September of that year he was once more on his way to Hollywood. His difficulties over tax were not ended, but there would be peace now until after the war.

During the early 1930s the Wodehouses spent some time in England—at least one summer at Hunstanton Hall—but most of their time in France. In 1934 they were living in Paris when Guy Bolton, with whom Plum was to collaborate on a musical play, *Anything Goes,* wrote saying that he could not work there, and suggesting that, since Plum could not go to London, they should meet at Le Touquet.

The Wodehouses had not been long at Le Touquet when they decided that in all the circumstances it was the ideal place for them to live. They liked it for itself and also for its nearness to London. Staying at first in a hotel, they soon began to look for a house and found one called Low Wood. This was a fairly typical seaside villa in a row of others with a garden. By August Plum was writing to Leonora:

> We are looking forward to getting into Low Wood. I think we have done wisely in only taking it for a year at first. One never knows how one will like a place. I must say, though, that it will be odd if we don't like it, as we shall be living just the sort of life we like best. It seems to me that our life will be very much the same as yours at the Grange, or as the life we led at Great Neck, which I loved.
>
> Winky and Boo have just been washed, preparatory to being exhibited with Mummie in the "Madame de 1934 et son chien" event in the local dog show. As far I can gather, this is decided partly by how the Madame is dressed and partly by personal influence with the judges. We have one of them in our pocket and are full of confidence. . . .
>
> The other night I went to the Casino, had a shot at Roulette, won three mille in two minutes and came home. At seven a.m. Winky was restless, so I took her out, and we had been out about ten minutes when Mummie arrived, having been at the Casino all night and lost three mille. So we took the dogs for a walk and went in and had breakfast.

Followers of the fortunes of Bingo Little and his wife Rosie M. Banks may remember the use that was later made of that incident.

A short time before this, Leonora had had her first baby, Sheran, and in this letter Plum also wrote: "We are simply enraptured by the photographs of Sheran. I never saw such a beautiful baby. What a change from the old Chinese Gangster who leered at us on your bed in April, fingering her gat under the swaddling clothes. You must have her photographed every year." Then in November he wrote:

> Just been reading your letter to Mummie. How splendid that you have taken up riding and enjoy it so much. Rather, as one might say, you than me, but I'm awfully glad you're doing it.

BOOKS. Yes, do send me the two Claudius books. I'd love to have them.

I had a letter from Denis Mackail, laughing heartily at me for saying I liked *Good-bye, Mr. Chips.* I still stick to it that it is a jolly good book. . . .

Have you read Evelyn Waugh's *Handful of Dust*? Excellent in spots, but he ought to have you to read over his stuff before he publishes it. You would have told him (a) that he couldn't have a sort of Mr. Mulliner farce chapter about the man going to Brighton if he wanted the story to be taken seriously and (b) for goodness sake to keep away from Brazil.

What a snare this travelling business is to the young writer. He goes to some blasted jungle or other and imagines that everybody will be interested in it.

Also that Dickens stuff. Marvellous as a short story, but much too much dragged in.

If you have *not* read Evelyn Waugh's *Handful of Dust*, by the way, not a little of the above will be lost on you. . . .

What about Wells' autobiography? I've got it and read most of it, but I don't know.

In his next letter (December 1934) he wrote:

Boo scratched at the door to be let in. I got up and let her in, and she waited till I had sat down again and then scratched to be let out. This is her favourite joke. I expect in a minute or two she will be scratching to be let in again.

Boo is the most extraordinary dog. In the morning I have breakfast in a lovely warm room with a fire, and she comes in for a minute but always wants to go out again. When I have finished breakfast I find her sitting in the fire-place in the drawing-room with her back against the fire. It is not lit and all the windows are open, so that the room is like an ice-house, but she prefers it to the breakfast room.

I believe she reasons as follows: I sit in here after dinner and it's warm and cosy. Therefore, this is a warm, cosy room. I admit that at the present moment I have an odd illusion that I am freezing, but that must be mortal error or something, because it has been definitely proved that this is a warm, cosy room. Either a room is warm and cosy or it is not warm and cosy. . . .

I must say Le Touquet, if you're all alone, is a quiet sort of spot. I would have liked it better, only I have just finished eight months of terrific strain, what with doing the novel, the novelette and the play and having all the income tax stuff as well, and I couldn't settle down to anything. I felt very let down and at a loose end, and would have loved a couple of weeks in London. I feel better now, and am getting ahead with some short stories. But I shall be glad when April comes and I can come over to England. . . .

I am very keen on getting the papers today, as I see that the Puss* and gang were riding at Derby. I hope they had a good day.

Isn't it amazing what a few books there are that one wants to read. Mummie sent me a list yesterday to choose from, and the only one I could even contemplate reading was *Moss Rose* by Joseph Shearer. One of them was that book of Phyllis Bottome's—I forget the title—which is about a lunatic asylum. It simply beats me why anybody should want to read it.

I must say the same thing rather applies to those Claudius books. I read *I, Claudius* and was interested, but I felt almost looney when I had finished. I haven't been able to bring myself to start the second one yet.

I absolutely agree with you about Wells' autobiography. I always maintain that what kills an author is complacency. I have watched Wells getting more and more complacent for years and going all to pieces as a writer. His autobiography, most of it, is simply deadening. You feel as if you had been buttonholed by an old bore to whom you had to listen politely.

Aren't writers extraordinary. I simply gasped when Wells said that the Bulpington of Blupp was as good a character as Kipps. It meant that his critical sense was absolutely dead. The Bulpington of Blupp isn't a character at all. I felt the same when Conan Doyle used to say that the later Sherlock Holmes stories were as good as the early ones. It's a relief to me to know that I've got you to tell me if I am going cuckoo in my work. I shall be interested to hear what you think of this last novel of mine. I think it's good. It certainly moves.

These last remarks were seriously meant. Plum took immense trouble to get his manuscripts to Leonora before they went to his agent, and he relied very much on her judgment. In January 1935 he wrote to her:

> I wrote to Westbrook the other day to send you my new novel, *The Luck of the Bodkins*. I want you to go over this very carefully and mark the bits you don't like. I have an uneasy feeling that I have made it too long, though I can't see that there is any deadwood, as the plot is so strong. The only thing, I may have overwritten the dialogue in spots. Mark cuts wherever you feel needed.

He also wrote: "That was a great boost Woollcott gave you. I wish there were more books like that." In *While Rome Burns*, describing what is clearly the Cazalet house, Fairlawne, in Kent, Alexander Woollcott had written that he had left it clutching in one hand a spray of priceless orchids from the nursery and in the other a forty-inch cutlass of sinister appearance, and then said:

> My host had heard me innocently admiring them, and to my genuine surprise had pressed them into my hand at parting. As I drove off into the

---

*Plum called Peter Cazalet "the Puss," probably because of a nickname that Leonora used when speaking of him.

night, I made a note to remember that on my next visit I must be heard expressing my admiration for several paintings by Augustus John and the late Mr. Sargent, for a small bronze head of Epstein, for the avenue of immemorial yews which glorifies the drive, for the bride of the younger son of the house, and for a small black spaniel bitch named, if memory serves, Tiny.[3]

In the letter quoted above, Plum said: "Mummie has just cut my hair with a safety razor and it looks fine. You ought to cut the Puss's hair with a razor. Don't you hate these early spring evenings, when there is a chill in the air and one bird is tootling away to itself. They make me feel old and forlorn." And then in June 1935:

> Sensational news. Yesterday we bought Low Wood!!! We have been changing our minds every day since we got back, and as late as yesterday morning had made an offer for another house. But it was refused, and then Mummie suddenly switched back to Low Wood.
>
> I must say I am delighted. I have grown very fond of the house, and with the alterations we are going to make it will be fine. We came to the conclusion that we wanted to live in Le Touquet and that Low Wood was the best bet on account of the position.

Le Touquet was the best bet not merely because of the tax rates in England, but also because of the quarantine laws. As Plum wrote to Leonora in January 1935:

> Mummie blew in on December 23 with a six weeks old Peke puppy so now we have three Pekes and are rooted here forever. It is an angel, a male this time, but Winks and Boo won't have anything to do with it. Boo sulked for four days after its arrival but has now accepted the situation. . . . We spend all our time spreading fresh paper.

This male puppy is never heard of again, and as some time after this Boo died of a tick-borne fever, it seems possible the puppy may have died too. Later Winkie died. "Winkie is dead," Plum wrote to Townend. "I can hardly bear to write about it. . . . The usual thing—tick fever. . . . We had the body taken down here, and she is buried beside Boo in the garden."

But before this happened, Ethel had bought a female puppy, which was given the name Wonder. Wonder survived to become the best known and most beloved of all the Wodehouse Pekes. She will be heard of again and again in Germany and France during the war years, and finally, in 1947, accompanying the Wodehouses to America.*

*In David Jasen's book he says that the male pup was Wonder, and he supports this statement with a sentence from a letter by Wodehouse to Leonora. In the original of that letter, which I have, the sentence does not occur. Wonder did not arrive until nearly two years after the male pup and was a female, as correctly stated by William Townend in *Performing Flea*, pp. 91–2.

In September the Wodehouses went to Hollywood, and in November
Plum wrote to Townend from a house in Angelo Drive, Beverly Hills:

> Well, here we are, settled in a house miles away up at the top of a
> mountain, surrounded by canyons in which I am told rattlesnakes abound
> and employing a protection agency to guard the place at nights! We
> looked at a lot of houses in the valley part of Bev. Hills, where we were
> before, but couldn't find one we liked, so took this one, which is a lovely
> place with a nice pool, but, as I say, remote. Still, that's an advantage in a
> way, as we don't get everybody dropping in on us. . . .
>
> Everything is very pleasant and placid here, and I am having a good
> time. But it doesn't seem as interesting as it was last time. I miss Thalberg
> very much, though I like Sam Katz, for whom I am working. I am
> collaborating on a musical picture with a man whom I last saw twenty
> years ago, when I was sympathizing with him for being chucked out of
> the cast of one of my musical comedies. He is a wild Irishman named
> McGowan, who seems to be fighting the heads of the studio all the time.
> I get on very well with him myself.[4]

To Plum's astonishment he was set to work with McGowan on the script
of *Rosalie*, the same story on which he had worked for so long five years
before. Nor was he any more successful. In the following March he wrote
to tell Townend that he had sold *Summer Moonshine* to *The Saturday
Evening Post* for $40,000. And he went on:

> Against this triumph I have to set the fact that Metro-Goldwyn-Mayer
> are not taking up my option, which expires in another two weeks. I have
> had another frost with them. I started gaily in working on a picture with
> Bill McGuire . . . and I gradually found myself being edged out. Even-
> tually they came out into the open and said they wanted McGuire to write
> the thing by himself all along! . . . There seems to be a curse over MGM
> as far as I am concerned.

And it was, as David Jasen remarked, "the Hollywood mixture as before. Once again he was on the MGM payroll without being asked to earn
his salary."[5] He did, however, do a picture for RKO, *A Damsel in Distress*.
And Ethel probably enjoyed Hollywood more than he did. She told Jasen:

> Parties were very easy to do if you had the money. We did, because Plum
> was getting $2,500 a week. I would go down to the supermarkets and buy
> a big saddle of lamb, vegetables, turkey, ham and chicken livers. We
> would have seven cases of champagne. Our butler, Arthur, would handle
> the floral arrangements. He could do the most amazing things with flow-
> ers. Then we hired a caterer and barman. He would supply the olives but
> we had to supply the liquor.[6]

But by May 1937 Plum wrote to Townend:

> I wish we had taken this house for six months instead of a year. There seems to be a probability that I shall do a four weeks' job on Fred Astaire's next pix based on *A Damsel in Distress,* but except for that nothing is stirring. I was told that I was going to do *The Earl of Chicago,* but I see Ben Hecht is doing it. The fact is, I'm not worth the money my agent insists on asking for me. After all, my record here is eighteen months . . . with only small bits of pictures to show for it. I would be perfectly happy if I could just be left alone to write stories, as I hate picture work.[7]

And in October 1937 he wrote: "Just a line to say that we are not staying here for the Spring, after all, but are sailing on October 28th, and I shall be back at Le Touquet on November 4th."[8]

Yet if the mixture was as before, it had once more left plenty of time for Plum to work on novels and short stories. In the ten years from 1930 to 1940, he published thirteen novels, a collection of essays called *Louder and Funnier* (originally written for *Variety*), and six collections of short stories. This decade saw the publication of *Right Ho, Jeeves* (1934), which I think his best book, *Uncle Fred in the Springtime* (1939), which I believe Bernard Levin has said is his best book, and *Quick Service* (1940), which Wodehouse thought was his best book. Few people would agree with Wodehouse about *Quick Service,* but it is still a very good book, and is interesting for two other reasons. The first is the unashamed plagiarism from Harry Leon Wilson. He takes a main strand of *Ruggles of Red Gap* and weaves it in as a substrand of his own. The second, and more important, is that here he reaches the complete development of a certain type of Wodehouse hero which he called a "buzzer." David Jasen describes him as a Psmith-type hero, but this is surely a misnomer. There are no Psmith-type heroes, although if one had to choose inherited characteristics, both Uncle Gally and Uncle Fred (to whom he devoted several other books, notably *Uncle Dynamite*) have the quality of using both courage and wit to extricate themselves from unpleasant situations they have wilfully created, while Hamish Beamish in *The Small Bachelor* is omniscient in a manner which is reminiscent of Psmith.

Joss in *Quick Service,* like Mycroft Cardinal in *Spring Fever* and Jeff Miller in *Money in the Bank,* is altogether less suave and less elegant than Psmith, and all three are more romantic. They resemble Psmith only in that a show of confidence is part of their stock in trade.

> He shut the door.
> "Now, then," he said, "what's all this nonsense I hear about you being engaged?"
> If a criticism could have been made of the tone in which he spoke, it

was that it resembled rather too closely that of a governess of rigid ethical views addressing one of her young charges upon whom suspicion of stealing jam has rested, and Sally gave a little gasp. Her full height was not much, but, such as it was, she drew herself to it. She had decided that cold dignity was what the situation demanded.

"I beg your pardon?"

"And well you may, if it's true. Is it true?"

"Perfectly true. May I ask what business it is of yours?"

"That," said Joss, more like a governess than ever, "is one of the silliest questions I ever heard. Considering that I'm going to marry you myself."

"Oh? I didn't know that."

"Well, you know it now. Why, good Lord, we were made for each other. I spotted it the minute you came into J. B. Duff's office. You don't mean you didn't get it, too? Why, it stuck out a mile. There were you, and there was I, and there we were, so to speak. My poor young fathead, I should have thought you would have got on to it right away." (*Quick Service*, Chapter 15)

There is a theory that every character in every novel is a fragment of its author—a very surprising theory if related to Plum and Joss.

The great event of 1939 was that the University of Oxford bestowed on him an honorary degree in recognition of his services to literature. He must have been overwhelmed. He had no ambitions of this sort, and only the constant praise of his books by the most difficult critics convinced him that he had succeeded in something he had never consciously tried to do, and entered the ranks of those who are valued for the quality of their work rather than for its popular appeal.

In June 1939 he walked in the academic procession from Magdalen College to the Sheldonian Theatre in the Encaenia at The University of Oxford to become an honorary Doctor of Letters. The Public Orator, Dr. Cyril Bailey, gave his address partly in Latin hexameters, partly in prose. This is a translation:

Here is a magical author, than whom no one is more expert at delighting men's minds and arousing laughter. He has introduced a new cast of stage characters and endowed each with his own comicality. Who is not familiar with his rich young man, good-natured and kindhearted, incapable of doing anything he wants to do without the help of a "faithful Achates" who is his deviser of stratagems and arbiter of dress? Or of the voluble and tubby companion whose uncle and nephew and all his relations have had, by his account, extraordinary experiences in life? Then there is the noble Clarence, owner of his father's ancestral estates and a distinguished sow; and Psmith ("leave it to him"); Augustus the expert on the love life of newts; and other people born under various stars. Our author does not turn up his nose at men's vices, but observes these with gentle affection, and laughs at their misdeeds. In addition, although his pages are full of everyday language, he does not let his words run on in unrhythmical disorder, but is neat and witty and "a lover of elegant speech."

Why say more? One known to all needs no testimony. I present to you a humorist—shall I call him our Petronius or our Terence?—Pelham Grenville Wodehouse, Fellow of the Royal Society of Literature, to be admitted to the Honorary Degree of Doctor of Letters.

The Vice-Chancellor of the University, George Gordon, then presented the degree and said in Latin: "Most pleasant, witty, charming, jocular, and humorous Sir, on my authority and that of the whole University I admit you with your retinue of Pleasantries, Witticisms, Charms, Jokes, and Humours to the Degree of Doctor of Letters *honoris causa*."*

That night at the Gaudy dinner at Christ Church Plum sat at the High Table and listened to the speeches customary on this occasion. After these were over, those seated at the lower tables began to bang on them and chant, "We want Wodehouse! We want Wodehouse!" Alas for the glitter of our story (as Winston Churchill once wrote): our hero disgraced himself. Rising to his feet, he barely mumbled the words "Thank you" and ungracefully and ungraciously sat down. Several stories have since been put about as to why he behaved so badly, but none are needed. Asked what he might do when unexpectedly faced with so massive a request for communication with the human race, anyone who knew him would accurately have predicted his behaviour.

In those years he came often to The Grange at Shipbourne to see "the gang"—Anthony Mildmay as well as Peter Cazalet and the beloved Snorky. He came alone, and I think he and Ethel seldom travelled together because they would not both leave their dogs (in that way showing them more consideration than many people showed their children). Plum found it easy to talk to Peter and Anthony, while, although not quite part of the gang, Jack and I were so often in the house and so close to the Cazalets that he was also on good terms with us. In this society he entered the conversation with far more than his usual confidence. However, this was a very long time ago, and there remains in my mind only one memorable thing he said.

The time was the early spring of 1939, and Neville Chamberlain had just made some optimistic public statement about the future. Jack cast doubt on this, and Peter Cazalet turned on him furiously.

---

*The original Latin of Dr. Bailey's speech is in Appendix B, but because the Vice-Chancellor's speech is in language which really has no English equivalent, I give it here: "*Vir lepidissime, facetissime, venustissime, iocosissime, ridibundissime, te cum turba tua Leporum, Facetinarum, Venustatum, Iocorum, Risuum, ego auctoritate mea et totius Universitatis admitto ad gradum Doctoris in Litteris honoris causa.*"

"You are becoming simply a bore," he said. "You prefer to take a gloomy view."

By now there was plenty of evidence of the German treatment of the Jews and of what happened to people in concentration camps. We ourselves had a German couple living with us who had until lately been inside one. But the vast majority of English people either did not read the books and papers which made this knowledge available or refused to believe it. The Germans have been much criticized for failing to see what was too unmercifully obvious, but this blindness was shared by the rest of the world. I can remember English people being enormously shocked in the middle of the war when they understood for the first time the extent of the German enormities, although these had been publicized for years. This should not be forgotten when considering the conversation which took place at The Grange.

I cannot remember the full details of this, but Jack must have said, in effect, that the Germans were determined to conquer Europe, and Peter must have argued this, when Plum made his memorable intervention.

"What I can't see," he said, "is what difference it makes. If the Germans want to govern the world, why don't we just let them?"

In the Wodehouse world the enemy is invariably and quite indifferently authority as such, and to understand him, one must again call in aid Rebecca West's striking reminder that the word *idiot* comes from a Greek root meaning "private person."

Nevertheless, Plum wrote two letters to Townend from Le Touquet after war was declared which suggest, in terms so artless they might almost be a parody of his own style, that he had changed his mind. "Didn't you think that was a fine speech of Churchill's on the wireless? Just what was needed, I thought. I feel we are a bit too gentlemanly. Someone ought to get up in Parliament and call Hitler a swine." And on 8 December: "I've been reading all Churchill's books. . . . They are terrific. . . . What mugs the Germans were to take us on again. They must have known we should wipe them out at sea, and that there never has been a war that hasn't been won by sea power."

I think no one has ever completely understood why the Wodehouses stayed on at Le Touquet, not merely after war was declared but even after the end of the "phoney" war, although they were begged by their neighbour and friend Lady Dudley to leave when she did, and also of course by Leonora. (Leonora later made an unavailing attempt to arrange through William Townend for a boat to be sent over to fetch them.) Plum was in the middle of a novel, and one can also be fairly certain that the difficulty of taking Wonder to England had something to do with it. Chiefly, they

seem not to have realized the danger. On 26 June 1945 Ethel wrote a very
long letter to her friends Denis and Diana Mackail in which she tried to tell
them all that had happened to Plum and herself since they last met. In this
she said:

Well! Starting at Le Touquet, there we were, having a very delightful
time, with our beloved RAF 85th squadron dropping in at all moments
for tea, staying on to dinner whenever they wished to, and as many as
they liked. We would turn up the rugs after dinner, and dance to "My
Heart Belongs to Daddy." We would listen to the radio, and hear that
there was a slight bulge but nothing serious, we believed that the Germans
were beaten already, had no boots, and didn't think they had a kick in
them, because we treated the BBC as our Bible at that time. Very few
residents were in Le Touquet. Then the Germans really got a move on,
and our RAF disappeared and were seen no more in Le Touquet. We
became a little anxious, but not seriously so, and Plum went on writing
his novel, and I tending my roses in the garden. Then things became
sticky and we heard the Germans were breaking through. Our neighbours
on each side of us left in their cars in a hurry, and we decided to leave the
following day, which was a Sunday. We only had two very small cars, the
tiny Lancia which I was to drive, and the luggage in the second car which
my little secretary, the daughter of the Golf Pro was to drive. She said she
would like to come with us. We were to leave at 2 o'clock. At the last
moment she changed her mind, so it took valuable time finding someone
else to drive, eventually we succeeded, and started. Got about fifteen
miles, when the Lancia broke down (we had had a bad accident in the
Lancia some time before, it was put right in the village, but apparently
badly done). However there we were, by this time the roads crammed
with people, cars, everything you could think of. We put the car in a
field, and decided to return to Le Touquet. We heard all the bridges were
being bombed, and we couldn't all get in the other car, so Plummie got
back somehow, and thankful we were to be in our house again, off those
dreadful roads. When we got home, we found at our house a large Ford
car, and people we knew, getting at the petrol we had left buried in the
garden. We filled her up, and then we started off once more, only to break
down again when we got to the golf club. We all returned and decided to
stay put, as it seemed the only thing to do. Then began a rather trying
time, with German planes over the house, circling around all night, and
we expected to be blown to bits any moment, as we had no cellars.
Nothing happened for a day or so, then Germans arrived on motor bicycles. I saw them, and very nervous they were, that first day, however
nobody took a pot shot at them, and they were in possession of Touquet.
We heard nobody must leave their garden after 9 o'clock, this didn't seem
too bad. Plummie got a little easier in his mind. Then we had orders to
report every day to the Commander at Paris Plage. It was gorgeous weather,

we had no idea what was happening, as we dare not listen to the radio any longer. A few days later three cars drove up and a German sergeant and soldiers marched in the house, and asked to see all our food supplies. They took practically everything, and I had masses of stuff, then asked for Plummie's tobacco, then my cigarettes!! I was livid. But I had to give it to them. The next thing was our bicycles, two new ones, which our beloved Leonora had just sent to us. Then the cars, I found four officers in the garage. I told them the cars were broken, but they said they could easily mend them! Then the radios. We had two French officers staying with us, they were taken to Germany eventually. One beautiful morning Plummie had just been down to report at Paris Plage. (I only reported on Saturdays.) I was arranging the lunch in the garden when he suddenly appeared and told me there was a German soldier in the hall with a gun waiting to take him to a concentration camp.* He only had ten minutes to pack a suitcase. I was nearly insane, couldn't find the keys of the room for the suitcase, and Plum went off with a copy of Shake-speare, a pair of pyjamas, and a mutton chop. I was left alone at the house for two days, then a German Major came with a General said he wanted to look over the house. He sat on the terrace the entire afternoon enjoying the view, then looked over the villa, and announced he wasn't going to move, and his soldiers brought over everything and put them in Plum-mie's bedroom. I could have killed him! Two days later the Major told me I should have to leave. Had I any where to go? The French officers had given me an address of some French people who said they would give me a room. They had a trout farm 50 kilometres from Touquet. I was allowed to go there and take my personal luggage with me in a small car which they provided. On my way to the trout farm, driven by a German soldier in the smallest car they could find, I could only take a few suit-cases, and had to leave most of my things, however I had Wonder and Coco the parrot. Nothing was allowed in front with the soldier driving. My hostess met me at the door at a rather dreary house in a neglected field, and I was shown into a small back bed-room, there I sat for an hour or so, wondering how I should keep up my courage and nearly out of my mind about Plummie. There was a little lane at the side of the house, and Wonder and I used to walk up and down waiting every day for the postman, and at last after about ten days, a card from Plummie telling me not to worry he was perfectly all right, and was at Lille.

---

*The Germans interned all Englishmen under the age of sixty. It is incorrect to speak of a "concentration camp."

II

THE GERMAN BROADCASTS

10

The Camp Note Book

During the whole of the time Plum was interned he made notes for a book on life in camp, which he intended to write after he was released. These are in the form of a diary, but it is not in strict chronological order. Sometimes he made a note to ask someone else something or to remind himself to write something in greater detail later on, and he seemed to do this when he had the leisure. For this reason I have sometimes altered the order of the diary, and I have also cut passages which are either incomplete or which I cannot understand myself. Otherwise what follows is exactly as he wrote it. It is sometimes inconsequent or repetitive, but these are notes for his own use. For the easier understanding of the reader, Plum spent the first week in Loos Prison, the second week in barracks at Liège, five weeks in the Citadel at Huy, and forty-nine weeks at Tost in Upper Silesia. He was fifty-eight.

"The Camp Note Book" is not to be confused with *The Camp Book*. "The Camp Note Book" was written in his own hand—a thing he never did unless he was without a typewriter—and is clearly not polished or written for publication. *The Camp Book*, which will be referred to again and again in quotations from his letters, was written up from these notes, was finally a full-scale manuscript for a book, and was seen and read by at least one person alive today (Anne Yorke, Denis Mackail's daughter); but it was never published and has now disappeared, possibly destroyed by Plum himself, or by Ethel.

From the beginning of these notes Plum refers to a companion he calls Algy. This was the nickname of Arthur Goddard, who had been the barman at Algy's Bar in Le Touquet. The other men from Le Touquet were George Ballinger, the proprietor of Algy's Bar, Arthur Grant, the golf professional, and Eric Moore, who had also been employed on the golf course.

The suggestion has been made that certain passages about the Jews in camp may give offence on the grounds that they are anti-Semitic. Yet, if one reads Plum's comments on the Belgians and the French, on the likeness of "Mr. Big," the camp commandant, to retired British colonels who live in Cheltenham or Bexhill, or, more especially, on the English (men holding British passports) at Liège, one cannot help thinking the Jews get off fairly lightly. Plum was born one hundred years ago, and these notes were not meant to be read by anyone but himself. The quality they chiefly exhibit is the insularity so common to Englishmen at that date. Today one cannot conceive, much less explain, how it was possible for intelligent and educated people never to question these assumptions of personal superiority. Yet such attitudes were widespread right up to the Second World War, and were adopted not merely towards "foreigners," but towards people of any class lower in the social scale than one's own, and to those who held different beliefs. If the "sixteen Jews, headed by a rabbi," to whom Plum refers, had been Plymouth Brethren or even Methodists, they might well have received the same treatment, while the Frenchman, "Guts and Gaiters," and a character called " 'My boy'—Young Petersen" are spoken of in terms not unlike those applied to the Jew with spectacles. All these things were for his own amusement, and Plum was not always funny when he meant to be.

I do not of course suggest that the contemporary attitude to Jews was only to be found in England, because it was widespread in the rest of Europe and in America, and in both places produced more serious results. But it could often be merely a manner of speaking, a kind of club talk, which had no bearing on actual relationships or emotions towards particular individuals. Plum was too little involved with real life to examine or reject traditional attitudes, but I very much doubt if he could be described as anti-Semitic. He had few friends, but many of the people he most liked and respected were Jews, while he was known to have real affection for several of them. Unlike contemporary writers such as Sapper, John Buchan, and Dornford Yates, he never made jokes about Jews (unless they happened to be the President of Perfecto-Zizzbaum Motion Picture Corp., when the joke was against Hollywood). Richard Usborne tells me that when he sent Plum the original draft of his book *Wodehouse at Work*, which contained a passage making this point, he scored it heavily in the margin, and in a scribbled sentence beginning "For God's sake . . ." wrote a comment to the effect that having spent thirty years in the American theatre, he was not likely to make jokes about Jews.

"The Camp Note Book" is headed "Germans reached Le Touquet on May 22nd" and reads as follows:

Sunday, July 21, 1940

Hot sunny day—walked to Commandature to report—saw Harrold coming along with suitcase—went in and interpreter said all English male civilians to be interned. Explained where I lived and was taken home by soldier in car. Ethel out with dogs—packed valise—saw Wonder crossing lawn—Ethel arrived. Hasty packing, forgot sponge, razor blades, identity card, brush.

Drove back to Commandature—motor bus there—long wait—eventually started off, wives waving goodbye—stopped at Etaples to pick up Cartmell— German sergeant very decent, also very pleasant German soldier who looked like young John Barrymore and gave us cigarettes—we were allowed out to buy wine. Stopped again at Montreuil. The drive took 8 hours to Lille.

Arrived Lille, and after delay drove to prison at Loos.

Algy, Cartmell, self were put in Cell 44 after registering at office and leaving all money except 500 francs, knives etc.

The cell, 12 foot long by about 8 foot wide, whitewashed walls, bed in corner under window. Large window about 5 foot by 3, air quite fresh. Granite floor. Table and chair chained to it—toilet in corner near door. Small basin in wall by toilet with tap, quite good running water. Overhead two staples in wall for chaining dangerous prisoners. In corner by door, oak shelf, half broken off by prisoners who beat in panels with it. One wooden hook.*

We arrived at 9 when it was almost dark and went to cell without fuss, but civilians who had got there earlier had to take off clothes and put them outside door.

Algy and I were given a thin straw-stuffed mattress each and two blankets— no sheets. We slept on these on floor.

(Amazing how soon one gets used to this. The first night it seemed impossible to get to sleep—slept in clothes. Later, beds seemed quite comfortable.)

PRISON ROUTINE

Called at 7 with bell—breakfast at 7:30. First the grille opens and three large loaves of brown bread (unleavened) handed in. This is ration for day. Then each prisoner is given a round tin and a tin spoon and attendant (also a prisoner) dishes out watery bouillon made from cube of Oxo or something.

At 8 exercise—This consists of going into a back yard about 20 foot by 12 at widest spot. Door locked on us. There we met rest of Le Touquet crowd— barely room to walk. This lasts for ½ an hour and we are taken back to cells and locked in for rest of day till 8 next morning.

At 11 lunch—a vegetable soup.

At 5 dinner—a vegetable soup but a bit thicker.

(When our soup was brought, Algy used to shove up the cover of the tiny

*No, merely for fastening bed up.

peephole over the hole in door, so that we could have at least a small view of corridor. Warder begs us not to as it will get him shot!)

After that no more visits from warders unless something exceptional happens. On Thursdays a sausage as extra at dinner. Friday morning—hot shower bath.

Algy complains to German Commandatur about our treatment as convicts by French prison "chef." Comm. furious with chef, insists on all cell doors being left open and us allowed stroll about corridors. It bewilders warders and nearly breaks their hearts, as if they had been golf pros obliged to watch people trampling over the greens.

The drawback to life since July 21 has been the uncertainty as to what is to happen to us next—shall we have to sleep on straw etc?

NOTES

1. *Monotony terrible for first day, but Algy in great form. One is wondering from the first when we will be shifted to prison camp and every footstep brings us up, listening.*

2. *Our smell. Good solid upstanding smell caused by drains. On last day German officers came and inspected cells and said: "Disgusting. How typically French!"*

3. *Soldier leaving with other soldiers on last day shakes my hand and says "Thank you for Jeeves!"*

4. *Prison brings out all that is best in us all.*

From Loos, which was merely a stopping place on a road which finally ended at Tost in Germany, the Le Touquet prisoners were moved to the Citadel at Liège. On the journey to Liège the men from Le Touquet joined men from other districts, and Plum continued as follows:

July 27

Our Paris Plage crowd comparing notes with crowd from Lille Caserne. They slept on straw but had room and freedom to play football. We are inclined to put on airs about our cells and confinement.

In train—400 of us, collected from everywhere, arriving in motor trucks.

In train—Journey of twenty-four hours—8 hours in train before it started. No food and drink except what we could buy at Lille before starting. The cattle truck (40 hommes, 8 chevaux au long) had no windows, and they broke a panel out to get air. They did journey in almost complete darkness.

In train—holes in floor, so afraid of draught, I sit on Snorky's case and get snatches of sleep. Eat at intervals during night—man in chauffeur's leggings

(Haskins) extraordinarily kind to me. Gives me tin of pâté, ½ a loaf, butter, radishes, salt and beer. We roll slowly to and fro through country and eventually get off at Liège at 12:30, exactly 24 hours in train. German guard very nice, let us off on [illegible].

I was first to alight from train. Nice old German general asked me how old I was, felt my suitcase and said it was too heavy to carry and sent for truck—asked me if I had had anything to eat or drink. Very sympathetic and kindly. We walked through Liège, whistling "Tipperary" and "The Barrel," and up a long steep hill which tested some of us pretty severely. Then parade. Then hot soup. Lovely day, so arrival was not depressing.

July 31, 1940

SERGEANT BARUTA

Liège. Parade 8 a.m. and 8 p.m.—like a lot of shuffling sheep. Sergeant calls "Form into fives"—the company, except for Dormitory 52B, which stands in perfect formation looking rather smug, instantly forms fours, then threes, eventually after a chaotic scramble fives. But is this the end? No sir! Old George in row 23 sees old Bill in row 42 and shuffles across to chat with him, with a cigarette end hanging from his lower lip. By the time he is ready to return to position his place has been filled up like a hole by the tide—he shuffles about trying to fit himself in elsewhere and finally forms up as sixth man of a row. Sergeant shouts and after long wait the ranks are in order. But is this the end? Again, no—the Sergeant and worried-looking pal in specs, plus French soldier interpreter who is popular with the masses and comes in for a lot of genial chaff, walk the length of the ranks, counting. They then step aside and hold a sort of Hollywood conference, while we wait eagerly for whistle. Long delay. Something wrong. Word goes round that we are one short. Has old Joe escaped? One pictures him filing through bars with file smuggled in by jailer's daughter in a meat pie.* But no—Here comes old Joe, sauntering along from the Red X block, where he has no business to be—he has a pipe in his mouth and an indulgent look on his face as who should say "Playing soldiers, eh?" He is thoroughly cursed in German and joins ranks. We are counted again after a long interval of forming fives on the sound old system of assembling in groups of sixes and threes, practically all the personnel having left the ranks to cluster round and listen to the Sergeant talking to old Joe. Another conference. This time mysteriously we appear to be five short. A discouraged feeling grows among us that we are losing ground. The Priest addresses us—he is a sort of spokesman or liaison officer between us and the Germans. He says: "Have the six men who came from Ghent registered at bureau?" He speaks accusingly and they seem wounded. "Si, si, si," cry these typical Englishmen, who suffer

---

**If she had smuggled in a file, he would have eaten it.*

from the disadvantage of not being able to talk English. * *Another conference. Parade has now lasted 40 minutes. Priest summons all room chefs to join conference, and it is then announced that we must all return to our rooms, where room chefs will make a list of their men and assemble them. Room 52B, rather overdoing the smug note, writes out a placard in chalk on cardboard— 20 Männer Stimmet (20 Men correct)—and when whistle blows again for renewal of parade I hold this in front of me like a sandwich man. It doesn't get a smile from Teacher, which is disappointing—he presumably being too busy trying to count us in our peculiar formation (old Bill having again sauntered off to old George and got into an argument about whether yesterday's coffee tasted more like coffee than this morning's). Another conference. Still five short. Situation appears at deadlock, till some bright person suggests "How about the men in hospital?" They prove to be 5 in number, and the whistle blows again for dismissal. We have spent an instructive and pleasant fifty minutes, and learned much about our fellow men.*

At Liège—At 7 we get cups of barley coffee. Man I meet says he hopes it isn't habit-forming, as he finds he's looking forward to it so eagerly each day.

Being in Citadel is rather like being on the road with a theatrical company— also like being at Hollywood where you feel humbly pleased if a director smiles at you and elated if by any chance you get a nod from an executive—thus, a smile from a German sergeant is as if you were smiled at by Capra, while a nod from Kommandatur is as if one of the head men of the big company smiled at you in the studio prison yard.

Liège Citadel. Great question is—is it better to queue up for your grub 1/2 an hour before time or to wait?

Kitchen Sergeant a worried-looking young man and I don't wonder, for if we are a little weak in keeping the ranks when standing still, we go all haywire when walking and not many steps are required to turn us into a football crowd coming out of stadium. Food queues bring out all our sick comedy. We jest

---

*In a note made later, Plum wrote: "At Liège Citadel an Englishman is anything from a Borneo head hunter/Malay to the illegitimate son of a Bulgarian who deserted the Polish mother and absconded to England. At least half those present can't talk English and converse in Flemish. I think they ought to release at least the baboons and anything that goes on all fours. A trained body of men like the Gestapo could easily weed out the doubtful cases. If they have tails, release them. (This happy breed of men. Shakespeare said some nice things about English but camp would have puzzled him.) Kandhu—a little Malay of 44 who looks 15, like a small monkey—has travelled all over world and has a wife in every port. Put his profession down in register as 'Bottlewasher and dancer in a circus.' One night he gave a native dancing exhibition in his dormitory—a ground floor one—very picturesque, with everybody clapping rhythmically and German guards looking on. He also played football all day, and next day had to report sick. Not so young as he was!"

lightly about eggs and bacon etc. (*This is the fundamental joke, one feels.*) Little brown dog hangs hopefully about cookhouse. What a hope!

Breakfast, 7 a.m. Two large ladlefuls of coffee made of oats, no sugar or milk, and a slab of black bread with a dab of lard, jam or honey on it—and damned good it is when you get used to it.

Lunch, 11:30 Two large ladlefuls of thick soup, with rice or potatoes or macaroni in it. This is the star meal. Very hot and good. Not much salt in it.

Supper, 7 p.m. Same as breakfast.

It's amazing how this diet, which looks meagre, is really all one wants. One feels marvellous on it.

Great variety of utensils—military dixies (mess tins), bottles, oil cans, almost flat bits of tins* etc. Nothing was issued to us and we had to go to the dustbin and rake it over and then scour what tins we found with sand from a grubby sand pile by the toilets. (Toilets, my foot! The Greeks had a word for it.)

(Algy's dixie was pinched, also his tin spoon. Great excitement.)

It takes about 1/2 an hour to get from end or near end of queue to cookhouse. Men there with cauldrons—the bread is in slices on a trestle beyond cauldron and you file past and grab your piece.

Everything in the camp involves hours of standing. Today, for instance, July 31, I stood 50 minutes on morning parade, 35 minutes in queue for morning coffee, 45 minutes for midday soup, 60 minutes for canteen and shall probably do another 45 minutes for evening coffee and evening parade: total of 4 hours odd. This, added to constant strolling during day and exercise walks at night, keeps one very fit. (You go for a long walk with one man after evening parade, he goes to bed, you team up with another. Bed at 9:30 or 10, pleasantly weary and get to sleep right away, in spite of bed having no springs, no pillow and straw mattress. I use my coat, suitcase and grey sweater for pillow, raincoat for extra blanket. No sheets. I sleep in grey flannel trousers, blue sweater and red cardigan.)

Odd, the tendency of the English lower classes to assemble in groups and stand absolutely motionless. Mostly our crowd do this—very exceptional to see anyone walking. When I did my daily dozen the first morning, a gaping multitude assembled. Our crowd wear caps, scrubby beards and shiny coats and trousers and look like a football crowd up north.

Only exception to this is a group of youths who have put up goal posts and dug up a football with rag in side and play footer all day. German guards join in.

*One swanker has a thermos flask.

Big cleaning up of dormitory. Everyone working, shining floors and squeezing dirty water into pails with old rags—two young Catholic priests in their flowing robes working away with brush and squeegee, bank manager stripped to waist, etc.

Difficulty of keeping clean is that nothing helpful is issued. We have to scrounge for old pails and rags and brushes. Sometimes one dormitory has a brush and lends it to another.

Tins of any sort or knives and forks as valuable as rubies.

The dormitory cleaning latrine. Genial white-haired Scotsman like Will Fyffe.

Cook Sergeant tells us as a great secret that tomorrow we shall be told "where we are going and when." This may mean we are going to be sent home but more likely that we are moving on to Germany.

The great drawback to life at Citadel is apprehension. One feels we are all right so far, but what about when it rains at food time, or if sickness breaks out. Some men have got toothache, and nothing to be done for them. Also apprehension about soles of one's shoes wearing out.

Wednesdays and Saturdays we get a warm shower. Very up-to-date, clean place in this rather out-of-date barracks.

On 3 August Plum and the rest of his companions were moved once more, this time to the Citadel at Huy:

JOURNEY TO HUY

August 3, 1940

Breakfast. Whistle goes at 6:30, parade at 7. We are told soup will be at 9:30 and we must be ready to leave by 11:30. We parade with baggage in boiling sun for an hour and drive down to station in covered wagons, 25 men to each—absolute Hole of Calcutta. Into cattle trucks at station. After 4-hour journey to do 25 miles.

Very hot.

Parade in street for almost 1/2 an hour, then march up to Citadel carrying baggage. Appalling trip—Citadel at top of steep hill with glorious view of Meuse.

No arrangements for sleeping. They start by putting 40 men into a room for 15, no beds, not even straw on floor.

Eventually some of us move to another room with straw in it, but so filthy we are not allowed to use it. I am writing this at 8:30 p.m. and it looks as if I shall have to sit up all night. Tomorrow we are promised beds or at least straw. Exercise ground very small. No room to move when we were paraded in it this afternoon. This is going to be hell.

August 4, 1940

The night of our arrival at Huy was not so bad as I had expected. At the last moment we found clean straw in a room upstairs and brought it down. (We did not dare use the old straw that was in our room for fear it might be lousy.) I slept in drawers, grey flannel trousers, a sports shirt, sweater and red cardigan, with my raincoat and grey tweed coat as blankets. (There were enough blankets for about 20 men, plus some old soldiers' coats which I didn't dare touch.) I used my other trousers, grey cardigan and briefcase as pillow. I was so tired, I could not get to sleep at once (we had to be in our rooms by 9)— also we were on ground floor and a sentry paced the stone flags outside all night. But I got to sleep eventually, but was woken by the cold at about 4 a.m. (got up at 5 and did my exercises). We got up at 6. At 7 chef de chambre (Monaghan now, Algy having had too much work at Liège) and helper go and get coffee in bucket and bring it back to room and we share it out, 19 of us. About twenty minutes later, Monaghan and helpers arrive with bread ration for the day, two loaves and a half, half of what we got at Liège, and jam. We also managed to get a little more coffee.

Parade was at 1/2 past 8 on the first morning. We formed up in fives, by rooms, and much less confusion and delay than at Liège. After parade, all men with one arm or leg or otherwise crippled were called forward and given option of having separate room. Chefs de chambres then summoned and told that there would be a room inspection at 9 (which there wasn't) and that we must stand to attention. Also we must salute non-coms and officers. A good job too, as we need discipline. The sentries are very friendly here.

The morning was given up to cleaning—I cleaned sills and a man in room above emptied a bucket of water all over me, silly ass. Volunteers were called for yesterday for cooking and today for potato peeling. We cleaned up passages and washroom. Now gradually being borne in upon us that we are a ruddy peripatetic fatigue party—we cleaned up Liège and they moved us on, and now we shall clean up Huy and presumably move on again.

A lovely sunny day—very exhilarating being up and out at 7 (i.e. by the sun, allowing for summer time and German time). Everything on a very small and compact scale here—the Germans have a guard down by gate and wash at the tap outside which we use.

Everybody one meets has a new story to tell of the cowardice of the Belgians and the lack of discipline in French army. Two old sweats I talked to on parade—one spoke of 100 Belgians coming into his village and 5 Germans arriving and the Belgians throwing down their arms, the other of a French officer in his village who left his post flat in order to evacuate his wife.

August 5

We hear that tomorrow all the Germans have been able to buy for us is 28 kilos of macaroni. (We get a thin sweet broth with prunes in it.)
Parade at 5—nice Sergeant announces that he is going home on leave for a few days and is loudly cheered, as we all like him enormously.

August 6

Boys of 16 sorted out—air of hope and excitement in camp—fear nothing will come of it.

August 7, 1940

Rainy morning—not cheered by rumour that someone has escaped. (This proves to be true.) Atmosphere that of Dotheboys Hall after escape of Smike.

Just after breakfast rumour spread through camp that one of the Belgian boys had escaped. Proved true. He had got through one of the slits (not more than 6-inch) in the wall at end of passage, leaving rope tied behind him to water pipe. Atmosphere like Dotheboys Hall after escape of Smike. At 11:30 whistle blew. All to their rooms.* Presently four German soldiers in tin hats and bayonets enter with interpreter—they take away all our washing cords and even small bits of string which we were saving for shoelaces—and there is a moment when it seems as if our belts will have to go, but this final disaster does not occur. We open our suitcases, which are searched (reminds me of first minutes with Customs men at New York—same sense of guilt). Then we have to pile our suitcases on table and turn over all the straw which forms our beds. We are told that "when we get out" the string will be returned. (Comedy touch to all this is that it happens just when we ought to be getting our lunch from cookhouse.) I must say that everything is being done to relieve the monotony!

Opinion is divided between appreciation of chap's enterprise and the feeling that he was a swine to leave us to be snootered [*sic*] for his crime. God knows what restrictions we shall have now. We had just got all set to ask the Kommandatur for more bread, but when we heard his voice outside we felt that it was not the moment. After lunch, Arthur Grant and I went to wash up the dishes at the pump next to guard room. I was feeling like a naughty boy after the search of room and was prepared to be told not to do something by anybody I met. At the pump was a very tough-looking German private and he said something to me in what sounded like a rough, annoyed voice, and I was just about to say "Yes, sir, very good, sir" and retire, thinking that he was

*Kommandatur heard issuing orders outside. Previous to this more troops arrive at guard house.

telling me I ought to be in my room, when I suddenly found that he was offering us his soup. He filled both our tins, and I've never tasted anything better—thick rice with strips of meat. This is the most touching thing that has happened to me since the invasion began.

August 8, 1940

Kommandatur takes parades. Announcement formally made—"It is forbidden to steal."

Great excitement this morning. Man named Wilcox called for by guard and suddenly released—he is an Antwerp bank manager. The rumour now is that very soon a lot of us are to be released. Rumours are our great standby here. One doesn't mind if they aren't true or couldn't possibly be true, the point is they buck one up for the day and then next day comes another rumour.

Horror is always lurking round corner. Today (August 5 [*sic*]), going down corridor to my room, I see door of room on right open—I didn't know there was a room there—and in it is a man with *scabies*. Isolated, but is it too late? At back of one's mind is always the thought—suppose an epidemic starts? The man attributes it to sleeping in straw!

August 11

For first time, I fetch soup in bucket from cookhouse. Frightful sense of responsibility—suppose I dropped it!

The canteen. Algy, Jock, the big man and others form a committee and are given an empty room—the big man is allowed downtown for $1\frac{1}{2}$ hours a day with soldier—comes back first day after three hours, sweating from the climb. There are about 20 rooms and the results are divided evenly between them. Each man gets a piece of cheese about $2\frac{1}{2}$ inches by $2\frac{1}{2}$ inches and it is amazing what a difference it made. Saved up, it sees one through the next day. From now on, it is announced, two or three men will be allowed out to make purchases. (The soldiers are all for this, as it means that more of them will get out. One tends to forget that they are just as cooped up as we are!)

A German soldier gave Algy a cigar—he hadn't the heart to smoke it in front of us, so put it up to drawing of cards, aces high. Farmer won and gave it back to Algy, who could now smoke it with a clear conscience.

Our chef de camp, Erike (who is now interpreter—gives our notices in English, French and Flemish), gets leave to break down a partition in wall next to infirmary and reveals labyrinth of disused rooms—lofts—which give the place a whole new aspect. There is one, No. 77, with a large unbarred window from which it is a drop only a few feet to hillside. I am scared stiff that we shall have another jail break and, feeling a bit like teacher's pet, get hold of Sherrer and show it to Sergeant. Sergeant seems unalarmed—says there is always a sentinel with a machine gun guarding the terrace, and I feel he has been warned and it is now up to him.

August 12

Today the bread ration failed and we had small biscuits. Rumour ran round camp that there would be no bread next day, and Sergeant made special announcement at evening parade that there would.* I think there was a distinct windy feeling that there might be a risk. The food situation is pretty dangerous. One epidemic of influenza would wipe half of us out, as our resistance power is so lowered.

It's extraordinary how one's whole soul becomes obsessed with food.†

It is divided up to the last millimetre, and one eats with relish chunks of lard etc. which would formerly have made one sick. Great problem is how to split up one's food—eat half your bread at breakfast (day's ration about half as thick as width of ordinary novel and about twice as long as that width)‡ or go easy at breakfast, relying on heat of coffee to give you the illusion of having fed, and go a buster at tea.

One's great worry is the thought of the wives, waiting for news and getting none. It stabs one like a knife sometimes, so that one has deliberately to school oneself to think of something else quick. August 12 on parade it was announced that letters written at Huy had "left here"—but this may simply mean that they have been taken from Citadel to the Kommandatur and may not get any further.

August 13

I have now been sleeping ten nights without a blanket, so I took Erike to Sergeant to complain. Sergeant very apologetic, but it seems there are none. Last night was bitterly cold. Algy has got me a thermos, so I shall save some of the evening coffee and drink it in the small hours.

I have a theory about these parades. I believe Mister Big is the German equivalent of the Colonel living at Cheltenham or Bexhill, they have dug him out after years of retirement and given him this fairly important job, and it has gone to his head—he loves the feel of strutting up and down in front of us and having interpreters give out orders. Specimens: We must shave every day—stand at attention on parade—not cluster round guard room, hoping for food

*He said this was more than they were getting in Germany before the war.
†Sherrer went to town today for canteen and bought me a pound of sweets. Heaven!
‡7 men to a loaf generally, but often 8.

from soldiers etc. (*These last two coldly ignored. Every day a line of boys sits on wall outside guard room, like birds waiting to be fed.*)

Mister Big is 62 and retired. Ex-inspector of police. Thinks everyone a crook (like Baxter). Volunteered for this job. Loves being a little king. Bexhill stuff.

August 14

A wonderful day! Oddly enough, it started badly, as it was raining during parade and I couldn't [illegible]. Then suddenly, for no reason, I got a sort of exalted feeling—definitely happy, as if a cloud had rolled away. I volunteered to help peeling potatoes in morning and loved it. Then I found I was on potato fatigue next day, and Moore came up and told me he didn't think it right for me to have to peel potatoes, so Erike would do it for me. Then in afternoon a man came up and paid back 5 francs which I had lent him a few days ago, he having no Belgian money. This touched me enormously, as I had lent him the money practically in darkness outside canteen and couldn't have recognized him again—also I had clean forgotten it. This made me feel how decent everybody is really. Then Algy asked me to join canteen committee, which means getting the run of the room. And finally, after evening parade, there was shouting for "Whitehouse" (a lot of people thought it was "Lights out"!) and I went to guard house and saw Sergeant standing there with my passport! And behind him I recognized one of the suitcases from home. Also a letter from my darling Bunny on table, which of course I wasn't allowed to read yet. But Sergeant let me look through suitcase and take it with me. Full of shirts and a lovely dressing-gown!! Dying to know if Bunny got my letter from Liège. Next morning man comes in at 6:30 and asks for me—little Jew linguist chap in specs—he is from Sergeant, who ought not officially to have let me have suitcase before Mr. Big inspected it—wants it back before he arrives.

Gradually the bores develop and it is hard to avoid them in this confined space. Wherever I go, Sherrer keeps bobbing up with his life story. I dash into room thru window.

August 15

Today, with one of those abrupt jerks which the Germans always seem to like doing, whole situation suddenly changed. Announced in parade that canteen is verboten, also that no letters and parcels may be sent or received—order from Kommandatur at Liège. Sergeant says I shall get my letter though. (I got it later in afternoon—a wonderful letter, which made me happy.)

The reason for forbidding letters is apparently that there has been a lot of sabotage at Lisle, people cutting telephone wires etc. so I am told by very nice, sympathetic German lieutenant,* who says he is to be our Kommandatur next week. He speaks English and is very guarded about Mister Big, but evidently thinks him a stuffed shirt. Things should be much better under him.

The great fear that haunts us all is that there should be a riot among the tougher crowd in the camp, which might mean machine guns being turned on us. I talked with a man named Thompson, who said there had been mutterings in his room but he had talked the malcontents out of it. He says interned civilians are by international law entitled to a room and toilet apiece and same rations as Germans! So they can't treat us like this really—but they do! (Like [illegible] story of the man in prison. "They can't put you in prison for that." "I know they can't—but they have!")

Met cook and congratulated him on today's soup. He was grateful, because his professional pride has been wounded by grumblers saying there wasn't enough. He said he could have made it more by adding water, which would have spoiled it. He takes me into cookhouse and shows me the dried vegetables in great pots soaking. Very ingenious—they come (German) in small packets, very compressed.

Food. Amazing how one comes to value all one can get. Sometimes small sort of dog biscuits are served instead of bread, and one watches like a hawk to see that one gets exactly one's share. I dropped one in a pile of dust and ate it with relish. Also "butter"—a sort of pale axle grease, at which I would wince in peacetime—I eat it and lick the knife—no fastidiousness here!

The Lily of the Field—Belgian boy of 19 in our room (34), who never offers to do a hand's turn, in spite of our stinting ourselves to give him an extra bit on account of being a growing boy!

August 16

After lunch three sudden whistles for parade—evidently something wrong and we all feel like schoolboys at Dr. Grimstone's—Sergeant and three men go down ranks with nervous-looking spectacled Jew who looks after electric lights. A long harangue in German from Sergeant. It gradually develops that the Jew was insulted by a boy who said he would "throw him in the river." The idea of this as a threat is comic—(a) it would need a damn fine throw, and (b) most of us would welcome being thrown into river. The BS 694s [sic] are paraded for about ¾ of an hour while the Jew seeks vainly for the boy. Finally those under 30 are lined up apart. Still no result. Then Sergeant says he had intended to bring the thing up to Kommandatur but will settle it amicably if we all promise not to do it again—we do, enthusiastically.

*Dr. Haas.

Nobody seems to know what the actual trouble was. One story is that the criminal spoke disparagingly of the Germans, when asked to do something.

At 3:30 another parade. It starts Sergeant and interpreters yelling for Hycock—Heycock—etc. with no result. We are then informed that we of the lost legion (our room No. 34 is last on list and is always served last) can have mattresses. We line up and collect them and stuff them with the straw in our room, each being scrupulously careful not to take any of his neighbour's straw. Bags long and limp and one wrestles with them like Laocoon. Air filled with straw.

At 5 another parade. Strange new Big Pot appears. We are all ordered to our rooms till 2 whistles blow. Big Pot goes round rooms—comes to ours—we are told to take off our coats—the linings of them inspected—also raincoats. Sergeant then goes round snipping off the maker's labels, if English. (Note that French ones are ignored.)* Big Pot then thanks us and exits. "Now," says Algy, "come and put your heads together. Why?" The procedure seemed loony. The conclusion we came to is that Big Pot is Gestapo man and they want these labels for parachute troops to be dropped in England—they will have German coats and these labels will be sewn in. But to me the thing remains a mystery.

August 17

Idleness makes us all obsessed with food—jealousy rankles—people stalk about telling stories of men seen coming out of cookhouse with six potatoes and a bit of meat. The trouble really is that the numbers of men in rooms vary—thus soup is doled out in buckets of equal size, with the result that a room of 10 men live the life of Riley, getting same amount as a room of 25 men. Also cookhouse men suspected of helping themselves on side. This afternoon after lunch I am trying to sleep and rolling German voice wakes me. It is Sergeant outside window explaining to group of us that what we want is more discipline and comparing us unfavourably with recent French prisoners.

Another unpopular man is he who does step dancing at weekly concerts. His turn bores everybody but he demands extra ration for doing it.

It is now decided that each room shall re-elect a chef de chambre (the present ones are incompetent ones chosen simply because they speak German), who will elect various committees. (Algy saw man with a pudding! We shudder.)

Rather gruesome, the way we all keep our eyes alert to see that the other fellow doesn't get a crumb of bread more than we do!

The real trouble is that we need someone or a committee with authority and

*No, some Arras ones were taken.

*power to impose penalties. At present, it is open to the corrected man merely
to tell the corrector to go to hell.*

August 18

*People are starting to experiment with foods—man gathering berries on bank,
probably poisonous. Parsons and a roommate club together their biscuit ration, add sugar, milk, jam, and cook bakes it for them and they hope to get a
cake, though I feel they are running an awful risk of wasting good biscuits.
Another man tells me he saves his second helping of soup, pours it on biscuits,
adds jam and eats result cold. Algy's pudding* consists of softened biscuits,
condensed milk, sugar, honey, jam. (Many men with false teeth find it impossible to eat the biscuits in their natural state.)*

*Another substitute now prevalent is tea† or straw instead of tobacco—tea
smoked has a horrible sweet, sickly smell and is very unpopular with rest of
dormitory.*

*Orders keep being given on parade—e.g., Boys must not gather round guard
room like pelicans in wilderness—but they still do. Also no smoking on parade, but we blandly roll up in a fragrant cloud of smoking tea. Also, we must
get on parade quicker—we must come at the Double. But we are like the Fifth,
who "don't dance"—we don't double—we still remain the languid saunterers
we have always been. Also no hands in pockets.*

August 21

*Sudden announcement that the water is going to be off for two days! Some-
thing is always going wrong in this damned place. This means presumably that
one won't be able to wash or shave for two days. (Main burst.) As it happened,
water came on again in afternoon—amazing how it bucked one up.*

96 steps down to the deepest cellars here at Huy.

*I wrote a letter to Red Cross (American) at Brussels, saying 700 men here,
many of them having been taken at moment's notice and so on rocks and we
haven't been able so far to communicate with our families. Mr. Big for some
reason went off deep end about it, said "mensonges" and tore it up! (Later on
heard that he got badly ticked off by Kommandatur for something and was
taking it out on us.)*

*Canteen started again. Jock got quite a lot of cheese. The man keeps pleading
for garlic, with a strong opposition in his room! Another wanted 50 kilos of*

---

*Wonderful!
†If one has tobacco, one has to be more or less a secret smoker.

potatoes!! Another asks Jock if he couldn't get him dog biscuits. Note—Bread, chocolate, tobacco, cake and biscuits are now rationed and cannot be bought without ration ticket, which of course we haven't got. And today (August 22) I hear the Holland frontier has been closed, so cheese will probably be unavailable. Ration of bread today for whole day is one loaf to 8 men—i.e., one slice about an inch thick for all day. For last three days we have been getting only biscuits—50 each per whole day, about as long and wide as a postage stamp. (N.B. We complained we were not getting enough bread, so they took statesmanlike course of giving us no bread at all.)

We are rather like Falstaff's army in *Henry V*.

New Sergeant starts parade by shouting "Good morning"—we shout back. A little like Captain in *Pinafore*.

Great Moment in day is when Jeff brings in bread ration—(a) Is it bread today or biscuits?—(b) If bread, how many men to the loaf?—If as low as six, it makes our day, as that means a slice for breakfast and a slice for supper. It has been as high as 8 to a loaf.

August 22

Big day. I am asleep in afternoon when soldier comes to window and says I am wanted. I go to guard room and there is my beloved Oberst, who has stopped off to see me on his way to Germany on leave.

Later we are told that two high officers from Liège are to inspect camp. Parade at 4:30, with our crowd straggling up as usual. Lieutenant Big once more pleaded with us to come on parade at double.* We are dismissed and immediately afterwards whistle blows again.—This time one or two of us actually do break into a dignified trot. We are dismissed as soon as assembled.

The Oberst tells me my poor Bunny is worrying, as I feared she might. He is going to tell her I am all right. He advised me not to make myself spokesman of camp—reference to that Red Cross letter. I said to him "Do you know, I still don't know your name." He said something about later on. I said "You're very mysterious about your name." He laughed and said that there was a war on. I said "I wish you would finish it off soon," and he said Before Winter.

He tells me all the Paris Plage wives of British subjects, whether English or French, have had to leave.

I say to Arthur that there has scarcely been a really dull eventless day since we came—always some parade or visit or excitement. I say the Germans must have an Entertainment Committee for our benefit.

Stray thought—How marvellous if the other 18 men in Room 34 suddenly decided to go on hunger strike and gave me their ration.

*To give the 2 officers an eyeful.

The General visits some of the rooms, but not ours. Unfortunately the two men whom he asked if the food were sufficient were (a) Erike, the stoutest man in the camp, who said it wasn't and received a sceptical glance at the tummy. Erike endeavoured by waggling his waistcoat to show what wastage there had been, but there was such a lot left that the demonstration was not impressive. (b) The Jew in spectacles (the one who was "threatened"), who said he had quite enough, omitting to add that he was getting double rations because he looked after the electric light, and thereby became the most unpopular man in camp. (c) The really shrewd tacticians were the Jew boys, who left their biscuit ration spread on table, thus causing General to enquire, and he was apparently shocked when told that this was instead of bread. We went to bed hopeful, but today (August 23) no bread, only biscuits. (This was the same General spoke to me on Liège platform. He came accompanied by a staff, one of whom went into latrines and staggered out again, then had another shot to see if it was as bad as he had thought. He found it was!)

Grass bank a good place for looking for cigarette stubs thrown away by old garrisons.

August 23

Sergeant announces that we must all clean our rooms, as a very big General is coming to inspect the camp. He doesn't turn up, and at evening parade Sergeant apologises for giving us so much trouble for nothing. Very decent of him.

August 24

Eighteen boys and men released. Also our names are being tabulated in age groups, which is promising.

A man who was once a windjammer sailor tells me that this is nothing to that life. His first voyage lasted 345 days! After getting down to one weevily biscuit and an inch of water per day, they reached Pitcairn Island.

August 25

In canteen room, looking at view and talking to Jock, Yule and Algy—when two men rush in. Their wives are down below, hundreds of feet. They lie on broad window sill, looking down and shouting, and we hear women's voices. Finally we drag them in, afraid they may lose their heads and jump, and Algy, wonderfully gentle, makes them sit on bench. They sit there with bowed heads, crying, and Algy talks to them like a mother, saying they know their wives are all right and we shall soon all be out etc.

We amuse ourselves in various ways: a man in Room 15 gives German lessons; physical jerks; Aunty Sally with tin cans.

Human nature peeps out under influence of hunger. Men volunteer to peel potatoes and sneak the skins to eat later.

Lots of ill feeling about the man in gaiters who voted himself into cushy job in hospital* —he goes to town daily for medicine and brings back steaks etc for himself—he has edged his two sons into cookhouse.

August 26

Parcels arrive. New Lieutenant—Mr. Big and entire company left yesterday—has them opened and everything in them opened—bread, sardine tins, everything. (Letters are destroyed after being read by recipient, for fear of code.)

It looks as if this new lieutenant may succeed in smartening us up, a task which has defeated hundreds. Sergeant on parade yells "Achtung" and startles me—spring to attention.

Then Lieutenant says stand at ease. After the counting, another "achtung," then dismissal, and we troop off a bit dazed.†

August 27

I am on potato peeling fatigue. Sergeant comes among us, patting our pockets to see we aren't pinching any! All very genial. One of the squad has an apoplectic fit and keels over. He had been smoking tea.

August 26

Man in corridor shouting down to his wife, who has come from Antwerp. He can see her, but she can't see him. She can only hear him.

"Scabies" is like an alley cat—he slinks about and you find him suddenly brushing against you. A friendly, gregarious soul, who has now got lice. His policy is to become such a menace that he will be let go. He refused to wash, and when given a second shirt promptly lost it. "Rabies," his loony roommate in straw-covered dungeon at end of passage, asked—not unnaturally—to be alone, and they rigged up a sort of cubicle at end of my strolling place on first floor.

*With double rations.
†Next day he and entire garrison suddenly leave.

August 29

Man comes up to me in upstairs corridor and asks me how Ukridge would have liked this life. He is ragged and down at heels but an OMT [sic]. (Another ragged man is Winchester and Oxford.) He says this life has completely cured his kidney trouble—he used to get out of bed all doubled up and now is lissome. I find, too, that my rheumatic finger, before quite stiff, is now flexible. We appear to be getting here sort of treatment you pay heavily for at places like Ruthven Castle. This man tells me you can sharpen a razor blade by filling glass with water and rubbing blade round inside under water.

We are told on parade not to parade with our hands in our pockets. Quiet amusement on our part and hands thrust deeper into pockets.

August 30

Sergeant wants us to do an hour's physical jerks—raised eyebrows, and Erike explains that on our present diet we are too weak and would be using up more calories than we have at our disposal. Sergeant reluctantly convinced, then next morning sees me doing my daily dozen and triumphantly refutes Erike. Result is that we are paraded and the younger men do jerks while we look on. Rich comedy, especially the Lily of Field. I feel sure the Germans have an Entertainment Committee.

Describe "House," popularly known as Ousey-Ousy. Cardboard cards and stones from courtyard.

August 31

Man gets letter from his wife, at Cambrai, written in Flemish. Lieutenant calls him in and makes him translate it—not allowing him to handle it. He reaches a pathetic bit about his little girl and breaks down and drops a tear on letter. Lieutenant ticks him off, says an elderly man like him ought to be ashamed of himself. Then he makes him read letter again, to see if he gives the same translation. Then he gives him letter and sends him off in to corner to read it to himself. When he has finished, he takes letter back and tears it up. (Note— the day he arrived here, Lieutenant was informed that his wife had been killed by an English bombing plane.)

Wife shouting to her husband, who hung at slit in wall, is reported to have said that the English radio had announced that War would end on October 9!! Smythe, the golf club secretary, in washroom tells me this morning that all the "over 50's" should have been released last week and are going to be this week! All this, added to fact that it is glorious day and one can sit in sunshine, make for a wonderful optimism. Plus fact that Algy and Jock and Arthur and I, by sacrificing our life's blood in way of breakfast biscuits, have managed to assemble two *puddings. We have them with a dixie-full of tea at 3:30 and at 5 swig a quart of near-coffee apiece!*

Man comes up to me and begs me, if I write a book about all this, to mention that it was Charlie who did my washing. You're right, Charlie it was. C. Westcott, gentlemen.

Misfortune at lunch. I put my dixie full of soup on suitcase and in sitting down kicked suitcase, not only spilling a quarter of it but having it soak through chinks of suitcase and stain shirts etc. Amazing that a mere splash of soup can spread itself so much. The world seemed to become all soup. (Algy gave me some of his potatoes to make up for it.)

The pudding question becomes more and more a difficulty. Today I gave up 15 biscuits, which I would have loved for breakfast, and I don't feel it's worth it, as one's helping of pudding just seems to slide down and be gone.

Guts and Gaiters, the Frenchman in leggings, who edged himself into hospital job, has been getting horse steaks up the funicular and selling them at 3 francs apiece. They are supposed to go to the men under 20, but sometimes there are some over.

Welcome gift of fruit from Belgian Red Cross this afternoon. Report says that Germans say this is not to occur again. Why, I wonder.

Talking to Reeves, the padre. He tells me that Kandhu, owing to cadging food from Germans, has acquired 128 biscuits as a sort of reserve of capital. All one's values change in a place like this—news like that makes me feel Kandhu is a millionaire—it is like hearing of the Duke of Westminster.

Note—he tells me the reason Kandhu's clowning has fallen so flat with this last lot of Germans is that in the recent fighting one of their company was killed by a Senegalese by having his throat bitten through. (When they saw our coloured contingent, they recoiled and asked "Are they dangerous?")

This new lot of Germans are simply baffled as to who the hell we are. A German Guard went to dentist's with a prisoner and, asked by dentist if we were prisoners of war, said "No." "Civil prisoners?" "No." "Then who are they?" "I don't know."

Situation is confused by fact that so many of our ragged regiment have been raiding the pile of military coats and caps left behind by Belgians, so now parade shows ranks dotted with these.

Morning parade. Names called out and letters distributed. Each man steps apart in group and reads letter, then has to hand it back to Corporal, who takes them all away and destroys them.

September 4

Jeff went to town to oculist's and came back with bread, given him by population. Divided among our 19, it ran to one small slice apiece, but very welcome.

Food—One sees a human document wandering about yard and says "Come on, you human document, tell me the story of your life"—but all he will talk about is the rations.

Going downtown. People are let out with guard or go to oculist's, dentist etc. At first, they smuggle in food like schoolboys—one man with a jam tart wrapped round his chest—then they get bold and go out with bags and sacks. Smythe tells me his guard was a married man with children and hadn't been home for two years—they all fraternized. Guard offered a drink, told them not to spend their money on him but to save it for food for themselves.

Eventually, people got too reckless and an unexpected General found them roaming about shops (September 5) and has now forbidden anyone to go to town. We are hoping this is only temporary, as it has happened before. Luckily Algy went down today (September 5) and came staggering back, loaded with food. (Algy's description of nipping into cafe with guard, having a drink, drawing blinds first, then peeping through door and nipping out.)

Crown v. Anchor. German sentry with bayonet joins crowd and puts his franc on with the best of them.

I reluctantly decide to stand out of the pudding quartette, finding the pudding too much of a vampire preying on one's substance. Pudding marvellous, but so good that one's share vanishes in a couple of gulps.

The smelly cheese in cigar box in one's suitcase.

Our room is scrupulously honest, but one hears of other rooms where you have to carry your bread ration about in your pocket all day. (Red-haired spectacled boy pinches father's biscuits.)

September 7

We wake this morning to find that 16 new prisoners have arrived in the night. All Jews, headed by Rabbi. Distinct lowering of the tone.

On 8 September Plum was moved to Tost in Upper Silesia.

September 8

The journey to Tost. 3 nights in train, no room for legs. We were given half a loaf on leaving and at Cottbris (1:45, after being 32 hours in train). Red Cross nurses brought half loaf. Excellent fresh bread per man, soup. Our dear old Sergeant is with us, and the sight of him does much to take away that lost feeling. He is more like a mother than a Sergeant, except at Sagan, where a man takes advantage, door being open to get out and pick up cigarette ends. Sergeant yells and brandishes revolver—temperamental mother, in fact more like an aunt. (We hear later that he is shortly to sit for his exam for a lieutenant and much depends on his getting us successfully to our destination. I hope he passed all right.) Frightful thing about these journeys is that you have no means of knowing how long they are to be.

Some humorist on parade: "When the war is over, if I have any money, I'm going to buy a German and keep him in the garden and count him!"

The animal howling at tables in dining-room if it looks as if wrong table were to be served first. Man jumps on chair and shouts that his bread ration has been pinched. He was only away from the table about 4 seconds.

German soldier who took Leonard Cook away from home gave him his raincoat when it came on to rain, and got wet himself.

THE MIGHTY FALLEN

1. The Major—full notes elsewhere.

2. The Cook—an autocrat at Huy, a nonentity at Tost.

3. Kandhu—No audience for his clowning at Tost.

4. Erike, undisputed chess champ—then Mackenzie arrives from Lake [illegible]—a wizard at chess—he takes on 12 men simultaneously, Erike one of them, and reads book in between moves.

October 8

Lovely day. Inoculation. As I was in line, stripped to waist, got into conversation with charming German corporal who spoke perfect English and had read all my books. Also another one had, which bucked me up enormously.

GENERAL NOTES

1. Camp an advertisement for instituting marriage. Not a single man I have met but is pining for his wife.

2. Write about feeling of living on capital—i.e. if one loses or breaks anything, impossible to replace it.

We are a motley crowd. We start out with ordinary [illegible]—after that we just don't make sense.

The yard at Huy, a fairly roomy cuspidor.

"Toffee"—*his mode of self-expression is to spit. Where you or I would throw off an epigram or utter a light laugh, Toffee spits. The Spit Courteous—The Spit Meditative.*

October 15, 1940

My 59th birthday! Great excitement, as after three months letters have arrived from wives. Parsons' wife wrote to him, posted in Belgium, enclosing letters from Mrs. Moore and Mrs. Webb. Mrs. Webb says she isn't going to send Charlie winter things, as, all over 38, she has been told by Commandature, are soon to be released! Also Mrs. Moore says she and the other wives, after being 3 weeks away, are now back in Le Touquet. I wonder if this is so, and if Bunny will go to Low Wood and if so will the General go elsewhere?

Owing to boiler bursting, no potatoes for lunch!! No words can overestimate the tragedy. Instead, excellent porridge but too little of it. In afternoon inoculation again. So I had a hell of a birthday.

October 16, 1940

Today, by contrast, was perfect. Gorgeous weather, cold in morning but boiling later. Heard that Jack White and his son were released today and have gone, so apparently people do get released. Then it was announced that we would get soup and potatoes for tea!! The result was that I was able to save all my bread for breakfast and still felt quite full after some swell soup and eight spuds. Then came the best thing of the day—Sandy Youl, Tom Sarginson and Briers all got letters from their wives posted in France!! so at last the ice pack has melted.

(Poor old Sandy was so hungry yesterday, he ate his breakfast bread at tea—I offered him a slice of mine this morning, but he nobly refused.)

Sandy's wife was 7 weeks as a sort of internee at St. Marc de Barrière in Lille, but is now able to go where she likes and is off to Paris. A terrific relief to me, as it means that Bunny presumably need not stay on at St. Georges if she wants to go elsewhere. (Commandant says War will be over in a month!)

The final batch of prisoners are now in. A few days ago we got 150 men from the Orama, sunk in June. Very breezy and rowdy for first two days but now toned down.

Then came about 50 more, including an inexplicable boy of 13 in bare knees and knickerbockers. Apparently the son of a Polish Jew—his father, mother and small sister are all in different camps. *

**Since writing this, lots more prisoners have come in. March 1941 total in camp is 1,240.*

October 19, 1940

We are first sitting this week—get up at 6, moon shining brightly—white frost on roofs. I am lying on my bed after breakfast, amusing to see different occupations of the men. Arthur sweeping floor under his bed, George Pickard darning sock, Scharny sewing vest, McCandless writing up diary, Smythe having back of his neck shaved by Rex Rainer, Tom Sarginson at table studying German, Erike and Mackenzie playing chess, Brimble darning his boots, more sweeping going on in middle of room. Tom Musgrove comes in from second floor with his daily rumour.

"Blessings on him that first invented sleep—it wraps a man all round like a cloak"—Sancho Panza.

ORDERS

1. *No food to be kept in dormitories—and then we are given two days' rations ahead.*

2. *No lights in dormitories in morning—How see to get up at 6 in winter?*

3. *Must get up at 6—yet if you are third sitting, you can't get breakfast till 8:30 and there are only 5 basins and 3 baths for 180 men, who, if all rise at same time, will all want to wash at same time.*

October 30, 1940

*We are third sitting and usually lie in bed till 7:30. This morning McCandless, chef de chambre, tells us that Algy told him last night that something was going to happen this morning and to get up early. Nothing broke till 8:15, when I was doing my exercises in my yard, and a man shouted for me out of window. I went up and found everyone lined up out in corridor. Long wait, then various soldiers arrived—our nice interpreter, who told us to go over to breakfast-room. We went and he came over and led us back, after a short wait. We found corridor full of soldiers. Men went into room, each with soldier. When I went in with my soldier, interpreter came too and everything was very pleasant. They looked at my papers, but most of them had been passed by censor already. Interpreter tells me he worked for Fred Harvey on news-stand—he is so bucked today as he got Reader's Digest through the mail from America. Scare over, we are told to stay in rooms—goodness knows how long! This means breakfast now out of question, so I eat my dry bread and drink ½ a pt. of beer. From a remark interpreter dropped, I fancy this search wasn't for anything specific but is a thing they spring on you at irregular intervals. But why do it just at our breakfast hour? Subita Germanorum sunt concilia.**

*Note the next search of this kind was on February 19, 1941.

Later, at tea, we managed to get some coffee. N.B. Our Commandant went off on 10 days' leave on Saturday and everything seems to have gone wrong since then. We became third sitting, which meant that on Sunday, with reveille at 7, we didn't get breakfast till nearly 10 and coffee was all cold. Then we had carrots on Sunday, and yesterday and today we had cabbage, and not much of it. Also potatoes undercooked. No tobacco as yet, and beer considerably diminished in alcoholic content. (Story is that the man who looks after our food calculated wrongly and used up all October supplies by October 28!)

"My boy"—Young Petersen. Orange hair, very close and sleek—beret—horn-rimmed spectacles—small perky nose—mouth very small and always half open. Worst scrounger in camp.

Kandhu's comedy has been practically nonexistent in the formal atmosphere of Tost camp, but today he perked up enough to imitate a spitting cat as he was passing group of German soldiers. They also imitated cats, and this encouraged him to do a barking dog. He went on his way, much strengthened.

I am very fond of the two interpreters I have talked with—one grey-haired (43), fresh face, veteran of last war, the other, the spectacled one, who learned his English in U.S.A. (He worked for Fred Harvey hotels at newsstand, and says "Have you got me, boys?") It bears out what I have always said, that Germans are swell guys, and the only barrier between us is the one of language. I have never met an English-speaking German whom I didn't like instantly.

November 1

Great row after evening parade—we have been third sitting all week, after being first last week, and Van Sammeren announces that next week we are again first—the Dutchmen being second for third week running. Howls of fury and almost a mutiny. (Our crowd is jealous of Dutch. When we were first, they kept crowding in on us after half an hour, when we were entitled to three-quarters, and Van Sammeren ticked us off for it.) Our crowd mostly cloth-capped and Dutch very genteel, elegant young lecturers and language-school proprietors. Note—We are men without women and it is interesting to note how we relapse into boyhood—all our emotions are boyish. We have become Penrods.

When we arrived, we found the Dutch already here—very well dressed, as they had been interned near their homes, and all getting regular parcels and they had pinched all the key positions.

All went fairly well till the Orama sailors arrived and caused third sittings, where you get lunch at 2 and tea at 6. Personally, I rather like third sitting—you get unlimited coffee at tea (though danger of it being cold) and you lie in bed till late, as it is at 8:30. (Only trouble is Sundays, when reveille is at 7, first sitting at 8, i.e. third sitting doesn't get breakfast till about a quarter to 10.)

Disgusted man on parade—Bloody goblins! (Hello Gnomes.)

November 11, 1940

Posted by Bunny on October 7, my first parcel (2 kilos) arrived today. My number was read out in dormitory and I had to parade behind barbed wire outside dining building at 3. About 20 of us. We were marched off by guards with bayonets to Post Office down the drive (men about to get parcels being notoriously apt to try to escape into Upper Silesia in Winter). Presently our Lieutenant arrives and goes into inner room, whence an interpreter appears at intervals and calls out numbers. My parcel consisted of gloves—these, after I had signed for parcel, very earnest soldier pinches thoroughly, presumably to discover concealed machine guns—2 cakes—these are cut in half—2 packets of French tobacco—these are opened—2 packets of cigarettes—ditto. It is the old story—too many Oppenheim stories, or else going to cinema too much to spy films. (As a matter of fact, I believe these searches are due to the boastful books published after last war by men who escaped from prison through messages in cakes etc. BUT—a fact not clearly understood by the Germans of 1940—these were soldier prisoners, young bachelors, not married men of 50 and over with their wives and families in German hands.) (Parcel-getting just like hampers of schooldays.)
Some men had sardines opened so they must eat them at one go.

A Thought—The irritating thing about life here is the way one is being always scolded and threatened. After parade Van Sammeren appears. We are not to look out of window, or we will be deprived of privilege [of] writing letters for a month. We are not to smoke in corridors, or something will be forbidden in building. We are not to move about on parade or we will be dragged out of bed and made to parade again. We are not to have dormitory light on in morning—not to have food in dormitories or eat. Exactly like short-tempered nurse with children. "See what internees are doing and tell them they mustn't."

November 14, 1940

I must make a note of this day as one of the absolutely flawless ones of my life. It started with a glorious golden sunrise and a warmth like Spring, with a gentle west wind blowing. I had a fine breakfast, bread and jam (I had saved almost all my bread)—then a good read and then news that there was a parcel for me. I went down expecting it to be 1 kilo and it turned out to be 5, and all the sorts of things I wanted, including chocolate and my turtle-neck sweater. Just before lunch, two letters from Bunny and then announcement that there was another parcel for me. I worked on novel in morning and it came out beautifully. At 4 I got my parcel, again just what I wanted—sardines, pâté, etc., and when I got back to dormitory Czarny gave me second volume of *Good Companions*. I had a lovely tea, helped by strong rumour that men of 60 and approx. were to be released. After tea, a walk with A. Grant in park, very nice. Then up to bed, with spuds saved from lunch and sardines to look forward to for supper. All through the day the west wind blew and it was as warm as Spring. I sat out in park for half an hour before getting my parcel. Bunny's letters were sweet and happy and I really felt she was all right and that we should be together again soon. A peach of a day! Horrible outcrop of beards. Theory is that men grow them to make themselves look older and get off fatigues.

December 6, 1940

Bitter wind and snow. After parade Haskin gave me jar of meat, tea, sugar, gingerbread, four large biscuits, bit of chocolate and a bit of barley sugar, also large chunk of bread. (He now works in cookhouse and gives me potatoes every night.) Heavenly fair, especially as Arthur had Bunny's parcels. We had each saved a bit of fish stew at lunch and had mashed potatoes with it, and I had a bottle of beer. Then smoke in corridor.

Instance of ingenuity in Camp. Dutch barber is asked by man accustomed to dye his grey hair every month if he can dye it. Later, barber is seen crouching on his bed, holding lighted match under jam jar of water, soft soap and boot blacking. He sells the stuff to man for 83 pfennigs and man is very satisfied.

Bores on parade. Great trap is getting next to a bore. We line up at least 1/4 an hour before Kommandant comes, so as to have us all in order and counted and announcements made, so one is at the mercy of a bore. There is one remorseless storyteller who breaks off story when we right turn into next corridor and then goes on with it. I shall never forget Butcher and the story of his cough, as Kommandant was late and we stood there 1/4 an hour and I was feeling weak with a cold.

General note. We lay great stress here on the morning greeting. One goes to breakfast in a flurry of "good mornings"! The manners of nearly all the men are charming—to me, at least. They beg your pardon when they pass you close and always stand aside for me to get through doors. I find myself liking them more and more.

December 11, 1940

Today was one of our fractious days, when we became more like small boys than ever. Word was brought by Corporal that a man from sailors' room was to come to sleep in our dormitory. Apparently he had asked Kommandant if he could, because he disliked the younger set in his room. Instantly we were up in arms. Erike, the old fool, taking advantage of being able to speak German, tried to show Corporal that by squeezing the beds on our side together there would be room for one more bed. (He has always been jealous of our beds.) Charlie Webb thereupon refused to move his bed—he said he was entitled to that amount of space between beds. Erike then said Charlie's chair wasn't Charlie's chair but a communal chair, and Charlie said he wasn't talking about the chair but about the space. Arthur Grant then urged Erike to stop being jealous of those who had merely had the luck of the draw. Erike said *"Well, you come over here and try one of these double-deckers,"* which enabled Arthur to score off him badly, by saying that he *had* slept over there for some nights till asked to move across. Erike then accused Arthur Grant of treating the radiator as a private radiator when it was really a communal radiator, and I told Erike to shut up. Erike said *"I won't shut up. Can't I talk?"* Upon which, Smyth, who was trying to write a letter, closed the debate by saying *"No you bloody well can't. Shut up and let me write my letter. You're always talking. When you're not talking chess, you're talking balls!"* Exactly like a row in a junior dormitory at school.

At lunch, another row. This time about working for the Germans. Tom Sarginson very truculent. Said he was sick of men saying they would work at their own job at home but not while in camp—pointed out that in former case they would still be working for Germans. He for some reason signalled out poor old George Pickard for attack. Sandy said he could work at his own job, but only in Calais. Then somehow Tom fell foul of Reggie Rainey, accusing him of being willing to accept money and food from England, thereby weakening England's resources. Reggie got very warm and said he didn't want money. Tom said then why was he always borrowing it. Sandy said there were 30,000 English prisoners in Germany—England was spending £11,000,000 a day on war, so a parcel for each wouldn't weaken her resources appreciably. Fortunately, just as we were all getting heated on about three different subjects at same time, the red-headed boy came in to fumble in radiator for his rags to clean table, and everyone turned on him, saying he had no business in here till everyone had left. (Maybe better to have him sneak in and sit down to his lunch.)

These rows start between A and B and then C butts in and takes fight away from A, mixing it with B till interrupted by D.

There are 64 men in our dormitory, the cream of the camp we think.

These have to be saluted:

All officers, officers of Medical Corps, also company Commanders and Guards posted about Camp (except Guards on duty).

In practice one merely beams at the Corporal who is our Company Commander, looking on him as an old friend. (Difficult to tell an officer from Senior NCO's, except by little sword.)

When Internees are standing about in groups, the first to see Officer shouts "Achtung!"* whereat all face officer at attention with hands on seam of trousers! (I am too apt merely to grin.) Alas when Officer enters room indoors, the head must then also be uncovered. Internees come out of saluting position at command "Ruhren" by the superior. (It sounds like "Rear Lights.") "Internees when passing a superior will look at him and assume an erect bearing." (When I do this, I look a perfect ass.)

DAILY TIMETABLE

6 a.m.	Reveille. (Sunday 7 a.m.)
6–7	Morning toilet, making of beds.
7–8:30	Breakfast, cleaning of rooms, bathrooms, lavatories, passages and staircases.
8:45	Morning parade on weekdays. (10 a.m. on Sundays.)
9:30	Inspection of the sick in hospital by camp doctor.
9:30–12:30 p.m.	Occupation of internees according to orders issued by the Lagerführer (i.e. fatigues).
12:30–2:30	Dinner and washing of utensils in three sittings.
2:30–4:30	Occupation etc.—as above.
4:30–6	Supper—in three sittings.
6–8	Free.
8–8:15	Evening Parade in corridors.
9:15	Lights Out.

Discs—*must* be worn round neck.

Sick—Sick men report after morning parade to their Company Commander, who enters them in the sick list and sends them, with the list, under guard† to Hospital. Doctor examines patient, inscribes against his name "fit for duty," "mildly ill" or "to be received in hospital." Dental patients are sent with guard to dentist—each getting about 5 minutes.

Clothes mending—small repairs done by internees—larger ones at tailor's shop.

Punishments—Smoking stopped, canteen closed, letter-writing stopped, solitary confinement. (Run of Cinderella interrupted by confinement of Cinder-

*This is good, but gives too much scope for humorists. A man can have a lot of quiet fun by shouting "Achtung" and watching his fellows assume an erect bearing when no-one there.
†You can't move a step without guard.

ella, *Prince Charming, Dandini and Fairy Godmother for singing provocative anti-G songs in corridor.)*

February 16

Parsons gets two days' solitary confinement for writing "That's What Italy Thought" on poster of bomb dropping on London, hung outside doctor's room. He comes out and tells us about what it is like. You get loaf of bread per day, beer bottle of water in morning and evening—plank bed with no mattress—no books, tobacco etc. Monotony very bad. He can see out of window, sees men carrying dixies, assumes it is lunch time, later sees them carrying potatoes and realises first time it was simply the 9:30 water for tea. Bitter disappointment.

Two blankets allowed, but taken away during day.

February 19, 1941

Typical bad day. We start by parading out of doors in cold mist and suddenly place becomes full of soldiers with bayonets, every officer on the list, and interpreters carrying large baskets, so we know there is going to be a search of dormitories. After standing for an age, while sailors' room is searched, we march back to our corridor and line up there for another age. Then we go in groups into room and a soldier accompanies each of us to his bed, where he examines books etc. (For some reason, haversacks are being confiscated.) I am all right, as everyone knows I am writing novel. Then we go into corridor again, and eventually all is over, but too late for hot water for making tea, work and so on, it being now about 10:45. So loaf about till lunch, feeling rottenly tired after a bad night and all this standing about. The next thing that happens is that White House is closed till 3—for no apparent reason—so I go to Room 404 to type and find church choir practice going on. I can't disturb them with clatter of typewriter, so I try White House again. It is open now and I settle down in my room. Suddenly a measured voice from outside— someone lecturing on paper manufacture. I feel my typing is interrupting lecture, so I hurry through and go out, to find it is merely a man rehearsing lecture to empty room! Then at end of day, as usual, everything comes right. I am told two parcels for me at 9 next morning, which means missing parade, and corridor very cosy, so all well.

February 22, 1941

Fifteen new internees have arrived, and once more the problem arises—where to put them? Again the sinister figures of Jock Monaghan, the Corporal and

George Travers are to be seen conferring in dormitory. Eventually, it is decided that two double-decker beds go in on our side, but Arthur and I are still safe. One takes a sort of melancholy interest in watching the dormitory become more and more like a box of sardines. One feels that we must soon reach saturation point. The maddening thing is that Lagerführer Buchelt realises we are overcrowded and he is always saying so—but there is some bland authority in Berlin who looks on this camp as composed of elastic or like one of those bookcases which expand.

March 2, 1941

I am just starting work. Arthur has just brought tea to dining-room, when Tom Sarginson comes in to say there is a special parade at 10:50. I assume a mere clothes parade with our corporal—instead, about 6 new officers come and inspect us—we have to turn to wall and raise right foot to see if boots all right—what is wrong with left foot apparently does not interest them.

I find standing next to me the new man, of whom we have heard. He has been here in a cell since Saturday—came from camp near Nuremberg and is very sniffy about conditions here. Very public-school manner—clipped Oxford voice. Apparently, at his camp lights out was at 10 and they sat up talking and cooking till 3 a.m. and got up in morning when they pleased—no parades—Red Cross parcels in great quantities. Odd effect on me is of feeling like a boy at school when oldish new boy arrives who has been at Eton or somewhere. I feel annoyed at aspersions he is casting on the dear old College and resent his talk of the superiority of his camp. "I'm not going to like it here," he says in a very superior manner. "What's the food like? How many to a loaf?" I say "Five." "At our place it was four." G. Pickard timidly says it used to be 4 1/4 but he brushes this aside. He asks "When can I get my tea in the morning?" This one we can answer, as it is our only strong point. It seems he likes his cup of tea at 9:30 ("When I have my breakfast") and we can do him this, as our hot water comes up then. "How do I manage for shaving water? Out of the tap?" I say "Yes, out of the cold tap." He is horrified. (No barbed wire at his camp.)

March 25, 1941

I found sailors playing cricket in my yard—real bat and stump. I hadn't played for 27 years and found it hard to get down to balls. I bowled and got one wicket, great fun. (Ball goes through barbed wire and slim sailor is shoved through after it.)

March 26, 1941

Mackenzie has been teaching red-haired Corporal enough English to get us up in morning. First time he tried it he just shouted "Get opp!" and Mackenzie spoke to him like a father, with result that next day he said "Get opp, gentlemans, if you please," causing great good feeling.

Arthur at dentist, sits next to sailor who is to have tooth out. Wilson comes in and says "Any here for extraction?" Sailor does not move. Arthur says "Weren't you going to have extraction?" Sailor: "What's that?" "Have a tooth out." Sailor: "Why the hell can't he speak English?"

March 27, 1941

Order on parade. We are to look at Officer and keep looking at him as he passes.

March 31, 1941

March has been the worst month so far—beastly weather and nothing good happening. Today was the climax. After an extra-long morning parade, I went over to dining-room and at 10:15 was told there was another parade. It seemed that the Snake (the man who was "threatened" at Huy) was working on radio in lower dining-room and claimed an electric switch had been stolen from his bag. Macintosh told us we had an hour for man to own up and he would not be punished. We lined up for an hour. Then we were told we were "confined to barracks" till further notice. We marched to and from lunch and tea with a guard—lots of chaos and delay of course. At about 6:30 we were told the ban was off. Trouble from authorities point of view is that we are already confined to barracks. We can be stopped walking in park but 90% of camp don't know there is a park and spend all their time in corridor. (Vast school of thought holds that Snake broke the switch and was afraid to own up, as this was the second one he had broken.)

"They won't kill us and they can't put us in the family way, so what have we got to worry about?"

The great war is not the one raging outside but the war in dormitory between fresh-air lovers and frowsters (opening window-door).

RANDOM NOTES

1. *Washing. Full dress the rule. One man washes with his hat on. 5 basins—3 baths—everybody has to get up at same time, so best way of securing bath is to get up earlier. Today (May 31) there were 19 men in room besides myself.*

2. *Morning hot water at 8:45. Today (May 31) for some reason none was*

issued. Terrific tragedy as it means not being able to fill thermos and so no afternoon tea.

3. Room 404. Sailors dancing—cricket.

4. Cricket in park—dirt pitch with pump, just where bowler runs—tree stumps— trees all round—ball goes out through barbed wire and we have to tie two bats together with handkerchief and grope for it: If it goes out at other end, sentry prods it back with bayonet. (Trees meet overhead, making light very tricky.)

Lanquer inspected dormitories and was horrified at tenement aspect of clothes line—made new rules* —no lines in dormitories and no longer lines scattered anywhere in grounds, but only in two courtyards. Terrific improvement of course. One can now walk about in dormitory without finding one's head draped by wet flannel drawers.

Rumour that all Red Cross tins are to be opened or stored!! Picture the colossal work of it. At least 8,000 tins every 10 days—it will take hours getting a small batch of men through parcels office. Probably only a rumour.

This morning (June 13) after parade Lanquer paid surprise visit to dormitories. A little like Royalty inspecting a model home exhibition, or the Earl judging cottage gardens. My bed was in rare shape and I stood by it proudly.

Another new order is that only articles of daily use are to be kept in dormitories.

There may I end what happened in Tost.

I have no entries between May 28 and June 20.

---

*No tins on window sills.

11

The Broadcasts: Berlin

Camp was really great fun. I played cricket again after twenty-seven years, and played havoc with the opposition with slow leg-breaks. I was in the middle of an over when they came and told me to pack. . . .

I really do think there is nothing on earth to compare with the Englishman in a cloth cap and muffler. . . . The War Graves Commission gardeners are the salt of the earth.

I got very religious in camp. There was a Salvation Army colonel there who held services every Sunday. There is something about the atmosphere of a camp which does something to you in that way.[1]

"Camp was really great fun!" And the amazing fact is that he meant it. Never since he left Dulwich had Plum attained full membership of any human society. In the camp, gallantry, endurance, and loyalty to the gang were more important than a capacity for intimate relationships; rumour and jokes took the place of conversation; and the schoolboy code of honour became once more a necessity in the face of the alien authority. Plum was in his element. Because of his age and fame, he was offered a room of his own at Tost, but he refused it, preferring to share the conditions of his comrades. During the period that a man named Buchelt was Lagerführer,* he was allowed the use of a hired typewriter, for which he paid 18 marks a month, but apart from this the only favour he accepted was that of a room where he could work, and even here he had to share it with a saxophonist and a tap dancer. If his temperament and the experiences of his youth had left him singularly ill-equipped for what lay immediately ahead, even the most censorious must reflect how admirably they had fitted him for the testing months which lay behind.

Internees were normally released at the age of sixty, but in June 1941, when he was sent for and told to pack, Plum was four months short of this

*The word *lager* can be translated in several ways. In this case it means "camp." The Lagerführer was in charge of the prisoners under the camp Kommandant.

age. The reasons for his early release have never been completely established, but the visit on 26 December 1940 to Tost of an American news-
paperman named Angus Thuermer must be regarded as the starting point
of two different but contributory series of events. Mr. Thuermer interviewed Plum and afterwards published a photograph showing him muffled
up in a dressing gown and looking extremely old and thin. Guy Bolton
and his wife saw this photograph and were very much distressed by it.
They organized a petition to the German authorities to secure his release,
Virginia Bolton going to enormous trouble to get a distinguished list of
signatories. She secured twenty-four names, including not merely those of
senators and congressmen, but of the president and secretary of the Authors' League, the secretary of the Dramatists' Guild, and others whose
names were well known in the theatre and in the literary world. The
petition, which was delivered to the chargé d'affaires at the German Em-
bassy in Washington, read as follows:

> We the undersigned seek your good offices in the forwarding of a plea
> to the appropriate authorities in your home country in reference to the
> writer, Mr. Pelham Grenville Wodehouse of Villa Low Wood, Le Tou-
> quet, France.
>   We are informed that Mr. Wodehouse is under detention by the Ger-
> man control and we, speaking for his American friends, his American
> readers, and the various literary societies of which he is a member, beg
> you, Sir, to employ your influence to obtain his release.
>   We believe that any restraint that may be placed on Mr. Wodehouse's
> movements is purely formal and is not based upon any act of his. Further
> than this, may we respectfully point out to you that Mr. Wodehouse is
> fifty-nine years of age, that he has never had any military or political
> connections and that without exception his writings are of a light, humor-
> ous order, completely free from propaganda. His friends are desirous that
> he should be permitted to return to the United States where he made his
> home for many years and we will be grateful to you if you can assist in
> bringing this about.

There is no evidence that this letter had any effect, but it was from
leading citizens of a neutral power which the Germans would still have
preferred to placate, and it must at least have drawn attention to Plum's
plight. He knew himself of other efforts being made on his behalf from
letters written to him by Mrs. Demaree Bess, the wife of the European
correspondent of *The Saturday Evening Post*. In the last of these she said:

> We have been assured that the Foreign Office is quite agreeable to your
> release, and it is only necessary to obtain the consent of the Army. Now,
> at long last, we have the satisfaction of knowing that the matter has been
> presented properly to the men in charge. There have been a number of

signs recently which cause us to think that our hopes may not be much longer deferred.[2]

For nearly forty years after these events the petition organized by the Boltons and the letters from Mrs. Bess have been regarded as the most likely cause of Plum's release four months before he was sixty, the plan to get him to broadcast following naturally and without previous calculation from it. From leading citizens of the United States, whom the Germans still hoped to keep neutral, they drew attention to the plight of a distinguished man of letters. However, with the publication of the Cussen Report we learn for the first time of a conversation which some commentators have believed to be evidence of a far more calculated sequence of events, also set in motion by Angus Thuermer's visit to the camp. Here is what Plum said in his statement to Major Cussen:

> The first time any question of broadcasting ever arose was in the course of a very brief conversation which I had with the Lagerführer in his office. This must have been some time in May 1941 because he left the camp towards the end of that month and his reason for sending for me was to tell me that I had to turn in the typewriter which he had hired for me. He referred to my article. This was an article which had been arranged for by Thuermer. It was to deal humorously with my camp experiences and was to appear, he told me, in the American magazine *Time*. What happened in America I cannot say—possibly *Time* considered the article too light— but it appeared in *The Saturday Evening Post* and was entitled "My War with Germany." Among the subjects I dealt with in it were the repulsiveness of the internees' beards, the probable effect on my table manners of the dining methods at Tost and other things of a similar kind. It was lighthearted throughout.
>
> The Lagerführer told me how much he had enjoyed the article and then said "Why don't you do some broadcasts on similar lines for your American readers?" I said "I should love to" or "There's nothing I should like better"—or some similar phrase. These remarks were quite casual and made no impression on my mind.[3]

Given that it was part of the German propaganda effort to persuade Englishmen to broadcast on their wavelengths, it seems at first unlikely that Lagerführer Buchelt's remarks were of a purely casual kind, or that having received Plum's answer, he made no use of it. Plum himself said (although three years later, talking to Cussen): "The inference I draw from this episode is either (a) that he had been told to sound me as to my willingness to broadcast or (b) that having been informed by me that I was willing—as I have described above—he reported to Berlin."

For these events and all those which immediately followed Plum is the chief witness, although the more important statements of his other accounts have been confirmed by Werner Plack of the German Foreign Office. There is no other evidence of this conversation with the Lagerführer, which cannot, in any case, be considered in isolation, but only in conjunction with the rest of his account. For the moment, it seems reasonable to assume that since it took place sometime in May, he had no reason to recall it when on 21 June he was suddenly sent for and told to pack his things. He had a companion with him who was being released because he was sixty, and he said to Cussen: "I also had in mind of course the activities of Mr. and Mrs. Demaree Bess."[4] There was therefore no reason why he should have felt surprise or suspicion when, after packing his bags, he was escorted with the other man by two guards on a night train to Berlin. Here is his account of what happened next:

> We arrived at the Friedrichstrasse station at about seven in the morning, and after a sketchy breakfast at the buffet trailing through the Mittelstrasse, began looking for a hotel. In Germany, for some extraordinary reason the football cup final is played towards the end of June, and this happened to be the day of the fixture. The city being in consequence full of out-of-town visitors, there were no rooms available at any of the five hotels which we tried, and the Gestapo men then decided to make for the Adlon.[5]

The statement that on 21 June 1941, the day Plum arrived in Berlin (and, incidentally, the day Hitler declared war on Russia), the German equivalent of the Cup Final was played there is true, the two competing teams being Schalke 04 and Vienna (Austria was then a part of Germany). However, this fact should not obscure the more important one that the Adlon had been taken over for the use of the Foreign Office, because Plum stayed there again from time to time until he left Germany. Speaking of later visits he wrote:

> We stayed at the Adlon because we were not allowed to stay anywhere else. We made several attempts to move to less conspicuous hotels and we also tried a number of *pensions,* but without success. At our first visit to these hotels and *pensions* we were always informed that we could have accommodation, at our second that they were full up.[6]

On 21 June, when Plum first arrived at the Adlon, he was allowed, after a wash and a rest, to walk in the courtyard behind it. Here he was presently joined by Major Baron Erich (called Raven) von Barnekow. Describing this meeting afterwards Plum wrote:

> Baron von Barnekow was one of my oldest friends, a German who had been living in America for the last twenty years and had, I learned, just returned to Germany to marry his cousin. We had seen a great deal of

one another during my last visits to Hollywood, where he had moved from San Francisco. He was, I think, the most confirmed anti-Nazi I have ever known. (A year later he was found shot outside his hunting lodge in Pomerania.)*⁷

And to Cussen he said:

With regard to Major von Barnekow I cannot remember where and when I first met him, but I think it was in New York in 1929. He was our great friend in Hollywood, paying long visits to us when he could get away from San Francisco where he was a stockbroker. He was completely American—nothing German about him. . . . He and I had a long conversation. He told me he had been trying to get me exchanged for a German manufacturer of screws who was an internee in England. He told me of his cousin the Baroness von Bodenhausen to whom he was engaged to be married. This surprised me as the last time I'd seen him he had been engaged to Kay Francis, the motion picture star.† He said he wanted me to go to stay at the Baroness's home "Degenershausen" in the Harz mountains about 17 miles from Magdeburg. She would be in Berlin in a day or two and would take me down there.⁸

No great imagination is needed to understand how immensely reassuring this meeting must have seemed to Plum, who had met no one from the outside world for almost a year, had no idea what the future held, and had neither money nor clothes. Nor would he have felt any apprehension when, as they went into the hotel, they were joined by Werner Plack, because Plack had also spent some years in Hollywood, where, failing as a film actor, he had become a wine merchant. The Wodehouses had known him slightly. "I remembered Plack from Hollywood," Plum told Cussen. "I had never known him very well but had met him occasionally at parties."⁹ Von Barnekow accounted for the otherwise suspicious fact that the two men were there together by explaining that Plack was now in the Foreign Office and had told him that Plum was coming. He then went off to the Hotel Bristol, where he was staying, to get both money and clothes for Plum, who had nothing but the suit he was wearing and two shirts. He left him talking to Plack. During this conversation Plack asked him whether he would like to broadcast, and Plum immediately replied that he would.

Plack then said that he would have Plum brought to his office the next

---

*Immediately after this meeting von Barnekow went to the Eastern Front, and a year later he committed suicide.

†The engagement to Kay Francis was broken by mutual consent on the outbreak of war. Von Barnekow had been an officer in the Richthofen squadron in the first war and returned to Germany to join the Luftwaffe.

day and hurried off to make the necessary arrangements. After he had gone, there occurred another meeting, one which Plum recounted without comment, but which must surely have seemed a strange coincidence even to his uninquiring mind.

> Shortly after this I met Lagerführer Buchelt in the lobby. He was in civilian clothes. He congratulated me on being released and I told him I was broadcasting my experiences. He made no reference to our previous conversation. He suggested a visit that afternoon to Potsdam.
>
> We spent the afternoon at Potsdam, returning in time for dinner—the party comprising [the man who left camp with Plum, whose name for reasons of security is blocked out on each occasion that it appears in this report], the two plainclothesmen and myself.[10]

Since the publication of the Cussen Report, all commentators have taken it for granted that the sequence of events began with the conversation with the Lagerführer, who naturally reported it to the Foreign Office, thereby prompting Plum's early release and accounting for the presence at the Adlon not merely of Werner Plack, but also of von Barnekow and Lagerführer Buchelt. At luncheon in Richard Usborne's house on 4 March 1981, Werner Plack categorically denied that the Lagerführer had made a report or that there was any reason for Wodehouse's release other than the petitions and the fact that he was within a few months of being sixty. When asked how it was, in that case, that von Barnekow went to the Adlon to meet Plum, he replied: "Because I told him he was coming." And he insisted that the broadcasts followed naturally and without previous intention on the conversation he himself had with Plum that day. When he was asked to explain how in that case Buchelt also came to be there, he seemed very much surprised and said he knew nothing of it. Herr Plack was speaking of events which had taken place almost exactly forty years before, but he was unshakable on his recollection of them.

On the morning of 23 June, the day after his arrival in Berlin, Plum was taken to Werner Plack's office, where he met Dr. Paul Schmidt, the head of the department, who said he had read his books and made some complimentary remarks.* Here it was explained to him that his broadcasts would be recorded on wax, and he almost certainly agreed to write and speak five.

The following day, 24 June, the plainclothes guards handed him his passport and disappeared from his life, as did the internee who had left camp with him. He was, within certain obvious limits, a free man.

---

*Dr. Paul Schmidt was the same man who acted as Hitler's interpreter; he was the author of the book *Hitler's Interpreter,* published in translation by Heinemann in 1951. He is not to be confused with Dr. Paul Schmidt the Press Director.

When he reached this point in his interrogation by Cussen, Plum said:

It is now that my recollection of events begins to get blurred, and it was at this point that the correspondents began to flock round me. I told them that I was going to broadcast. I can remember broadcasting with Flannery, but I cannot remember the date and I recall meeting one of Hearst's men and arranging to write an article on camp life for the *Cosmopolitan* magazine.[11]

Harry Flannery, to whom he refers, was the correspondent of the Columbia Broadcasting Company, and had been informed by Plack that Plum was expected in Berlin. He is important because in a book called *Assignment to Berlin*, which contains inaccuracies of a damaging kind, his was until now the only published account of the events connected with Plum's broadcasts from Germany.* Earlier in his book Flannery had written of a previous meeting with Plum, when he visited the camp at Tost at the beginning of 1941. Speaking of this, he gave a not very recognizable description of Plum's appearance and then wrote:

"Suppose you were talking to a Columbia audience, what would you say?" he was asked.

Wodehouse beamed. He rubbed his hands together, raised his voice, and acted as if there was a microphone in front of him.

"Hello," he said, "hope I'll be seeing you soon. Anyone in America who would like to send me some chocolates can do so without offending me. I want to make the United States my headquarters from now on, and I'd be there now if it hadn't been for that income-tax trouble in 1936." He added: "That's all settled now."

Flannery goes on to say that Wodehouse dropped his act for the microphone and, after saying that he was writing a novel called *Money in the Bank*, gave a description of the conditions in which he wrote. He then continues:

Wodehouse asked if there were any motion-picture offers for his latest novel. "I hope my agents know I'm receptive," he declared. "And say," he went on, "what does the United States government do about the income tax of a person in one of these places? How do I pay my income tax?"

It was suggested that the government might be left to worry about that.

"But they find you, you know," said Wodehouse.[12]

In the course of time Plum grew to dislike Flannery almost more than anyone else he met in his life. "I couldn't contradict lies being told about me at the time," he wrote to Townend. "Flannery, for instance, not a

---

*I accept David Jasen's account, which is short and written to a brief supplied by Plum himself.

word of truth. . . . And all the conversations he repeats as taking place between himself and me are non-existent. . . . I wish, by the way, that when people invent scenes with me they wouldn't give me such rotten dialogue. Can you imagine me saying some of the things Flannery puts in my mouth?" And in a different context, he also wrote:

> In the whole course of my literary life the only interviewer who ever quoted with absolute accuracy what I said was Milton Mackaye about twenty years ago. All the others have altered and embroidered.
>
> As a rule, this does not matter much. If an interviewer says to you, "What do you think of our high buildings?" and you reply, "I think your high buildings are wonderful," and it comes out as "I think your high buildings are wonderful. I'd like to see some of those income tax guys jump off the top of them," no harm is done. The sentiment pleases the general public, and even the officials of the Internal Revenue Department probably smile indulgently, as men who know that they are going to have the last laugh. But when a war is in progress, it is kinder to the interviewee not to indulge the imagination.[13]

In this second passage, Plum is voicing a common complaint of people who are interviewed by the press. The trouble is not, as he wrote to Townend, that pressmen invent the whole thing, but that they embroider the truth in a manner that is invariably annoying and can be damaging. Thus no one who had ever met Wodehouse would believe in the description of the act with the microphone in Flannery's account, or that Plum began a sentence "And say . . ." (to the end of his life he spoke as an Englishman). But the introduction of the subject of income tax rings true, in particular the remark "But they find you, you know." In this way, with a mixture of truth and invention, Flannery succeeded in belittling Wodehouse—probably for no better reason than to make his own account more interesting. Far worse, he leaves the reader in doubt about what is true and what false. Plum was justified in complaining of Flannery, because he wrote his equally colourful account of their second meeting with even less regard for the facts.

He interviewed Plum at the Adlon and cabled a story to his office, and he writes: "Late the next day a cable came from Paul White asking me to put Wodehouse on the air in an interview." Flannery says that he therefore wrote a script and checked it with Wodehouse.

> Among other questions, I planned to ask him what he thought of the Russian Campaign. Wodehouse proposed saying: "The bigger they are, the harder they fall." I cautioned him against that. "That predicts a Nazi victory," I said. "You can't do that."
>
> "Why not?" he asked.

"We're fighting the Nazis. Any such reply would be propaganda or worse, coming from you. You can't say that."

Wodehouse thought a moment.

"Do you know," he said, "I wouldn't have thought of that."*

The Flannery interview, as it went on the air, was as follows:

FLANNERY: What is your status now, Mr. Wodehouse?

WODEHOUSE: Well, I must say I really don't know, Mr. Flannery. I'm still a prisoner, I suppose, more or less. I mean, if I wanted to go to Switzerland or somewhere, I imagine there would be objections. But I'm living here at the Adlon—have a suite up on the third floor, a very nice one, too—and I can come and go as I please.

FLANNERY: Do you mind being a prisoner of war in this fashion, Mr. Wodehouse?

WODEHOUSE: Not a bit. As long as I have a typewriter and plenty of paper and a room to work in, I'm fine.

FLANNERY: I believe you wrote a book while you were in the internment camp.

WODEHOUSE: Yes, the only one in thirty years which I've written by hand and not on the typewriter. It was slow work at first, but I gradually got used to working with a pencil. *Money in the Bank* I called it, and I've just heard that the script has been safely shipped to the United States, which is a load off my mind. After I'd done that one, I wrote a hundred pages of another. I call it *Full Moon*, because my characters are more moonstruck in it even than usual.

FLANNERY: Do the books tell anything about the life of a prisoner of war, Mr. Wodehouse?

WODEHOUSE: Good Lord, no, Mr. Flannery. There are enough other people writing about the war, and my readers, I believe, would rather have something different. But I'll tell you something about the war and my work that's been bothering me a good deal. I'm wondering whether the kind of people and the kind of England I write about will live after the war—whether England wins or not, I mean.

FLANNERY: Your characters will always live, Mr. Wodehouse. Maybe just in a different setting.

WODEHOUSE: That's interesting. I've been wondering.

FLANNERY: What do you think of the new phase of the war—the German-Russian—Mr. Wodehouse?

---

*It must be remembered that until the day before Plum had been interned for a year and knew little of the progress of the war.

WODEHOUSE: Well, the thing that strikes me most is how little worked up the German people get about it. I'd have thought they would have been feverishly excited, but they don't even seem to talk about it. And the guards who were looking after me that Sunday never even so much as bought an extra.

FLANNERY: You had guards, then, Mr. Wodehouse, when you first came to Berlin?

WODEHOUSE: Yes, a couple of chaps who brought me here from the camp. They left the other morning. It was sort of funny, you know. They took me around and showed me Berlin, and they hadn't even seen it before themselves. We went to the Olympic Stadium and down to Potsdam and back on a steamer on the Wannsee. The Wannsee made me feel I was back in the United States. It was just like Lake Hopatcong, or one of those places.

FLANNERY: Did your guards speak English—or did you speak German, Mr. Wodehouse?

WODEHOUSE: No. That was another funny thing.

FLANNERY: How did they show you around, then?

WODEHOUSE: Oh, they just poked me in the ribs and pointed at things. I understood.

FLANNERY: About the camp—the prisoners there were all English, I suppose.

WODEHOUSE: Technically English, yes, but two thirds of them couldn't speak a word of English. They came from all over the place—Norway, the Netherlands, Belgium, France, and parts of Germany. They spoke all kinds of languages—people with English passports for one reason or other, I suppose.

FLANNERY: Up here in Berlin do you find that many people speak English?

WODEHOUSE: In the time I've been here, it seems as if everyone does. I've met dozens of people—most of them in the last few days, correspondents from every country in the world, I think. There was one to see me this morning from Iceland, I think it was. Charming fellows, but such an awful lot of them.

FLANNERY: Anything you'd like to say, Mr. Wodehouse, about the United States?

WODEHOUSE: Yes, I'd like to be back there again. You see, I've always thought of the United States as sort of my country—lived there almost all the time since 1909—and I long to get back there once more. But I guess there's nothing I can do about that now, except write stories for you people. I hope you continue to like them. Well, good night, everybody.

DAVIES [from America]: Mr. Wodehouse's many friends here in the United States will be glad to know that he is free and that he is apparently comfortable and happy. Mr. Wodehouse seems to be more fortunate than most of the other Englishmen in his internment camp, whose release would perhaps have had less publicity value for the Germans, and, of course, he was only in an internment camp to begin with, which is a very different thing from a concentration camp. People who get out of concentration camps, such as Dachau, for instance— well, in the first place, not a great many of them get out, and when they do, they are seldom able to broadcast.

In his book Flannery quotes this broadcast interview in full and then goes on:

> Columbia signed off. I complimented Wodehouse on adjusting himself to the shifts in the script and said he was a good broadcaster. He said nothing. He was lost in thought. As we walked from the booth to leave the building, Wodehouse revealed that he was thinking of Davies's remarks.
> "Nasty of him, wasn't it?" he said.

Flannery goes on to say that he accompanied Wodehouse back to his room, where he heard him answer a call from a representative of the Associated Press.

> "Why am I going to broadcast for the Germans? Well, they asked me; that's all. No, there are no other reasons. Good-bye."

Flannery says that Wodehouse was puzzled by the question, and he decided to explain it to him.

> "It's none of my business," I said. "You can broadcast for the Nazis if you wish; that's up to you. But none of us Americans would do it. The mere fact of our being on a German radio programme, even if we didn't speak, but played a piano or violin, would be propaganda. We would be aiding the Nazis. They would make capital of it."
> Wodehouse was not convinced.
> "But we are not at war with Germany," he said, considering himself an American. (He had not been in England for seventeen years but had neglected to apply for United States citizenship. "I just put it off," he said, "it was so much bother.")
> I replied to his remark on the war.
> "Officially we are not at war with the Nazis, but actually it's about the same."
> "But," Wodehouse protested, "my scripts won't be censored. I can't, for the life of me, see what all the fuss is about."

Flannery says—and this is significant—that he thought Wodehouse must have talked to Plack about this, because soon afterwards Plack suggested to him that the idea of broadcasting for the Germans be dropped in favour of a series over Columbia. He asked Plack whether he had also offered the series to NBC, and on Plack replying that he had, he cabled Paul White. The representatives of both American wavelengths refused to do it. Now Flannery goes on:

> By this time the Wodehouse plot was evident. It was one of the best Nazi publicity stunts of the war, the first with a human angle. That was because it was not the work of Dr. Goebbels, but of Hollywood-wise Plack instead. Plack had gone to the camp near Gleiwitz to see Wodehouse, found that the author was completely without political sense, and had an idea. He suggested to Wodehouse that in return for being released from the prison camp he write a series of broadcasts about his experiences; there would be no censorship and he would put them on the air himself. In making that proposal Plack showed that he knew his man. He knew that Wodehouse made fun of the English in all his stories and that he seldom wrote in any other way, that he was still living in the period about which he wrote and had no conception of Nazism and all it meant. Wodehouse was his own Bertie Wooster.
>
> Plack knew that the stories would tell some unpleasant truths about the Nazis, but that they would all be lightened by the Wodehouse wit. He knew that Wodehouse would not be dangerously critical; he never was. He could be trusted to write an uncensored script, and since he was Wodehouse he would gain an audience for the Nazi programmes. Thus people might be lured into hearing the general Nazi propaganda line, but even if they heard no more than Wodehouse, some of the criticism of the Nazis would be averted by Wodehouse himself. [14]

The last two paragraphs make Flannery's account of the first importance. He states unequivocally that Plack went to Tost, saw Wodehouse, and suggested to him that if he would make a series of broadcasts he would be released to do this—the most damaging statement that has ever been made about the whole affair, and one that until now has not been answered publicly. Here are the facts.

In 1945 Wodehouse wrote from Paris to Michael Joseph, Flannery's London publishers, a letter in which he quoted the paragraph in Flannery's account which begins, "By this time the Wodehouse plot was evident," and then went on:

> I understand that *Assignment to Berlin* had a wide circulation in England and that the passage which I have quoted has done me a great deal of damage. I have not read the book, but I was told by a friend of mine in Berlin, an Englishwoman, the widow of a German, that words to this

effect occurred in it, and I immediately, anticipating what the effect would be of such an accusation, took the precaution of obtaining signed statements from Herr Plack and from the Lagerführer of my camp, denying that any such meeting had taken place. I had never seen Herr Plack in my life until I was released and taken to Berlin, when we were introduced by the late Baron von Barnekow, an old Hollywood friend of mine. In short, my agreement to broadcast my camp experiences was made after my release and not as the result of a bargain with the German authorities.

The only explanation I can think of is that Mr. Flannery misunderstood Herr Plack. On the occasions when I met him, I always found Herr Plack's English very difficult to follow. If Mr. Flannery cares to write me a letter admitting that he was mistaken, I shall not pursue the matter.

The end of the letter is characteristically amiable, and the statement that Plum had never seen Plack is untrue. Since it does not materially alter anything, it seems to be the kind of exaggeration of a point common in conversation but more unusual in writing. Because of this, it must be emphasized that Plum denied to the end of his life that Plack went to Tost, and Herr Plack also denied it, in letters to Richard Usborne and in conversation with him and with me. In the course of time (5 September 1945) Flannery replied:

> Your letter of 16 July 1945 denies that Werner Plack, of the German Foreign Office, met you while you were in the internment camp near Gleiwitz, and declares you did not meet Plack until you were brought to Berlin.
>
> That may be true. Whether Plack went to the camp himself, had someone else go, or arranged your release on information otherwise obtained from the camp, is irrelevant. In any case, Herr Plack told me that he had not only arranged your broadcasts but those of others to follow planned to attract listeners to the Nazis' programs.

That is really not good enough. The question of whether the agreement for Wodehouse to broadcast was made before or after his release cannot be irrelevant, since on it depends the question of whether the broadcasts were made in return for his release. Flannery's credibility as a witness is destroyed partly by the facts, but altogether by his attitude to them. It is astonishing that having written and published two paragraphs about Plack's visit to the camp, he thought it sufficient, in answer to the complaint that there was no truth in them, to say, "That may be true," but it is "irrelevant."

However, with the publication of the Cussen Report, Flannery's account loses some of its importance, because we now know that the question of broadcasting first arose in the conversation with the Lagerführer while Plum was still in camp. The Lagerführer himself was not in a position to do more than pass on the information that Plum had said he was willing to broadcast, but if one choses to believe in a deal, it could obviously have been proposed without the outside intervention of Plack or anyone else.

All the evidence, both from Plum's accounts and from Plack's, and all the behaviour of everyone concerned at the time, suggest that it was not. This is the only known time that Plum mentioned this conversation, and throughout his interrogation by Cussen he seems anxious to give complete information whether it is relevant or not. In all other respects the account he gave then is the same as he gave again and again, whether on guard or (as with Townend and Guy Bolton) off it. He always strenuously denied any question of a deal, while his fury against Flannery was concentrated entirely on this point. His whole behaviour throughout suggests a man innocent of anything except stupidity and, perhaps, a too great insensitivity to the world outside his own concerns. All those who knew him have believed that the Germans showed unusual good sense in their handling of this matter. He had a strong, rather schoolboyish sense of honour, and had a deal been proposed to him he would almost certainly have rejected it.

Why, then, did he do it? The answer he gave again and again was that he saw no harm in it and that, having received so many letters and parcels from America, he had always felt embarrassed by being unable to answer them.* He made the broadcasts to reassure his well-wishers and to thank them.

Here is what he said to Cussen:

> I should like to deal with my motives. . . . I was feeling intensely happy in a mood that demanded expression and at the same time I was very grateful to all my American friends and very desirous of doing something to return their kindness in sending me letters and parcels.
>
> There was also, I am afraid, a less creditable motive. I thought that people, hearing the talks, would admire me for having kept cheerful under difficult conditions but I think I can say that what chiefly led me to make the talks was gratitude.[15]

It is quite easy to believe that statement and to understand that he might have thought he was simply showing the right spirit in treating his experiences with good humour. Nevertheless, although it is dangerous to surmise on a matter of such importance, there may well have been a motive stronger than any of these. For more than a year he had been starved of publication. He was the most professional of writers, and while not all professional writers write for money, they almost all write for publication. To achieve it, he had always been ready to write such things as the "By the Way"

---

*All his life he answered fan letters personally, and one cannot doubt the truth of this remark.

column, plots for *Mugsey's Magazine*, "slush" for women's papers—anything that came along. Initially this may have been because he needed money, but he did not change when he had made a great deal of it. To the end of his life he was prepared to cut seventy thousand words down to forty thousand, or vice versa, to please some editor, to make alterations to the plot or the sequence of subplots, even to rewrite whole episodes. My husband was one of the first people to meet him after the liberation of Paris (where he then was), and speaking to him of the broadcasts, Plum said sadly, "They were one of the best things I ever wrote." For a year he had been denied any outlet for the stuff which bubbled up inside him, and he simply jumped at the only opportunity he had to release it. If he could have done it for an article in *Punch* or *The Saturday Evening Post*, he would have preferred it. As it was, he accepted without thought the only medium offered him.

George Orwell puts the same point a little less kindly in his essay "In Defence of P. G. Wodehouse": "To judge from the broadcasts themselves, Wodehouse's main idea in making them was to keep in touch with his public and—the comedian's ruling passion—to get a laugh."[16]

The broadcasts were not transmitted live, but recorded. The first seems to have been both written and recorded on the day after Plum met Plack and Schmidt at the Foreign Office, and before the Flannery broadcast. Plum told Cussen:

> As regards the making of the record for the first broadcast, I wrote it on the typewriter which Mrs. Bess had by now sent me and handed it to Werner Plack at the Adlon. I was driven by Plack to the broadcasting place where the manuscript was censored by three officials each representing a branch of the authorities and then I spoke it into the device, the actual recording taking place in an adjoining room. Plack preceded me by putting on to the record the introduction to my talk.[17]

On 27 or 28 June Plum went to the Harz mountains, where according to his statement he remained until the end of November "with the exception of two visits to Berlin to make four other records."

In the outside world it was not understood that the broadcasts were recorded, and it was thought that Plum continued to broadcast week after week in spite of evidence that he knew of the dismay and disapproval his talks had caused. In fact, from the time they were recorded he had no control of what happened to them, although he was allowed to speak two paragraphs in self-justification before the fourth talk. In Richard Usborne's words:

> Plack, for the German Foreign Office, had five funny talks on gramophone records. It was his job to make the best use of them. Like a literary

agent, but serving German propaganda purposes rather than his client's profit, Plack tried to place the talks where they would find the biggest audiences in America. So he offered them to the two American broadcasting companies, ABC and CBS, through their representatives in Berlin. Neither company wanted to run the talks, so Plack put them into the Foreign Office's own programmes to America.[18]

The first talk went out on short wave to America on the evening of 27 June and, because of the difference in time, was heard in England by the BBC monitors in their hut at Evesham and by hardly anyone else. The BBC made a full record of this talk, either in shorthand or mechanically, but the last four they only summarized. At the conclusion of his interrogation three years later, Plum gave the scripts of all five to Colonel Cussen. These were filed with the report, and since Plum kept no copy, for nearly forty years the exact text of the last four was not available to anyone, not even to Plum himself.

During the intervening time there has been some speculation among the few people who knew the inside story as to how, if Plum had not expected to give them, he had managed to write the five talks so quickly. With the publication of the scripts, which are attached to the Cussen Report, it becomes obvious that with the exception of the first talk, which describes his experiences in Le Touquet before the actual internment, they follow very closely the notes he made in "The Camp Note Book," which forms Chapter 10 of this book. The text of the last four will be found in Appendix C. The first, which was introduced by Dr. Paul Schmidt, was as follows:*

It is just possible that my listeners may seem to detect in this little talk of mine a slight goofiness, a certain disposition to ramble in my remarks. If so, the matter, as Bertie Wooster would say, is susceptible of a ready explanation. I have just emerged into the outer world after forty-nine weeks of Civil Internment in a German internment camp and the effects have not entirely worn off. I have not yet quite recovered that perfect mental balance for which in the past I was so admired by one and all.

It's coming back, mind you. Look me up a couple of weeks from now, and you'll be surprised. But just at the moment I feel slightly screwy and inclined to pause at intervals in order to cut out paper dolls and stick straws in my hair—or such of my hair as I still have.

This, no doubt, is always the effect of prolonged internment, and since July the twenty-first, 1940, I have been spending my time in a series of Ilag. An Ilag must not be confused with an Offlag or a Stalag. An Offlag is where

---

*I have compared the monitored version of the first talk with the manuscript version attached to the Cussen Report. There is virtually no difference, but where words were inaudible, or, in the manuscript version, there were typing errors, I have corrected one from the other.

captured officers go. A Stalag is reserved for the rank and file. The Civil Internee gets the Ilag—and how he loves it!

Since I went into business for myself as an internee, I have been in no fewer than four Ilags—some more Ilaggy than others, others less Ilaggy than some. First, they put us in a prison, then in a barracks, then in a fortress. Then they took a look at me and the rest of the boys on parade one day, and got the right idea at last. They sent us off to the local lunatic asylum at Tost in Upper Silesia, and there I have been for the last forty-two weeks.

It has been in many ways quite an agreeable experience. There is a good deal to be said for internment. It keeps you out of the saloon and gives you time to catch up with your reading. You also get a lot of sleep. The chief drawback is that it means your being away from home a good deal. It is not pleasant to think that by the time I see my Pekingese again, she will have completely forgotten me and will bite me to the bone—her invariable practice with strangers. And I feel that when I rejoin my wife, I had better take along a letter of introduction, just to be on the safe side.

Young men starting out in life have often asked me, "How can I become an Internee?" Well, there are several methods. My own was to buy a villa in Le Touquet on the coast of France and stay there till the Germans came along. This is probably the best and simplest system. You buy the villa and the Germans do the rest.

At the time of their arrival, I would have been just as pleased if they had not rolled up. But they did not see it that way, and on May the twenty-second along they came—some on motorcycles, some on foot, but all evidently prepared to spend a long weekend.

The whole thing was very peaceful and orderly. Le Touquet has the advantage of being a sort of backwater, off the line of march. Your tendency, if you are an army making for the coast, is to carry on along the main road to Boulogne, and not to take the first turning to the left when you reach Etaples. So the proceedings were not marred by any vulgar brawling. All that happened, as far as I was concerned, was that I was strolling on the lawn with my wife one morning, when she lowered her voice and said, "Don't look now, but there comes the German army." And there they were, a fine body of men, rather prettily dressed in green, carrying machine guns.

One's reactions on suddenly finding oneself surrounded by the armed strength of a hostile power are rather interesting. There is a sense of strain. The first time you see a German soldier over your garden fence, your impulse is to jump ten feet straight up into the air, and you do so. About a week later, you find that you are only jumping five feet. And then, after you have been living with him in a small village for two months, you inevitably begin to fraternize and to wish that you had learned German at school instead of Latin or Greek. All the German I know is *"Es ist schönes Wetter"* and this handicaps conversation with a Bavarian private who knows no English. After I had said *"Es ist schönes Wetter,*" I was a spent force and we used to take up the rest of the interview in beaming at one another.

I had a great opportunity of brushing up my beaming during those two months. My villa stands in the centre of a circle of houses, each of which was occupied by German officers, who would come around at intervals to take a look at things, and the garden next door was full of Labour Corps boys. It was with these that one really got together. There was scarcely an evening when two or three of them did not drop in for a bath at my house and a beaming party on the porch afterwards.

And so, day by day, all though June and July, our quiet, happy life continued, with not a jarring incident to mar the serenity. Well, yes, perhaps one or two. One day, an official-looking gentleman with none of the Labour Corps geniality came along and said he wanted my car. Also my radio. And in addition my bicycle. That was what got under the skin. I could do without the car, and I had never much liked the radio, but I loved that bicycle. I looked him right in the eye and said *"Es ist schönes Wetter"*—and I said it nastily. I meant it to sting. And what did he say? He didn't say anything. What could he have said? P.S. He got the bicycle.

But these were small things, scarcely causing a ripple on the placid stream of life in the occupied areas. A perfect atmosphere of peace and goodwill continued to prevail. Except for the fact that I was not allowed out of my garden after nine at night, my movements were not restricted. Quite soon I had become sufficiently nonchalant to resume the writing of the novel which the arrival of the soldiery had interrupted. And then the order went out that all British subjects had got to report each morning at twelve o'clock at the Kommandantur down in Paris Plage.

As Paris Plage was three miles away, and they had pinched my bicycle, this was a nuisance. But I should have had nothing to complain of, if the thing had stopped there. But unfortunately it didn't. One lovely Sunday morning, as I was rounding into the straight and heading for the door of the Kommandantur, I saw one of our little group coming along with a suitcase in his hand.

This didn't look so good. I was conscious of a nameless fear. Wodehouse, old sport, I said to myself, this begins to look like a sticky day. And a few moments later my apprehensions were fulfilled. Arriving at the Kommandantur, I found everything in a state of bustle and excitement. I said *"Es ist schönes Wetter"* once or twice, but nobody took any notice. And presently the interpreter stepped forward and announced that we were all going to be interned.

It was a pretty nasty shock, coming without warning out of a blue sky like that, and it is not too much to say that for an instant the old maestro shook like a badly set blancmange. Many years ago, at a party which had started to get a bit rough, somebody once hit me on the bridge of the nose with an order of planked steak. As I had felt then, so did I feel now. That same sensation of standing in a rocking and disintegrating world.

I didn't realize at the time how much luckier I was than a great many other victims of the drag-net. All over France during that Sunday, British citizens were being picked up and taken away without being given time to pack, and for a week those in Boulogne had been living in what they stood up in at the Petit Vitesse railroad station. For some reason, Le Touquet was given a substantial break. We were allowed to go home and put a few things together, and as my home was three miles away, I was actually sent in a car.

The soldier who escorted me was unfortunately not one of those leisurely souls who believe in taking time over one's packing. My idea had been to have a cold bath and a change and a bite to eat, and then to light a pipe and sit down and muse for a while, making notes of what to take with me and what could be left behind. His seemed to be that five minutes was ample. Eventually we compromised on ten.

I would like my biographers to make careful note of the fact that the first thing that occurred to me was that here at last was my chance to buckle down and read the complete works of William Shakespeare. It was a thing I had been meaning to do any time these last forty years, but somehow, as soon as I had got, say, *Hamlet* and *Macbeth* under my belt and was preparing to read the stuffing out of *Henry the Sixth, Parts One, Two, and Three*, something like *The Murglow Manor Mystery* would catch my eye and I would weaken.

I didn't know what internment implied—it might be for years or it might be for ever—or it might be a mere matter of weeks—but the whole situation seemed to point to the complete works of William Shakespeare, so in they went. I am happy to say that I am now crammed with Shakespeare to the brim, so, whatever else internment has done for me, I am at any rate that much ahead of the game.

It was a pang to leave my novel behind, I had only five more chapters of it to do. But space, as Jeeves would have pointed out, was of the essence, and it had to go, and is now somewhere in France. I am hoping to run into it again one of these days, for it was a nice little novel and we had some great times together.

I wonder what my listeners would have packed in my place—always remembering that there was a German soldier standing behind me all the time, shouting *"Schnell"* or words to that effect. I had to think quick. Eventually what I crammed in were tobacco, pencils, scribbling blocks, chocolate, biscuits, a pair of trousers, a pair of shoes, some shirts and a sock or two. My wife wanted to add a pound of butter, but I fought her off. There are practically no limits to what a pound of butter can do in warm weather in a small suitcase. If I was going to read the complete works of William Shakespeare, I preferred them unbuttered.

In the end, the only thing of importance I left behind was my passport, which was the thing I ought to have packed first. The young internee is always being asked for his passport, and if he hasn't got it, the authorities tend to look squiggle-eyes and to ask nasty questions. I had never fully realized what class distinctions were till I became an internee without a passport, thus achieving a *social position somewhere in between a minor gangster and a wharf rat.*

Having closed the suitcase and said goodbye to my wife and the junior dog, and foiled the attempt of the senior dog to muscle into the car and accompany me into captivity, I returned to the Kommandantur. And presently, with the rest of the gang, numbering twelve in all, I drove in a motor omnibus for an unknown destination.

That is one of the drawbacks to travelling, when you are an internee. Your destination always is unknown. It is unsettling, when you start out, not to be sure whether you are going half way across Europe or just to the next town. Actually, we were headed for Loos, a suburb of Lille, a distance of about a hundred miles. What with stopping at various points along the road to pick up other foundation members, it took us eight hours.

An internee's enjoyment of such a journey depends very largely on the mental attitude of the sergeant in charge. Ours turned out to be a genial soul, who gave us cigarettes and let us get off and buy red wine at all stops, infusing the whole thing with a pleasant atmosphere of the school treat. This was increased by the fact that we all knew each other pretty intimately and had hobnobbed on other occasions. Three of us were from the golf club—Arthur Grant, the Pro., Jeff, the starter, and Max, the caddie master. Algy, of Algy's bar in the rue St. Jean, was there, and Alfred, of Alfred's bar in the rue de Paris. And the rest, like Charlie Webb and Bill Illidge, who ran garages, were all well-known Paris Plage figures. The thing was, therefore, practically a feast of reason and a flow of soul.

Nevertheless as the evening shadows began to fall and the effects of the red wine wore off, we were conscious of a certain sinking feeling. We felt very far from our snug homes and not at all sure that we liked the shape of things to come.

As to what exactly was the shape of things to come, nobody seemed to know. But the general sentiment that prevailed was one of uneasiness. We feared the worst.

Nor were we greatly encouraged when, having passed through Lille, we turned into a side lane and came through pleasant fields and under spreading trees to a forbidding-looking building which was only too obviously the local hoose-gow or calaboose. A nasty-looking man in the uniform of the French provincial police flung wide the gates and we rolled through.

Next week—the Rover Boys in Loos Prison.

All five talks were in this vein and had no word of propaganda. Very few people in England heard them, and even fewer have read them until this day. That they were harmless in themselves and harmless in intention is established beyond doubt. A BBC commentator, after a summary of the first talk, made the following remarks:

> The general atmosphere he seemed to give was one of kindly and reason-
> able treatment; but woven into the humorous style—and perhaps dis-

guised in it—were pictures of "an official-looking gentleman" who demanded his car, radio and his bicycle; a German sergeant who hurried him on his packing, shouting "*Schnell*" behind him so that he had to think quick; and a "nasty-looking man in the uniform of the French police" at the gate of Loos Prison.

Wodehouse introduced the fourth talk himself. He said:

The Press and public of England seem to have jumped to the conclusion that I have been in some way bribed or intimidated into making these broadcasts. This is not the case. I did not make a bargain, as they put it, and buy my release by agreeing to speak over the radio; I was released because I am sixty years old, or shall be in October. The fact that I was freed a few months before that date was due entirely to the efforts of my friends, people like Demaree Bess of *The Saturday Evening Post*. As I pointed out in my talk, if I had been sixty when I was interned I should have been released at the end of the first week.

My reason for broadcasting is a simple one. In the course of my period of internment I received hundreds of letters of sympathy from American readers of my books who are strangers to me, and I was naturally anxious to let them know how I had got on. Under existing conditions it was impossible to answer these letters, but I did not want to be so ungrateful and ungracious as to seem to be ignoring them, and the radio suggested itself as a solution.

In August 1941 the broadcasts were repeated on long wave to England, this time not by the Foreign Office but by Goebbels's Propaganda Ministry. Richard Usborne, who talked to Werner Plack, says that it was no part of the original intention and to this day Plack does not know why Goebbels's Ministry decided to do it. Before the first one, Wodehouse was heard saying:

The five talks that will follow are word for word as they were delivered over the radio by me to the United States. They were designed simply as a way of acknowledging the hundreds of sympathetic letters which I received during my internment from American readers of my books— letters which I had no other means of answering. They have caused violent attacks on me in England, but I still cannot see that there's anything in them which could not have been printed if I had been in a position to write for English newspapers. It never occurred to me that there could be anything harmful in such statements as that when in camp I read Shakespeare, that the Commander at Huy had short legs and didn't like walking uphill, that men who had no tobacco smoked tea, and that there was an unpleasant smell in my cell at Loos Prison.

12

The Broadcasts: England

On 27 June the English national newspapers announced that P. G. Wodehouse had been released from internment and had agreed to broadcast once a week from Germany to America. The reaction was instantaneous. On 28 June the *Daily Mirror* was the first in the field with an article which carried the headline THE PRICE IS?, and on the same day William Connor, who wrote a column for the *Mirror* under the name "Cassandra," set the tone for a great deal of the comment which was to follow:

> P. G. Wodehouse, to use his own words, has been *"browsing and sluicing"* with the Nazis in Berlin's biggest and best hotel—the Adlon. Bertie Wooster's owner and sole proprietor is now nesting in a suite on the third floor which he describes as "very nice too."* It appears that Mr. Wodehouse is to broadcast once a week to the United States. "General chats, entirely nonpolitical," explained the Great Wag. He then went on: "I am quite unable to work up any kind of belligerent feeling—really. Just as I'm about to feel belligerent about some country, I meet a decent sort of chap—we go out together and lose any fighting thoughts or feelings."
>
> Mr. Wodehouse is fortunate.
>
> He hasn't seen great areas of London, Coventry, Liverpool and other cities flattened by his Hunnish hosts. He hasn't heard the rattle of machine-gun fire as the gorillas of the Luftwaffe spray bullets at British seamen struggling in the water.
>
> No doubt Goebbels thinks he's being particularly smooth in using Wodehouse on Deutschlandsender. Unbiassed stuff. Reasonable stuff. Can't-you-see-our-side-as-well-as-yours stuff. But even if he sings with the tongue of angels this clubfoot from hell will fool none of us. Jeeves may speak softly to us from the radio masts of Berlin. The world's greatest gentleman may purr as he never purred before.

---

*This is from Flannery's interview. Any reader wishing to see what the press can do without altering a word should look back to p. 197.

> But the lads down at the Drones Club will never approve.
> Never, never, never.

That is exceedingly clever, because it blurs the distinction between the personalities of Wodehouse and the club-footed Goebbels, and immediately links the offence of broadcasting to some of the worst excesses of the war. The sentence quoted from Wodehouse as beginning "I am quite unable to work up any kind of belligerent feeling . . ." is repeated from the report of an interview Plum gave an American correspondent, and he was later to deny that he ever said it. Quoted extensively, it aroused the most intense hostility towards him among all classes of Englishmen. The Second World War was not notable for hysteria of the kind which, deliberately whipped up, so disgraced the civilian population of the First World War, and the storm of disapproval aroused by this remark is for that reason all the more illustrative of the climate of opinion which naturally and necessarily prevails in wartime in even the most civilized societies. The sentiment attributed to Wodehouse is one without which international relations could hardly survive in peacetime, and, moreover, it is noticeable that in war it is one that is increasingly felt the nearer men get to their enemies. (On Christmas Day in the First World War the troops of both sides fraternized along the narrow line between the trenches.) And if his critics had no experience of life in an internment camp, it was true that Wodehouse knew nothing of the bombing of English towns.

Nevertheless, although Cassandra's comments made it plain that the anti-Wodehouse propaganda would be both savage in tone and cleverly handled, the *Daily Mirror* was not alone either in the attitude it took or in small but immensely damaging misrepresentations. On 1 July the *Daily Express* printed some extracts from the first broadcast (as monitored by the BBC) and slightly but vitally misquoted it. Wodehouse had referred to a "beaming party" at his house (those who have read the last chapter will remember the context); and by dropping the word *beaming*, the *Express* gave the sentence a different—and in the circumstances, far more damaging—meaning. This was to stick, and it was often repeated that Wodehouse was giving a cocktail party at Low Wood when he was arrested along with the rest of the civilian population.

However, it is only fair to say that the feeling both newspapers hoped to arouse would have been given expression even if their accounts had been more scrupulous. On 1 July a long correspondence in the *Daily Telegraph* was opened by a viciously worded letter from a Mr. George Williams. The correspondence was continued for some weeks, and all sides of the case were represented. Today the letters that remain of interest are chiefly those of Wodehouse's fellow authors. On 2 July Ian Hay, his old friend and collaborator in plays and musical comedy, after saying that while Wode-house's innumerable friends must rejoice at his release, continued:

> We are less happy that he is to give a weekly broadcast from Berlin. To put it frankly . . . we are horrified.
>
> No broadcast from Berlin by a world-famous Englishman, however "neutral" in tone, can serve as anything but an advertisement for Hitler; as a testimonial to Nazi toleration, as a shining instance of Nazi consid-eration and humanity towards prisoners of war—an ingenious dose, in other words, of soothing syrup for America, designed to divert American thoughts from the horrors which are being perpetrated in German prison camps today upon thousands of persons less happily situated than Mr. Wodehouse.
>
> There is no doubt that Mr. Wodehouse was deliberately released for this purpose. It was a brilliant idea, and unfortunately my old friend seems to have fallen for it. I have no hesitation in saying that he has not the slightest realisation of what he is doing. He is an easy-going and kindly man, cut off from public opinion here and with no one to advise him; and he probably agreed to broadcast because he saw no harm in the idea, and because, after long captivity, he is thus enabled to resume relations with his friends of the English-speaking world.
>
> But one thing is plain. No word of his can help our cause, and hardly any word can fail to help the enemy. The broadcasts must stop for the sake of our country and for the sake of Wodehouse himself; for if he goes on he will lose every friend he has, and their name is legion.
>
> I therefore suggest that immediate steps should be taken through some friendly neutral authority in Berlin, to drop a hint to our much beloved but misguided "Plum" to lay off.

Hardly had Plum's friends had time to wonder why Ian Hay—clearly a person of considerable influence—had not made his plea more privately and in a manner more likely to be effective, when he forever lost the limelight to Plum's other old friend, A. A. Milne. Milne wrote:

> The news that P. G. Wodehouse had been released from his concentration camp delighted his friends; the news that he had settled down comfortably at the Adlon made them anxious; the news that he was to give weekly broadcasts (but not about politics, because he "had never taken any inter-est in politics") left them in no doubt as to what had happened to him. He had escaped again.
>
> I remember that he told me once he wished he had a son, and he added characteristically (and quite sincerely) "but he would have to be born at the age of 15, when he was just getting into his House eleven."* You see the advantage of that. Bringing up a son throws considerable responsibil-ity on a man; but by the time the boy is 15 one has shifted the responsi-

---

*A cricket term.

bility onto the housemaster, without forfeiting any reflected glory that may be about.*

This, I felt, had always been Wodehouse's attitude to life. He has encouraged in himself a natural lack of interest in "politics"—"politics" being all the things which grown-ups talk about at dinner when one is hiding under the table. Things, for instance, like the last war, which found and kept him in America; and postwar taxes, which chased him backwards and forwards across the Atlantic until he finally found sanctuary in France.

An ill-chosen sanctuary it must have seemed last June, when politics came surging across the Somme.

Irresponsibility in what the papers call "a licensed humourist" can be carried too far; naivety has been carried too far; Wodehouse has been given a good deal of licence in the past, but I fancy that now his licence will be withdrawn.

Before this happens I beg him to surrender it of his own free will; to realise that though a genius may grant himself an enviable position above the battle where civic and social responsibilities are concerned, there are times when every man has to come down into the arena, pledge himself to the cause in which he believes, and suffer for it.

The whole of this letter was unexpected from a man who had seemed to be a friend, and the last part is inexplicable. What licence had Wodehouse ever sought or been given? He was not a womanizer and he did not drink. He had made an enormous fortune, but by talent and almost unparallelled hard work. These words have—and since there is some real animus behind them, are clearly intended to have—the effect of a smear, while very few people would pause to ask themselves exactly what they mean. Probably Milne did not ask himself, but if he did, he could only be referring to the old income tax canard. On the same day W. A. Darlington, having expressed himself on the subject of the broadcasts, continued with an equal disregard for the facts: "He was equally easygoing in his money affairs, for he came into the public eye . . . when the United States authorities demanded £50,000 of unpaid income tax from him."

Wodehouse's friend William Townend replied to these letters in the *Daily Telegraph*, but, as happens in these cases, his letter was published (on 9 July) only after an interval had passed. He wrote:

In April [1917] when the United States entered the war, a recruiting office was set up for Britons resident in that country. Wodehouse offered

*Years later Richard Usborne wrote to Wodehouse that the remark Milne quoted actually appeared in *Psmith in the City*. Wodehouse replied, "You have cleared up a mystery that has been puzzling me for years. The thing he quoted me as saying . . . seemed familiar, but I was certain I had never said it to him. Evidently he must have read it in *Psmith in the City*. . . . Odd chap, Milne. There was a curious jealous streak in him which doesn't come out in his writing. I love his writing but never liked him much."

himself for enlistment but was medically rejected as quite unfit for military service.

That he had trouble with his income tax has often been brought up against him. As Mr. W. A. Darlington says, the U.S. Government demanded £50,000 of unpaid income tax from him. What Mr. Darlington omits to say is that the U.S. Government after prolonged negotiation accepted one seventh of the sum asked for.*

And he made the obvious point that they would not have done that if they could have proved the claim for the larger amount.

There were many other people who, even if they did not condone Wodehouse's actions, tried to explain them. Ethel Mannin wrote suggesting that judgment should be withheld until the facts were known—"Judge not that ye be not judged"—and Dorothy Sayers wrote as follows:

> In the discussion about Mr. P. G. Wodehouse's unhappy broadcasts, there is one point of which we ought, I think, to remind ourselves. At the time of the Battle of France, when he fell into enemy hands, English people had scarcely begun to realise the military and political importance of the German propaganda weapon. Since then we have learned much. We know something of why and how France fell; we have seen disintegration at work in the Balkans; we have watched the slow recovery of American opinion from the influence of the Nazi hypnotic.
>
> But how much of all this can possibly be known or appreciated from inside a German concentration camp—or even from the Adlon Hotel? Theoretically, no doubt every patriotic person should be prepared to resist enemy pressure to the point of martyrdom; but it must be far more difficult to bear such heroic witness when its urgent necessity is not, and cannot, be understood.

Two days later someone who signed himself "Disinterested"—but who was apparently in a position to have received information—gave some of the facts of what had happened in Germany. He ended his letter:

> I have no right or desire to comment or pass judgment on Mr. Wodehouse's action, but I would add the remarks made by someone who knew him in Berlin. They agree with Mr. A. A. Milne that he is politically naive, and with Miss Dorothy Sayers that he is unconscious of the propaganda value to the Germans of his action. It sprang, they say, from his desire to keep his name before his American reading public. But they do add, most emphatically, that he did not buy his release from prison camp by agreeing to broadcast. Anxiety for his wife, whom he had left near Lille, may have led him to press for his release several weeks before it would normally have been granted him.

*In fact, it was just under a third; see p. 140.

On the whole his brother authors supported Wodehouse. Both Monckton Hoffe and Gilbert Frankau suggested that much of the fuss was created by people who envied his gift for making money, and Sax Rohmer wrote:

Mr. W. A. Darlington's reference to a claim for £50,000 made by the United States Revenue upon P. G. Wodehouse is calculated to mislead. I would like to point out that a similar claim (in my own case for a less staggering sum) was made upon all English novelists and playwrights, or all of those with whom I am acquainted, who derived any considerable revenue from the U.S.A.

However, it fell to Wodehouse himself to immortalize the only letter in the *Daily Telegraph* correspondence which is remembered today. On 8 July Sean O'Casey wrote:

It is amusing to read the various wails about the villainy of Wodehouse. The harm done to England's cause and to England's dignity is not the poor man's babble in Berlin, but the acceptance of him by a childish part of the people and the academic government of Oxford, dead from the chin up, as a person of any importance whatsoever in English humorous literature, or any literature at all. It is an ironic twist of retribution on those who banished Joyce and honoured Wodehouse.
If England has any dignity left in the way of literature, she will forget forever the pitiful antics of English Literature's performing flea. If Berlin thinks the poor fish great, so much the better for us.*

One unpublished letter deserves attention. This was sent to the editor of the *Telegraph*, who replied that he could not publish it for lack of space. Its author had other means of making himself heard, and in Octave 8 of his autobiography and again in *Homage to P. G. Wodehouse* Compton Mackenzie quoted what he wrote then:

There is a curious infelicity in Mr. A. A. Milne's sneer at Mr. P. G. Wodehouse for shirking the responsibilities of fatherhood. Such a rebuke would have come more decorously from a father who had abstained from the profitable exhibitionism in which the creator of Christopher Robin has indulged.
I gather that Mr. Wodehouse is in disgrace for telling the American public over the radio about his comfortable existence at the Hotel Adlon. Not being convinced that I am morally entitled to throw stones at a fellow author, and retaining as I do an old-fashioned prejudice against condemning a man unheard, I do not propose to inflict my opinion upon the reading public, beyond affirming that at the moment I feel more disgusted by Mr. Milne's morality than by Mr. Wodehouse's irresponsibility.[1]

*Sadly, E. C. Bentley of clerihew fame also expressed this point of view.

Inevitably questions were asked in the House of Commons. On 9 July Mr. Mander (Liberal member for Wolverhampton) asked the Foreign Secretary, Mr. Eden, if he had any statement to make with reference to the release from internment in Germany of Mr. P. G. Wodehouse and the arrangement for him to give a weekly broadcast from Germany to the United States of America. And Mr. Eden replied: "Yes, Sir. His Majesty's Government have seen with regret the report that Mr. Wodehouse has lent his services to the German propaganda machine." Mr. Mander then asked whether the Foreign Secretary would take such steps as were available to him to bring to the attention of Mr. Wodehouse and others the grave peril in which they place themselves by playing the Nazi game during the war. Mr. Eden replied: "I will certainly have in mind the honourable member's suggestion." And in answer to a question about the arrangements made for recording broadcasts by British subjects under enemy auspices, Mr. Peake, Under-Secretary at the Home Office, made it plain that such broadcasts were recorded. A Colonel Evans then asked if the Home Office would consider the advisability of broadcasting an appeal or warning to British subjects resident in enemy country against any broadcasts they might be inclined to indulge in as a result of bribery held out by the enemy, so that their position would be quite clear upon their return to England. After Mr. Peake had said that he would pass the suggestion on to the Minister of Information, Earl Winterton asked: "Will the Minister make it clear by Order in Council that these people will be liable to prosecution, whoever they are and whether they are famous writers or anybody else?" Mr. Peake replied: "I think that the situation is already perfectly clear. Anybody who assists the enemy by broadcasting in their programmes is obviously liable to prosecution if sufficient evidence can be brought after the war. . . ."[2]

In spite of all this there was a considerable amount of understanding in the country, and this was also expressed in articles in the press. Thus a leader in the *Yorkshire Post*, after referring to both the main charges and subsidiary charges which had been brought against Wodehouse, went on:

We are confident that Wodehouse is at least no Haw-Haw. That creature Joyce* hates this country, would like to see Hitler destroy it and is doing his odious utmost to help the work of destruction. . . .

Wodehouse, dreamily casual, belongs to a different world of ideas, a luxury world of happy humour. There is no reason to suppose that he detests or despises his own country. Why should he scorn it when it has given him wealth, honours and popularity? He is far more fool than knave. He is behaving as his own Bertie Wooster might behave if lacking

*William Joyce ("Lord Haw-Haw") broadcast propaganda for the Germans throughout the war.

the guidance of Jeeves. Cut off from what we are thinking he may not realise that his talks will do the Germans great good in America by spreading the legend that his captors are really nice, large-minded people victimised by circumstances beyond their control.

Now that everybody had had his say, it was possible that public interest might have waned and the broadcasts become no more than a blurred memory in the minds of those top people who actually read the national newspapers—but for two things. The first was that excerpts from the article which Angus Thuermer had taken from camp (first published in *The Saturday Evening Post*), and which may be said to have been the first in the chain of events leading to the broadcasts, now began to appear in English newspapers. Like the broadcasts, it was an account of life in camp intended to amuse, but the excerpts which appeared in England merely served to destroy any hope that the feeling against Plum might die down. It was entitled "My War with Germany" and began:

> On the lips of everybody today, from Berlin to Vladivostok, from Peebles to Mattahamquehasset, Maine, there is a question. It is the question: "Afterwards—what?" Everywhere, thinking men are looking to the future, asking themselves what it will bring forth; and it is pretty generally agreed that at the conclusion of hostilities we shall see many changes from the old familiar conditions of the days before September 1939.

After several paragraphs of this sort of thing, he made it clear that the changes he is speaking of are changes in himself. Thus: "If at some aristocratic board you hear a protesting voice shouting 'Hey! That bird's been given one more spud than I got' and see a flushed face glaring down the table, that voice and that face will be mine. We learn to watch our interests in camp."

None of this would have done much harm (though not much good) if it had not been for the last paragraphs of the article:

> Mind you, if I were a bachelor without dogs I should be in no particular hurry to leave. In many ways Tost is a home from home. We eat well, we sleep well, and as for trembling when we see a job of work, there is no necessity, for those of us who are over fifty, to do this, as all fatigues are performed by our juniors. . . .
>
> Furthermore, the air you get in Upper Silesia is magnificent; the sentries are models of manly beauty at whom it is a treat to look, and you soon become accustomed to finding yourself hung up on the barbed wire like a hat on a hatstand.
>
> Nevertheless, being a married man with a Pekingese and a German boxer, I am in favour of moving elsewhere if it can be arranged. The only

thing I can suggest is that Germany and I get together at a round table and discuss the terms for a separate peace.

It should be simple to arrive at some settlement which would be satisfactory to both parties. The only concession I want from Germany is that she give me a loaf of bread, tell the gentlemen with the muskets at the main gate to look the other way and leave the rest to me.

In return for this I am prepared to hand over India and an autographed set of my books and to reveal a secret process for cooking sliced potatoes on the radiator known only to internee Arthur Grant and myself. This firm offer holds good till Wednesday week.

Since this article was written while Plum was still in camp and had no hope of early release, no one can deny his gallantry. But his tone was disastrous, and even those people who were not offended were not amused. However, the publication of excerpts did no more than keep the story going. Something infinitely worse was being prepared. In an autobiographical work entitled *Off the Record,* written in the form of diary, Charles Graves, who was present as a journalist, recorded the circumstances in which it was first suggested that the Wodehouse broadcasts should be the subject of a "Postscript" after the nine o'clock news. (This was the same Charles Graves for whose book Plum had written an introduction, claiming that his qualifications to do so were unexceptionable on the grounds of his friendship with him.) Graves said:

> Lunched with Duff Cooper in a private room at the Savoy.*
>
> It was a curious party—six professional individualists. Cassandra, whose real name is Connor, of the *Mirror,* spectacled, with blue lidless eyes and an unidentifiable accent, Francis Williams . . . Michael Foot . . . A. J. Cummings . . . Hannen Swaffer.†
>
> I raised the subject of P. G. Wodehouse and said that Ronald Squire or Cecil Parker‡ should be put up to a reply, speaking as Jeeves about their poor Master. Duff Cooper said that nobody could imitate Wodehouse. I said this was unnecessary. We could take complete sentences of real Wodehouse out of his various novels and make them fit the case. Cassandra then offered to broadcast to America himself, knocking Wodehouse for his tax evasion. I regard this as silly but Duff Cooper jumped at it.³

*Alfred Duff Cooper, later Viscount Norwich, was at that time Minister of Information, although shortly to give way to Brendan Bracken.
†William Connor told Richard Usborne many years later that he remembered the luncheon party as taking place soon after Germany's invasion of Russia because they drank vodka. The others were Francis Williams of the *Daily Herald,* later a Life Peer; Michael Foot, journalist and politician, later Leader of the Labour Party; A. J. Cummings of the *News Chronicle;* and Hannen Swaffer of the *Daily Express,* a "well-known figure" in London.
‡Well-known actors of the day.

Charles Graves seems to have had no particular animus against Wodehouse, because he later confided to his diary:

> As for P. G. Wodehouse, the photographs of him as a prisoner of war in Germany show that he has lost at least four stone in weight. At the outbreak of war he looked like a rubicund archbishop, now he looks like a Trappist monk! Poor old boy. I *mean* it. He was cut off from the rest of the world at England's darkest hour—Dunkirk. Since then he has heard nothing except what Goebbels has pumped into him, and it would not surprise me in the least if he genuinely thought he was doing us and the U.S.A. a good turn with his talks. . . . He is the last man in the world to do what he is doing if he really knew the truth.[4]

Graves nevertheless was responsible for the conversation which led to Connor's infamous broadcast. The talks after the nine o'clock news known as "Postscripts" were a feature of wartime Britain, and it was estimated that they were heard by upwards of ten million people. Many of the most successful were given by J. B. Priestley, and the week before, Quentin Reynolds, the famous London correspondent of *Collier's*, had delivered a talk in the form of an open letter to Dr. Goebbels. Speaking in a particular sneering drawl, he had constantly addressed his remarks to Dr. Goebbels, and the following is a fair sample of what he said:

> Have you heard about the RAF, Doctor? I thought so. Have you heard about the RAF night fighters? I spent a night with them last week. It was a night of stars.
> One hates to spoil the Sabbath, Doctor, with stories of death. But that night, Doctor, many of your bombing planes stayed in England.

None of the facts of what happened after the meeting at the Savoy have previously been made public, although it became known that the Directors of the BBC allowed Connor to broadcast only after protest and under pressure from the Minister of Information.

The sequence of events was as follows. When Connor delivered his script to the BBC, it was immediately objected to and alterations were asked for. On 7 July 1941 Connor wrote to Duff Cooper:

> Dear Mr. Duff Cooper,
> I am sorry to say that I don't think I shall be doing the Wodehouse broadcast to North America, which you suggested to me on Friday. The B.B.C. rang me up and it immediately became apparent that I should not have the liberty of saying exactly what I think—a privilege this newspaper grants me every day. It is not possible to discredit Wodehouse's action with soft words delivered in the accents of Mr. Stuart Hibberd.* This

*Stuart Hibberd was a BBC newscaster.

swift check to your proposal is disheartening and disappointing to me for I felt I could have done a good job.

Sincerely yours,
William N. Connor

To this Duff Cooper replied on 8 July:

Dear Cassandra,

I am sorry that there seems to be some misunderstanding with the B.B.C. according to your letter of yesterday.

The fact is that everybody has to submit texts of what they are going to say—even Cabinet Ministers—the idea being that inadvertently some security rule might be broken otherwise.

If you will send your script to me personally, I will hand it on to the B.B.C. and will undertake not to interfere with the strength or violence of anything you care to say. Once I have passed it the B.B.C. cannot interfere. I hope you will agree to do this.

Yours sincerely
Duff Cooper

On 12 July he wrote again:

My dear Cassandra,

I received your text which I find wholly admirable. I have sent it straight on to the B.B.C. without altering a comma and with instructions that they should arrange for it to be delivered to the United States with the least possible delay. I am afraid it will mean for you sitting up to an unpleasant hour. That is a sacrifice I am sure you will be glad to make. I also suggested that you should be consulted as to the desirability of giving the same stuff in the Home programme, either as it stands or slightly altered for home consumption. You will, no doubt, discuss this possibility with the B.B.C.

Many thanks for your effort.

Yours sincerely
Duff Cooper

Duff Cooper apparently believed that he was acting under the wartime powers of the Minister of Information to direct the war effort of the BBC, although he may have exceeded those powers in directing that any person should broadcast. The Director General* and the Governors of the BBC then objected on three grounds: (1) Evidence of what Wodehouse had done was scanty and in a different category from what William Joyce (Haw-Haw) was doing; Wodehouse had merely done something ill advised. Also, there was no evidence as to whether he was under compulsion or not. (2) The talk was right out of key with anything the BBC had ever done before.

---

*Frederick Wolff Ogilvie, LL.D.

It was a personal attack and might excite pity for the victim. Wodehouse was extremely popular in England and in America, and it was a journalist with a notorious reputation who was attacking him. (3) The success of the attack would be short term. The Director General added that he deplored the whole broadcast and would certainly not transmit it on the Home Service without definite orders in writing from the Minister.

Duff Cooper then ordered the broadcast, in writing for the Empire Service and verbally for the Home Service.

In the meantime the Governors of the BBC had taken Counsel's Opinion, which was that Connor's text was clearly libellous—if broadcast, slanderous—and given the extent of Wodehouse's assets in this country, might be the subject of enormous damages. This opinion was communicated to the Minister, and it is recorded that he understood that if an action was brought against the BBC after the war, the BBC would be sued for doing something on formal Government orders, and that any expenses incurred by the BBC in damages and costs would presumably be a charge on the state. The Minister's instructions were to go ahead without further consultation except with Mr. Connor. Counsel's Opinion was read to Mr. Connor, who said he was still willing to go on.

The Governors of the BBC made one more attempt. They stated that having examined the script, they had come to the conclusion that it was undesirable to broadcast it (a) because of Counsel's Opinion and the use by the BBC of material so described, and (b) because of the possibility that this script, with its many exaggerations, might provoke reactions in America and at home opposite to those desired. They then said that while they would carry out the Minister's instructions, they thought they might properly ask him to reconsider his decision for the reasons given.

A message was then sent to the Governors that their views had been conveyed to the Minister and that he adhered to his instructions. The necessary direction was therefore given for the broadcasts to go out on the Home and Overseas services.

Connor's "Postscript" was as follows:

> I have come to tell you tonight of the story of a rich man trying to make his last and greatest sale—that of his own country. It is a sombre story of self-respect, of honour and of decency being pawned to the Nazis for the price of a soft bed in a luxury hotel. It is a tale of laughter growing old and of the Judas whine of treachery taking its place. It is the record of P. G. Wodehouse ending forty years of money-making fun with the worst joke he ever made in his life. The only wisecrack he ever pulled that the world received in silence. The last laugh bought from him by that prince of innocent glee—Dr. Paul Joseph Goebbels.
>
> Pelham Grenville Wodehouse is in his sixtieth year—a British subject

now held prisoner of war in Nazi Germany. When the war broke out Wodehouse was at Le Touquet—gambling. Nine months later he was still there. Poland had been wiped out. Denmark had been overrun and Norway had been occupied. Wodehouse went on with his fun. The elderly playboy didn't believe in politics. He said so. No good time Charlie ever does. Wodehouse was throwing a cocktail party when the storm troopers clumped in on his shallow life. They led him away—the funny Englishman with his vast repertoire of droll butlers, amusing young men and comic titled fops. Politics, in the form of the Nazi Eagle, came home to roost. Himmler took the place of Jeeves—and he didn't even knock on the door before he came in.

Bertie Wooster faded and Dr. Goebbels hobbled on the scene. Goebbels who is as quick as he is evil—and that is very fast indeed—had an idea. He saw in P. G. Wodehouse a useful weapon to wield against the outraged people of America and Great Britain. All the blood of Poland still stained the earth. The blood of murdered Czechs, and Norwegians, and Dutchmen, and Belgians, and Frenchmen and of Englishmen cried out. Goebbels wanted the place tidied up a bit. He needed a human blotter to dry up the blood. He found a sponge in his hands. He now wanted his audience—the millions of people who read and admired Wodehouse's writings. He wanted YOU—the people who are listening to me. So he treated his prisoner gently. He sent him to an internment camp in Upper Silesia and saw to it that he was put in charge of the library. A soft job to breed sweet reasonableness. Six months later the plan began to show the first signs that it was working. "I am quite happy here," wrote Wodehouse, and Dr. Goebbels knew that things were on the move. Far away in Washington, Dr. Hans Thomsen fitted in *his* piece into the crafty jigsaw. He wrote to Senator Barbour and assured him that the Führer's prisoner was "quite comfortable." Wodehouse was being stealthily groomed for stardom, the most disreputable stardom in the world—the limelight of quislings. On the last day of June of this year, Dr. Goebbels was ready. So too was Pelham Wodehouse. He was eager and he was willing and when they offered him Liberty in a country that has killed Liberty, he leapt at it. And Dr. Goebbels taking him into a high mountain, showed unto him all the Kingdoms of the world . . . and said unto him: "All this power will I give thee if thou wilt worship the Führer."

Pelham Wodehouse fell on his knees.

Perhaps you have heard this man's voice reaching out to you from his luxury suite on the third floor of the Adlon Hotel. It comes across the Atlantic from our war-torn continent to you in America, still at peace. Maybe you can forgive this old man now wedded to the worst tyranny that ever scourged mankind.

We who remember Dunkirk will neither forgive nor forget.

Fifty thousand of my countrymen are enslaved in Germany. They fought their way across the northern plains of France so that their comrades could escape to England. They went through an inferno of flame and steel so that democratic England might live. How many of them are in the Adlon Hotel tonight?

How many of them are sailing on the pleasant lakes around Berlin, as Wodehouse did the other day?

Barbed wire is their pillow.

They endure but they do not give in.

They suffer but they do not sell out.

Perhaps you sympathise with anyone faced with the hideous apparatus of Nazi persecution. You are right to do so. But between the terrible choice of betrayal of one's country and the abominations of the Gestapo, there is only one answer.

The gaols of Germany are crammed with men who have chosen without demur. They have lost everything. Many of them are dead. But they have something that Wodehouse can never regain. Something that thirty pieces of silver could never buy.

In two paragraphs in the same style Cassandra proceeded to compare Wodehouse disadvantageously to a man named Dimitroff, temporarily very popular with the British because he had defied the Nazis. (In the light of subsequent history, this was an unlucky choice; Dimitroff was a Bulgarian Communist who later earned unpopularity in England.) He then continued:

Pelham Wodehouse is well known in the United States. He was with you in New York when during the last war we were muzzling another Führer by the name of Kaiser Wilhelm who also ran amock against the world.

YOU made Wodehouse rich.

YOU brought him fame.

Hundreds of thousands of American dollars poured into his pockets.

Two thousand dollars a week was the price of this Jester. But he was too quick for you. A smart guy . . . when the Internal Revenue Department called around for a slight item of one hundred and twenty-five thousand dollars of income tax owing, [they] found that the Fun-doctor had flown.

Maybe you'd care to hear the sequel to this, for it occurred in that same villa at Le Touquet. They rang him up and told him that he owed the United States more than a hundred thousand dollars. "Do I," said Wodehouse with careless ease. "Oh, I thought the amount was more. It certainly used to be."

Mr. Wodehouse must have been thinking about a little piece he wrote in 1928. It was called *Money for Nothing*.

Before I end this broadcast I wish to speak directly to Mr. Wodehouse sitting up there in his suite overlooking the Unter den Linden.

Cassandra then adopted the voice and manner of Quentin Reynolds in addressing Dr. Goebbels the week before.

> Mr. Wodehouse, you said the other day that you were "quite unable to work up any kind of belligerent feeling about this war."
>
> Do you know Dulwich, Mr. Wodehouse? Of course you do. It is the suburb of London where you went to school. I was there one night not very long ago, Mr. Wodehouse, and something happened that might interest you, who feel so calm and so imperturbable about this war.
>
> It was a peaceful night. Soft and gentle until the quiet was splintered and torn into a thousand screaming shreds as a thousand pounds of explosive travelling at seven hundred miles an hour hit the ground with appalling violence.
>
> It was soon silent again. Near me under five, fifteen, fifty tons of rubble lay human beings. Most of them dead. Some of them alive. A few of them dying. YOUR countrymen, Mr. Wodehouse. It was quiet. The contrast was rather shocking. One expected noise and excitement. Instead of that, there was a silence that was too reminiscent of the grave. The rescue squad began to work. Someone called for silence. No one spoke. We listened and with growing horror I knew we were waiting to hear cries of agony and pain from underneath those crushing loads of battered masonry and brickwork. Trapped, Mr. Wodehouse. That was it—trapped in a man trap. A ghastly evil cage of pain Made in Germany. MADE IN GERMANY! The words we knew as kids stamped on toys. Something savage and something unspeakably cruel. You should have been there Mr. Wodehouse, you with your impartiality, your reasonableness and perhaps even one of your famous little jokes.
>
> Good-night, America.
>
> And good-night to YOU, Mr. Pelham . . . Grenville . . . Wodehouse.

The reaction to this vicious calumny, in which all the important facts were unchecked and untrue and violently emotive language was used in an attempt to connect Wodehouse in the minds of listeners with all the blood-stained horrors of war, was immediate, and, as the BBC had predicted, largely the opposite of that intended. This time many newspapers besides the *Telegraph* received letters on the subject, and these were not, as before, mainly from writers and other public figures, but from the ordinary citizens of the land. On 19 July, four days after the "Postscript," *The Times* published a selection of readers' letters, all of which were adverse to Cassandra, and of which the following is representative.

> Will you allow me space to protest against the broadcasting by the BBC after the 9 o'clock news of the recording by Cassandra? I think I have never heard a meaner piece of invective given such publicity before all the facts and circumstances are known on which a fair judgment might be formed.

On this occasion, too, almost every newspaper carried articles of adverse comment. (Hannen Swaffer was one of the very few journalists who supported Cassandra.) This extract from the *Spectator* (18 July 1941) covers most of the points that were made:

> Nothing I have heard on the wireless for a long time involves the BBC in greater apparent discredit—I emphasise the adjective for reasons that will appear—than the broadcast on P. G. Wodehouse on Tuesday night. The announcement that the news would be followed by a talk on Wodehouse by "Cassandra," of the *Daily Mirror,* must have caused some surprise, but it was nothing to the astonishment of every listener who heard the talk—cheap, slanderous, feeble-violent, calculated inevitably, if it had any effect at all, to create a reaction sympathetic to Wodehouse—must have felt that the BBC should ever have passed such a script. "Pelham Grenville Wodehouse," we were told among other things—to be called Pelham Grenville is evidently a serious aggravation of other offences—when the war broke out, was living at Le Touquet "gambling." I should like to know the authority for that. There are other things I should like to know too. Every listener I have spoken to so far had one word for the broadcast—outrageous. Disgust with the thing, I understand, at Broadcasting House from top to bottom was universal. If the BBC had been a free agent it would have been turned down at sight. But over a wide and undefined field the BBC must take orders from the Ministry of Information, and the orders in this case were imperative. Whether the mandate was Mr. Duff Cooper's personally, I have no means of knowing. But the responsibility is clearly his. If he has decided that the *Daily Mirror* is the glass of fashion and the mould of form, most of the hard things that have been said about his Ministry seem considerably too mild. As for Wodehouse, his case has been adequately dealt with in temperate comment from many quarters. To revive it at all was idiotic psychology.

In the House of Commons a Captain Cobb asked the question: "Would it not be a good thing to replace the official of the BBC who was responsible for passing the filthy postscript to the news on Tuesday night?"[5]

The Governors of the BBC quite reasonably objected to the adverse publicity they were receiving, and Sir Walter Monckton, Director General of the Ministry of Information, told the Director General of the BBC that in correspondence and other forms of publicity about this broadcast the BBC might say that it had been given under the direction of the Minister of Information. The Governors were not satisfied by this, however, and at a meeting on 17 July, at which the Minister was present, they pressed him to announce publicly that Cassandra's broadcast had been given under his direction and against BBC advice. Duff Cooper then wrote to *The Times:*

> In justice to the Governors of the BBC I must make it plain that mine was the sole responsibility for the broadcast which last week distressed so

many of your readers. The Governors indeed shared unanimously the view expressed in your columns that the broadcast in question was in execrable taste. *De gustibus non est disputandum.* Occasions, however, may arise in time of war when plain speaking is more desirable than good taste.

In this letter, quoting a Latin tag to add authority, Duff Cooper relied on the old trick of answering a minor charge while letting the real one go by default. His taste, as he suggested, was his own affair, but the real issue was the one of truth. As Minister of Information, he insisted on a broadcast in which highly defamatory and improbable statements were made before all the facts could be known, and the impression deliberately given that the Wodehouse broadcasts contained propaganda for the Germans, although the monitored scripts were available to him. No one has ever attempted to explain or justify his behaviour, but several people who knew him well have agreed that he may simply have lost his temper. The only Minister to resign at Munich, he was well known for his strong anti-Nazi stance, but also for fits of uncontrollable rage. He would have been angry when he first heard of the Wodehouse broadcasts, and he would no doubt have found the opposition of the BBC extremely provoking. He never thought it necessary to make amends.

Connor jumped at the suggestion that the accusation against him was merely one of taste. Duff Cooper's letter appeared on 22 July. On the following day Cassandra wrote as follows:

I had not intended to intervene in the controversy about my recent broadcast on the subject of P. G. Wodehouse, but the relish and the perseverance with which you seek to discredit me necessitates an answer. I have been condemned on the grounds of bad taste. Since when has it been bad taste to name and nail a traitor to England? The letters which you have published have only served as a sad demonstration that there is still in this country a section of the community eager and willing to defend its own quislings.

You claim that there has been a "storm of protest" against this talk. I wonder. Of the letters received by the *Daily Mirror* over 90 per cent have completely approved of what I said. The remainder expressed the point of view to which you have given so much publicity. The correspondents of the *Daily Mirror* are not yours, but as a sample of general public opinion they are far more reliable than any mass readership index to which *The Times* may lay claim. By pure reasons of circulation they come from a representative slice of the community which out-numbers your readership by 10 to 1. The people who approved of what I said about P. G. Wodehouse are pre-eminently among the vast masses of fighting men, factory workers, miners, and the ordinary common people who are carrying the burden of this war. However, I do not begrudge you the "storm of protest" which you have so diligently fanned, for it compares favourably with the flat calm of acquiescence which was such a prominent feature of your correspondence before and up to the year of Munich.

I learn with interest that the Governors of the BBC share your views of what you describe as a "notorious" broadcast. However, I accurately anticipated their reaction, and it is to the credit of Mr. Duff Cooper that he insisted beforehand that the BBC should have no say whatsoever in the script of this talk. It would certainly not have been possible for him to have adopted this point of view, had it not been that their lamentable Governorship had rendered matters of propaganda demonstrably outside their scope.

To the accusation that this broadcast was vulgar, I would remind you that this is a vulgar war, in which our countrymen are being killed by the enemy without regard to good form or bad taste. When Dr. Goebbels announces an apparently new and willing propaganda-recruit to further this slaughter I still retain the right to denounce this treachery in terms compatible with my own conscience—and nothing else.

Yours faithfully,
William N. Connor
("Cassandra")

The following day he received one more letter from Duff Cooper.

Dear Cassandra,

I was glad to see your letter in *The Times* this morning. I hope you have been no more worried than I have by the carefully stirred-up agitation which that most unrepresentative paper has been conducting. I feel sure that even they received many letters on the other side, but they have long abandoned publication of letters that do not coincide with their own policy.

It may interest you to know for your private information that somebody who did not like the broadcast showed the text of it to the Prime Minister, who expressed the view that he could find no fault with it, except that the language seemed rather too mild.

Yours sincerely
Duff Cooper

There is no supporting evidence that Churchill saw the broadcast script, or that he made this comment. Equally there is no evidence to refute it, although the word somebody in Duff Cooper's letter may not be thought very strong. In any case, in spite of the storm of protest provoked by Cassandra's broadcast, the effect of the smear remained. Detail is quickly forgotten, but some of the general effect is remembered, and it is likely that this broadcast more than anything else accounts for the belief still held by some people that Wodehouse wittingly betrayed his country in return for a room at the Adlon, and that he broadcast propaganda for the enemy.

So much for the public record. One of the most illuminating letters was written privately. On 21 July Leonora Cazalet wrote to Denis Mackail:

Dearest Denis,

Thank you very very much for your really sweet letter, it was nice of you and it did make me feel quite cosy for a bit. It really is horrid about Plummie, and of course not for me to use obscene language about Mr. Milne but I can't help being pleased when other people do it; so your letter being on those lines was doubly pleasant. Actually if you would like to know truthfully my own reactions, I am absolutely certain without any trace of doubt that he has no idea that he is doing anything wrong. I have heard records of all the broadcasts to date, and he is so clearly speaking to what he imagines to be a sympathetic and interested audience that, apart from anything else, it's tragic that he should have so little idea of how flat his jokes are going. I almost believe that he probably even thinks he's being rather clever with the Germans in being able to talk to his friends, as of course the context is absolutely harmless. You probably saw excerpts from an article published in America, most of the good bits left out and in it he is so definitely making light of rather obviously bad conditions and not minding them. Behaving in fact like an Englishman should. . . . Any way, it's not much good airing my views to the general public as of course very reasonably I'm considered biased & any way it isn't helping our war effort so naturally is judged accordingly. I also feel a bit like a mother with an idiot child that she any way loves better than all the rest. . . .

Thank you and Diana again for your sweetness,

Yours,
Snorky

13

The Broadcasts:
The Aftermath

On the day that Baron von Barnekow met Plum in the courtyard of the Adlon and later left him with Plack, he was evidently serving his country. He made what amends he could to friendship. He now arranged for his fiancée, Baroness Anga von Bodenhausen, to come to Berlin to meet Plum. Towards the end of the week (on 27 June, Plum said) she drove him back to her estate, Degenershausen, in the Harz mountains, where he was to spend so much of his time while he was in Germany.

He returned to Berlin twice in July, each time to record two of the broadcasts which had in the meantime been written in the country. On the second occasion, after he had recorded the fifth broadcast, he went to the Adlon. Here presently Ethel arrived, bringing Wonder, the Peke, and they returned together to Degenershausen, where they spent the whole of the first summer.

There remains a considerable correspondence between Plum and Ethel Wodehouse and Anga von Bodenhausen, and also some letters to the latter's daughter, Reinhild. In these letters Plum always addressed the Baroness as "Dearest Anga," and Ethel wrote her as "Dearest" or "Darling," so it is apparent that a great affection sprang up between the Wodehouses and their hostess. The Baroness von Bodenhausen was a rich woman, and her husband had had estates in Kenya as well as in Germany. She spoke excellent English, while Reinhild, then a child, showed extraordinary facility in learning to speak to "Onkel" Plummie. The Wodehouses were treated as honoured guests, and the Baroness would accept no payment from them. From odd remarks in the letters it is apparent that she had a large and beautiful house in its own park in the lovely country of the Harz mountains.

Attached to the letters between the Wodehouses and the Baroness von Bodenhausen there are some notes which she made and which contribute much to the picture of Plum's life in her house and her relationship with him. The following are exact quotations:

> On his side one feels a very kind and light and large personality, he never could hurt, he never could be narrow or disturbing, soft, kind, unselfish, I dont know any fault in his character, a bit vague perhaps.
>
> Then yesterday he was so openhearted and confidential as never before all of a sudden telling me: You see, Anga, Degenershausen is just like a dream, but you always have it in your mind, things are quite wrong in the world and it suddenly grips you.
>
> Plummie is as light as a feather in his attitude with other people, he never approaches too near, he dislikes pathos, he never tries to be impressive or funny and his regularity of habit is without the slightest pedanterie and makes life quite smooth and clear cut. You grow your roots in a place like this. Yes, Plummie lives in a dream world and he charmingly forgets all you have told him to repeat it all over and then he just says: Oh, no really and polishes his eyeglasses. . . .
>
> I know exactly what will happen next: he will come upstairs to settle in his armchair next to the fireplace and continue some talk we had at dinnertime. We then listen to the German news on the radio with his comments and just by talking on he sort of mysteriously gets out of the room—talking meanwhile, and all of a sudden, like a conjurer he is outside and you are left alone.

There is also a note made by Anga von Bodenhausen of greater importance:

> When in the evening I returned from Berlin with all the news for Plummie I met him downstairs in the almost dark entrance hall. "Don't tell me anything, you first have a bath and a rest, Anga." He was very reserved and shining with kindliness and I was glad to have undertaken this most unpleasant journey and told the people in the Ministry in Berlin: Mr. Wodehouse would not come anymore, he was ill and his radio speeches were stopping immediately.[1]

There is no reason to doubt the authenticity of these remarks. In Plum's statement to Cussen he spoke of a series of cables between himself and Wesley Stout, editor of *The Saturday Evening Post*, of which he said he remembered the gist and which were presumably in the *Post*'s files.

> (1) Stout to me:
> "Deeply concerned by reports in press that you are about to broadcast on German Radio. Destroys value of article now beyond recall and may jeopardize serial."
>   The word *article* evidently refers to the one arranged by Thuermer when he visited me—though I was puzzled at the time.*

---

*And the word *serial* refers to *Money in the Bank*.

(2) Myself to Stout:

"Talks cannot possibly hurt serial. Simply comic accounts of my camp life in lightest possible vein."

(3) Stout to me:

Repeated his warning against broadcasting and ended "people here resent what is considered your callous attitude towards England. Like serial and want to buy it but can only do so on your giving definite undertaking to stop broadcasting."

(4) Myself to Stout:

To the best of my recollection:

"After the fifth talk will not speak again in any circumstances on any subject whatsoever. Cannot understand what you mean by callousness. Mine simply flippant cheerful attitude of all British prisoners. It was a point of honour with us not to whine."

My telegrams seem to me to show (a) my definite intention to make only the five camp talks and (b) the absence of any bargain to obtain release by carrying on German propaganda. For my refusal to do so at this stage, had such a bargain existed, would have involved my being sent back to internment. Had there been a bargain five talks would never have satisfied the German authorities.[2]

So it is not unlikely that Anga, who spoke the language and knew some of the people at the Ministry, should be the one who travelled to Berlin to tell them that Mr. Wodehouse would not come anymore.

At the end of July, Ethel arrived. When last heard of she was in a small back bedroom on a trout farm about 50 kilometres from Le Touquet, in the company of Wonder the Peke and Coco the parrot (as described in a letter to Denis and Diana Mackail).* She had just heard from Plum, who told her he was all right and at Lille, and she continued her letter to the Mackails by describing Plum's experiences as she afterwards learned them. Then she wrote:

> During this time I spent three months at the trout farm, then I thought they were getting tired of me, so I managed to get a permit to go to Lille. My host drove me there on a very wet day in his truck, then I started to find a room wandering all over Lille in the pouring rain with little Wonder, everything requisitioned, not a hotel anywhere.* After 8 o'clock I gave it up and went to a restaurant, sat in a corner and shed a few tears. The cashier talked to me, and took me to her landlady after the restaurant closed, and she gave me her daughter's room for five nights, later I found a room, and stayed at Lille for three months, cooking on a little gas ring in my room for Wonder and myself, then I would go to all the shops and

*Coco was left behind, I think, at the trout farm.

*See pages 150–51.

pick up odd food for Plummie, and in the afternoons go to the hospital there as there were some of our men there. Later I went back to the country to the same little village as before, but this time I stayed with some charming people, French, a dear old lady, her son, and daughter, as a paying guest, because they hadn't too much money. A charming house with a huge park, and letters every week from Plummie telling me all the time that he was working on a novel and not to worry about him.

Ethel then returned to an account of Plummie's life, and after describing his release, she went on:

The first person he ran into was Raven Barnico [*sic*]—a German that we had known in America for years, and lived in Hollywood when I was there, and always came to our swimming parties. He nearly passed out when he saw Plummie, and they had a long talk and then Raven went off to the Bristol, where he was staying, to get Plummie some clothes.

Ethel described the arrival of Werner Plack, and then:

Raven left him [Plack] talking to Plummie, and this man, after Plummie had been telling him about his camp experiences, said to him "Why don't you do some talks to America about camp on the lines of what you have been telling me?" Well, it struck Plummie as a most excellent idea, silly ass, because while he was at Tost he had been receiving lots and lots of letters from American readers and also parcels, and he hadn't been able to acknowledge any of them and he felt that the people who had written to him might be thinking him rather a louse for not answering. . . . So he thought that if he did five talks covering five chapters of his camp life it would please his readers over there, and so he went and did them. He hadn't a notion that there was anything wrong in talking on the German radio, so long as you simply did the sort of thing he was going to do. It wasn't till I got to Berlin, when the five talks had been made, that he knew he had made a bloomer, and then of course it was too late.

Predictably, this account is not completely accurate—in particular, it is obviously untrue that Raven von Barnekow was surprised to find Plum in the courtyard of the Adlon—but it is true that Plum had recorded all five broadcasts before Ethel arrived. There is no explanation in the Cussen Report or anywhere else of how or when he broadcast the introduction to the fourth talk, in which he showed knowledge of what had been said in the English newspapers, but this was monitored by the BBC.

The Wodehouses spent just over two years in Germany. All the first summer they were at Degenershausen, but in the winter the Baroness shut the house because it was impossible to heat it, and they returned to the Adlon. The following year, 1942, Plum returned alone to Degenershausen in April, but Ethel stayed in Berlin until July, when she once more joined him. The third and final summer both of them went as paying guests to a Graf Wolkenstein in Upper Silesia, probably because the Baroness von Bodenhausen by then had other people billeted upon her. Writing later to Townend, Plum said:

> I suppose I was in the middle of all sorts of interesting things, but they didn't touch me. We had a few friends, English and American women married to or the widows of Germans, and we saw them, but apart from that I lived the life of a hermit, plugging away at my writing. . . . I was right out of the world. My Upper Silesian host . . . lived a great part of his life in England, and . . . I found in his library five years of *Punch* and the *Saturday Review* and also great masses of *Cornhill.*

Where did their money come from? They always said they paid all their own bills and all their expenses at the Adlon, and that to do this they sold Ethel's jewels and also borrowed money. In the statement to Cussen Plum was more exact. He said they received 40,000 marks from the sale of a bracelet; borrowed 10,000 marks from a Frau Harbach (who, Ethel said in her account, had a son and daughter living in London to whom they were to return the loan in English money after the war); borrowed 5,000 marks from Raven von Barnekow; sold a wristwatch for 5,000 marks; received 8,000 marks in exchange for cheques on their American account; while in his possession at the time of his release Plum had 1,000 marks received from America. He received a sum of about 1,000 marks from Tauchnitz for book royalties. Later he amended the statement of receipts to include a further 40,000 marks (less 10 percent commission) received from a German film company for the right to make a film of one of his novels. The money spent in Berlin, he said, amounted to about 25,000 marks, although he again amended his statement after conversation with his wife, and said he thought the sum for expenditure was too small, although he was unable to deal adequately with this for the moment.*

He did not include any sum for payment for the broadcasts, but he had said earlier in his statement that Plack had given him 250 marks for the five.

The meaning of the Trading with the Enemy Act of 1939 was discussed in the House of Commons in a debate which will be quoted later. But since its meaning is often misinterpreted (various interpretations were put upon it in the House of Commons), and since Wodehouse has sometimes been accused of an offence, either technical or moral, in receiving a fee for

---

*In Paris he received from a Count Sollohub 140,000 francs, from his Spanish publisher 320,000 francs, and from Rotje, a picture dealer, 25,000 francs. The first of these sums was probably, and the third certainly, a loan to be repaid in English currency in England.

the broadcasts, at the risk of some slight repetition these accusations must be considered.

What should someone do who finds himself in an enemy country during a war and is forced to live at an expensive hotel (or even if he is not)? Wodehouse was a professional writer, and if he had refused money for the broadcasts it might with some plausibility have been suggested that he was being paid in a different way. Again, the fact that he sold the scripts of his novels for filming was not known in England, and in this he was certainly trading with the enemy. But what was Ethel doing when she sold her jewels? And what would have been the case if Plum had been a carpenter instead of a novelist? How does anyone not bent on suicide avoid trading with the enemy on enemy territory in wartime? If he refuses payment and lives on the generosity of his hosts (or at least on their generosity after he has made five broadcasts on their wavelength), is that more honourable? One must accept that there are situations from which there is no right way out, and whatever one does can be used against one.

And yet the Wodehouses behaved very well in their own fashion. They did not grumble or complain, and they did not give way to despair. Plum lived as he would have anywhere else in the world, with the hours not at his typewriter spent either reading or taking Wonder for a walk. (In a letter to Townend he said: "Wonder (the Peke) is in terrific form. Ethel brought her from France and she has settled down splendidly. All the children in the Tiergarten admire her enormously and follow her about shouting 'Kleine hunde.' " And he says again and again that Wonder would not eat anything but meat, so they had to give the whole of their ration to her.) Ethel behaved without much discretion, but with considerable gallantry. There is a story of a German General on leave from the front who came to the Adlon with his wife and his dog, to be told by the desk clerk that dogs were not allowed in the hotel. At that moment Ethel walked through the foyer with Wonder at her heels. "Why is that dog allowed?" the General asked. "That," the clerk replied, "is Mrs. Wodehouse's dog."

This story, which is almost certainly apocryphal, was told as evidence, if not exactly of corruption, at least to illustrate a favoured position. Yet anyone who knew Ethel would have known that it would be impossible to get Wonder out of the Adlon unless Ethel went too. And this is exactly what happened. When the hotel manager's complaints grew too numerous, Ethel moved to the Bristol, leaving Plum at the Adlon. Malcolm Muggeridge, who came to know her well, has described her as "a bad sleeper, accustomed to wander about during the night, polishing tables and planning to pull down whatever house they happened to be occupying and rebuild it nearer to her heart's desire; a mixture of Mistress Quickly and

Florence Nightingale, with a touch of Lady Macbeth thrown in—I grew to love her."³

When I asked him why he loved her, he replied: "She was so *game*." Someone has said that Victor Gollancz used to walk up and down trying to imagine what it would be like to be in a concentration camp. Plum's critics never seemed to wonder what it would be like, after a year in an internment camp, to be in a country where you knew almost no one and could not speak the language. How were they all so sure they would have known how to behave?

14

The Cussen Report and Parliament

By 1943 Berlin was being bombed night and day, and in September Paul Schmidt agreed that the Wodehouses should be moved to Paris. Ethel wrote later to the Mackails:

> The air raids [on Berlin] were frightful—buildings tumbling down in all directions. People in a panic trying to get on trains to get out of the city. It was frightful. . . .
>
> After an awful lot of trouble we finally got permission to go to Paris as they didn't really know what to do with us. We stayed two nights at the Hotel Bristol [in Berlin] on our way through, and I shall never forget those two nights! However we got out of the city. The Bristol later was bombed, everybody killed including many French maids. . . . We came to the Hotel Bristol in Paris, where we stayed until the Liberation, leading a very quiet life. As soon as the British arrived, Plummie at once reported to them. Our first visitor was a most delightful Major in the BIS. We talked over the whole affair and it was agreed that Plummie and I should see an official of the FO and go through the whole tiresome business. This we did, answering every question satisfactorily. Where we got our money from, who our friends were in Berlin etc. All went well. . . .

Plum did send a message to the British authorities through an American Colonel the day after General de Gaulle's official entry into the city in August 1944. The "most delightful Major" was Malcolm Muggeridge; the official of the FO was Major Edward Cussen, not of the FO but of Military Intelligence, whose report is constantly quoted here.

Muggeridge has written several accounts of his association with the Wodehouses, all of which are very much to be recommended to the general reader, the most easily available being in his book *Chronicles of Wasted Time.* His job seems to have been merely to keep an eye on them until Cussen arrived, but this he did in the most genial spirit. He writes: "My feelings about him [Wodehouse] on first making his acquaintance were, I should say, that he was a distinguished and original writer who had given a great deal of pleasure to a great many people, and that, as such, he was entitled to be kept clear of the monstrous buffooneries of war."

He describes Plum at that time as "a large, bald, elderly man, wearing grey flannel trousers, a loose sports jacket and what I imagine were golfing shoes, and smoking a pipe; a sort of schoolmaster's rig."[1] And he says of Ethel that "she turned out to be a spirited and energetic lady trying as hard to be worldly wise as Wodehouse himself to be innocent."[2]

Muggeridge had tragic news to tell them for which they were in no way prepared. In the previous May, Leonora had gone into the London Clinic for a small operation, thought necessary because she wished to have a third child and had failed to conceive. During the following night she rang the bell twice; once she asked for a hot drink, but the second time when the nurse reached the room Leonora was dead. Sir Bernard Spilsbury, who did the post mortem, said that she died of "early atheroma of the arteries." The shock that these words may convey is only a faint oscillation from the shock felt by her friends and relations at that time. Leonora was under forty and had been in perfect health. She was mourned by everyone who knew her.

Her sister-in-law, Thelma Cazalet-Keir, wrote at once to the Wode-houses giving them the details, but it fell to Mr. Muggeridge to be the first to break the news. He wrote that after a long pause Plum said: "I thought she was immortal."[3] To Townend Plum himself wrote: "We are quite crushed by the dreadful news about Leonora. I really feel that nothing much matters now." And to Thelma: "Your sad news came as a terrible shock and has stunned me. Poor Ethel is prostrate."

As is well known, the Wodehouses spent the last thirty-odd years of their life in America, and he finally became an American citizen. One cannot help believing that if Leonora had lived, they would have spent some of this time, if not in England, at least in France. Plum seldom spoke of her in later years, but he wrote regularly to her children. The earlier letters written from France were for the most part of that lumpish kind everyone writes to schoolchildren (and to fans), telling them of his own doings and trying to take the right interest in theirs. But as soon as they grew up, they visited him regularly at Remsenburg, and his letters from there are a valuable source of all that will ever be known about him.

In his official capacity Mr. Muggeridge was soon succeeded by Major Cussen, but he remained in touch with the Wodehouses and looked after them until he left Paris.

Major Cussen was in charge of the interrogation of "renegades," and because he reported himself, Wodehouse was the first of these. Both be-

cause of the importance of the man and to test the working of the rules he
had laid down, Cussen decided to fly to Paris and conduct the interrogation
himself. He questioned the Wodehouses for two or three hours a day for
ten days, and his report is now lodged at the Public Records Office.

By the time the Cussen Report was released in 1980 almost everything
about the events connected with the German broadcasts was already known,
partly through Plum's own accounts in letters and in the typescript "Now
That I've Turned Both Cheeks," and partly through Richard Usborne's
researches. Yet, although the Report contains few surprises, the account
Plum gave Cussen is different in tone from any other. He obviously found
the whole situation intensely humiliating, and to friends and in interviews
he naturally made the best of everything, seldom altering the truth, but
occasionally improving upon it. (An obvious example is the letter to Michael Joseph in which he said that he had never met Werner Plack before.
This alters nothing fundamental or important, because he scarcely knew
Plack in Hollywood except by sight, but it would have taken much tiresome explanation, of a kind which would not necessarily have been believed, to establish this. Very many people in the circumstances would have
done as he did and strengthened the truth.) In the statement to Cussen he
gives the impression of a man not merely telling the truth to the best of his
ability but struggling for accuracy even in small details.

He had one awkward and rather sad fact to explain. On 21 November
1942 he addressed a letter to the British Foreign Office through the Swiss
intermediary in Berlin. This is a very long letter setting out the facts of his
internment, his release, and the reasons which led him to broadcast. The
second paragraph and the beginning of the third read as follows:

> In the press and on the radio of Great Britain it has been stated that I
> bought my release from internment by making a bargain with the German
> Government, whereby they on their side were to set me free and I on
> mine undertook to broadcast German propaganda to the United States.
> This I can emphatically deny. I was released, as were all internees who
> had reached that age, because I was sixty years old.

In his statement to Cussen, in a paragraph which is slightly confused but
which plainly refers to this letter, he said: "I have thought this matter over
very carefully and where the account I have just given differs from that
contained in my letter to the Foreign Office I wish the former to be
accepted. At the time when I wrote to the Foreign Office I was very
worried." And at the end of the whole statement, he said: "I should like
to conclude by saying that I never had any intention of assisting the enemy
and that I have suffered a great deal of mental pain as the result of my
action."

He convinced his interrogator, as the Report would convince most people today, that he was an essentially innocent man. Cussen died in 1973,
but before that, writing to Richard Usborne and speaking of *Performing
Flea*, he said: "Having read p. 107 and the subsequent pages of the book,
and bearing in mind its general tenor, I have no doubt that PGW would
do well to set out his full account of the years 1939 to 1945—before it is
too late." Nevertheless, it must be emphasized in view of later events that,
although Malcolm Muggeridge records his satisfaction that Cussen told
him "Wodehouse must be exonerated of everything but foolishness and
one or two minor technical offences," he adds: "Nonetheless, blowing
down his nose, in a legal way, he [Cussen] delivered himself of the opinion
that, for the time being, Wodehouse 'should be kept out of the Jurisdiction'; meaning, I assumed, out of England."[4]

The general tone and conclusion of the Cussen Report agree with what
Major Cussen said at the time to Malcolm Muggeridge and later to Richard
Usborne. However, he remarked several times that the evidence he had
received would have to be checked with the Germans concerned, if and
when they were found, and there is no record that this ever occurred. And,
while throughout he gave the impression of believing in Wodehouse's innocence of the main charges, he did make one or two observations of a
different kind.* Paragraph 48 states:

> It will be necessary to make enquiries in Germany in due course as to
> the conduct of the Wodehouses while they were in that country after the
> broadcasts. I fear that we shall find that their behaviour has been unwise.
> From what I have seen of Mrs. Wodehouse I expect to learn that she
> conducted herself in a flamboyant manner and that she accepted all the
> attention which was no doubt paid to her by German officials. Apart of
> course from the unwisdom of such conduct, if it took place, the basic
> matter with which we are concerned is not affected. Indeed, it seems that
> Mrs. Wodehouse was escorted from France to Germany by a Foreign
> Office official and that a good deal of fuss was made of her during the
> journey and upon her arrival in Berlin. She has, if anything, less political
> sense than her husband and I fear that she would not know how to
> conduct herself in the circumstances which arose. She did, however, real-
> ise quite clearly the harm the broadcasts had done to Wodehouse.

And part of paragraph 50 reads:

> Though the information thus obtained from people who knew the Wode-
> houses in Paris is favourable to the Wodehouses, I shall not be surprised

---

*In view of the importance of the matter, it seems reasonable to repeat that Werner Plack
did confirm the more important parts of Wodehouse's statement to Richard Usborne and
later to me.

if we receive complaints as to their conduct while in Paris and these will, of course, be investigated. Such complaints will no doubt arise from the attention paid to them by German officers and officials. I think that Wodehouse may have been in rather a difficult position in this regard because it was not easy for him to ignore a German who might choose to speak to him, and the same applies, perhaps to a greater degree, to Mrs. Wodehouse.

Various documents are attached to the Cussen Report, the most important of which was signed with an illegible initial above the typed initials "D. of P.P.," and this read:

> Having considered Major Cussen's report, I have informed M.I.5. that I am satisfied, on the present material, that there is not sufficient evidence to justify a prosecution of this man.
>
> It is possible that information may subsequently come to light, which will establish a more sinister motive for this man's activities in Germany but, having regard to the nature and content of his broadcasts, there is, at the moment, nothing to justify any action on my part; nor do I consider that the Trading with the Enemy Regulations would apply to this man's business transactions with the enemy while he was in enemy or enemy-occupied territory.

One or two other documents, although of minor importance compared with the statement of the Director of Public Prosecutions, throw further light on this whole affair. The first is quoted more for the eloquence and humour with which one of the civil servants to whom it was circulated sums up her opinion than for any other reason (not all of her colleagues agreed with her views). She wrote:

> The report, combined with Wodehouse's statement and his radio script, gives the impression that he lives in the same world as his characters, a cosmopolitan, apolitical place, into which conceptions such as the state and the nation do not intrude. He seems to be keenly interested in individuals but to have little sense of collective entities (other than "My American Public"), and while he would probably not help "the enemy" he has no very clear idea what the enemy is and has difficulty in recognising as such the individual Germans with whom he finds it easy to get on. Even, therefore, if he was specifically invited to broadcast and not given the impression, as his statement suggests, that he was being allowed to do so as a favour, he would be much more likely to think of himself as doing a good turn to the friendly Plack than as "assisting the enemy." Had he seriously wished to assist the enemy he could have given them much more help than we have any indication of; and it is difficult to believe that he would have thought it worth making such a bargain with them in order

to get out of internment, when he was reasonably content in camp (there could have been little hardship during the summer) and believed that he would be automatically released in four months' time.

In more than one memorandum attached to the report an official expresses anxiety that Wodehouse should not be short of money and therefore tempted to come "into the jurisdiction" in order to get released the considerable sums he had in England. This will be seen as an excellent example of how in government the right hand has no idea of what the left hand is doing.

Finally a telegram from the new Ambassador to Paris had a direct bearing on the Wodehouses' lives. Headed "Mr. Duff Cooper" and sent by bag on 29 September 1944, it reads:

> I think you should know that Mr. and Mrs. P. G. Wodehouse are staying in Paris at the Hotel Bristol which is supposed to be reserved for the Corps Diplomatique and where I myself together with the majority of the Foreign Representatives are living. . . . In view of the difficulties that might arise if the press were to get hold of the story, I am trying to arrange for Wodehouse to be moved to another hotel.

Returning now to Ethel's account to the Mackails of the Wodehouses' lives in Paris, we find that "our friend the Major" (in this case Muggeridge) suggested to them that they should move to the Lincoln, a quieter hotel, in order to avoid the attention of reporters. Soon after they moved to the Lincoln they were arrested by the French. Here is Ethel's account of what happened:

> We stayed quietly at the Lincoln, seeing no one. Then one night at 12:30 when we were asleep, we were suddenly arrested by the French! Plum was on the floor above me. I suddenly woke up and saw a sinister man leaning over my bed with his hat on and coat collar turned up exactly like a movie. I was told to dress immediately. I produced my British passport. Useless. I was told if I didn't dress at once, I should be taken in my nightgown!! Off we went to the Palais de Justice, not really frightened, but mad! When we got there we sat in a little passage on two wooden chairs for 17 hours before we were taken upstairs for interrogation. Two young men with type-writers then started to ask our name and address. They couldn't speak any English. I asked what the charge was, and was told Plummie had spoken on a German radio but they didn't know what about. I asked why I was arrested and they shrugged their shoulders. I asked to see my paper with the charges on it, there was nothing on it completely blank. I managed to make them understand they must get in touch with our embassy, eventually they did, our beloved Major came round at once with food and wine.

Malcolm Muggeridge's account is as follows:

Early one morning . . . I got a message from Jacqueline de Broglie, whom I had met with the Wodehouses, telling me that the previous night they had been arrested by the French Police. . . . It seemed that at a dinner party given by the then *Prefet de Police*, Luiset, an English guest had remarked on how scandalous it was that two such notorious traitors as the Wodehouses should be at large in Paris; whereupon Luiset gave orders there and then that they should be arrested. . . .

I located them at a police station on the Quai d'Orleans. No one seemed to know why M. and Mme Wodenhorse (as they appeared on their warrant) were there, and I had no difficulty in arranging for Ethel's immediate release. It appeared that, using her highly individual and idiosyncratic French at its shrillest, she had reduced the whole station to a condition of panic; aided and abetted by her Peke, Wonder, whom she had insisted on taking with her when she was arrested. By the time I arrived on the scene, the police, I could see, were desperately anxious to get Ethel and Wonder off the premises as soon as possible.[5]

To arrange Plum's release proved more difficult, and the only way it could be done was on grounds of health. "An amiable prison doctor," shaking his head after taking Plum's pulse, arranged for Plum's transfer to a clinic, the only one available proving to be a maternity home. He was not released for two months, and then he and Ethel went to a hotel at Fontainebleau.

On 6 December 1944 questions were asked in the House of Commons about the reasons for the Wodehouse arrest and surveillance by the French, to which the Foreign Secretary, Anthony Eden, replied that he was asking the French Government to state the legal grounds on which residence under surveillance was being maintained.

Sir J. Lucas: May I ask whether a British subject can be tried by Great Britain or France, for an offence in Germany?

Mr. Eden: My honourable and gallant Friend will see that there is no question of trial and no question of a charge. . . .

Captain Gammans: Did not the right honourable Gentleman give an assurance some time ago that any British subject suspected of Quisling activities should be brought to this country for investigation, and, if necessary, trial? Did not the Foreign Secretary give that assurance two weeks ago?

Mr. Eden: Does my honourable and gallant Friend mean that we should take positive measures ourselves to bring Mr. Wodehouse to England? If so, I can tell him—though it is not a matter for me but for the Home Office—that that matter has been gone into and, according to the advice given, there are no grounds upon which we could take action. . . .

Mr. Hogg: Is it not obvious that a person who broadcasts on the enemy wireless and receives a fee, either in kind or money, is trading with the enemy, and is punishable under the Act which deals with that offence?

Mr. Eden: Really, that is not a matter for me. It is a matter for the Home Office.

In reply to other questions, Eden asserted once more that the case had been considered by the appropriate authorities, who had advised that information at present available afforded no grounds for legal proceedings in this country, and he said again: "I have explained that the question whether there are any grounds for legal proceedings against Mr. Wodehouse is not a matter for me, but I have answered the question because the matter has been gone into, and it has been agreed that there are no legal grounds."[6]

There it might have been hoped the matter would rest. Yet Hogg, the Member for Oxford, had not been satisfied. On 15 December he initiated a short debate in order to pursue the matter. After mentioning a Colonel Rocke and Mr. P. G. Wodehouse by name and referring to the fact that twice during the preceding months Government Departments had said, replying to questions, that the legal advisers to the Government had assured His Majesty's Ministers that it was not per se an offence to speak on enemy wireless, Hogg went on to say that if it was not an offence to speak on enemy wireless during wartime, it ought very soon to be made one. In the preamble to his argument, he said that "we are not here concerned with penalties" and explained:

If it be that these gentlemen [Colonel Rocke and Wodehouse] have incurred the punishment for high treason, I should be the first to say that theirs was not a serious example of a terribly serious offence, and to ask for penalties to be remitted under the prerogative of mercy; or that they should be prosecuted for something less than high treason within the discretion of the learned Judge trying the case. I am not here to call for blood . . . but to vindicate the law.

Turning then to the Treason Act of 1351 (which, he remarked, was so well drafted by our predecessors that it remains the basis of the law today), he said that an authoritative pronouncement had been given in the *King* v. *Casement* case on those words from it on which he relied. This was:

If the British subject tends to act in a way which strengthens, or tends to strengthen, the enemies of the King in conducting war against the King, or which weakens, or tends to weaken, the power of the King and country to resist or attack the enemies of the country, he gives aid or comfort to the King's enemies within the meaning of the Act.

He then continued:

> The question is whether the person who happens to have performed on the enemy wireless has committed an act which strengthens the King's enemies, and has tended to weaken the country. I am astonished that one should have to argue this question to this House. What does the Attorney General think is the purpose of the German wireless? Is it not to build up a listening public in order that that public may have its morale sapped by tendentious broadcasts?

Hogg said that it did not matter whether the actual script of the broadcast was tendentious or not, and he said: "A person who happens to clown on the enemy wireless, instead of producing directly anti-British propaganda, is committing just as much an act of treason towards this country as 'Lord Haw-Haw' himself, although the punishment might well be less." And he added: "There can be nothing but contempt for the action of a man who, in order to live in a hotel more comfortably than his fellow prisoners, did that kind of thing against his country."

Hogg then turned to the point that in order to be guilty of the crime of high treason or any other crime there must be a guilty intention, and on this he said:

> A man, according to the law of England, is presumed to intend the consequences of his own action, and nobody, short of a lunatic, who broadcasts on the enemy wireless would fail to realise that the consequences would be to strengthen the King's enemies, and it follows that he should be condemned as having intended the inevitable result.

The Trading with the Enemy Act of 1939, he said, was a milder statute designed to prevent actions which might be technically treasonable but do not merit the penalty for high treason under modern conditions. It says that a person shall be deemed to be trading with the enemy if he has commercial or other intercourse or dealings with the enemy for the benefit of the enemy. "I submit," Hogg said, "that this broadcasting on the enemy wireless was having intercourse of the kind referred to in that section."

At this point Hogg finished with Wodehouse and spent the rest of his speech taking the Director of Public Prosecutions and the Attorney General to task for what he saw as "a little laxness in their application of the criminal law."

He was followed by Harold Nicolson, who said:

> I have been into the P. G. Wodehouse case with the greatest care. He gave six talks in Berlin directed to the United States when the United States was not at war with Germany. There were a great many American correspondents, many of whom I could cite as witnesses if necessary, in

Berlin at the time, and after Mr. Wodehouse's third talk they received telegrams from their newspapers to interview him and say that this was having a very bad effect in the United States. Therefore, after his third talk he was warned, but he continued and gave three more.

Then the Attorney General (Sir Donald Somervell) rose to reply. He dealt first with the Trading with the Enemy Act, and he explained that it applied to people and acts done within the jurisdiction of England:

> The trading which makes it criminal is the trading or attempting to trade by someone in this island with someone in Germany. That it does not apply to British subjects everywhere will be obvious to anyone who cares to look at Section 14. . . . If a British subject, for one reason or another, when war broke out happened to be in Germany, he must, of course, buy food and clothes in order to live, and anyone can see that it would be absurd to suggest that that was a criminal offence.

He went on to deal with the question of intent, and he said: "My honourable friend, to my mind, dismissed far too lightly and summarily the vital ingredient of the offence of the treason, which is the intent to assist the enemy."

The Attorney General then cited the leading case concerning intent in illustration of his point, a case which went to the Court of Criminal Appeal; but he was interrupted by Harold Nicolson, who said: "Suppose in this case it had been proved by the prosecution that three or four persons had come to him and said: 'What you are doing is assisting the enemy,' and if, having been warned, he had then persisted, surely the Court of Appeal would not have taken that view." In the course of the Attorney General's reply he said: "If my honourable friend has evidence which he thinks ought to be considered in regard to Mr. Wodehouse, I shall be glad to consider it."

"The Attorney General has got it," Nicolson asserted.

The Attorney General said that he had to deal with the points raised by Hogg, and he was sorry that Nicolson had intervened, as he had not the time to deal with his point. And, although again interrupted, he continued to discuss the question of "intent to assist the enemy" in the Treachery Act of 1940, and said: "With regard to the case of Mr. Wodehouse, we investigated it and considered the evidence. The Director came to the conclusion, and I read the papers and I agree with him, that on the evidence we have there is not sufficient evidence of intent to assist the enemy to justify proceedings."

The Attorney General also dealt with an objection by Viscount Hinchingbroke that "all a man has to say on being charged with treason is 'I never intended to do any wrong.'"

"I am glad my Noble Friend interrupted," the Attorney General replied. "I would like to dispose of that. Of course there are cases in which facts speak for themselves, in which they are obvious." (He took an extreme case of a man who had a gun and served in the German Forces.) He then went on:

> If he has donè propaganda of the kind which some of us have heard over the wireless, it is no use his saying, "I did not intend to assist the enemy." If he tried to persuade people to join the German Forces it is no use his saying he did not intend to assist the enemy. The problem and the difficulty for those who have to consider the matter only arises in cases where one cannot say that that ends the argument.[7]

The time limit for the debate having been reached, it was adjourned (in mid-sentence while Clement Davis was speaking) till the following Tuesday "without Question Put." It was never resumed, and for the time being this was virtually the end of the matter. (Not quite the end, because it was raised again at Question Time on 21 December, when some of the same questions were asked, and the Home Secretary, Herbert Morrison, gave virtually the same replies.)[8] Nothing had been achieved except a further smear on Wodehouse's name. Nevertheless, no serious objection can be made to any of the speeches except Harold Nicolson's.

Nicolson twice interrupted when the Attorney General had no time to answer him, in order to give an account which is inaccurate in almost every detail. He said that Wodehouse had made six broadcasts when in fact he had made five, a small point, but typical of the kind of incompletely informed gossip on which he appeared to be relying. More importantly, he said that after the third talk American journalists received telegrams from their newspapers to warn Wodehouse, and he went on: "Therefore, after his third talk he was warned, but he continued and gave three more." Nicolson was clearly referring to the time at which the third talk went on the air, unaware that all the talks were recorded for transmission at a later date. In fairness, it must be pointed out that since Plum went from Degenershausen to record the second and third talks and then again at a later date to record the fourth and fifth, it is not impossible for him to have met the journalists after he had finished the first of these two sets of recordings. But there is no evidence that he did, and no reason to assume it.

If he was ever warned, the most likely time would have been when the journalists surrounded him on his first day at the Adlon, an occasion about which he said to Cussen, rather unfortunately, that his memory was blurred. But this suggestion is negated by Flannery's evidence that several days later, in answer to a question from Plum, Flannery decided to explain the situation to him.

Harold Nicolson repeated these charges in an article in the *Spectator* and never at any time withdrew them.*

This is what Wodehouse himself had to say on the matter:

> I received absolutely no warning against making the broadcasts. The talks were delivered on the radio once a week, starting, I think, in July, which presumably gave the impression that I was in Berlin and coming regularly to the microphone, and that I was meeting newspaper correspondents all that time and being warned. What actually happened was that I wrote the first two talks in Berlin, recorded them on wax, and then left for the country to stay with relatives of von Barnekow—three days after I had arrived in Berlin. I then wrote the other three, came up to Berlin from the country for the night, recorded the talks on wax and went back to the country again, where I remained until December. When I learned about the furore the broadcasts had caused, it was too late.[9]

Wodehouse was speaking from memory, but he can hardly have forgotten that he came up twice to Berlin, because, apart from anything else, on the second occasion Ethel arrived. This seems an unfortunate moment for his memory once more to become blurred, but one must remember that Plum found this whole incident so humiliating that, while the centrepiece of his story never changes, he shows a constant tendency to alter small surrounding details, although for what reason or in what direction is never very clear. One must also remember that this typescript was, as far as we know, never published, while to what potential readership it was addressed is also unknown.

When in 1958 Richard Usborne began to make very serious and detailed researches into the question of the Wodehouse broadcasts, he corresponded with and talked to Judge Cussen (now dead) and Werner Plack (alive) and corresponded with Harry Flannery (now dead). No evidence to support Nicolson's statement or to contradict the essential part of Plum's has ever emerged. Rather to the contrary: Flannery, for instance, wrote a long letter in reply to one from Richard Usborne, and, although this is in his usual slovenly style, so that his statements are often ambiguous, he did say unequivocally: "It was only right that he should have been exonerated as he was after the war. He was caught. He was innocent. Anyone who knows Wodehouse knows that. I met some other Englishmen and Irishmen over there, with whom I wouldn't even talk, and Americans too, but there was no such reaction to Wodehouse."

---

*In this article Nicolson says that the first broadcast was not monitored but the other four were, which today seems to be the opposite of the truth. But he quotes from the last four correctly, and Leonora Cazalet also said she heard them. The explanation is that they were recorded on some kind of impermanent wax and have since disappeared, while the incomplete transcripts remain.

Wodehouse made an extraordinarily stupid mistake and may have committed a technical offence. (It should never be forgotten that the first Director of Public Prosecutions and the first Attorney General to read the Cussen Report thought not.) He may be considered unlucky to have paid for it with what, however sympathetic to him the surroundings, was a lifetime of exile. Yet, because a great effort of imagination is necessary to understand and sympathize with temperamental difficulties different from one's own, even if Duff Cooper had not insisted on the violent distortions of the Cassandra broadcast, some people would have been unable to comprehend how Plum came to broadcast on the German wireless, however harmless his text. There would nevertheless have been those who found the proceedings taken against him even more distasteful; and others who felt passionately in his defence.

15

Paris

When Malcolm Muggeridge secured the Wodehouses' release from the French police, Ethel went back to the Hotel Lincoln, but Plum, it may be remembered, was kept under surveillance and taken to a hospital. Here he stayed for two months, December 1944 and January 1945, after which he was freed and he and Ethel went to the Hôtel les Charmettes at Barbizon. This was almost immediately requisitioned by the army, and Plum and Ethel returned to the Hotel Lincoln. This in its turn was requisitioned. Writing to Denis and Diana Mackail from the address 78 Paul Doumer, Ethel thanked them for their sweet letters to her and apologized for the time she had taken in answering them:

> When they arrived we were just about to be thrown out of the Lincoln, as the hotel like every hotel in Paris was requisitioned. . . . We couldn't find a hotel or apartment in Paris, then by the most amazing luck a friend had an apartment she didn't want, and asked me if I would like to have it. I dashed round and took it at once, otherwise we would have been on the street! It's terribly expensive, 16,000 francs a month, 20,000 with gas and electricity thrown in, not to mention telephone. However, here we are! I haven't had one single second to sit down and breathe. Up in the morning early, preparing Plummie's breakfast, then all the flat to clean, then the lunch to prepare, Plummie's clothes to keep in order, tea, and in between times standing in queues trying to get a few vegetables for two hours at a time. Usually returning with a bit of salad and a few carrots. Dinner and then I could only fall on the bed exhausted. We have now managed to get a little maid. Her name is Anita, and she is very sweet, but can't cook and can't get up in the morning, but she can wash dishes better than Plummie could, and it's a great relief to have her.

After the liberation of Paris Plum wrote hundreds of letters to all sorts of people, and these letters tell better than anything else could the story of the Wodehouses' life in that impoverished city. During the periods he spent in Berlin, and again in Paris right up to the liberation, Plum wrote regularly to "Dearest Anga" von Bodenhausen. On 3 May 1944 he wrote:

> How is my darling Reinhild? I will write to her very soon. . . . I think so much about Degenershausen. How nice it is to feel that my tree in the middle of the park will soon be coming to life again. I do hope that Degenershausen will always remain an oasis of safety and happiness and that you will be able to spend one of the old time summers there. I wonder if you have been running off the African and Degenershausen films lately. It's so sad that Ethel has not seen the coloured ones with her and all the dogs.

After the liberation of Paris these letters ceased. There is a suggestion that Degenershausen was taken over by the Allies when they reached Berlin, and the Wodehouses may for a while have lost touch with Baroness von Bodenhausen, while it is understandable that during the period of the Cussen interrogation and until he was free to go to America, Plum should not have wanted to stress this friendship. But it is curious—yet characteristic of Plum, who lived in the present—that the generous Baroness and her daughter never heard from him again.

In 1945 the bulk of his letters were to Denis Mackail, William Townend, Guy Bolton, and Thelma Cazalet-Keir. The most descriptive and the most entertaining were to Denis Mackail. Thus, on 16 February 1945 he wrote from the Hotel Lincoln: "I hope everything is all right with you and that you are turning out the stuff with your usual zeal. I find that increasing age has slowed me up a lot, and I can no longer do what I used to consider a decent day's work. I have to force it out in drops, relying on technique instead of exuberance."

He went on to say that he had started to do the *Times* crossword puzzles again, and then he said:

> I like being back in Paris, and I think we shall stay here till the Spring and then go to some friends in the country. The only catch is that it is so difficult to work here, as we have to go out for all our meals such as they are, and whenever I really get going Ethel comes in and says that Wonder has to go for a walk *immediately.*
>
> I spent December and January in a clinic, where I was very comfortable, as we had heat (unknown now in Paris except in clinics and hotels where the diplomats live). I managed to do a lot of writing, although a bit hampered by the *inspecteurs* who would keep popping in and asking how I was getting on.*
>
> There were always two of them in residence, changing every three hours, so I now number quite a lot of *inspecteurs* among my friends. I

---

*He remained under the surveillance of the French police while in hospital.

was great pals with all of them, even the two whose corkscrews I broke. They were always delighted to nip out and buy me bread and wine and to open the bottles when bought. It is râther nice to think that I could walk into the Palais de Justice at any moment and be warmly greeted as an old buddy by at least twenty *inspecteurs.* . . .

Ethel has just been in to say that Wonder has to go for a walk immediately, so I must end.

On 22 May he wrote: "Of course, our real trouble is that while Ethel and I are perfectly content to be vegetarians, Wonder won't look at anything except meat, so we have to get it for her somehow." And on 7 November, from Boulevard Suchet:

First of all, observe and jot down in your tablets the above address. It is a new flat into which we move as soon as we can get our packing done. Very posh being right on the Bois (wonderful facilities for Peke exercising) and two doors from neighbour Windsor, who lives at 24 and will no doubt be dropping in all the time. We got it through Bea Davis, the owner being a friend of hers, and the price is almost the same as we were paying for the Paul Doumer hovel.

Talking of books, as we so often do when we get together, ought I to be ashamed of confessing to you a furtive fondness for Angela Thirkell? You told me once that she bullied you when you were a child, and for years I refused austerely to read her. But recently *Wild Strawberries* and *Pomfret Towers* have weakened me. I do think she's good, though if we are roasting her I will add that *August Folly* was rotten and I couldn't get through it.

And on 27 November:

I don't know if it is a proof of my saint-like nature, but I find that my personal animosity against a writer never affects my opinion of what he writes. Nobody could be more anxious than myself, for instance, that Alan Alexander Milne should trip over a loose bootlace and break his bloody neck, yet I re-read his early stuff at regular intervals with all the old enjoyment and still maintain that in *The Dover Road* he produced about the best comedy in English.

Referring then to a press report that they had fed pork chops to their dogs in Berlin, he went on:

How on earth the writer was supposed to have got his facts, I don't know. Actually we used to victual Wonder just as you in similar circumstances would have victualled Tan [the Mackail Peke]. We had an allowance of meat each daily and we gave this to Wonder and ate vegetables ourselves. I don't think I ever saw a pork chop when I was in Germany.

The new flat is a stupendous success. It is like living in the country with all the conveniences of town. We are right on the edge of the Bois, and every morning I put on plus fours and a sweater and go and do my Daily Dozen under the trees before breakfast. The improvement in my health has been immediate. I am now very fit, and my eyes, which had been troubling me owing to the bad lighting at 78 Paul Doumer, are now all right again. One thing I love about the French is that they are not hicks—I mean that if they see anything unusual they accept it politely and don't guffaw. Not a single pedestrian who has passed me during my morning exercises has even turned his head. They see a man in a white sweater and golf bags bending and stretching and they say to themselves, "Ah, a man in a white sweater and golf bags bending and stretching. No doubt he has excellent motives, and in any case it has nothing to do with me." This sort of attitude reconciles one to some of the things they don't do better in France. On November 17th, for instance, I went to the post office and filled in a form notifying them that I had changed my address and wished all mail to be sent to 36 Blvd. Suchet. It still goes regularly to 78 Paul Doumer.

And on 14 December:

I am feeling a little exhausted at the moment, because a French gentleman blew in unexpectedly and stayed to tea and I have been trying to talk French—and what is even more fatiguing, trying to understand French—for an hour and a half. This chap came originally when we were at Paul Doumer to inspect the electric light meter. Ethel, the silly ass, revealed to him that I was an écrivain Anglais, très connu, and he immediately whipped out of a back pocket the script of a play which he had written, and I had to read it. My courteous words of praise led to him producing another at his next visit, and in some mysterious way I apparently undertook to translate it. His visit today was to find out how I was getting on, and of course I hadn't started. Now I suppose I shall have to. As a matter of fact, it is quite a good play, about racing at Auteuil, but I can't see it being produced in London or New York. Still, translating it will be a good thing for my French. But what a mug one is ever to promise to do anything . . .

I wish I could get the glimmering of an idea for a novel. I don't seem able to get going these days, probably because I've got four novels in the drawer and my subconscious self feels what's the sense of sweating to dope out anything more till those are disposed of. Also, what the devil does one write about these days, if one is a specialist on country houses and butlers, both of which have ceased to exist?

On 23 December 1945 he introduced a theme which recurs again and again in his letters:

The last words in your second letter struck home. Though, as a matter of fact, I haven't anything much against Christmas Day itself. The time to keep cool is about a week before, when you realise you can't postpone the buying of presents another day. Ethel and I had our purgatory about three days ago, when we went down to the Rue de Rivoli and I waited interminably outside shops with Wonder in my arms and we then fought our way back in the metro where Wonder was nearly squashed. Anything that happens now seems all right in comparison. We gave a dinner last night, and we go out three times next week. After that things will get normal again. Thank God Ethel had the courage to refuse an invitation which would have involved dancing, of all ghastly things. But who am I to talk to a man with a wedding looming up on the horizon?

There was a dark side to all this gaiety. For many years Plum was quite unable to understand that his offence had been anything worse than a technical one which had been misrepresented in England and America, and which would be forgiven not merely by people who knew and understood him, but by the public at large, if it could be explained. On 29 November 1941, referring to the article "My War with Germany," he had written to his literary agent, Paul Reynolds:

> You know I still cannot fathom the mystery of that article of mine in the *SEP.* You said in your letter of June 17, 1941, "The *Post* was very pleased with your article," and I got a cable from [Wesley] Stout not more than a month later which ended, "Your article strongly resented by many." Why anyone should resent a harmless humorous article about men in camp growing beards and servers at meals hitting the bowl with fish stew four times out of five, it is beyond me to imagine. Evidently the *Post* people didn't on June 17. Amazing that an article which pleased them at the end of June should have roused indignation at the end of July. It seemed to me, when I wrote it, that I was doing something mildly courageous and praiseworthy in showing that it was possible, even though in prison camp, to keep one's end up and not belly-ache.

And he also wrote to Stout in the same strain: "I read it as a paper in the camp to an audience of several hundred, all rabid patriots, and had them rolling in the aisles. And they not only laughed but applauded. So what *can* have gone wrong?"

Astonishing as the question may seem, no one had the heart to explain to him that what had gone wrong was that between June and the end of July he had been heard delivering five broadcasts on German wavelengths. Reynolds did try to make him realize that the feeling in America had become very strong against him, but Plum continued to believe that if he were given the opportunity to explain that he had not broadcast in order to exchange camp for the Adlon Hotel, nor spoken a word of propaganda, all would be forgiven. While in prison he had written *Money in the Bank*, and in Germany he had very quickly finished *Joy in the Morning*, which he had been writing in Le Touquet before he was interned and the manuscript of which Ethel had brought with her when she joined him. In another letter (27 November 1941) he wrote to Reynolds:

> I have also written half of a novel about Lord Emsworth and his pig called *Full Moon*. This I have shelved for the time being in order to work on a book of Camp reminiscences. This will be good, but shortish. . . . I think I can make it 35,000 words without an effort, 45,000 by brooding over it. . . .
>
> Also do you think it ought to be published while the war is on? If people in America resented the article in *SEP* they would enormously resent a book of the same tone. It is very funny, a little vulgar in spots, and contains a chapter where I state my case to my English critics and—I hope—make them feel pretty foolish.

Now, in Paris in February 1945, he wrote to William Townend:

> In 1941, when I was in the Harz mountains I wrote a comic book about my adventures in Le Touquet and my camp experiences. . . . At that time I saw the situation thus: There had been a terrific outcry in England about the talks, but it had happened before I made the talks. They were then relayed to England, and I supposed that everybody had heard them and had realised that they were harmless, so I took rather an airy tone in my book, all having a good laugh together at the whole amusing misunderstanding sort of thing. Now it seems that practically nobody heard the talks, so that the bulk of the populace are under the impression that I did propaganda. In other words, I shall have to assume that 90% of my readers will be hostile. In which case a humorous treatment might be resented. It's all very difficult. But Malcolm Muggeridge insists that I shall be making a mistake if I try to write differently from my usual style, and I feel he's right.
>
> One thing against a serious treatment is the fact that everybody in England has been through such hell . . . that it would be simply ludicrous if I made heavy weather over the really quite trivial things that happened to me. It isn't pleasant to travel for three days and nights in a third class compartment, with wooden seats and four a side, and almost nothing to eat and drink, but I don't see how I can attempt to make a tragedy of it when writing for an audience which have been under fire from V bombs for months. That's the sort of attitude I must avoid at all costs.

For months, even years, Plum agonized over this. Particuarly he worried about the "tone." Reynolds, who was against the whole enterprise—although too sorry for Plum to say so—had written (8 September 1944):

> I approached the *Post* as to whether they would be interested in one or more articles by you on your experiences in Germany and Ben Hibbs,

the editor in chief, said that he was afraid your name was under too much of a cloud for him to publish you now but he hoped to be able to at some later date. I approached the *Reader's Digest,* who are paying enormous prices for articles, and they felt the same way.

Reynolds also wrote that if Plum did want to write about his experiences, "they should be in the first person and serious, not humorous, and pretty factual."

Reynolds was probably right. Apologizing for the nondelivery of an article, Plum had once written: "I have tried and tried and nothing will emerge in the shape of a humorous biography. . . . My form of humor is entirely objective. When I try to make it subjective, it just goes cold on me. I can't write humorously about myself. I'm sorry but there it is. It's just a knack I haven't got." If he had published unpolished the innocent diary which forms Chapter 10 of this book, accompanied by some statement to the effect that his broadcasts had contained no propaganda, there is just a chance that the absolute purity of tone he there achieved might have been found irresistible even in the hysterical atmosphere of the time. But he spent months ruining it. (That is surmise, but the seven pages of the manuscript of *The Camp Book* which by an accident survive seem to bear it out.) For he was right in thinking that the "subjective style" did not come naturally to him, although since he seldom used it, when he did it passed muster with the undiscriminating and was forgiven by the discriminating. On this occasion, he was too much out of tune with the public mood for it to be sympathetic to either.

He worried very much about opinion at Dulwich. He wrote to Townend in February 1945:

> I wonder how I'm regarded at Dulwich. Have you any means of finding out? Mine is a curious position, as I meet nobody but friends and keep getting encouraging letters, so that sometimes I get the illusion that everything is all right. I have to remind myself that there must still be an enormous body of public opinion which is against me. . . . Unpleasant things still appear from time to time in the papers. . . . I'm afraid there's a long way to go before things can come right, but I haven't a twinge of self-pity. I made an ass of myself, and must pay the penalty.

And in May of the same year he wrote again to Townend:

> I have just written a long letter to Rees [the man at Dulwich], giving him the facts about my release, and I hope he will get it published in the *Alleynian.* . . . I fortunately have positive proof that I never made any sort of bargain with the Germans in order to get out of camp. . . . The editor of the *S. E. Post* cabled me that he wanted to buy *Money in the*

Bank but could do so only [if] I would stop talking on the German radio. . . .* I didn't realize even then that I had been doing something which would outrage public feeling. I thought ye Ed was just being fussy! . . . What now seems like inexplicable idiocy was [because] for a year I had been completely out of touch with the world. . . . I have met at least a hundred Englishmen and Americans . . . since the liberation and every one . . . has been perfectly friendly. It seems so odd that I shouldn't have run up against a single person who shares the feeling that undoubtedly exists in England.

Watt† thinks that if I published the . . . book you want me to . . . it would lead to attacks. He may be right, but . . . it would make my position better.

He was advised by everyone who knew of it not to publish *The Camp Book,* and publishers both in England and in America refused to have anything to do with it. But he persisted. In September 1945 he wrote to Townend:

The Camp Book will settle it. If it goes then everything will be well.

I think I've made out a very good, very solid case—it is simply an elaboration of that letter in the *Alleynian* giving the facts and supporting them with a lot of documents—and I hope it will get across. My trouble has been to get the right tone. . . . One's mood changes from day to day. I go for a walk, and work up a spirit of defiance and come home and write a belligerent page or two indicating that I don't give a damn whether the public takes a more favourable view or not, because all my friends have stuck to me and it's only my friends I care about. Then I sleep on it and wonder if this is quite judicious! Also comedy will keep creeping in at the most solemn moments. I wrote this yesterday: "The global howl which went up as a result of my indiscretion exceeded in volume and intensity anything I had experienced since the time in my boyhood when I broke the curate's umbrella and my aunts started writing letters to one another about it." I showed the script to Ethel, making sure that she would swoon . . . and insist on it coming out, and she thought it marvellous. . . . What do you think? Will the reaction be "Ha, ha, I don't care what the chap has done. He makes me laugh." or: "Mr. Wodehouse appears to imagine that his abominable action is a subject for flippancy.". . . I can't tell in advance.

---

*He continues to describe the series of cables to Stout as he did to Major Cussen, and it is typical of the whole affair that his worst worry at that time was about the serialization of *Money in the Bank.*
†W. P. Watt, his English literary agent.

On 8 November he wrote:

> Yielding to the overwhelming pressure from Watt etc., I have decided to
> postpone publication of the camp book. . . . Everybody (but you) is so
> insistent that it should be held back until this Belsen business has become
> a thing of the past that I am pigeonholing it for the time being. What
> decided me was a letter from Ian Hay. . . . "Something quite unique in
> the annals of prisoner-of-war history . . . the first time that genuine suf-
> fering and hardship . . . have been described with resolute cheerfulness
> and humour. . . . A most moving blend of frivolity and fortitude. . . ."
> But he goes on to say: "I agree with Watt that publication should be
> delayed for some time . . . until the present witch-hunt for scapegoats has
> subsided."

Plum did not finally abandon the idea for another six months. Then he
wrote in a letter to Townend: "On *The Camp Book* there seems to be a
universal attitude of obstruction, and I'm tired of trying to buck it."

He also worried for some time about the publication and sales of his
novels. Sales of his back books dropped to almost nothing in 1942, and in
Britain certain public libraries—chiefly in Northern Ireland, but also at
Sheffield and Southport—went so far as to place a general ban on his books.
But by 1945 he was able to write to Townend:

> My cheap editions have suddenly taken a tremendous jump, starting about
> a year ago (Spring '44 that would be). The end of 1942 was a bad period—
> sales down to about 6 of each book. In the first part of 1943 sales rose to
> about 100 of each book, first half of 1944 from there to 900 of each book.
> In all, cheap editions seem to have sold about half a million in three years,
> which looks as though people have had a change of heart. Of course they
> may be buying my books with one hand and hating my insides with the
> other. But I hope not.

He was strongly advised against the publication of *Money in the Bank*,
but here—quite rightly, as it turned out—he overrode his advisers and
insisted on publication.

He was subject to great harassment over money. On 8 September 1944
he heard from Reynolds that the American Government had seized all the
money they held for him. "They took it by law and by force. . . . There
is no danger of their seizing further money for anything you write as you
are no longer a prisoner of war." However, in 1945 the U.S. Government
placed a total embargo on his funds pending settlement of tax said to be
owing since 1937. (Since Plum has been so much the subject of defamation
in relation to tax, it must be said in anticipation of the outcome that after
the war he was once more taken to court by the U.S. Federal authorities

and once more reached a reasonable settlement.) His funds in England were also frozen, because of a wartime ban on taking money out of the country. He was forced to write to thank Thelma for arranging for the transfer of £90 apiece from his and Ethel's London accounts, and to say that if this was to be a monthly payment they would be able to manage on it. As late as January 1946 he wrote to Denis Mackail:

> My failure to send a wedding present was not due to parsimony but to the fact that the authorities in the old country have suddenly concentrated all their energies on doing me down financially. I think I told you that the Bank of England would not allow me either to maintain my overdraft at its present figure or reduce it by selling securities. They have now attacked from another angle. Watt paid in a cheque into my account the other day and a few days later wrote me to say that it had been bounced back at him and he would have to fill up all sorts of forms and get permission from all sorts of people before he could pay me money. So I don't know where I am. Fortunately Ethel is in the chips so I can sponge on her for a while.

Worse was to follow. In 1945 there was a change of Government, and with it Sir Hartley Shawcross replaced Sir Donald Somervell as Attorney General. In the autumn of that year William Joyce (Lord Haw-Haw) was tried for treason. Addressing the jury in his final speech for the prosecution, Sir Hartley said: "I invite you to say that the mere act of broadcasting as applied to the German radio system was an act of adhering to the King's enemies irrespective of the subject matter of any political broadcast." And Lord Justice Tucker, summing up, said:

> Do you think it is essential for propaganda that it should be either false or true? Propaganda may be true and some may be false, may it not? Does it matter if it be false or true if it is broadcast over the enemy radio system? What is the purpose and object of a broadcast from Germany in English? Is it to assist the Germans or to assist the English?

This heralded no alteration in the law (as has sometimes been thought), but it was an unpropitious circumstance, and an indication that the new Attorney General's interpretation of the existing laws might differ from his predecessor's. On 13 March 1946, in the House of Commons, he was asked whether he would "take proceedings against P. G. Wodehouse for treasonable acts committed during the recent war." He replied: "The question of instituting proceedings against this man will be reconsidered if and when he comes within the jurisdiction of our Courts."[1]

This short answer, so mildly phrased, altered the course of Plum's life. Raymond Needham, who had acted for him against the Inland Revenue in 1934, was asked for an opinion as to what it meant. He consulted (in a professional sense) Christopher Shawcross, the Attorney General's brother.

Mr. Shawcross produced five pages of Advice in which he made it clear that the new Attorney General could be assumed to be taking a different view from Sir Donald's, that the debate initiated by Quintin Hogg was "very instructive as to the facts which the prosecution might be able to prove against Mr. Wodehouse and as to the view which the jury might take," and that the unsupported charges made by Harold Nicolson would have to be answered.* He then went on to say that Mr. Wodehouse should provide a complete statement of his prewar residential history (what were his knowledge of and visits to Germany?) and of all the circumstances of his going to Berlin and of how he came to broadcast. After Wodehouse had supplied this, the two Counsels issued a Joint Opinion, of which the most important paragraphs were:

> The present Attorney-General, in answer to a question which, in Mr. Wodehouse's interests, had better not have been asked, felt constrained to say that if Mr. Wodehouse returned to England the question of proceedings against him would be re-considered. We take this as a clear indication that he did not agree with the view of his predecessor that there was no evidence to justify such proceedings, and that proceedings would probably be started if Mr. Wodehouse came within the jurisdiction of the English Courts.
>
> We do not think that Mr. Wodehouse would be prosecuted for treason (as were Joyce and Amery) or for an offence under the Treachery Act, 1940 (which is not applicable). We think it more likely that he would be indicted under Regulation 2A of the Defence Regulations, for which a small penalty may be imposed—e.g. two months' imprisonment—although the maximum is penal servitude for life. Under this Regulation any act likely to be of assistance to the enemy is punishable, if done with intent to assist the enemy. If prosecuted under this Regulation, Mr. Wodehouse's guilt or innocence would be left to the Jury to decide. The Jury would have to decide whether his broadcasts did assist, or were likely to assist the enemy, and they might well decide this question against Mr. Wodehouse. The Jury would also have to decide whether Mr. Wodehouse made these broadcasts with intent to assist the enemy. In coming to the latter decision they would no doubt be influenced by Mr. Wodehouse's Statement on Oath that he had no idea at all that his talks could be of the slightest use to the Nazi war-effort and that his only motive in giving them was a perfectly innocent and proper one. They would no doubt listen to all the arguments in his favour such as those put forward by Mr. George Orwell in the article which is quoted in "Wodehouse in Wonderland." Nevertheless it would be open to the Jury to come to the conclusion (and we think they *might* come to the conclusion) that, in spite of all these considerations, Mr. Wodehouse must have known that broadcasting

---

*They would also have had to be proven.

by a person of his reputation would attract listeners in America to tune-in to the Nazi radio, and that that fact would help the Nazis, who obviously broadcast to America for no other reason than to let Americans hear what they had to say.

The verdict of the Jury would depend to some extent upon the character and pre-conceived notions of its individual members and also upon the kind of summing up which it received from the particular Judge trying the case. These are matters which nobody can predict.

Unable to come to England, the Wodehouses toyed for a while with the idea of restoring the much-damaged Low Wood and continuing to live in France. They decided in the end against this; the necessary work would have been too expensive. They then turned their minds to the country which had always been a second home, and immediately after receiving the Counsel's Opinion, they applied for visas to enter America. Here again they were thwarted for many months, probably not through any bad will, but through the slowness of the political machine in time of war. On 29 May 1946 Plum wrote to Thelma:

> The position is this. Visas are granted by the U.S. Embassy here. If they feel in doubt about an application, they ask Washington for advice. What I want is to get the machinery working so that the Embassy here get all the facts they want from London, so that they will be in a position either to give me a visa or else apply to Washington for advice.
>
> The moment they apply to Washington I can get things moving, for I have a number of friends over there who will take action on my behalf but who can't start anything until the Paris Embassy makes some move.

All through that summer Plum wrote to Thelma in the same vein, later adding that the "agony of the situation" was being increased by letters from Guy Bolton telling him there would be plenty of work for him in the theatre if he could go to New York. But, although harassed and thwarted on every side, he never despaired, and continued to read, work, and write letters. "I've been looking through my diary," he wrote to Denis Mackail, "and I realise that I must be one of the world's great correspondents. This is the 43rd letter I've written this month, and my monthly average for the last year has been over thirty. . . . I love getting letters, so I get a reward for my large output." He wrote continuously to Guy Bolton—letters which were, as they always would be, almost entirely about work on lyrics or on the books of musical comedies. In January 1946 he wrote to Bolton:

> And now how are the chances for a musical by us? I have abandoned all other forms of work and am spending my whole time working on

lyrics and am pleased to report that the old Muse is in the real 1916–1918 form. So far I have completed three really good ones, a couple of light comedy duets and one of those trios for three men which used to go so well. . . .

A fear that haunts me, of course, is that I may be thirty years behind the times and be turning out stuff that would have been fine for 1917 but no good for 1946. But I don't believe there is any reason to feel this. The numbers I hear on the radio sound exactly like those of twenty or thirty years ago.

The letters to Guy also concern an "imbroglio" about the lyric "Bill," but this is best explained in a letter to Denis Mackail:

That "Bill" thing is quite a drama. As you say, I wrote it in 1917 for *Oh, Lady!* Right. But, as always happens when you get a real winner, it was cut out. I think it was considered too slow or something and I wrote a lousy waltz thing instead. . . . Well, when *Show Boat* was in preparation Jerry asked me if he could use "Bill," and I said Yes, and he did. But Oscar Hammerstein went and changed about three words in it and for twenty years has been getting half the publishing royalties. I didn't pay any attention to this, not being particularly interested in lyrics during those years, but Guy Bolton, to whom—in exchange for a share of the book rights—I had given half my publishing royalties, started kicking and kept at it so assiduously that a few days ago I heard from America that Oscar has now relinquished all rights in the thing and in addition has coughed up $5000 in back payments.

In January 1946 he wrote to Mackail about his money troubles: "I don't get this Bank of England business at all. And the maddening thing is that none of the people in England who could tell me what it is all about—my accountant, my bank, etc.—will ever answer letters."
But mainly his letters were about his daily life:

The dog situation has become very complicated. I am now pledged to take the concierge's terrier out with Wonder in the morning, and unfortunately there's a female hound down in the direction of Port St. Cloud and the terrier legs off to her and comes back with the milk. So I ought to be following his every movement. But when I try to keep an eye on him Wonder goes off in the opposite direction. The thing always ends in my coming home without the terrier and saying to the concierge that Teddy has been "pas sage" and leaving it up to him to do something about it.

A passage occurs in a letter to Mackail dated 1 March 1946 which must be of major interest to all Wodehouse scholars:

Lindsay is the man who was given the job of re-writing *Anything Goes* (Bolton and Wodehouse) for New York and after terms had been arranged he wrote to me, apropos of his share, that he was not disgruntled but, on the other hand, not gruntled. I have used this once in a book and I see that Guy has used it in the play he sent me the other day, but if you would care to have it, help yourself. It's good.*

And on 20 April:

. . . What I want to know is, Is one missing lots of good books simply through the fatheadedness of reviewers? Can't these blighters even put over the books they like? Of course the bright side is that more and more critics are becoming ignored and will shortly disappear altogether. Arising from this, don't you think film critics are the most futile people in the world? Do they really think that the public reads their criticisms and is influenced against a picture—because they are always against—by them? Pshaw, if I may use the expression.

Well, what I was saying before lunch was that, reverting to *The Camp Book,* I think that what kept one cheerful when behind barbed wire was partly the fact that one was one of thirteen hundred men all having the same experience and partly that one felt so frightfully well all the time. I used to spring from my plank bed feeling terrific, and the way the old bean worked was nobody's business. If you want to experience real enjoyment when writing a novel you have to be in a position, as I was, when for all I knew I had three years or so to do it in. There was none of that nerve-racking stuff of having to do so much per day. I could be a Flaubert whenever the mood took me, taking a day over a paragraph.

Speaking of *Money in the Bank,* he wrote on 7 May 1946:

I can't remember what stage the drama had progressed to and I may be repeating myself. But, if I remember rightly, I left off with the battle at its height and the Jenkinses still dubious about postponing publication of *Money in the Bank.* Any way, I wrote them a forceful letter saying it was a straight issue between publishing in May and not publishing at all, and I have had an enthusiastic communication from Smith of Jenkins (and a rather wry one from Watt, whose views had been overridden, if that's the word) to say that the book will appear on May 27th. Smith says that the advance orders have been fine and that he expects to unload 25,000 within a week or so of publication, so what I feel is What the hell? If a section of the press gets up and howls, it won't affect me, because I shan't read what is written. I'll tell you one thing. If *Money in the Bank* . . . gets over, I intend to do a bit of Russian expansionism and throw my weight about. And by "gets over," I mean if it sells. Slams from the baser element don't matter a damn so long as the heart of the Public is sound. . . . As a matter

---

*"He spoke with a certain what-is-it in his voice, and I could see that, if not actually disgruntled, he was far from being gruntled." *The Code of the Woosters* (1938). Quoted in *The Oxford Dictionary of Quotations.*

of fact, if this book gets over with the public, I'm going to suggest to the Jenkinses that in future we deal direct with ye pub and ignore the critics. Marie Corelli did it, without, I believe, the slightest effect on her sales. Don't you loathe critics? I don't know whether I hate them more when they praise me or when they roast me. Their appearing in the matter at all always seems to me an impertinence. . . . I find I can't do anything in the writing line these days, except letters. I don't seem to get any ideas for a story. I've got a Jeeves novel mapped out but I'd like to get something else going so that I can be brooding on it in my spare time. The actual writing of a story always gives me a guilty feeling as if I were wasting my time. The only thing that matters is thinking the stuff out.

And in a postscript to this letter:

Oh I was forgetting. A most satisfactory review of A.A.M.'s *Clary Marr* in the *Daily Mail*. In case you missed it, it said that it was the silliest book of the year. . . . Yes, you were right. I lifted *Penneyfather* out of *Happy Thoughts.* I had no idea that even you with your encyclopaedic knowledge of English literature would remember *Happy Thoughts*. By the way in another opus entitled *Uncle Dynamite* the names of the girl's publishers are Potwood and Drooley.*

Plum, like the rest of us, was not so hostile to favourable criticism, as is illustrated by the following letter to V. S. (now Sir Victor) Pritchett, written in June 1946:

36 Boulevard Suchet
Paris

June 15, 1946

Dear Mr. Pritchett,

A friend of mine has just written to tell me of the kind way in which you spoke of my *Money in the Bank* on the Home Service on the night of the 12th, and I am kicking myself for having missed it. I really don't know how to thank you enough. It will mean everything to the book, and I am tremendously grateful.

Apart from the *réclame* (as we call it over here) it is a joy to know that a critic of your standing liked the story. I am particularly pleased that Lord Uffenham amused you. I had great luck with him. There was a man in camp with me who was Uffenham to the life, except for the murky past and the conviction that he was irresistible to women. All the Uffenham obiter dicta were thrown off by this man from time to time in the dormitory. I simply had to drink the stuff in and write it down.

The whole story was thought out and written while I was in camp. I had to do it in pencil in a room where a hundred men were playing darts

---

*With his usual shameless attitude towards plagiarism, Plum had lifted these names from *Happy Thoughts* by F. C. Burnand, editor of *Punch*.

and ping-pong, with generally a lecture on Beowulf going on in the background, but oddly enough it came out quite easily, though a bit slowly. Until I tried, I wouldn't have thought it possible for me to write a story by hand, as I have worked on the typewriter since 1911, but it turned out to be perfectly simple. It just meant being satisfied with doing a page a day instead of my usual eight.

You can probably imagine how I felt when I heard of your talk, for it was not without diffidence that I agreed to the publication of the book. I saw myself rather in the position of a red-nosed comedian who has got the bird at the first house on Monday and is having the temerity to go on and do his stuff at the second house, outwardly breezy and cheerful but feeling inside as if he had swallowed a heaping tablespoonful of butterflies and with a wary eye out for demonstration from the gallery. And now comes this applause from the stalls, thank God! Bless you.

Best wishes
Yours sincerely
P. G. Wodehouse

III

AMERICA

16

New York

All things come to an end, and in July 1946 the Wodehouses received visas for America. This surprising couple then delayed going there for nearly eight months. Their lease of the flat at Boulevard Suchet ran out during this time, and they moved to St. Germain-en-Laye, nine miles from Paris. In a letter to his publisher Plum gave two reasons for the delay:

> My main idea in planning to be in New York before Christmas was to be on hand to help in the production of the Psmith play. When I found that the production wouldn't take place for quite a while, probably not till next season, I thought it would be wise to dig in some quiet spot and finish the Jeeves novel, *The Mating Season*, because once I was over in N.Y. I might not have had time to concentrate on it. Also I hated the idea of leaving my wife all alone here, and she refuses to sail till she has got some clothes.[1]

It is significant, nevertheless, that in a letter to Guy Bolton Plum wrote:

> I am hoping that when I get Ethel to America she will like it so much that she will decide to make it our home. The scheme at the moment is to rebuild Low Wood, but after all Le Touquet is a summer place and one might well have an apartment in New York as well and come over to Le Touquet from April to the end of August.

Feeling against Plum had been extremely strong in America immediately after the publicity given to the Berlin broadcasts, but it very quickly died down. As early as 1946, reviewing *Joy in the Morning*, a writer in *The New York Times* said:

> Maybe Wodehouse uses the same plot over and over again. Whatever he does, it's moderately wonderful, a ray of pale English sunshine in a gray world. . . . There is, of course, the question of Mr. Wodehouse's "war guilt." Upon mature post-war reflection, it turned out to be about equal to the war guilt of the dachshunds which were stoned by super-heated patriots during World War I.

And on 11 May 1947 Plum wrote to Townend:

Well, sir, my visit to N.Y. has proved a sensational triumph. . . . There hasn't been a vestige of a stinker in the Press. . . . On the second morning . . . I held a formal "Press Conference"—no less!—at the Doubleday offices. . . . On Wednesday I was interviewed on the radio, reaching three hundred and fifty stations. I wrote the interview myself and made it as funny as I could, and it was a terrific success, so they tell me. I confined myself to funny cracks about New York and my books, making no mention of the broadcasts. . . . Ethel was . . . delighted with the thing and told me I had been fine.

One thing which helped Plum's worldwide rehabilitation was that, strangely enough, whatever else had suffered from his imprisonment and the terrible troubles following it, his muse had remained in glorious form. In Le Touquet immediately before he was interned, he had been writing *Joy in the Morning*, and when Ethel joined him in Berlin, she brought the manuscript with her. He finished this in Germany, where he also wrote *Full Moon* and *Spring Fever*. Before this he had written *Money in the Bank* while actually in camp.* In Paris he wrote *Uncle Dynamite* and *The Mating Season*. All of these are vintage Wodehouse, while the last two may be said (at the risk of mixing the metaphor) to be of the first water.

These books appeared gradually over the first years of his return to America, and all over the world they proved irresistible. This was the end of the matter in all countries except England, where his more censorious countrymen divided into three groups of opinion—which have remained until this day. There are those who, like Evelyn Waugh, feel that he was treated barbarously for a venial fault; others who, for want of evidence to the contrary, believe he agreed to broadcast in return for a room at the Adlon; and a third group who, while understanding that he did not speak propaganda or take part in a deal, nevertheless find the act of broadcasting on enemy radio an offence which, while not of the first magnitude, is nevertheless irredeemable. The third of these groups is the stiffest and may never change. One can only hope that the innocence and individuality revealed in his own writings on the subject will convince them that his faults sprang from the same source as his supreme talents, and that both were probably fixed in his childhood.

·   ·   ·

Money in the Bank must have been taken out by Demaree Bess while America was still neutral, because, although it was not published in England until 1946, it was serialized in *The Saturday Evening Post* and then published by Doubleday, Doran in 1942. The character Lord Uffenham is well known to have been based on a fellow internee, and Anthony Lejeune tells me this was an uncle of his named Max Enke.

When Plum first arrived in New York, although his four novels (five if one counts *Money in the Bank* in England) appeared one after the other and achieved sales which often exceeded those of his prewar books, he himself seemed chiefly interested in work in the theatre. Probably, as he had said earlier, he had no heart for a new novel while he still had four in a drawer. He had been writing excitedly to Guy Bolton from Paris about one idea or another for some time, and although he was disappointed to find the latter in England when he first arrived in New York, he quickly became involved in various theatrical propositions.

He wrote to Guy:

> The theatre here has me absolutely squiggle-eyed. I keep getting things offered to me, but I can't make out if they're real solid propositions or not. I have adapted a Molnar play and am to adapt his new one when he gets it finished, but as far as I can make out nothing is settled about the production of either. Now a manager wants Ogden Nash and me to make a musical of *Enter Madame*. I believe the money end is all right, but he doesn't seem able to get a composer and I'm darned if I can see how you can make that play into a musical.
>
> I can't get used to the new Broadway. Apparently you have to write your show and get it composed and then give a series of auditions to backers, instead of having the management line up a couple of stars and then get a show written for them. It's so damn difficult to write a show without knowing who you are writing it for. It's like trying to write lyrics without a book. I feel lost without you.

Nevertheless, in the first years back in America Plum had some success in the theatre. Gilbert Miller revived *The Play's the Thing* in 1948, and this had a considerable run of 244 performances, although a revival of *Sally* by a different management at the same time was a flop. *Don't Listen, Ladies,* an adaptation with Guy of a Sacha Guitry play, was produced in London in 1948, and in 1950 Plum worked on someone else's play called *The House on the Cliff* which he had been asked to rewrite. This remains of interest today only because it involved him in one of the last journeys he would ever take. He wrote to Denis Mackail:

> I got back the day before yesterday from a five weeks' tour with a play on what they call the Summer circuit and it has practically wiped me out. I started by going to Skowhegan in Maine, arriving there at 5:30 a.m. We had 11 days of rehearsals, and then opened, and were then informed that our next stop would be Watkins Glen, N.Y. and that we would motor there on the Sunday in two station wagons, a distance of 560 miles. Have you ever motored 560 miles in a day? It's roughly equivalent, I imagine, to starting from Land's End and fetching up at Edinburgh. Our next jump was only 150 miles, and then the company—not me, I went back to New

York—proceeded to dash up to the suburbs of Chicago, roughly 700 miles. Next Sunday they go from Chicago to East Hampton, Long Island—about 1100 miles. The poor devils have got to fly. And on top of all this the play was no good and won't come into New York unless I can effect some radical changes, which I can't. I tell you, this has cured me of being stage struck.

The last sentence was not true. Plum's great days in the theatre were over, but it would be many years before he accepted the fact. He seems really to have enjoyed this work. Partly this was for relaxation, as a tennis player plays golf on holiday. "I hate working on a musical unless it's with you," he wrote to Guy once. "When you and I talk a plot over, we diverge into all sorts of outside topics and the old brain, rested, comes up with something." Partly, too, it was because Plum, alone in the world except for Ethel, received real pleasure from Guy's company. "I do hope you're coming back soon. Life is very dull without you." But there is no doubt that he also had a zest for the work. When Guy was away (and he often went to England), Plum wrote to him regularly. Over the next thirty years he wrote him hundreds of letters, but these—which one might have hoped would be a gold mine—are full for the most part of out-of-date theatrical shop.

I have chosen the following examples more or less arbitrarily from dozens of the same kind of thing written over the years.

Your letter arrived when I was in the middle of working against time, so I haven't been able to see Hans B. yet, but will do so next week. I am pretty dubious, though, about this *Waltz Dream* proposition as long as Hans is mixed up in it. He seems to me one of those maddening people who are never satisfied with anything. I am having this trouble with Sidney Harmon, Jack Wildberg's partner, over the Conkle thriller which I adapted. (Has J.W. shown it to you, by the way?) I have done version after version according to his specifications, and finally we agreed on a scenario. I completed the script and sent it to him in Hollywood, and he telegraphs that he likes the dialogue and some of the scenes but "has reservations about the play." In other words, he has got a new batch of crazy ideas and probably wants the heroine turned into a male negro and the hero split into two Irishmen named Pat and Mike. I have written to Conkle asking him to what extent he is tied up with the Harmon-Wildberg management. If he is in a position to take the play away from them, I am all for it, as I know of another management who would probably grab it.

Or like this:

One thing, though, strikes me and that is that I think Jed has the right idea. He said "Make it a vehicle for Ray Bolger," and I see what he means. The interest is too evenly split up between—Oh, hell I can't remember their current names—between Willoughby Finch and the part Brown played—Ham and Jeff or whatever it is. And the reason it's so evenly split up is that Ham has such a big love story. Is there any way of playing down the Ham-Jane story and bumping up Willoughby and Kim? It's the fact of them doing so many numbers together that's the trouble. We could cut "There Were You" and give the Greenwich Village number to Tom.

Occasionally there is a reward, as, for instance, in a letter of 24 November 1948:

> I take it you will come back with the company. I shall meet you at the pier and immediately start to discuss Shelley with you. Entirely on account of the many plugs you have given Percy Bysshe, I went out and blew three dollars on a book containing all his poems and Keats's, and I want you to tip me off as to which are his winners. I have always liked "Epipsychidion" and "Ozymandias," but last night I tackled "The Revolt of Islam" and it was like being beaten over the head with a sandbag. I'm afraid I have got one of those second-rate minds, because, while I realise that Shelley is in the Shakespeare and Milton class, I much prefer Tennyson, who isn't.
>
> Incidentally, what lousy prose Shelley wrote. I do hate the way people wrote in those days. "It is an experiment on the temper of the public mind, as to how far a thirst for a happier condition of moral and political society survives, among the enlightened and refined, the tempests which have shaken the age in which we live. I have sought to enlist the harmony of metrical language, the ethereal combinations of the fancy, the rapid and subtle transitions of human passion, all those elements which essentially compose a Poem, in the cause of a liberal and comprehensive morality." Block those double adjectives, Perce!
>
> Why will people collect ALL a poet's work into a volume instead of burying the bad stuff? It's a nasty jar, after reading "The Nightingale," to come on the following little effort of Keats:—
>
> > There was a naughty boy,
> > And a naughty boy was he,
> > He kept little fishes
> > In washing tubs three
> > In spite
> > Of the might
> > Of the maid
> > Nor afraid
> > Of his Granny-good—
> > He often would
> > Hurly burly
> > Get up early . . .

I can see Keats shoving that one away in a drawer and saying to himself "Thank God no one will ever see *that* baby!" And then along comes some damned fool and publishes it.

Yet if the theatrical work he did with Guy had surprisingly little direct success, two very important things came out of it. The first is that he was seldom short of a plot. He busied himself turning plays into novels, sometimes novels into plays, and even occasionally these back into novels. And in the second place it set the future course of his life.

When the Wodehouses first returned to New York, they moved about— from hotel to apartment house and on to another. Finally they settled more permanently in an apartment at 1000 Park Avenue. This had a terrace on the rooftop where Ethel made a garden and where they sometimes had meals. Plum loved this terrace, and left to himself, he might have looked no further. But Guy had a house in a Long Island settlement called Remsenburg, and, staying there with the Boltons in 1952, Ethel walked in one evening and in characteristic fashion announced that she had bought a house. In the first years of their ownership the Wodehouses used this house only in the summer, but in 1955 they gave up the Park Avenue apartment and spent the rest of their lives at Remsenburg, seldom leaving it, and never for more than a night or two at a time.

But all this was in the cloudless future. From 1947 until 1949 Plum continued to be harassed by the seemingly endless restrictions on his money supply. He wrote to Townend in December 1947:

My financial position is maddening and tantalising. Lots of money in England but I can't touch it. Over here it's O.K. but the Income Tax trouble means I've got to watch expenses. In 1943 the Government pinched 40,000 dollars and froze my funds. So nobody who owes me anything can pay it. The case has come on and the verdict so far is that I owe the Government 20,000 dollars on one account (we're appealing). The rest of the case has to do with my 1921 tax. They say I didn't pay it and that plus interest and fines it comes to 28,000 dollars. So at worst that's 48,000 dollars, at best I'll win the 1921 case and would be repaid my 20,000 and Doubledays would pay me the 15,000 they owe me and Harms (that's the musical outfit) the 2,000 or 3,000 for music publishing. So at any moment I might be in the chips with 40,000 dollars in my kick. Meanwhile there's the weary waiting and I can't seem to click with the U.S. magazines. The only real bit of goose was when a man wrote a book called *Mr. Blandings Builds His Castle* and my lawyer took a flying leap and landed on the back of his neck and choked 1,500 dollars out of him for the infringement of copyright. I am sticking him on to the Kleenex people who have been using Jeeves in their ads and I hope to collect a bit more. I'm all for this business of cashing in on one's nuisance value. I lie awake at night trying to think of fresh victims. In 1924 I wrote a song called "Bongo on the Congo" and now a revue has a smash hit called "Bongo Bongo Bongo, I'm here upon the Congo," and I'm licking my lips and wetting the knife.

The United States's demands were settled in court in December 1949 after two appeals. Four different points were under review, and Plum won in all but one of them. He lost in what seems to have been an attempt on the part of his lawyer to refight an issue already decided in a test case brought by Sax Rohmer in an attempt to establish that royalties paid in advance for serial or book rights should be regarded for tax purposes as capital rather than income.*

This ended the tax troubles which had haunted so many years of Plum's life and which seemed to have been due as much to the insensate claims of the United States Federal authorities as to his own mismanagement. The truth is that his difficulties would have been not much different from those suffered by most artists working in more than one country in those days of unregulated international arrangements, but for the size of his income and the extra publicity given to him. In 1951 he wrote to Denis Mackail:

> What crooks Governments are. In 1943 the U.S. Govt. pinched 40,000 dollars of mine, claiming that I owed them a lot for back income tax. I fought and won three of the four cases, and they owe me about 30,000 dollars but not a penny from them yet, and they make me pay my 1951 tax in advance. . . . One of the claims they made against me was for income tax for 1921. Of course, neither side could produce any evidence, and after two years the judge decided in my favour.†

Also at the end of 1949 the Wodehouses got on the American quota, and as a result the British Government redesignated their bank accounts as American accounts. In 1950 Plum wrote to Denis Mackail:

> You ask me what I'm using for money. I'm rolling in the stuff. When I came in on the quota at the end of 1949, I was allowed by the Brit. Govt. to take my English money over here in dollars. Why, I can't imagine, as

---

*Plum's own views on this matter had been written to Guy Bolton from Paris in 1946: "Talking of the Treasury and my tax trouble, Washburn has just written that the Court has decided unfavourably in what is known as the Sax Rohmer Appeal—that is to say, alien authors *do* have to pay tax on the sale in America of serial rights and cannot laugh things off by claiming that they are lump sales. I must say I'm not surprised. I'm pretty optimistic by nature, but I never expected that my entire income for the last twenty years would turn out not to have been subject to tax at all! All I hope is that what seem to be the quite illegal claims the Government are making on me will be decided in my favour. I wish they would hurry up and come to a decision."

†Earlier Plum had written to Townend: "Income tax. They say I didn't pay in 1921 or 1923. Neither side can prove anything but there was a rule that you couldn't leave the country unless you had paid your income tax, and I certainly left the country."

no one else seems able to. I believe it's because I was not a British resident after 1939. Any way, though I can't touch my investments in England, I can bring over the interest on them and everything I make from books (which is considerable). All this, added to what I get here from American investments—sales of serials . . . puts me in a position where my last year's income tax was 20,000 dollars. If I could find some way of doing down the income tax hell hounds, I should be on velvet. (I pay American tax not English.)

Sometime in the early fifties he had a small stroke, and the letter B. H. Kean, the doctor who attended him, sent to me describes what happened so graphically that I have thought it worth including.

One day in the early 50s, a "bum" stumbled into my office, then located at 81st Street and Park Avenue. It was quite obvious that he was either very drunk or seriously ill. First aid measures were not helpful, so I called an ambulance to take him to Bellevue Hospital where derelicts are often sent for medical care. In an effort to identify him, we went through the pockets of his baggy, worn trousers and dilapidated corduroy jacket; in the process, my secretary remarked, "He's not a bum, he's an Englishman!" The jacket, although very old indeed, had been tailored in Savile Row, and further inspection revealed that his scruffy shoes were of very good quality. Above all, his nails were manicured! The ambulance was directed, therefore, to take the patient to Doctors Hospital, a private institution.

Some hours later, my secretary was seen meditating rather than working. Chided, she replied "I've seen that man before, and I know with whom: Oscar Hammerstein." I called Oc and asked him if he knew an Englishman and provided a superficial description. He said, "Of course, that's P.G. He's just arrived in America. He and his wife (was her name Penny?) live a few blocks up on Park Avenue.* He was probably taking his daily stroll. I'll call his wife." She met me at the hospital.

P.G. recovered from what was a minor stroke. They settled in the United States and lived happily for many years afterwards in the little town of Remsenburg on Long Island.

It is hardly necessary to say that this stroke had no serious consequences and was not repeated.

In the years while he was living in New York Plum published a collection of short stories called *Nothing Serious* and four novels: *The Old Reliable*, *Barmy in Wonderland* (*Angel Cake* in the United States), *Pigs Have Wings*,

---

*Plum called her Bunny.

and *Ring for Jeeves*. The last two were both part of a series, *Pigs Have Wings* being a Blandings Castle book, and *Ring for Jeeves* being rewritten from a play of Guy Bolton's called *Come On, Jeeves;* it was the only failure of the Jeeves series. Of *Nothing Serious* he wrote to Denis Mackail:

> I say the Jenkins people sent me the reviews of *Nothing Serious* and I note a distinct improvement in tone. I seem to be practically back to the "Dear old P. G. Wodehouse" days. My loathing of the critics, however, continues unabated. Damn their impertinence for praising my books. Don't they know that I just write them for you to read? What one strives for is some system by which one can print a maximum of six copies and still get paid thousands a year.

And of *The Old Reliable* he wrote to the same correspondent:

> *The Old Reliable.* Full of good gags, yes, but not really out of the top drawer. I keep being a little ashamed of it and wishing I had held it back till I could have done something about ironing out what they call over here the "bugs" in it. As your discerning eye will have spotted, it is a play turned into a novel and much too hastily done. This was the one which I had to write in a hurry in order to get it into *Collier's* as a serial, and I ought to have taken my time after that and rewritten it. But the Jenkins people were cabling to ask when the new novel would be in their hands, so I had to rush it. Never again. The only thing I am proud of about the book is that it is simply *Spring Fever* written again but so shrewdly that I don't think anyone will notice it. . . .
>
> The curse of this book is that when I was doing it as a play I shoved in every good gag I could find in all my other books and a whole lot of them still remain in the text. That stuff about measuring time, by the way, is lifted entirely from *The Small Bachelor*.

About *Pigs Have Wings* he wrote again to Mackail:

> Galahad—Of course you are entitled to your view of him, but if you think him a swine, how do you feel about Falstaff and Mr. Micawber and, for the matter of that, Fred Barfield in *Bradsmith Was Right*? Do you consider Falstaff a drunken lout, Micawber a petty swindler, and Barfield a selfish hound? Don't you make *any* allowances for the fact that a character is supposed to be funny?

Barmy in Wonderland was a novel written from a play by George S. Kaufman called *The Butter and Egg Man,* and when a critic complained that Wodehouse had never learned to write American dialogue correctly, Plum was able to reply that all the dialogue was Kaufman's.* All the usual

---

*Plum offered Kaufman his first net American payment on the novel ($2,700) for permission to use his play. Kaufman gave permission, but refused to take the money. This was sent to

Wodehouse characters are present, but, in addition, there is a marvellous new invention bearing the name Mervyn Potter. Potter is an American, a world-famous movie star, and a hopeless alcoholic, but he is a descendant, if only through a collateral branch, of that most attractive of all Wodehouse characters, Psmith. On his first appearance, he arrives in the office of Mr. Anderson, a hotel proprietor, in one of whose attached bungalows he is for the time being residing in. Having seen to it the night before that the desk clerk, Cyril Fotheringay-Phipps, should not be in a condition to fulfill his duties on that morning, he has taken his place, and his manner of answering a telephone call to the desk by Mr. Anderson has resulted in a summons to the presence.

A knock on the door broke in on his [Mr. Anderson's] reverie, one of those cheery, exuberant knocks which are practically bangs. It was followed, even before he could say "Come in," by the entrance of a figure at the sight of which, had his conscience been less clear, Mr. Anderson might have started apprehensively. . . . His visitor was wearing a policeman's uniform, complete with cap, belt and pistol.
The face beneath the cap was one of singular beauty, lean, keen and finely chiselled, with eyes, slightly bloodshot at the moment, which over a period of years had shaken more women to their foundations than any pair of eyes since those of the late Valentino.

In the course of time this conversation occurs:

"What a beautiful world it is, is it not? One of the nicest I ever came across. But you are wondering why I am here, no doubt, though delighted, of course, to see me. Well, when we were chatting on the telephone just now—and what a wonderful invention that is, the telephone. Good brains there, I always say when they bring up the subject of Alexander Graham Bell—I suddenly remembered that there was something I wanted to tell you. Not that it was a beautiful world. Something else. Some little secret that I wanted to share with you. So up I came, going hoppity-hoppity-hop."
A disturbing thought struck Mr. Anderson.
"You haven't been sitting at the desk, dressed like that?"
"I have indeed," said the human sunbeam, blowing a jovial smoke-ring, "and I was a sensational success. It was pretty to see my public's enthusiasm. I got writer's cramp, signing autographs. This costume is part and parcel of my story. Anderson, my poor old deadbeat, you have had a bereavement. I burned my bungalow down last night." (*Barmy in Wonderland*, Chapter 1)

---

him all the same. The cheque was not cashed and Kaufman, finding it in his pockets some months later, inquired what it was for. In the end he accepted it.

During this time Plum also worked hard on two books of an unusual kind. In January 1946 he had written to Guy Bolton from Paris:

Listen. I've suddenly got the most terrific idea—a book of theatrical reminiscences by you and me to be called

BOOK AND LYRICS
by
Guy Bolton and P. G. Wodehouse

I only got the idea an hour ago, so haven't thought out anything about the shape of the thing, but I believe we could make a big thing out of it. You have an enormous stock of theatrical stories and I have a few myself. My idea would be to make it a sort of loose saga of our adventures in the theatre from 1915 onwards, studded with anecdotes. Think of all the stuff we could put into it! I remember you telling me a priceless story about Bill McGuire, but I've forgotten the details, and between us we must have a hundred unpublished yarns about Erlanger, Savage etc. Do you think in your spare time you could dictate a few to a stenographer—quite in the rough, just the main points for me to work up? Meanwhile, I'll be trying to shape the vehicle. I see something on the lines of Woollcott's *When Rome Burns*—I mean *While Rome Burns*. Don't give away the title to a soul, as it seems to me a winner and somebody might pinch it. A book like this would be a cinch for serial publication. . . .

This book was published as *Bring On the Girls*. For years I have believed that it had been written almost entirely by Guy Bolton, with Plum merely lending his name and a few jokes, but this was simply wishful thinking. All the evidence shows that Plum was at least equally involved; and while he always bowed to Guy's judgment over plays, it is unlikely he would have been so accommodating where a book was concerned. In any case, *Bring On the Girls* is not really any worse than *Over Seventy* or *Louder and Funnier,* for which Guy cannot conceivably be blamed. The last two are told in the first person, *Bring On the Girls* in the third, and all are based on heavily embroidered incidents from real life. Like Guy, Plum believed that it is anecdotes that make a book.

Whether he liked the finished product is uncertain. He wrote to Guy: "I must say it reads magnificently," but in two letters to Denis Mackail he seems less certain. On 1 May 1954 he wrote:

I wrote to Pop Watt yesterday telling him to send you the English version of *Bring On the Girls*. . . . I am a bit dubious as to whether you will like it. All that stuff about "said Guy," "chuckled Plum with a merry twinkle in his eyes" and so on may jar on you. Of course, what we ought to have done was to have one of us write it in the first person. Hesketh Pearson and Hugh Kingsmill wrote two books of the said Hesketh type, but I don't think it's good. I wouldn't have minded so much if we'd called ourselves "Bolton" and "Wodehouse," but Guy says it's an insult to a man in America to call him by his surname. Did you know that? You either have to call him "Mr. Smith" or "Percy." Not if his name is George Brown, of course, but you know what I mean.

And in answer to a letter from Mackail which appears to have been critical, he wrote:

> I agree with everything you say about the *Girls* book. I must say I am surprised at the enthusiastic tone of the reviews. I was expecting to get slated on all sides, but I've had about twenty so far and all good.
>
> It's an odd book. Of course, the things we say happen to us didn't really, but they did happen to somebody and are all quite true. Thus it was Fred Thompson who used to throw his letters out of the window, Arthur Hopkins who played golf with Ziegfeld in the dark and so on. Legitimate, I think. Anyway, we have avoided that awful "We opened in Philadelphia with the following cast . . . that sterling actor George Blank as the Prince," which makes theatrical reminiscences so boring.

Performing Flea is a very different kind of book. The title is a quotation of Sean O'Casey's remark in the letter he wrote to the *Daily Telegraph* at the time of the Berlin broadcasts. About this Plum wrote: "With Sean O'Casey's statement that I am 'English literature's performing flea,' I scarcely know how to deal. Thinking it over, I believe he meant to be complimentary, for all the performing fleas I have met have impressed me with their sterling artistry and that indefinable something which makes the good trouper."[2]

Plum had been writing regularly to William Townend ever since they left Dulwich, and Townend wrote to him in 1951 suggesting that a selection of these letters would make a book. This collection is more than just the letters of one writer to another who is less successful and less talented; it is, as has already been said, a manual for the writing of popular novels. Extremely revealing of Plum's kindness and generosity to Townend, it is also a record of his own methods and to a lesser extent of his life. What it is not is what it appears to be—a selection of original letters which have been given an introduction and footnotes. On 16 October 1951 Plum wrote to Townend:

> I think the letter scheme is terrific. . . . The great thing, as I see it, is not to feel ourselves confined to the actual letters. I mean, nobody knows what was actually in the letters, so we can fake as much as we like. That is to say, if in a quickly written letter from—say—Hollywood, I just mention that Winston Churchill is there and I have met him, in the book I can think up some amusing anecdote, describing how his trousers split up the back at the big party or something. . . . Also, these letters give me a wonderful opportunity of shoving in thoughts on life to a much greater

extent than I do in my actual letters. . . . I have always wanted to write my autobiography but felt too self-conscious. This will be a way of doing the thing obliquely.

And in fact Plum did call in the letters and largely rewrote them.*

Originally it was intended to include in the book the scripts of the Berlin broadcasts. The difficulty was that Plum had never had more than one copy, and this he had given to Major Cussen at the time of the interrogation in Paris. On 7 April 1952, he wrote to Townend:

> There probably remains in existence no official record of the broadcasts. All the Home Office have are the rough copies I gave Cussen, and I can always say that those were simply rough copies and that I actually spoke a little differently. . . . I can quarry the stuff out of the camp book, but I can't be sure that it will be word for word what I spoke on the radio. . . . If I get a line or two wrong, the Home Office aren't going to issue an official protest, and if they do, I can say that the script I gave Cussen was changed a little. I mean, it isn't as if I were going to say in the book things which would have altered the tone of the talks. . . . [Although] I may put in a gag or two which I didn't actually speak but invented later. . . . Thus, in the second talk, about Liège barracks, I remember saying on the radio as a wind-up "Without wishing to be indelicate, I may say that until you have helped to clean out a Belgian soldiers' latrine, you ain't seen NUT-TIN." I can remember the exact tone of voice in which I said it. But in the camp book I go on "When I meet my grandchildren, I shall say 'Ask me what I did in the great war, kids,' and they will say 'What did you do in the great war, grand-daddy?,' and I shall say 'I helped to clean out the latrine at Liège barracks.' And it is extremely probable that their reply will be 'We thought as much,' for even now you can still get an occasional whiff, if the wind is in the right direction.". . . Now, did I actually say that on the radio? I can't remember. But I don't see that it matters whether I did or not. Do you? In other words, I'll dig the talks out of the camp book and trust to luck that they are accurate in small details like that.

Clearly, the marginally more sophisticated Townend must have taken the trouble to discover that the broadcasts had in fact been monitored, and that the whole of the first and parts of the others remained.† In his next letter, Plum wrote: "In *Performing Flea* I am sorry to say that Grimsdick (that's the head of Herbert Jenkins) insists on printing the broadcasts word for word as I spoke them, leaving out the funny bits I shoved in later." And in a letter written on 8 July 1953 he says:

> The proofs of the Letter book have arrived and I have been shuddering over some of the things I said in the broadcasts. . . . I describe myself as

---

*The original letters have disappeared, no one knows how.
†At that date more of the others may have remained.

"beaming" at the Germans and I talk about "fraternising" with them. I have added a bit to my letter to you, saying that I was trying to be subtle and sarcastic, but I'm afraid the critics will tear me to pieces. I'm wondering if it might not be better to cut the broadcasts altogether. . . . Except for that passage and a nasty crack about the Belgians, the stuff is very harmless, but the critics may ignore the harmless stuff and concentrate on the bad bits.

And then on 29 July:

I decided to cut the broadcasts out of the Letter book. There were bits in them that would have been dangerous, but my chief objection to them was that they were inferior work and compare badly with the extracts from *The Camp Book*. I had to write them in a hurry and wasn't able to polish, and my stuff depends so much on polishing. I feel very much relieved that they are out. We now have a good book.

Richard Usborne told me that when he discussed with Plum the idea that he might include a chapter on the Berlin incident in his book *Wodehouse at Work*, Plum told him that it was ten years before "the penny dropped" about the broadcasts (Mr. Usborne's phrase, I think, not Plum's), but that when it did, he felt completely sickened and never wanted to hear of or speak of them again. I think this moment obviously occurred when he read the transcript of what he actually said in the first broadcast. Most people have had the experience at some time in their lives of being unable to understand how they came to do something which afterwards seems obviously and unbelievably tasteless and foolish. The words *beaming* and *fraternising* caused the detached and unbelligerent Plum an instant understanding, emotional as well as intellectual, of what others had felt at the time. In any case, he withdrew the broadcasts and *The Camp Book* from private as well as public circulation and refused to discuss the matter again.

All that is comprehensible. What follows defies understanding. A section at the end of *Performing Flea* includes a written-up account of that part of Plum's internment which took place in Huy prison, and a refutation of certain of the charges which had since been made against him. In this he said:

Some of the charges made against me at the time of the broadcasts were, of course, quite true. W. D. Connor, for instance, in his article in the *Daily Mirror* and subsequent speech on the B.B.C., accused me, not mincing his words, of having the Christian names of Pelham Grenville, and he was perfectly right.

In the year 1881 I *was* christened Pelham Grenville—after a god-father, and not a thing to show for it except a small silver mug. I remember protesting at the time, vigorously, but it did no good. The clergyman stuck to his point. "Be that as it may," he said, having waited for a lull,

"I name thee Pelham Grenville." All that I can do is to express regret to Mr. Connor, coupled with the hope that his Christian names are Walpurgis Diarmid or something of that sort, and that someday he will have to admit it in public.[3]

Performing Flea was published in London on 8 October 1953. On 9 October, under the headline "Call Me Another Name, Mr. Wodehouse," Cassandra revived all the old charges in the *Daily Mirror* in the same emotive terms. "London was being bombed unmercifully. The ragged remains of little children were being dragged from under tons of rubble; hundreds of thousands of decent kindly Britons were crouching in cellars. . . ."

However, at the end of the article he answered the Walpurgis joke: "Dear Mr. Wodehouse—Mr. Walpurgis Diarmid Connor presents his compliments. But I feel disgruntled or at any rate far from gruntled—you may recall the phrase—at the choice of the name Diarmid." He then says that his second initial is not D but N. "So cannot we both start again? W for Walpurgis—but N for what? You must help me. N for Nebuchadnezzar?

"Not very good. N for Neanderthal? An improvement, I think. Walpurgis Neanderthal Connor. . . . But you can do better. You suggest what N stands for and I will come to a fair compact with you."

Within a few days, he continued, he would be travelling through many of the main towns of America, and if Wodehouse could suggest a good name for the N, "to the hotel clerks I will announce myself as Walpurgis-Connor. That ought to shake 'em and will also fulfill your wish that someday I will have to admit to such a string of formidable names in public. I shall enjoy it immensely. Come now, Mr. Wodehouse, N for what? Yours sincerely, Walpurgis Connor."

He ends the article by saying that he has sent this letter to Mr. Wodehouse but has had no reply. Connor must have been a man of quite exceptional hardihood, because immediately after this Ralph Champion, then chief United States correspondent for the Daily Mirror Group, received a cable from London asking him to arrange a luncheon for William Connor with P. G. Wodehouse. This he succeeded in doing without any apparent difficulty.

Describing this meeting to me nearly thirty years later, Mr. Champion said it took place at the Warwick Hotel, where "the usual porterhouse steaks" and plenty of wine were consumed, and that after a slightly uneasy start, conversation flowed. When I asked what the two talked about, he replied about the book that Plum was then engaged upon, about the New York theatre, about the state of London, and about cats. William Connor had succeeded in finding the only subjects on which Plum was a ready conversationalist.

Soon after, Plum wrote to Townend:

> I never have been able to like Churchill. Every time I've met him he has had a silent grouch on. One of the few really unpleasant personalities I've come across. By the way, it was Churchill, even more than Duff Cooper, who egged Connor on to make that broadcast, so Connor tells me. . . .*
> I gave Connor lunch when he was in New York and we got along together like a couple of sailors on shore leave. We parted on Christian name terms, vowing eternal friendship.

And: "The most extraordinary result of *Performing Flea* is the starting of a beautiful friendship between self and Cassandra Connor! He has just sent me Cudlipp's history of the *Daily Mirror, Publish and Be Damned* (what a good title!) with a charming inscription."

It would be a brave man who attempted to analyze the emotions which prompted Plum to friendship with someone who had so damaged him. David Jasen, who came to know him very well, once made the perceptive remark that he *had* to like everyone. Yet it is difficult to understand how this compulsion could be carried as far as Connor.

*A considerable exaggeration. See p. 227.

17

Remsenburg: Over Seventy

The Wodehouse estate at Remsenburg, on Long Island, consists of twelve acres, of which seven are wooded, and runs down to the sea. (Plum could walk by himself with the dogs running loose.) As one drives through Remsenburg, apart from an occasional man working in a garden and large cars at all the front doors, it seems strangely deserted. On a visit to Ethel in 1980 we could not find the house or anyone to ask about it. (In fact, we might have recognized it by a small attempt at a privet hedge.) This is because there are no small houses, no children on the roads, no one walking, no sheep or cattle being moved from one field to the next.

In letters Plum always described the house as much bigger than it is. "Ethel has made great changes at the Remsenburg house," he wrote to my husband, Jack Donaldson, "and it is now quite a show place. Think of Knowle or Blenheim and you will get the general idea. You know, large sun parlours protruding in all directions and the sitting room enlarged to about the size of the Albert Hall." In fact, by the time Ethel had finished with it, it had a reasonably large sitting room, at one end of which they dined, a study and bedroom for Plum, a large double spare room, and the kitchen, all on the ground floor; and above, a large bedroom and bathroom for Ethel and a small maid's bedroom. Like so many twentieth-century houses all over the world, it has little natural style, but Ethel, who owned some very good furniture and had a penchant for artificial flowers, made it pretty and comfortable and also individual. As Plum wrote to Denis Mackail in 1950:

> Ethel has had an awful job of it and is at present in one of her depressed moods when she says "Why did I do it? Why *did* I do it?" But I think this will wear off. Credit side: lovely grounds of about 4 acres, including a wood, through which one walks down to the water. Also everything like heating system, gadgets and so on perfect. . . . Further to credit side:

lovely air and comparative coolness even in the hottest weather. Yesterday it was 93 degrees in New York but down here quite all right.*

Here Plum lived happily for the last twenty-odd years of his life. After 1955, when they gave up the Park Avenue apartment, he seldom left Remsenburg even for a night. Every day he followed the same routine: writing in the morning, walking with Guy (when he was there) and the dogs in the afternoon, thinking about work after tea, cocktails, dinner, and a book, and early bed. He always did his daily dozen every day, and we know from his letters to Sheran he regularly did crossword puzzles. "Thanks for the crossword puzzles. But doesn't the *Times* man madden you? I can't understand the way his mind works. Take this last batch. One clue was 'This turn is rather offensive'—4 letters—and the solution is 'star.' I don't get it. Why is a star turn offensive?"† And later in life his simple routine was seriously broken up by an addiction to television serials.

He made two new friends, to both of whom he was genuinely attached: Scott Meredith, who wrote him a friendly letter while he was still in trouble over the broadcasts, and whom he rewarded by making him his agent, and Peter Schwed of Simon & Schuster, who published his books from the early 1950s to the end of his life. Peter Schwed wrote this description of his first meeting with him.

Plum used to toddle into the Simon & Schuster office himself each year and deliver his new manuscript by hand. I rather wondered why his first experience didn't discourage him. That year we had a not very literate receptionist who not only didn't recognize his name but had an intriguing habit of wiping her memory and slate clean of anything that took place before she went off on a coffee break. When Plum arrived that day she seated him in a dark corner and dashed off to get hers before the Danish pastry ran out. Plum, ever a courteous and philosophical man as well as a shy one, sat in his corner and puffed his pipe. And sat. And sat.

I had been in a meeting out of which I expected to be called immediately upon the Great One's arrival, but when the meeting ended and there had been no word, I went out to the receptionist's desk to see if there had been a message about Mr. Wodehouse's being delayed. The receptionist was still mulling this difficult query over in her mind when the elderly gentleman emerged from his dark corner beaming, and came towards me with one outstretched hand and a manuscript held in the other. He had been waiting patiently without ever inquiring about the delay for almost

---

*Originally there were four acres, but Plum bought more land. Jasen says the estate runs down to a river, but I think it is a salt-water creek.

†Apparently anyone ordinarily competent at crossword puzzles can give the answer to this without pause for thought. A *star* turned becomes *rats*.

an hour but he shook off all my apologies. "I've had plenty of practice," he said, "in doctors' waiting rooms."

That quiet, good-humored acceptance of the chips as they happened to fall was typical of Plum. He was not only a gentleman, he was a gentle man who never used his sharp wit as a weapon in personal relationships. He saved that for his writing and among friends in a living room or around a dinner table he invariably was the appreciative listener, laughing approvingly of others' feeble *bon mots*.

For the main, however, Plum's life was without events, except those which occur in the mind; yet he never ceased to write letters, and because so many of these have been preserved, there is a more vivid picture of him from this period than from any other time of his life. Apart from punctilious replies to every fan letter, these were written, as before, mainly to Guy Bolton, Denis Mackail, William Townend, and his grandchildren, Edward and Sheran.

Then there were the dogs and cats. Wonder lived to a great age and was certainly still alive in 1951. Curiously, her death is not recorded in any letter, although it must have been the occasion of deathless sadness. She was succeeded by Squeaky (who actually arrived while Wonder was still alive). Squeaky seems to have belonged in the first place to Guy and Virginia Bolton and to have been left in the Wodehouses' care while they were in England. Squeaky was white, and Plum wrote to Sheran: "She really is an angel, and everybody loves her. I think we told you that she screams at the top of her voice when she is pleased about anything. When the Boltons had her in Hollywood, the neighbours reported them to the police, saying they had a dog which they were torturing." And he wrote to Guy:

Well, first of all Squeaky has been a stupendous success. I thought Wonder would have thrown her weight about, but they get on together like Klaw and Erlanger.* The only moment of tension is when I put on Squeaky's harness. . . . When Squeaky screams, Wonder edges up looking tough, and says "Ah, shut up!" out of the side of her mouth. But now I seem to have cured Squeaky of screaming. She lets me put her harness on without a murmur. She really is the most angelic dog in existence. She loves everybody. . . . Her passion for me, which one noticed at Remsenburg, is now stronger than ever, and she won't let me out of her sight. If I sneak down to my study and start working, I hear yells of agony on the stairs and have to go and open the door, and then she rushes in and I have to nurse her on my lap for about ten minutes before she will settle down in her armchair (where she sleeps at night). Yesterday she insisted on lying on my desk when I was writing.

*Marc Klaw and Abraham Lincoln Erlanger were theatrical agents.

Then there was Bill, the foxhound, who made sure of a haven for life by turning up irresistibly covered with ticks and half-dead from hunger. Ethel de-ticked him and fed him, and Plum took him for walks. Several cats also turned up, but only one achieved a separate personality. She was called Poona and regularly walked with Plum and the dogs. Unless one understands that Plum's and Ethel's affection for these animals was at least as great as most people's for their children, one misses the whole flavour of life at Remsenburg, as well as one of the two main reasons for it. "The whole point in our buying this house," Plum wrote to Mackail in 1950, "was that we would have a place where we could turn the key and go away whenever we wanted to. Now I don't see how we're going to move even for a day."

As before, Plum's letters to Denis Mackail are the most amusing, and if one constantly halves the animosity, they are the most revealing. Thus, although a great reader, Plum always had trouble finding books he liked. Writing to Mackail from New York in 1950, he said:

> Getting back to writing, my trouble—and it's probably yours—is a sort of scornful loathing for the reading public. One feels What's the use of strewing one's pearls before these swine? I mean, if they like the muck which they apparently do like, why bother? I don't think it's quite so bad in England, where somebody does occasionally produce a decent book, but over here it's incredible, the awfulness of the bestsellers. I go for my books to a library round the corner, and every time I scan the shelves and go out without anything, feeling that I'd rather read nothing than American bestsellers. I just go home and read the forty-year-old books on my shelves.

And he wrote to Sheran:

> What do you find to read these days? I simply can't cope with the American novel. The most ghastly things are published and sell a million copies, but good old Wodehouse will have none of them and sticks to English mystery stories. It absolutely beats me how people can read the stuff that is published now. . . . I am reduced to English mystery stories and my own stuff. I was reading *Blandings Castle* again yesterday and was lost in admiration for the brilliance of the author.

From New York in 1951 he wrote to Mackail:

> Another book I have re-read is George Orwell's *Dickens, Dali and Others*, in which he has a long article entitled "In Defence of P. G. Wodehouse" which is practically one long roast of your correspondent.* Don't you hate the way these critics falsify facts in order to make a point? It's perfectly all right for him—or any other critic—to say that my stuff is

---

Dickens, Dali and Others was published in England as *Critical Essays* (Secker & Warburg, 1946).

Edwardian and out of date. I know it is. But why try to drive it home by saying that my out-of-touchness with English life is due to the fact that I did not set foot in England for sixteen years before 1939?

If only these blighters would realise that I started writing about Bertie Wooster and comic Earls because I was in America and couldn't write American stories and the only English characters the American public would read about were exaggerated dudes. It's as simple as that.

Another thing I object to in these analyses of one's work is that the writer picks out something one wrote in 1907 to illustrate some tendency. Good Lord! I was barely articulate in 1907.

Orwell gave me lunch in Paris in 1944, and I liked him. Dead now, poor chap.

Probably Orwell's real offence was that he attempted a defence of the Berlin broadcasts. He was not the last writer to do so, or the last to incur resentment against what Plum instantly detected as a form of patronage.

Other things he disliked at this time were *The New Yorker* and, oddly enough, the theatre. Of the first he wrote (to Mackail):

> I wonder how you're going to like having to read *The New Yorker* every week. As it only costs 15 cents, I buy it weekly, but it's a long time since I found anything in it worth reading. I think what I hate most are the stories. Why do they all begin: "When my father and I were living in Singapore, my aunt Georgina used to stay with us. She had grey ringlets and a pug dog"? I thought that sort of thing went out in the eighties. And what price those Letters from Czechoslovakia and other places? And those yards of stuff about shops? And the profiles of dull people you've never heard of? I think you are darned lucky if only the wrapper arrives.

And of the theatre:

> Of course, if you hate going to the theatre, as I do, it cuts you off a good deal of the London whirl. . . . The other day a kind friend—equivalent to your Yorks—dragged me off, kicking and screaming, to see Rex Harrison and wife in a bloody thing (by an obviously bloody author, Christopher Fry) called *Venus Observed,* and I never suffered so much in my life. To start with I dislike Rex Harrison on the stage more than any other actor—I except actresses as that would include Beatrice Lillie, to avoid seeing whom I would run several miles—and I can't stand Lilli Palmer (Mrs. R.H.), and I think Christopher Fry ought to be shot. I tried to go to sleep, but the noise from the stage was too much. Incidentally, don't you hate most of all created things actors and their wives who announce, as the Harrisons did, that they cannot play this play for more than sixteen weeks. They are sorry, they know this will be a disappointment to their public, but they really must take the thing off at the end of the sixteenth week. I was delighted when *Venus Observed* came off at the end of the eighth week for lack of popular support.

And of *My Fair Lady* he wrote:

> I thought it was the dullest, lousiest show I had ever seen. Even as *Pyg-malion* without Rex Harrison it was pretty bad, but with Rex Harrison it is awful. Whoever started the idea that he has charm? I had always consid-ered Professor Higgins the most loathsome of all stage characters, but I never realised how loathsome he could be till I saw Sexy Rexy playing him. Why everyone raves about the thing I can't imagine.

The only current musical he approved of was *Annie Get Your Gun,* which he thought excellent.

However, there were better things. On 25 December 1950 he wrote to Mackail from Park Avenue: "Oh, glory, glory! I feel like a Salvation Army Colonel seeing a sinner come into the fold. Yours of Dec. 1 announcing that you have at last seen the light and resigned from the Pest Hole. Golly, what a club!, as R. L. Stevenson said of your other haunt, the Athe-naeum."*

But mostly his letters are about Remsenburg, about books, about critics, and about his work.

> Ethel has been buying trees like a drunken sailor—if drunken sailors do buy trees—and though we shall have to go on the dole very soon the result is rather wonderful. The garden is beginning to look like something, and as I write hammering comes from the next room, where a squad of workers are putting up mirrors on the walls as first step to turning room into a bar, if you will believe it. I know quite well that when we have our bar Ethel will continue to make the cocktails in the kitchen. But I think the idea is to be prepared in case the Quality comes pouring in. Ethel, who loathes seeing a soul except me and the dogs, can't shake off those dreams of being the centre of a rapid social circle. (Good line in my forthcoming Jeeves novel about Bertie's Uncle Tom. "His face wore the strained, haggard look it wears when he hears that guests are expected for the weekend." Don't you hate having people about the place?)

And in another letter:

> This house really is fine now. Ethel's new sun parlour is terrific. Huge windows on every side and a great view of the estate. This morning they are putting in the bar in a small room on the other side of the house. God knows why we want a bar, but E. thought it a good idea. What is supposed to happen is that the County saunter in for a drink, and we mix it at the bar. The County little knows that if they come within a mile of us we shall take to the hills. But that's Ethel. She really loves solitude as much as you and I do, but she has occasional yearnings to be the Society

*Readers who have followed this chronicle with sufficient care will have no difficulty in identifying the Pest Hole as the Garrick Club.

hostess and go in for all that "Act 2, The terrace of a Meadowsweet Manor" stuff.

And in 1956:

> I have now completed a full year at Remsenburg. . . . I have only spent one night away. . . . Always something to do—e.g. letting Bill the fox-hound out and letting him in again, ditto with Poona the cat. Both are now out, and in a minute I shall hear a moaning at the side door like a foghorn, which will be Bill wanting to come in, and soon after that Poona will appear at the window. It all helps to pass the tikm—haha—!time.

Among Plum's unfailing interests was his typewriter. Thus:

> I'm writing this on my new electric machine which arrived yesterday and I'm feeling very lost on it. It has more gadgets than you would believe possible. One of its features is that the slightest touch on the wrong key and the fatheaded machine types the letter, though knowing perfectly well that you didn't mean it. I seem to be all right so far but you'll probably get a lot of tiknes for times and rightd for rights. What advantage it has over my old one I haven't yet discovered.

Chiefly, however, he wrote about the books he read and those he wrote. Of the former he said (speaking of the McCarthy investigations): "It's like Bardwell v. Pickwick; which reminds me, do you hate Dickens' stuff? I can't read it." And in a later letter:

> Well, sir, I'm giving Dickens a last chance. I'm reading *Bleak House* for the first time and it isn't as lousy as I had expected. But, oh, my God, why can't he ever draw a straight character? Most of it is told by Esther Summerson and every single character she meets is a freak of some kind. There is a boy who decides to become a surgeon so a big surgeon is introduced. There's no earthly reason why he shouldn't be a straight character, but Dickens—you can see the sweat starting out on his brow—feels he's got to have a whimsical comedy, so he gives him a wife who's always talking about her two previous husbands, Captain Slogger of the navy and Professor Dingo.
>
> "When I was with Professor Dingo,"—said Mrs. Badger, "a man of European reputation . . ."
>
> Fine if the Badgers were the only comic characters but there are at least a million others, even worse freaks.

Then, on Christmas Day 1954, after some of the usual remarks about Christmas:

> How I agree with you about the BBC. A loathsome institution and one only gets about thirty quid for their starriest productions. Yes, I too have had my fill of Maugham. There's a book just published called *Mr. Maugham Himself* and it consists of all his old stuff dished up again. A deliberate swindle, I consider, because it suggests some sort of autobiography and I

must say I do like M's autobiographical stuff. But Max. What a louse. Simon & Schuster gave me his fat volume of dramatic criticisms, and that supercilious attitude of his made me sick. And do you realise that but for Max there would have been none of this *New Yorker* superciliousness. They all copy him.

In a later letter he said: "The catch about Max Beerbohm is that just as one is about to dismiss him as an overpraised fraud one remembers something really good that he wrote. Did you ever read *Seven Men?* It's excellent." Almost two years later he reverts to this theme: "I'm still reading Max Beerbohm's dramatic criticism book, as it is in short spasms easy to read at breakfast before the papers arrive. I dislike it more every morning. What lice dramatic critics are especially if they start off by being lice like M.B."

Of *Tom Jones* he wrote: "I've been trying to re-read *Tom Jones,* and my opinion is that it is lousy. Do people really think it's the greatest novel ever written? What I felt after reading a few pages was that if this son of a bishop goes on being arch like this, I'm through. And I was through. Can you stand him?"

And of Thomas Hardy:

Clemens.* He wrote me the other day—a letter almost exactly the same as he wrote you, except that in my case it was Thomas Hardy not Belloc. He said he believed I had said I had modelled my style on Thos.—or words to that effect—and that T.H. had always expressed great admiration for my work (of which I should be surprised to hear he ever read a line). I had to break it to him that I had never so much as opened a book of Thomas Hardy's and never intended to. His answer was to send me a book he had written about Mark Twain. . . .

This letter went on:

We are having the most superb weather, which of course means there is a drought all over the country, ruining thousands. Unfortunately the garden is in a hell of a mess, Ethel having got it right up her nose. Today there are five gardeners sweating away, moving shrubs and generally messing up everything. But I must say the place will eventually look like a million dollars.

Of modern English writers, he wrote:

I say, what about these younger English novelists? The last time I was in New York I bought two of Kingsley Amis's books, though I've never been able to get through *Lucky Jim.* I haven't been able to get through these either, and yet the critics say how screamingly funny they are. Do you get a laugh out of them? Nancy Mitford, too. I couldn't read her last, which the critics say is the funniest she has written. Very dull and no story, it seemed to me. On the other hand, I like Noel Coward's novels.

*Cyril Clemens, president of the International Mark Twain Society.

His views were not influenced by any personal emotion. Of Milne, he wrote: "Any news of A.A.M? You know he did write some damned good stuff. I can re-read a thing like *Two People* over and over again and never get tired of it."

The critics were a constant theme.

I tell you how I feel about reviews. I read one that says this work of genius tells of the half-brutal life of the miners of West Virginia and I say No, not for me. Just as in, am I right, *Greenery Street* your hero said "Oh! my God. There's an Irishman in this book" and put it down. Whereas, if they say this lousy, badly written novel, without a spark of interest in it, is about the London stage or something like that, I'm on it like a shot. Recent discovery. Any English mystery story, however bad, is better than any American mystery story, however good.*

And about a book of his own, he wrote: "I've just finished my new novel. Fairly good, I think, but what does it *prove?*"

The 1950s may well have been the lowest point in Wodehouse's popularity measured purely in terms of volume of sales. Although there was no moment in his whole career when his prestige dropped or when he was not collected and read by addicts of his work, he was at this time a moderate seller in America; and even in England, although there was usually a good sale for a new book, the reissues of today were unknown. In 1956, in a letter discussing the title *Something Fishy*, which his English publisher thought too much like *Something Fresh*, he wrote: "I pointed out to him that the damn thing [*Something Fresh*] only sold 35 copies last year and it is forgotten except in a very small circle of fans."

The beginning of the revival in sales may well be attributed in large part to Penguin. In 1948 they had begun the practice of issuing ten titles by one author simultaneously, and in this way a million books by one author (Shaw, Wells, Waugh, Agatha Christie) were published on the same day. In 1953 Penguin brought out five P. G. Wodehouse titles simultaneously, an accolade which must have aroused much public interest.†

In terms of a sedentary life, the 1950s were full of events. In 1953 Malcolm Muggeridge became editor of *Punch* and immediately invited Plum to contribute to it. For several years he wrote regular articles, and in 1956 he drew extensively on these for a semi-autobiographical book called *America, I Like You*. Altered and extended, this book appeared in England a year later as *Over Seventy*. Both versions have a certain value for scholars,

---

*This must have been written before he discovered Rex Stout.
†The books were *The Inimitable Jeeves; Right Ho, Jeeves; The Code of the Woosters; Leave It to Psmith;* and *Big Money*.

as so much of the material, although heavily embroidered, is founded on fact. In all other respects, they illustrate again that this writer, whose humour so delights the civilized world that at all levels of intellectual attainment men recognize kindred spirits by their choice of quotation from it, laboured, when he turned his attention to essays in the "subjective" vein, like a carthorse under a heavy load. As usual, he seemed aware of this himself, although again as usual he accepted the commissions with all the willingness of a literary hack. "I'm glad you like my *Punch* stuff," he wrote to Mackail, "I went into it gaily and now find it's a hell of a sweat. Still it's all good practice in technique and what not." (He was at this time seventy-four.)

For the rest, the fifties were not an especially distinguished period. Plum wrote a book called *French Leave*, the plot of which was originally Guy Bolton's, and which between them they used a good many times. When Plum received an invitation to turn *French Leave* into a film script, he wrote to Guy:

> We now come to a moot point. Do we coyly reveal the fact that your play on which the book was founded has already been made into a picture three times? I strongly advise not. As far as I know, nobody except you and me and Watt knows that *French Leave* is not my own unaided work. And in any case the novel—what with Old Nick, Clutterbuck etc.— deviates so much from your original that I don't think it is necessary to say anything. It's a pity the hen stuff at the beginning is almost word for word from your play, but that's the only thing anyone could spot. So secrecy and silence, I think, don't you? All moneys will be paid to me as apparently the sole author, and I will slip you yours—in pounds, if you are still in England when the advance comes in, or in dollars if you are over here.

Guy's play was called *Three Blind Mice*, and he left a note on the letter quoted from Plum saying that three films, *Three Blind Mice, Moon over Miami*, and *Three Little Girls in Blue*, were made from it for one payment, so that when Plum was offered a large sum for the film rights of *French Leave*, they were sorely tempted. "But eventually truth prevailed."

After Plum died, Guy said that they had had an agreement to go fifty-fifty on eight of his books, on the grounds of collaboration of one sort or another. There is ample evidence that in some cases Plum passed half the royalties he received on to Guy; but Guy had difficulty in proving this, because the secret had also been kept from Ethel, who might well have regarded the arrangement as overgenerous. *The Small Bachelor* was founded on the musical *Oh, Lady! Lady!*; *If I Were You*, although based on *Vice Versa* by F. Anstey, was rewritten from a dramatized version in which Guy had collaborated called *Who's Who?*, and *Do Butlers Burgle Banks?*

(again according to a note of Guy's) was based on a play of his—although this was called by the suggestive title *Money in the Bank*. I have not been able to find any clue to the other four, even in Mr. Jasen's book, as secrets from Ethel would also have been kept from him.

The other books of this period were *Jeeves and the Feudal Spirit; Something Fishy,* in which Lord Uffenham reappears, as also Keggs the butler; *Cocktail Time,* the third of the Uncle Fred novels; and a collection called *A Few Quick Ones.** None showed any real falling off in standard, yet none were of the best.

However, the most notable publication of the fifties was not a novel, but the appearance in *Encounter* of five articles of the humorous autobiographical kind under the title "Berlin Broadcasts." These appeared in two successive months, October and November 1954 (two the first month and three the second). These articles have since been accepted as the scripts of the actual broadcasts from Germany, but in fact they were the versions he had written for inclusion in *Performing Flea* and which had been deleted after his publisher's insistence "on printing the broadcasts word for word, leaving out the funny bits I shoved in later." The last four are amazingly similar to the broadcast versions, but this is not surprising, since they were taken from "The Camp Note Book." The first one, describing events before he began the "Note Book," differs considerably although, apart from the deletion of the whole of the "beaming" episode, not importantly from what he actually said in Berlin. This article is given in Appendix D.

In November 1954 Plum wrote to Townend: "I'm being egged on to become an American citizen. Do you think it would hurt me in England if I did? I don't want to let Jenkins down by suddenly ruining my sales, but it seems to me that, if sales survived all that other business, I ought to be all right." And in October 1955 he wrote to Mackail:

> As far as I can make out, I don't actually become a citizen [of America] till the middle of November . . . but I gather that I . . . am set.
>
> The morning after the proceedings I was rung up on the telephone by the *Mail,* the *Express, The Times,* the Associated Press and others. They all wanted to know why I had done it, and it was a little difficult to explain without hurting anyone's feelings that, like you, I don't feel it matters a damn what country one belongs to and that what I really wanted was to be able to travel abroad without having to get an exit permit and an entrance permit, plus—I believe—a medical examination.

Since by then Plum had arranged his life so as not to have to travel even as far as New York, except under the greatest pressure, the first reason he

---

*Lord Uffenham appeared in *Money in the Bank,* and Keggs appeared first in a story called "The Good Angel" in the collection *The Man Upstairs* and then in *A Damsel in Distress.*

gave for changing his nationality carries more conviction than the second. However, he had a third reason which probably carried more weight than either. It has often been assumed that after a quite short passage of time he could have returned to England without risk of legal proceedings. This, sadly, is not true. Following the change of Government in 1951, discreet inquiries were made of the new Attorney General, Sir David Maxwell-Fyfe, who replied in private, as Sir Hartley Shawcross had in public, that this could not be guaranteed.

In the fifties Plum reached a peak fame on which he became a subject for other writers. The first in the field was Usborne, and Plum has been quoted much earlier here as saying he found Usborne's book a little unsettling. All authors must regard it as some sort of a compliment to be thought worthy of analytical comment, yet all feel, I think, a little uneasy about what these subliminal probings may reveal, since no personal statement or denial is relevant evidence. Plum seemed aware of this, although his response was characteristically naive. In letters, he referred to both Usborne and Jasen as "my biographer," although I think he really understood the difference in their approaches. Writing to Mackail, he said of the former:

> He keeps shooting in at me letters which have to be answered at great length. He seems to think that I must have suffered greatly from tyrannical aunts in my childhood, having written so much about them, and I have just sent him a four-page letter explaining that in a humorous story you can't have an unpleasant mother so it has to be an aunt. Why do these fellows always think that there is something hidden and mysterious behind one's writings? . . . Isn't it extraordinary how these fellows always want to dissect and analyse? I should have thought that anyone who wrote himself would realise that a writer just sits down and writes.

The 1950s were also enlivened by the beginning of a pen friendship with Evelyn Waugh. (They met once, but only once, when Evelyn personally asked for Plum to be invited to a luncheon given in his honour by the editor of *Vogue*.) Evelyn, having a much greater capacity for appreciation, probably admired Plum's work more than Plum admired his, but Plum returned his immense loyalty and willingness to rush to his defence by doing the best he could ("I always like his stuff").

In the mid-fifties both writers were incensed by the *Daily Express*, Evelyn managing a small but protracted war against it which turned into a *cause célèbre*. A *Daily Express* reporter called Nancy Spain turned up at Piers Court, Evelyn's house in Gloucestershire, with a friend named Lord Noel-Buxton but without an appointment, and was refused permission to enter the house or to see Evelyn. She wrote an article describing this visit and was instantly attacked by Evelyn in an article which—refused by *Punch*, probably on the grounds of its being too libellous—was printed in full in the *Spectator*. Plum then joined in the fray with a set of verses on the same theme (not, probably, among his best), sent first to *Punch*, where they suffered the same fate as Evelyn's article, and then to the *Spectator*, which once more printed them.* He appears to have sent the manuscript of these verses to Evelyn, because the latter addressed him from the Grand Hotel at Folkestone (where he had gone to work) as follows:

Dear Dr. Wodehouse†

I waited for *Punch* to thank you for your letter and the superb song of Lord Noel Buxton. I was afraid they would not publish it. They had refused the original *Spectator* article. So now I am proud in possessing the only copy of one of the Master's works. I show it to favoured friends to their huge delight.

Thank you very much indeed for the kind things you say about *Officers and Gentlemen*. I hope very much that it goes down with the Americans. They have shown distinct signs of getting bored by me lately. In England a few loyal old soldiers seem to like it—not the reviewer.

I don't think Mikes is worthy of your attention.‡ I will give him a crack on the nut if I sight him. In fact I will go now and make sure that he isn't staying in this hotel. Come to think of it many of the clients might be he.

Yours ever
Evelyn Waugh

Soon after this episode Plum was called on by an *Express* journalist named Rene McColl, whom he treated with greater kindness than Nancy Spain had received, but who subsequently wrote a long article in which the following passages occur:

Mr. W., whose mien, although at all times charming and pleasant, had about it a faint hint of gentle melancholy, is at present bashing out his autobiography at an observed speed of 2,000 words *per diem*.

"Wodehouse, Esq.," I observed, "could I, to use the vernacular of this our host nation, pop the jolly old 64-dollar question?

"If you were back in Germany, a prisoner, and you had it all to do again—would you do it?' "

---

*These verses are reprinted in *Over Seventy*.
†I have written elsewhere *(Evelyn Waugh: Portrait of a Country Neighbour)* that although Plum addressed Evelyn quite simply by his Christian name, Evelyn felt that he could not call Plum by his, since he did not know him, or address him as "Wodehouse," because that would seem too cold. He believed that he had solved the problem neatly by addressing him as "Dr. Wodehouse."
‡George Mikes, like Sean O'Casey, believed that Wodehouse was a very overrated writer and had said so in an essay in *Eight Humorists* (Wingate, 1954), pp. 153–75.

The melancholy that I had observed settled down more thickly.

"No, I wouldn't," he replied in low-key tones. "I never thought there would be any trouble about those broadcasts—honestly not. They were—they were just a description of life at the camp. No harm meant—absolutely not."

"Were you paid for them?" went on Quizzer Wooster austerely.

"No," said Wodehouse.

"Will you ever come back to England? Is there any obstacle that you know of hindering the jolly old return trip?"

"There's no obstacle that I know of, but I'm afraid there's only a very slight likelihood of my return," said Woders, staring sadly at the floor.

"Why, dear?" Mrs. W. now inquired.

"Because there is nothing to go back to," said Woders. He said it very mildly because, you know, mildness is the main thing you notice about him.

Please on no account tell any of my fellow members at the Drones Club, but at this point Wooster felt somewhat sorry for Wodehouse Esq.

"He won't go back unless he's welcomed back," went on Mrs. W. "Plummie" (that's a pet name) "Plummie is terribly hurt."

"No, I'm not," said Woders, still so quietly.

"There were ridiculous stories about me too," said Mrs. W., "about my trunks and my evening dresses in Germany. Absurd!"

"Darling, we aren't trying to defend ourselves," said Woders, "there's nothing to defend."

Woders—and Wooster is not a sentimental sort of chap—Woders at this point somehow got one.

Grey-haired bloke. No longer young. Looking miserable. If Wooster had been sitting in judgment on the Bench, Wooster would have had difficulty in maintaining that stern, objective approach which magistrates and co. so require.

For all his natural humility, Plum always recognized impertinence when he met it. He wrote to Townend:

I frothed with fury, of course. The bastard had rung up saying he was a great friend of M. Muggeridge's and could he come down and have a chat, so we of course laid down the red carpet for him. He tucked into a fat lunch with cocktails and white wine, and was all cheeriness and dear-old-pal-ness, and then he went off, bursting with my meat, and wrote that horrible article. I'm not sure that what didn't wound me most was his thinking he was writing Bertie Wooster dialogue. . . . Well, this settles it. Any newspapermen who want to interview me in future get the Waugh treatment. What a wonderful thing that was of his in the *Spectator* that you sent me. I wrote a polite stinker to McColl saying I was sorry my guilty conscience had made me a melancholy host, but was glad that he had enjoyed eating my bread and salt. I enclosed the Nancy Spain verses and said how glad I was that Waugh had torn those two to ribbons, adding—in a sinister way—that I thought people were fools who played filthy dirty tricks on humorists, because the humorists could always get back at them. I don't imagine he has the slightest idea that he did anything contrary to the manners and rules of good society. I thought Waugh made an excellent point when he said that nothing the *Express* could write about an author had the slightest effect.

Then in 1957 Nancy Spain unwisely and inaccurately compared the sales of Evelyn Waugh's books with those of his brother Alec's, to Evelyn's disadvantage. He instantly sued the *Daily Express* for libel, Alec appearing as a witness on his side. On 2 March he wrote to Plum from Combe Florey House, near Taunton, to which he had now moved:

> Thank you very much for your letter. The verdict last week was a great surprise and delight to me. . . . Damages for libel are the only tax-free earnings possible now. The Spain case was a close thing. At any time in the last six months I would have settled for £500. At the end of the first day's hearing I would have taken a fiver gladly. The judge was a buffoon who invited the jury to laugh me out of court. But they were a fine prejudiced body who were out to fine Beaverbrook for his rudeness to the Royal Family quite irrespective of anything Miss Spain had said about me or me about her.

Much to both authors' delight, Evelyn had been awarded £2,000 in damages against the *Daily Express*.

But these, although not necessarily the high spots, were the excitements of life, the normal course of which is better illustrated by any of the following:

> How about old S. Maugham, do you think? I've been re-reading a lot of his stuff, and I'm wondering a bit about him. I mean, surely one simply can't do that stuff about the district officer hearing there's a white man dying in a Chinese slum and it turns out that it's gay lighthearted Jack Almond, who disappeared and no-one knew what had become of and he went right under, poor chap, because a woman in England had let him down. Why, it's almost exactly like Captain Biggar's story in *Ring for Jeeves*.

Or:

> Conditions here are against solid work. At ten in the morning our maid turns up in her car with the papers and mails so of course I never get settled at the desk till about 11. 11:30 I'm interrupted by Ethel waking up and wanting me. About a quarter to one she brings Squeaky down and I have to go out into the garden with her.

In the afternoon I walk to the Post Office and back, three miles, for the afternoon mail and try to resume work at four. But am generally too tired to do much. Also sometimes *Punch* and *Spectator* are apt to arrive by second post and then I get into an armchair to glance through them and then find it's a quarter to six when it's cocktail time. I just plug along these days and by dint of working every day manage to accomplish something. But I am sometimes thinking wistfully of the Norfolk Street days when we dined at eight and I could do half a dozen pages between tea and dinner.

Or (to Mackail):

Life has become slightly hectic now because Ethel makes me rake up the leaves. It strains all sorts of unexpected muscles. Wonderful exercise of course. Yesterday I worked for two hours and got every lawn and the drive cleaned up. Today the lawns are a mass of leaves and all the weary work to do again. That's life of course.

Life also held other sources of happiness. Thus:

I've discovered another gem in Keats. As follows:

> When wedding fiddles are a-playing
> Huzza for folly O!
> And when maidens go a-maying
> Huzza etc.
> When Sir Snap is with his lawyer
> Huzza etc.
> And Miss Chip has kissed the sawyer
> Huzza etc.

Well, John, I'll tell you. It's got the mucus,* but it needs a lot of work.

And greatest pleasure of all (again to Denis Mackail):

I wrote a short story in 1947 for the *Cosmopolitan*. Subsequently writing a Jeeves novel, I needed what we call in the tayarter a block comedy scene, so I took out the middle part of the short story and bunged it into the book. A month or so ago I thought up a new middle and sold the new-middle story with the old beginning and end in England. And I have now devised a new beginning and end for the new-middle story and sold it over here. Quite a feat, don't you think?

---

*In a story called "The Castaways" Mr. Schnellenhamer of the Perfecto-Zizzbaum Motion Picture Corporation asks Bulstrode Mulliner whether he has seen *Scented Sinners*.

"Bulstrode said he had not.

" 'Powerful drama of life as it is lived by the jazz-crazed, gin-crazed Younger Generation whose hollow laughter is but the mask for an aching heart,' said Mr. Schnellenhamer. 'It ran for a week in New York and lost a hundred thousand dollars, so we bought it. It has the mucus of a good story. See what you can do with it.' "

18

Remsenburg: Over Eighty

In 1960 Plum's American publishers, Simon & Schuster, brought out an anthology called *The Most of P. G. Wodehouse,* and on 14 October as a public salute they took a two-column advertisement in *The New York Times.* It was left to Plum himself to explain that they had mistaken the year of his birth, and the wording of the spread was then slightly altered. Headed "Publisher's Salute," it read:

> Whereas P. G. Wodehouse is tomorrow entering his 80th year and Whereas none of us has come of age without having read anywhere from one to eighty of his books with profit and delight and Whereas P. G. Wodehouse is an inimitable international institution and master humorist: We the undersigned salute him with thanks and affection.

Among the eighty names affixed to this statement were those of leading writers, lyricists, librettists, and poets of England and America. So distinguished is the list that one hesitates to single out individual names, but among the English who signed were W. H. Auden, John Betjeman, Ivy Compton-Burnett, Graham Greene, Nancy Mitford, Stephen Spender, V. S. Pritchett, Evelyn Waugh, and Rebecca West, and from America S. N. Behrman, Leon Edel, Ira Gershwin, Moss Hart, Ogden Nash, S. J. Perelman, Richard Rodgers, James Thurber, Lionel Trilling, and John Updike.

In England celebration was contained until 1961, the actual year of his eightieth birthday. Then the press treated him to his due as an international figure. Most famous among the tributes paid was the broadcast made by Evelyn Waugh on the Home Service of the BBC on 15 July and printed the next day in *The Sunday Times.* Coupled with Hilaire Belloc's preface to *Week-end Wodehouse,* this is one of the two most famous essays on Wodehouse, and excerpts from it usually occur in the work of everyone who writes about him, as well as in all volumes of the Penguin edition of his books. The quotations are from the second half of the broadcast, however, in which one writer renowned above all else for his style paid tribute to another. The first half of the broadcast was devoted to what Waugh described as "An Act of Homage and Reparation."

Referring to the fact that the Americans, "with their natural, exuberant generosity," celebrated his eightieth birthday when he reached the age of seventy-nine, Waugh went on: "Now with the real occasion almost on us, we, his former compatriots, may prepare our own proud, national salute, but first there is some unfinished business between us, an old and lamentable quarrel to be finally made up and forgotten."

He went on to record that Wodehouse had twenty years before "from his captivity in Germany made five recordings describing his experiences as a civilian prisoner of war," which were heard "by a negligible number of people in this country." All we knew, he said, was what we were told by "the journalist who acted as spokesman for the Minister of Information," and he quoted some of the more offensive passages from Connor's broadcast, although throughout his talk he did not mention Connor by name. He revealed (for the first time) that the Governor of the BBC had protested against the famous Cassandra "Postscript": "They were rebuffed and the incident provides a glaring example of the danger of allowing politicians to control public communications, a power they had usurped during the war and have now, as we all know, relinquished."

He said that the broadcast did not have the effect designed for it, and went on: "Some innocent hearers believed what they were told and were incensed. Some high-spirited young airmen set out for Le Touquet to demolish Mr. Wodehouse's villa, but, as sometimes happened, they pranged the wrong target." And he said, which was true, that a great volume of protests came from the universities and from fellow writers, but that they were not unanimous, and "it is significant of that shabby time that most of those few who supported the attack did so on the grounds not of patriotism but of class," a statement he went on to elaborate, but which contains only a minimum of truth. Not until 1954, he said, when *Encounter* published the broadcasts, did the full truth become clear. As his friends had always confidently believed, there was in them no political implication of any kind, no mention of Hitler or of the Nazi system. The nearest he came to comforting the enemy was to suggest that they were human beings, neither admirable nor lovable, but human. . . .

> Mr. Wodehouse's broadcasts were not calculated to engender respect for the Germans, nor hate. That was his offence in the eyes of the official propagandists of the period. He revealed that civilian prisoners had slightly endearing nicknames for their gaolers—"Pluto, Rosebud, Ginger and Donald Duck"; that like most prisoners of war they were able to organize

some modest recreations for themselves. Our rulers at the time, like our enemies, were dedicated to fomenting hate. They would have had us believe that the whole German nation comprised a different order of creation from ourselves. Mr. Wodehouse's simple diversion from their party line was what was represented as "kneeling in worship" of Hitler.

And he ended this part of his talk:

"It is now time to regard the incident as closed." George Orwell wrote that in 1944, but there is a hideous vitality in calumny. Justice *seems* to have been done. Innocence *seems* to have been established. But always there is some mean and ignorant mind ready to reassert the lie. . . .

It is therefore with great pleasure that I take this opportunity to express the disgust that the BBC has always felt for the injustice of which they were guiltless and their complete repudiation of the charges so ignobly made through their medium. If Mr. Wodehouse is by any chance listening in his distant western island of refuge, I would say: You have always given great evidence of magnanimity. You tell me you have met and conceived a liking for the man who twenty years ago did you so grave an injury. Will you please extend your forgiveness to everyone whoever spoke or thought ill of you?

Evelyn Waugh then went on to record what is, without question, not merely the most felicitously phrased but also the most penetrating appreciation of Wodehouse's talent that has ever been made. This is what is remembered today and what is of lasting importance. At the time, however, the first part of the broadcast attracted the most attention, and in spite of the strength of Evelyn's opinions and the lucidity with which he expressed them, it did not end the matter. He had successfully denied the worst charge—of knowingly putting over propaganda for the Germans in return for some personal gain—but he had failed altogether to deal with the argument that to broadcast on the German wavelength in wartime was in itself an offence. He left the way wide open for the reply (duly made in a letter to *The Sunday Times* the following Sunday) that he had let this charge go by default.

He was not the first or the last writer who would cause Plum unhappiness by an attempt to explain his character or to clear his name. Plum understood full well by now what his offence had been, and understood too that he could never be completely exculpated. But he might, he felt, be left alone. If his friends could not celebrate his talents without dragging this whole unhappy incident into the open again, he would willingly have foregone the celebrations. In this case he had other and more complicated reasons for regretting Evelyn's attempt to defend him. On 10 May he wrote the following letter to his new friend, Cassandra.

Dear Walp.

A rather embarrassing situation has arisen. (For me, I mean. I don't suppose you'll turn a hair over it.)

Some time ago I had a letter from Evelyn Waugh, saying (quote) "I have arranged for the BBC to make an act of homage to you on July 15th, the twentieth anniversary of their attack on you."

I thought that was fine, but I have just had a letter from Guy Bolton, recently arrived in London, and he says that somebody told him "that Evelyn Waugh is making a TV appearance which will be an attack on Cassandra in answer to what he wrote of you."

Well, dash it, you and I are buddies, and if the above is correct, I don't want you thinking that I had anything to do with this. I value our friendship too much. I'll do what I can to halt the proceedings, though, as I say, you probably won't give a damn.

Even before I met you, I had never had any ill-feeling about that BBC talk of yours. All you had to go on was that I had spoken on the German radio, so naturally you let yourself go. And what the hell! It's twenty years ago.

I hope the cats are flourishing. We have just had to add a stray Boxer to the establishment. So now we have two cats (both strays), a dachshund and this Boxer. Fortunately they all get on together like old college chums.

When are you going to make another of your trips to this side?

Yours ever

Plum

And at the same time he wrote to Evelyn Waugh:

Dear Evelyn

I'm a bit concerned about this TV appearance of yours on July 15. I've just had a letter from Guy Bolton, who said that somebody had told him that you were going to make an attack on Cassandra of the *Mirror*. And the embarrassing thing (to me) is that for several years past he and I have been great friends. I had a very amiable letter from him one day when he was over here and we lunched together and got on fine. He sent me that *Mirror* book with a charming inscription, and since then we have been on first name and Christmas card terms. So I am hoping you will see your way to make your talk not so personal as you had planned. Is this possible? If not, okay. But I thought I would mention it. . . .

Yours ever

P. G. Wodehouse

This letter explains why throughout the broadcast Evelyn did not mention Connor by name. His biographer Christopher Sykes said in a letter to Richard Usborne that Evelyn had told him "that P. G. W. had patched up his quarrel with the repulsive Connor, which I [Sykes] thought very feeble and so did Evelyn." And he said that Evelyn had said: "P. G. Wodehouse was not made to take part in the war. He got everything wrong. The truth is he is not a very warlike man"—a surprisingly tolerant attitude for Evelyn to take, since he was a very warlike man.

One would like to believe that Plum was partly motivated by the knowledge that if Connor were attacked he would attack back, since to me at any rate it seems not so very pusillanimous that the object of all these attentions should prefer not to be trapped between two such warlike men. Yet it seems more likely that his reasons were both more complicated and more "feeble." In any case, neither Christian name nor Christmas cards prevented Cassandra returning, without regard for friendship or for truth, to all the old charges on the following day. Once more he linked his new friend's name with the rubble in London, with the death of six million Jews, and with "the same evil gang which had decided that when Britain was conquered every able-bodied man between the ages of seventeen and forty-five would be deported as slave labour to Estonia."

Then there was one further cause for sadness. Evelyn had said that some RAF pilots had attempted to "prang" the Wodehouse villa at Le Touquet. Richard Usborne took immense trouble to investigate this statement and established that it could not possibly be true. No one knows where Evelyn heard it, but he undoubtedly believed it. So, unhappily, did Plum, who was disturbed by the story at the time. One must nevertheless question Usborne's statement in his book, *A Wodehouse Companion*, that "it hung like a cloud in Wodehouse's mind till his death fourteen years later." Usborne gives Guy Bolton as his authority for this statement, but Guy was well known for his conversational exaggerations, and I think—as do those who knew him best—that to believe this is entirely to misunderstand Plum's character. He did not continue to dwell on any aspect of the German affair with this degree of melancholy. He was sick to death of the whole thing, but, essentially a happy man, when left to himself he forgot about it.

Plum celebrated his eightieth birthday in his own way by publishing *Ice in the Bedroom*. In a review in *Punch* (25 October 1961), Eric Keown wrote: "P. G. Wodehouse, just turned eighty, can still work miracles. At any point in his long career *Ice in the Bedroom* would have struck the harshest judges as spot on. The old deftness of manipulation is still there, and on every page are phrases which bring one up short with admiration."

Ice in the Bedroom is indeed a miracle. One is constantly asked by people who have never read Wodehouse where to begin, and it would be easy if the reply were definitely in the great period of the twenties and thirties. But the books he wrote when he was in Germany and France, and the output of the ten years of his life between seventy and eighty, make it impossible to do this. In his ninth decade he published *Ice in the Bedroom, Aunts Aren't Gentlemen,* and *Do Butlers Burgle Banks?*—all, as Keown puts it, "spot on."

In reading the reviews of the last period I have been struck by the fact that both Auberon Waugh and Anthony Lejeune are inclined to complain when Wodehouse departs, as in *Ice in the Bedroom* and a book called *Bachelors Anonymous,* from the well-known cast of characters of his major series books. Yet I have enjoyed *The Small Bachelor, Ice in the Bedroom, Do Butlers Burgle Banks?,* a collection of short stories called *Indiscretions of Archie,* even *French Leave* and *Barmy in Wonderland,* as much as any of his books except the two masterpieces *Right Ho, Jeeves* and *The Mating Season.* This may be because, coming to Wodehouse late and reading most of his novels in a short time, I am able to transfer more easily from one set of names to another. But I think not. I think here the difference between male and female humour becomes apparent. The Jeeves books, if not the Blandings, are drier and more purely humorous than most of the non-series books, in which Wodehouse allows the characters not sentiment (in which I have made it plain I do not think the Master excels), but a slightly romantic panache. They descend in a collateral line from Psmith, and I love them more.

The other work of this period was *Author! Author!,* a book in which at the instigation of his American publisher he rewrote *Performing Flea* for the American market. Considerably altered, with the editing overtly done by Wodehouse himself instead of Townend (as we know, he was actually in charge in *Performing Flea*), it is more contrived and less interesting, the connecting notes being in the style of his *Punch* articles. A certain self-consciousness has crept into the formerly hearty style of the letters. Thus, page 1 of *Performing Flea:*

> Gosh, what a time since we corresponded! When you last heard from me, I was living in Bellport, wasn't I? Or was it Central Park West? Anyway, I know that wherever I was I was having the dickens of a job to keep the wolf from the door. No one would buy my short stories. I couldn't sell a damn one anywhere. If it hadn't been for Frank Crowninshield, the editor of *Vanity Fair,* liking my stuff and taking all I could do, I should have been very much up against it.

The same thing in *Author! Author!* becomes:

> Since we last corresponded, all sorts of things have been happening to me. At the beginning of the war I struck a bad patch and had grave doubts as to whether I would be able to keep the wolf the right side of the door. I

had a certain facility for dialogue and a nice light comedy touch—at least, I thought it nice—but I couldn't sell a story anywhere.[1]

There are then five lines of that sort of thing before we reach Frank Crowninshield.

However, Plum was egged on to this by his publisher, and one must not complain, since this work probably gave his mind the rest it required between one inspired novel and the next.

His health had begun to deteriorate. Ever since the small stroke of the early fifties he had been subject to giddy fits, and he had a certain amount of arthritis. He was marginally lazier than he had used to be, and he spent more time on television serials, crossword puzzles, and two-handed bridge (with Ethel in the evenings, an innovation introduced by Edward Cazalet).

But he still did the daily dozen, and he still walked with Guy when he was there, alone when he was not. "I miss you sadly on my walks. It'll be fine if you don't get too involved with rehearsals in September. It's extraordinary how dull that round is without you. I do it twice daily, but I don't enjoy it." And he still had the same difficulty over books:

> How do you feel about literary classics? [he wrote to Guy] I have come to the conclusion that there must be something wrong with me, because I can't read them. I tried Jane Austen and was bored stiff, and last night I had a go at Balzac's *Père Goriot* and had to give it up. I couldn't take the least interest in the characters. Give me Patricia Wentworth!

Then there was David Jasen. I have already expressed the view that the literary world and all Plum's readers owe an everlasting debt to Jasen for his persistence in eliciting and recording the facts of Plum's life. But one would have been surprised to hear that Plum himself had enjoyed it. He wrote to Denis Mackail:

> We had my biographer to lunch on Saturday—his invitation not mine—and he made me sit and talk about myself from 1:30 to 5:30, by which time I was nearly dead. What a ghastly bore it is having to talk about oneself. I always thought I was about the dullest subject there was; but he drinks in my every word, blast him. I can't imagine what he thinks he's going to do with the book if he ever writes it. Publishers may be asses, but surely they aren't asses enough to spend money on a thing like that. He threatens to come again in about two weeks from now and Ethel means to get tough and tell him that he's got to be out of the place by 3:30 at the latest.

Why, then, if he so much disliked the inquisition, did he allow Jasen to come? There could never be more than one answer to this question—because Ethel thought a biography a good idea. All decisions were Ethel's.

"Ethel likes it," "Ethel thinks it funny," "Ethel let him come," "Ethel will tell him to go." According to Guy Bolton (never a very reliable witness), at the end of his life she reduced Plum's pocket money to five dollars a month.

As the years wore on, Ethel grew lonely and bored at Remsenburg, and, never very easy, she became considerably more difficult. "She really loves solitude as much as you and I do," Plum wrote to Denis Mackail. But this was not true. She had an enormous zest for life, and she loved a party. When she was just on ninety-five we wanted to visit Remsenburg, and she said she would be glad for us to go and see the house and garden, and she would arrange for someone to show me where Plum worked and where he walked; but she herself was not up to seeing anyone. No sooner had all this been agreed than she telephoned across the Atlantic to ask us to luncheon. In New York we got another message, suggesting we stay the night. When we arrived at the house, she came down the stairs, specially dressed and made up, in a royal manner to welcome us. She gave us drinks at the bar, talked all through an excellent lunch, loaded us with presents of Plum's books, and clearly had the jolliest time.

When she decided to get rid of the apartment in New York, it was as much for the sake of the dogs as for Plum. In the early years at Remsenburg she had much scope for her natural inclination "to pull down whatever house they lived in and rebuild it nearer to her heart's desire," and afterwards she altered the garden on a grand scale. Then in the late sixties she found a new interest. She persuaded Plum to donate $35,000 to an institution for sheltering stray dogs and cats, rejoicing in the name (surely to be found nowhere but in America) of the Bide-a-Wee Association. A shelter for one hundred dogs and cats called the P. G. Wodehouse Shelter was built at Westhampton (the nearest town). Ethel took great interest in this, visiting it nearly every day for long periods and feeding and petting the inmates. All this came to a sad end on an occasion described to me by Virginia Bolton, who was on the committee and present at the time. A new manager had been appointed, and he announced at a meeting that under new rules no one but the staff could feed the animals or stay in the shelter after 5 p.m.

"Does that apply to everyone?" Ethel asked, and he replied that it did.

"Bang went the $300,000 the association would have got when Plum died," Virginia Bolton remarked.

Bang, too, went Ethel's last interest.

She slept badly and late, with never fewer than two dogs on her bed, and her health was not good. "Bunny would be writing," Plum wrote to Sheran, "but she has been quite ill for a long time and has a continual pain which keeps her more or less in bed." "Poor Bunny has not been at all well lately. She can't get rid of her bronchitis and this keeps her awake at night." "Bunny is not too well and has a good deal of trouble with not sleeping. But she always bucks up at night and is out in the garden now, doing watering." Malcolm Muggeridge had described her as "a mixture of Mistress Quickly and Florence Nightingale, with a touch of Lady Macbeth thrown in." In these days, Florence Nightingale was fast disappearing and Lady Macbeth grew apace.

No one lasted very long. "Ethel has a new lawyer," "Ethel has a new maid," and complete loyalty to the new and a breaking-off with the old were expected of everyone. After Armine died, Nella, his widow, went to live with them, an arrangement which seems to have worked for some time.

Ethel spent most of the day in her room, and to the very end, whenever she wanted him, although crippled with arthritis, Plum climbed the stairs.

"What did she do up there all day?" I asked someone who knew the household.

"Well, she tidied her drawers and her cupboards and she counted her things. 'There's a pair of gloves missing,' she would say, and she had to be reminded that she had given them to the maid."

"But why?" I asked. "Why?"

"She was so *bored.*"

Plum kept aloof from it all. A visitor who was present when a dog-fight began in the sitting-room described a scene which seems symbolic. Ethel and Nella got up at once and seized the dogs to separate them, but Plum went on talking as though nothing had happened.

"Did he love her?" I asked Guy Bolton, and he shrugged his shoulders as though to express "Who shall say?" But I think there's no doubt that he did. "My own precious darling Bunny," he wrote to her when she was away,

> this is just to tell you how much I am missing you and praying that you will soon come back safe to me. I love you, darling, more than a million bits.
>
> Oh, how lonely it was without you last night! The house was like a morgue. . . .
>
> I am looking after your birds. I gave them seed and water at lunch time today and at five o'clock yesterday. So they are all right. . . .
>
> Poor darling, you must be having a ghastly time. I do hope they won't exhaust you with those X-rays, but I'm afraid it will be very painful. But I know they will find that everything is all right and you will come back to me in a few days. . . .

All my love, angel, and remember that I never stop thinking of you and how much I love you.

Your Plummie

My own precious darling Bunny

I am writing this to tell you how much I love you and how miserable I am when you are not with me. . . . I turned in at eleven, and when I hadn't got to sleep at two-thirty I got up and took a pill and went to sleep after that. Due to worrying about you, of course. . . .

What a sad thing it is being alone. Ordinarily hours pass without my seeing you, but just knowing you're there makes it all right. Now I keep thinking "I'll go and see my Bunny," and then I realize that you aren't there. I do miss you so, darling. . . . Oceans of love, darling. I'm thinking loving thoughts of you all the time. I love you more and more every day.

Yours
Plummie

Darling Angel One

Life's a terrible blank without my Bunny, I think you're quite right to stay in N.Y. another week. Dash it, it's about ten years since you were out of Remsenburg and you certainly deserve a change.

Spend money like water, because we are simply rolling in it. . . .

Gosh, how I am missing my loved one! The house is a morgue without you. Do you realize that—except for two nights I spent in N.Y. and the time you were in hospital—we haven't been separated for a night for twenty years!! This morning Jed waddled into my room at about nine, and I said to myself "My Bunny's awake early" and was just starting for your room when I remembered. It's too awful being separated like this.

Nor is there any doubt that, in her own fashion, Ethel loved Plum. She had the habit of leaving notes for him all over the house:

My darling Bless you. I love you more than ever *but* it's not possible. Just going up stairs. Nothing to tell you *but* I'm in love, I'm in love, I'm in love, I'm in love, I'm in love with a wonderful guy. Bunny.

My darling Bless you. I love you more than ever. Poona has just dined on chicken livers and is now fast asleep in cupboard where flash lights are kept. Don't close door and smother Poona.

My darling Plum. How am I going to tell you how much I love you. We have been married for 53 years and "It don't seem a day too long." Love and love again. Bunny.

And if, in these notes, there is, unlike Plum's pure affection, a note of reassurance, Plum was her life and the only person she bothered to reassure.

Both of them received real pleasure from the visits of their grandchildren. After the war they did not see them until they grew up, but they had corresponded regularly, and through a mixture of instinct and hearsay Sheran and Edward understood how to treat them. Edward talked to Plum about racing and cricket, and Sheran sent him books and crossword puzzles and shared his interest in the theatre and in TV serials. Neither of them either expected or received great demonstrations of affection in return, but Plum felt at ease with them, and Ethel grew to depend on them. "We have got Edward with us," Plum wrote to Guy, "but unfortunately he has to go and settle down in N.Y. as he is joining some legal firm till October. But we shall have him for weekends. He's wonderful to have staying with us and we both love him." And he wrote to Sheran in the style he reserved for intimates: "Your ghastly Sixteen books have turned up. Guy brought them round. I will send them to you by Edward, though feeling strongly that it would be much better to burn them." And speaking of his current novel:

> Still it's progressing, though slowly because of soap operas. I used to watch just *Love of Life*, and now I have got hooked to *Edge of Night* and *Secret Storm*, which come on from 3:30 to 4:30, so I have to do my writing after dinner. Also, at 11:30 in the morning I have to watch *The Dick Van Dyke Show*. Have you seen it? It's easily the best thing on television.

Edward called Ethel "the Colonel," a joke after the Master's heart and one he adopted himself. Nevertheless, this tolerance was not extended outside the family. When a friend of Edward's sent a letter of introduction and asked to be allowed to visit them, Plum wired—to the joy of everyone—that he was terribly sorry but he and Ethel had to go to Boston for the weekend.

In 1965 Edward married Camilla Gage, and he hoped that Plum and Ethel might come to England for the wedding. He therefore made inquiries for the third time as to whether Plum could be assured that he would be safe from legal proceedings if he came. The question was not officially put and the answer was unofficial, but for the first time it was in the affirmative.

Whether Edward seriously believed Plum would come, I do not know, but he cannot have been very much surprised when Plum ran out at the last moment. He was too old now to visit his native land, and too set in his ways to leave Remsenburg.

.　.　.

Plum must have received a great many letters from distinguished contemporaries, but unfortunately very few remain. There is a bundle of letters from Agatha Christie, in the most interesting of which she complains, as so many lesser mortals have, of the attentions of publisher's editors:

> Before that [publication], no doubt there will be some periods of rage at the, to my mind, unnecessary corrections made by proof readers to my grammar. And as that is usually wrong in the personal remarks made by the characters it really does enrage me, because few people I ever met do talk grammatically, and this includes myself.

Another letter that he kept concerns a rather elaborate but very good joke made by Sir Robert Birley. While Headmaster of Eton, Sir Robert spent all his leisure hours cataloguing the marvellous and rather neglected library of historical books and papers. He sent Plum a copy of the catalogue, in which Item 17 reads as follows:

> 17. The Gutenberg Bible or 42-line Bible. Fo. Mainz c. 1455: The first printed book, of which 48 copies (if some seriously imperfect examples are counted) have survived; twelve of them printed on vellum.

Having described in some detail the Eton copy, the catalogue continues: "To the recorded copies of the Gutenberg Bible should be added one in the library of Blandings Castle."*

In the letter accompanying the catalogue, Sir Robert said:

> I am very hopeful that some German professor will write to me asking what he should do to inspect the book. I shall, of course, suggest to him that he catches the 11:18 or the 2:33 p.m. train from Paddington Station for Market Blandings, having secured a room at the Emsworth Arms Hotel and making use of the services of Mr. Jno. Robinson and his station taxi-cab.

And in a letter written to my husband, giving me permission to quote from this letter, Sir Robert said that although he had failed to trap a German professor, he had succeeded in considerably worrying the great New York bookseller H. P. Kraus.

In his letter to Plum Sir Robert told of an occasion when he was in the study of the Provost of Eton, Dr. M. R. James, "the most learned scholar I have ever known." The Provost had referred to a house where Queen Elizabeth I had stayed. "I said, under my breath, 'One of those houses, no doubt,

---

*"In the museum at Blandings Castle you might find every manner of valuable and valueless curio. There was no central motive, the place was simply an amateur junk-shop. Side by side with a Gutenberg Bible for which rival collectors would have bidden without a limit, you would come across a bullet from the field of Waterloo, one of a consignment of ten thousand shipped there for the use of tourists by a Birmingham firm. Each was equally attractive to its owner." (*Something Fresh*, Chapter 3)

at which Queen Elizabeth had spent a night in her snipe-like movement about the country.' 'What, my dear Birley,' he said. 'Do you read him too?' It became a great bond between us."

In 1965 the first and best of the Wodehouse television series appeared on the BBC. This was *The World of Wooster,* in which Ian Carmichael played Bertie, and Dennis Price, Jeeves. Carmichael was older than Bertie is intended to be, but with the aid of a slight stammer he conveyed the essence of the role. *The World of Wooster* achieved immediate success and was followed by a series called *Blandings Castle,* in which Sir Ralph Richardson played Lord Emsworth; Meriel Forbes, Lady Constance; and Stanley Holloway, Beach. This series was also very popular, although not considered to have hit off the spirit of the thing so certainly as its predecessor. Further television series appeared and continue to appear, and there is no doubt that, while they have done nothing to increase Plum's literary standing, they, like the Penguin editions, have ensured something equally important: that he is read.

But the most extraordinary thing about Plum's ninth decade is that in it he wrote almost as much and quite as well as in any other. He continually complained about slowing up, and he had adopted the method of writing in an armchair with his feet up and then typing only from a forward draft. "It doesn't work badly," he wrote to Guy.

> I did four pages in the armchair yesterday, and can always improve them when I type. The novel is coming out fine so far, and I think it will be all right to the end, but the blood sweat and tears are awful. When I remember that I wrote the last twenty-six pages of *Thank You, Jeeves* in a single day, I sigh for the past. Pretty darned good if I get three done nowadays.

He had also, as we know, become much more susceptible to such outside attractions as *The Edge of Night.* Yet his output was phenomenal. In the ten years from 1960 to 1970 he produced seven novels and one collection of short stories. These were *Service with a Smile* (America, 1961; England, 1962); *Stiff Upper Lip, Jeeves* (America, 1963; England, 1963); *Biffen's Millions* (America, 1964), appearing in England as *Frozen Assets* (1964); *The Brinkmanship of Galahad Threepwood* (America, 1965), appearing in England as *Galahad at Blandings* (1965); the collection of short stories *Plum Pie* (England, 1966; America 1967); *The Purloined Paperweight* (America, 1967), appearing in England as *Company for Henry* (1967); *Do Butlers Burgle Banks?* (America and England, 1968); *A Pelican at Blandings* (England, 1969), appearing in America as *No Nudes Is Good Nudes* (1970).

All these books are up to standard, but in particular *Service with a Smile* and *Do Butlers Burgle Banks?* (written when he was eighty-seven) have the extreme sensibility and the sure humorous touch of their most inspired predecessors.

19

Finale

Plum died on 14 February 1975. Before that date, on or after the celebrations for his ninetieth birthday, he performed the astonishing feat of publishing four more novels. According to Jasen, *Much Obliged, Jeeves* (*Jeeves and the Tie That Binds* in America), published on his birthday in 1971, was his ninety-third book, and if this is correct, he published altogether ninety-six, or more than one for every year of his life. The other three in this decade were *Pearls, Girls and Monty Bodkin* (1972), *Bachelors Anonymous* (1973), and *Aunts Aren't Gentlemen* (1974).

More surprising even than the quantity is the quality. Reviewing his last book in the *Evening Standard*, Auberon Waugh wrote:

> After a sticky period in his late 80s, P. G. Wodehouse has sailed out into the sunshine again. The new Wodehouse, *Aunts Aren't Gentlemen*—a Jeeves and Bertie Wooster offering—is as funny, elegant and as light of touch as anything we have seen in the last 70 years. If there are no memorable set-pieces which would be included in a Wodehouse album, the backchat is better than ever with scarcely a line in it which does not have the authentic touch of the Master.

And he ended his review with words which might serve as an epitaph: "Nobody deserves any sympathy in these hard times if he has not at least tried to banish his cares by applying himself to this latest in the long line of masterpieces."

In his tenth decade this writer, revered in his time by Asquith, Belloc, M. R. James, and Ronald Knox, read and admired by every succeeding generation of learned men, was honoured by some of the leading writers of our own day in a symposium of essays edited by Thelma Cazalet-Keir and called *Homage to P. G. Wodehouse*. This was presented to him in 1973.

Then in 1975, in the New Year's Honours List, Pelham Grenville Wodehouse was created a Knight Commander of the British Empire—an act, if

not of reparation, of honourable renewal of his ties with his native land—
and one that came just in time, for two months later he died. On the
occasion of his knighthood he received letters of congratulation from all
over the world, many of which, collected in a large packing case and given
to me when I visited Ethel, now reside in the Pierpont Morgan Library in
New York.

Since the time of his stroke in 1951, Plum had been subject to occasional
unexplained giddy fits. He suffered also from arthritis and from his heart.
"You ask about my health," he wrote to Guy in 1971.

> Well, there's nothing much the matter with me except that if I go upstairs
> to Ethel's room I pant as if I had been running to catch a train. This passes
> off after a few puffs, and today I went up the stairs without panting so
> probably it was just a passing malaise. I am quite okay when sitting or
> walking and it doesn't affect my doing exercises, so there can't be much
> to worry about.

And in a later letter: "I feel pretty awful after all the fuss about my birthday, and the interviewers and particularly the BBC nearly killed me. I
couldn't walk a step without having to stop and gasp." (He also wrote:
"About coming back for my birthday. If it is possible for you to stay on
in London, I wouldn't leave if I were you. Ethel is having a huge party at
the Henry Perkins Hotel in Riverhead, and I doubt if you would enjoy
it.")

Then in 1972:

> A nasty thing happened to me a couple of weeks ago. I was taking a walk
> in the grounds, and just as I got opposite the Gonell house I staggered
> sideways and came down a hell of a whack on the side of my face. No
> reason that I can see. I was walking slowly and didn't trip over anything.
> It was like a stroke, though of course it wasn't one. Like a chump I was
> without a stick which I am never now even indoors. I suppose one just
> has to reconcile oneself that this sort of thing comes with the package deal
> of being over ninety. Fortunately my brain continues at the top of its
> form. But my legs have definitely gone back on me.

To the end of his life he did his exercises every day, although he could
no longer walk, and the present generation of dogs were so old that they
could not either. Nothing else changed. He still staggered up to Ethel's
room whenever she called him, he still complained of the difficulty of
finding anything to read, and he still watched television. He wrote Guy:

> Here's a commission for you when you see Pat Smith. Tell her that by
> sailing when she did she missed the colossal punch in *Edge of Night*. You
> won't understand a word of this, but tell her that Uncle Charles phones
> Keith, and Keith (who is supposed to be dead) . . . and blow me tight if

he doesn't turn out to be the bearded hippie who is trying to seduce
Lavinia. He confesses to having done all the murders which have been
perplexing us, and then murders Uncle Charles.

Most unexpectedly of all, in spite of the fact that—apart from the musical *Leave It to Jane,* which had had considerable success off Broadway,
and a Jeeves play, which was a flop in London—the partnership had had
nothing produced in the theatre for years, he still spent much of his working day on lyrics, and did so with all the enthusiasm of old. He wrote to
Guy in 1971:

> You're absolutely right, of course, about the inconsistency of the "Find a
> Girl" number, but it seems to have got by all right in all these years. Don't
> you remember it in the original, it was done by Oscar Shaw, Olin How-
> ard and an Ollie with a small moustache. Each did a single dance with a
> girl and it was terrific.
>
> But for all we know people may have noticed that it wasn't consistent,
> so I have re-written it, as enclosed. I think it will be all right now. I have
> kept Bub's lines in verse two, as they are in character for him.

Wodehouse was probably more *loved* than any other writer since Jane
Austen, and certainly more quoted. Wherever I go people anxiously press
on me their preferences. I must not underrate the Mulliner stories; or
overlook Lord Ickenham on his way to the bathroom "armed with his
great sponge, Joyeuse";[1] or forget the best of his dedications: "To my
daughter Leonora without whose never-failing sympathy and encouragement this book would have been finished in half the time";[2] or his capacity
to create humour by using terms appropriate to one thing to illustrate
another, as in "He folded her in his arms using the interlocking grip"[3] and
also in "That 'To-morrow and to-morrow and to-morrow' thing. Some
spin on the ball there."[4]

On my own account I choose two more quotations, the first to show
the suppleness of his prose and the shrewdness of his humour when just
on ninety, the second to give an example of what after all for most people
is "the essence." In the first, Lord Emsworth, otherwise alone at Blandings
Castle, has been visited by a friend of his son, Freddy.

> He had had to ask him to stay, but he had neutralized the man's menace
> by cleverly having all his meals in the library and in between meals keeping
> out of his way. A host can always solve the problem of the unwanted
> guest if he has a certain animal cunning and no social conscience. *(A
> Pelican at Blandings,* Chapter 1)

In the second example Bertie is in a hubristic mood:

> "To be quite candid, Jeeves, I have frequently noticed before now a
> tendency of disposition on your part to become—what's the word?"

"I could not say, sir."

"Eloquent? No, it's not eloquent. Elusive? No, it's not elusive. It's on the tip of my tongue. Begins with an 'e' and means being a jolly sight too clever."

"Elaborate, sir?"

"That is the exact word I was after. Too elaborate, Jeeves—that is what you are frequently prone to become. Your methods are not simple, not straightforward. You cloud the issue with a lot of fancy stuff that is not of the essence. All that Gussie needs is the elderly—brotherly advice of a seasoned man of the world. So what I suggest is that from now onwards you leave this case to me."

"Very good, sir."

"You lay off and devote yourself to your duties about the home."

"Very good, sir."

"I shall no doubt think of something quite simple and straightforward yet perfectly effective before long. I will make a point of seeing Gussie tomorrow."

"Very good, sir."

"Right ho, Jeeves."

But on the morrow all those telegrams started coming in, and I confess that for twenty-four hours I didn't give the poor chap a thought, having problems of my own to contend with. (*Right Ho, Jeeves*, Chapter 2)

In February 1975 Plum went into a hospital on Long Island, suffering from a severe skin disorder called pemphiguf—a name he might have invented himself—which involves the whole circulatory system. He took with him the manuscript of the novel he was working on and which was published posthumously with notes by Richard Usborne as *Sunset at Blandings*. On 14 February, he got out of bed and, crossing the room, he died.

His death was mourned, as his successive birthdays had been celebrated, in most countries of the civilized world. Yards of newsprint proclaimed the love and admiration felt for him and the years of pleasure he had given. Indeed one might say that if all the columns of his obituary notices were placed end to end, they would reach part of the way to the North Pole.

He was not a saintly man, because he could not love the human race. But he had many of the qualities of a saint. Kind, modest, and simple, he was without malice or aggression. He gave happiness to others as few people are privileged to do, and he was happy himself.

Appendix A

The Works of P. G. Wodehouse

BOOKS*

Title	Date	Place	Publisher
The Pothunters	1902	UK	A. & C. Black
A Prefect's Uncle	1903	UK	A. & C. Black
Tales of St. Austin's	1903	UK	A. & C. Black
The Gold Bat	1904	UK	A. & C. Black
William Tell Told Again	1904	UK	A. & C. Black
The Head of Kay's	1905	UK	A. & C. Black
Love among the Chickens	1906	UK	George Newnes
	1909	USA	Circle Publishing
	1921	UK	Herbert Jenkins
The White Feather	1907	UK	A. & C. Black

*With acknowledgements to David A. Jasen, Joseph Connolly and the Pierpont Morgan Library, and a word of caution from Peter Schwed of Simon & Schuster, who wrote: "In recent years there have been several scholarly volumes devoted to the writings of P. G. Wodehouse, and these naturally include in one way or another a complete list of his books. I tip my hat in admiration in the direction of anyone who actually has succeeded in scoring a perfect mark in that undertaking because I, admittedly no professional bibliographer, have tried to do it more than once over the past quarter of a century or so when I have been his American editor. It's a little like trying to square the circle. The works of Wodehouse, like the flowering gardens of England (a paradise he is believed by some to have invented and populated almost entirely with bachelors, butlers, aunts, the peerage, clergymen, jolly girls, some of whom have demoniacal ideas of fun, and golfers), are not numerically infinite but, whether for good or bad reasons, English and American editions frequently bear different titles."

Title	Date	Place	Publisher
Not George Washington	1907	UK	Cassell & Company
The Globe By the Way Book	1908	UK	Globe Publishing
The Swoop	1909	UK	Alston Rivers
Mike	1909	UK	A. & C. Black
The Intrusion of Jimmy	1910	USA	W. J. Watt
A Gentleman of Leisure	1910	UK	Alston Rivers
Psmith in the City	1910	UK	A. & C. Black
The Prince and Betty	1912	USA	W. J. Watt
	1912	UK	Mills & Boon
The Little Nugget	1913	UK	Methuen
	1914	USA	W. J. Watt
The Man Upstairs	1914	UK	Methuen
Something New	1915	USA	D. Appleton
Something Fresh	1915	UK	Methuen
Psmith, Journalist	1915	UK	A. & C. Black
Uneasy Money	1916	USA	D. Appleton
	1917	UK	Methuen
Piccadilly Jim	1917	USA	Dodd, Mead
	1918	UK	Herbert Jenkins
The Man with Two Left Feet	1917	UK	Methuen
	1933	USA	A. L. Burt
My Man Jeeves	1919	UK	George Newnes
Their Mutual Child	1919	USA	Boni & Liveright
The Coming of Bill	1920	UK	Herbert Jenkins
A Damsel in Distress	1919	USA	George H. Doran
	1919	UK	Herbert Jenkins
The Little Warrior	1920	USA	George H. Doran
Jill the Reckless	1921	UK	Herbert Jenkins
Indiscretions of Archie	1921	UK	Herbert Jenkins
	1921	USA	George H. Doran
The Clicking of Cuthbert	1922	UK	Herbert Jenkins
Golf without Tears	1924	USA	George H. Doran
Three Men and a Maid	1922	USA	George H. Doran
The Girl on the Boat	1922	UK	Herbert Jenkins

Title	Date	Place	Publisher
The Adventures of Sally	1922	UK	Herbert Jenkins
Mostly Sally	1923	USA	George H. Doran
The Inimitable Jeeves	1923	UK	Herbert Jenkins
Jeeves	1923	USA	George H. Doran
Leave It to Psmith	1923	UK	Herbert Jenkins
	1924	USA	George H. Doran
Ukridge	1924	UK	Herbert Jenkins
He Rather Enjoyed It	1926	USA	George H. Doran
Bill the Conqueror	1924	UK	Methuen
	1925	USA	George H. Doran
Carry On, Jeeves	1925	UK	Herbert Jenkins
	1927	USA	George H. Doran
Sam the Sudden	1925	UK	Methuen
Sam in the Suburbs	1925	USA	George H. Doran
The Heart of a Goof	1926	UK	Herbert Jenkins
Divots	1927	USA	George H. Doran
The Small Bachelor	1927	UK	Methuen
	1927	USA	George H. Doran
Meet Mr. Mulliner	1927	UK	Herbert Jenkins
	1928	USA	Doubleday, Doran
Money for Nothing	1928	UK	Herbert Jenkins
	1928	USA	Doubleday, Doran
Mr. Mulliner Speaking	1929	UK	Herbert Jenkins
	1930	USA	Doubleday, Doran
Fish Preferred	1929	USA	Doubleday, Doran
Summer Lightning	1929	UK	Herbert Jenkins
Very Good, Jeeves	1930	USA	Doubleday, Doran
	1930	UK	Herbert Jenkins
Big Money	1931	USA	Doubleday, Doran
	1931	UK	Herbert Jenkins
If I Were You	1931	USA	Doubleday, Doran
	1931	UK	Herbert Jenkins
Louder and Funnier	1932	UK	Faber & Faber
Doctor Sally	1932	UK	Methuen
Hot Water	1932	UK	Herbert Jenkins
	1932	USA	Doubleday, Doran

Title	Date	Place	Publisher
Mulliner Nights	1933	UK	Herbert Jenkins
	1933	USA	Doubleday, Doran
Heavy Weather	1933	USA	Little, Brown
	1933	UK	Herbert Jenkins
Thank You, Jeeves	1934	UK	Herbert Jenkins
	1934	USA	Little, Brown
Right Ho, Jeeves	1934	UK	Herbert Jenkins
Brinkley Manor	1934	USA	Little, Brown
Blandings Castle	1935	UK	Herbert Jenkins
	1935	USA	Doubleday, Doran
The Luck of the Bodkins	1935	UK	Herbert Jenkins
	1936	USA	Little, Brown
Young Men in Spats	1936	UK	Herbert Jenkins
	1936	USA	Doubleday, Doran
Laughing Gas	1936	UK	Herbert Jenkins
	1936	USA	Doubleday, Doran
Lord Emsworth and Others	1937	UK	Herbert Jenkins
Crime Wave at Blandings	1937	USA	Doubleday, Doran
Summer Moonshine	1937	USA	Doubleday, Doran
	1938	UK	Herbert Jenkins
The Code of the Woosters	1938	USA	Doubleday, Doran
	1938	UK	Herbert Jenkins
Uncle Fred in the Springtime	1939	USA	Doubleday, Doran
	1939	UK	Herbert Jenkins
Eggs, Beans and Crumpets	1940	UK	Herbert Jenkins
	1940	USA	Doubleday, Doran
Quick Service	1940	UK	Herbert Jenkins
	1940	USA	Doubleday, Doran
Money in the Bank	1942	USA	Doubleday, Doran
	1946	UK	Herbert Jenkins
Joy in the Morning	1946	USA	Doubleday & Co.
	1947	UK	Herbert Jenkins
Full Moon	1947	USA	Doubleday & Co.
	1947	UK	Herbert Jenkins
Spring Fever	1948	USA	Doubleday & Co.
	1948	UK	Herbert Jenkins

Title	Date	Place	Publisher
Uncle Dynamite	1948	UK	Herbert Jenkins
	1948	USA	Didier
The Mating Season	1949	UK	Herbert Jenkins
	1949	USA	Didier
Nothing Serious	1950	UK	Herbert Jenkins
	1951	USA	Doubleday & Co.
The Old Reliable	1951	UK	Herbert Jenkins
	1951	USA	Doubleday & Co.
Barmy in Wonderland	1952	UK	Herbert Jenkins
Angel Cake	1952	USA	Doubleday & Co.
Pigs Have Wings	1952	USA	Doubleday & Co.
	1952	UK	Herbert Jenkins
Ring for Jeeves	1953	UK	Herbert Jenkins
The Return of Jeeves	1954	USA	Simon & Schuster
Bring On the Girls	1953	USA	Simon & Schuster
	1954	UK	Herbert Jenkins
Performing Flea	1953	UK	Herbert Jenkins
Author! Author!	1962	USA	Simon & Schuster
Jeeves and the Feudal Spirit	1954	UK	Herbert Jenkins
Bertie Wooster Sees It Through	1955	USA	Simon & Schuster
French Leave	1956	UK	Herbert Jenkins
	1959	USA	Simon & Schuster
America, I Like You	1956	USA	Simon & Schuster
Over Seventy	1957	UK	Herbert Jenkins
Something Fishy	1957	UK	Herbert Jenkins
The Butler Did It	1957	USA	Simon & Schuster
Cocktail Time	1958	UK	Herbert Jenkins
	1958	USA	Simon & Schuster
A Few Quick Ones	1959	USA	Simon & Schuster
	1959	UK	Herbert Jenkins
How Right You Are, Jeeves	1960	USA	Simon & Schuster
Jeeves in the Offing	1960	UK	Herbert Jenkins
The Ice in the Bedroom	1961	USA	Simon & Schuster
Ice in the Bedroom	1961	UK	Herbert Jenkins
Service with a Smile	1961	USA	Simon & Schuster
	1962	UK	Herbert Jenkins

Title	Date	Place	Publisher
Stiff Upper Lip, Jeeves	1963	USA	Simon & Schuster
	1963	UK	Herbert Jenkins
Biffen's Millions	1964	USA	Simon & Schuster
Frozen Assets	1964	UK	Herbert Jenkins
The Brinkmanship of Galahad Threepwood	1965	USA	Simon & Schuster
Galahad at Blandings	1965	UK	Herbert Jenkins
Plum Pie	1966	UK	Herbert Jenkins
	1967	USA	Simon & Schuster
The Purloined Paperweight	1967	USA	Simon & Schuster
Company for Henry	1967	UK	Herbert Jenkins
Do Butlers Burgle Banks?	1968	USA	Simon & Schuster
	1968	UK	Herbert Jenkins
A Pelican at Blandings	1969	UK	Herbert Jenkins
No Nudes Is Good Nudes	1970	USA	Simon & Schuster
The Girl in Blue	1970	UK	Barrie & Jenkins
	1971	USA	Simon & Schuster
Much Obliged, Jeeves	1971	UK	Barrie & Jenkins
Jeeves and the Tie That Binds	1971	USA	Simon & Schuster
Pearls, Girls & Monty Bodkin	1972	UK	Barrie & Jenkins
The Plot That Thickened	1973	USA	Simon & Schuster
Bachelors Anonymous	1973	UK	Barrie & Jenkins
	1974	USA	Simon & Schuster
Aunts Aren't Gentlemen	1974	UK	Barrie & Jenkins
The Cat Nappers	1975	USA	Simon & Schuster
Sunset at Blandings	1977	UK	Chatto & Windus
	1977	USA	Simon & Schuster

COLLECTIONS

Title	Date	Place	Publisher
Jeeves Omnibus	1931	UK	Herbert Jenkins
Nothing but Wodehouse	1932	USA	Doubleday, Doran
A Century of Humour	1934	UK	Hutchinson
Methuen's Library of Humour (PGW, edited by E. V. Knox)	1934	UK	Methuen

Title	Date	Place	Publisher
Mulliner Omnibus	1935	UK	Herbert Jenkins
Week-end Wodehouse	1939	UK	Herbert Jenkins
	1939	USA	Doubleday, Doran
Wodehouse on Golf	1940	USA	Doubleday, Doran
The Best of Wodehouse	1949	USA	Pocket Books
Best of Modern Humor (edited by PGW)	1952	USA	Washburn
The Week-end Book of Humor (edited by PGW & Scott Meredith)	1952	USA	Robert M. McBride
	1954	UK	Herbert Jenkins
Selected Stories by P. G. Wodehouse	1958	USA	Modern Library
The Most of P. G. Wodehouse	1960	USA	Simon & Schuster
A Carnival of Modern Humor (edited by PGW & Scott Meredith)	1967	USA	Delacorte
	1968	UK	Herbert Jenkins
The World of Jeeves	1967	UK	Herbert Jenkins
The World of Mr. Mulliner	1972	UK	Barrie & Jenkins
The Golf Omnibus	1973	UK	Barrie & Jenkins
The World of Psmith	1974	UK	Barrie & Jenkins
The World of Ukridge	1975	UK	Barrie & Jenkins
The World of Blandings	1976	UK	Barrie & Jenkins
The Uncollected Wodehouse	1976	USA	Seabury Press
Vintage Wodehouse	1977	UK	Barrie & Jenkins

PLAYS AND
MUSICAL COMEDIES*

Date	Play	Details	Number of Performances	Place
1904	Sergeant Brue	Book: Owen Hall; Lyrics: J. D. H. Wood (1 by PGW); Music: Liza Lehmann	152	Strand, London

*With acknowledgements to David Jasen.

Date	Play	Details	Number of Performances	Place
1905	Sergeant Brue	Book: Owen Hall; Lyrics: J. D. H. Wood (1 by PGW); Music: Liza Lehmann	152	Knickerbocker, N.Y.
1906	The Beauty of Bath	Book: Hicks & Hamilton; Lyrics: Taylor (one lyric by PGW with music by Kern); Music: Haines	287	Aldwych, London
1907	The Gay Gordons	Book: Hicks; Lyrics: Wimperis (two lyrics by PGW); Music: Jones	229	Aldwych, London
1911	A Gentleman of Leisure	Book: PGW & Stapleton	76	Playhouse, N.Y.
1913	A Thief for a Night (same play retitled)	Book: PGW & Stapleton	?	McVickers, Chicago
1913	Brother Alfred	Book: Westbrook & PGW	14	Savoy, London
1914	Nuts & Wine	Book: Bovill & PGW; Lyrics: Bovill, Jones, & PGW; Music: Tovis & Gideon	7	Empire, London
1916	Miss Springtime	Book: Bolton; Lyrics: PGW & Reynolds; Music: Kalman & Kern	227	New Amsterdam, N.Y.
1916	Pom Pom	Book: Caldwell & PGW; Lyrics: Caldwell & PGW; Music: Felix	114	Cohen, N.Y.
1917	Have a Heart	Book: Bolton & PGW; Lyrics: PGW; Music: Jerome Kern	78	Liberty, N.Y.

Date	Play	Details	Number of Performances	Place
1917	Oh, Boy!	Book: Bolton & PGW; Lyrics: PGW; Music: Jerome Kern	463	Princess, N.Y.
1917	Leave It to Jane	Book: Bolton & PGW; Lyrics: PGW; Music: Jerome Kern	167	Longacre, N.Y.
1917	Kitty Darlin'	Book: Bolton & PGW; Lyrics: PGW; Music: Rudolf Friml	?	Teck, Buffalo, N.Y.
1917	The Riviera Girl	Book: Bolton & PGW; Lyrics: PGW; Music: Kalman & Kern	78	New Amsterdam, N.Y.
1917	Miss 1917	Book: Bolton & PGW; Lyrics: PGW; Music: Herbert & Kern	48	Century, N.Y.
1918	Oh, Lady! Lady!	Book: Bolton & PGW; Lyrics: PGW; Music: Jerome Kern	49	Princess, N.Y.
1918	See You Later	Book: Bolton & PGW; Lyrics: PGW; Music: Schwartz & Peters	?	Academy of Music, Baltimore
1918	The Girl behind the Gun	Book: Bolton & PGW; Lyrics: PGW; Music: Ivan Caryll	160	New Amsterdam, N.Y.
1918	The Canary	Book: Harry B. Smith; Lyrics: Caldwell & PGW; Music: Caryll, Irving Berlin, & Tierney	152	Globe, N.Y.

Date	Play	Details	Number of Performances	Place
1918	Oh, My Dear!	Book: Bolton & PGW; Lyrics: PGW; Music: Louis Hirsch	189	Princess, N.Y.
1919	Oh, Joy! (Oh, Boy! retitled)	Book: Bolton & PGW; Lyrics: PGW; Music: Jerome Kern	167	Kingsway, London
1919	Kissing Time (The Girl behind the Gun retitled)	Book: Bolton & PGW; Lyrics: PGW; Music: Ivan Caryll	430	Winter Garden, London
1919	The Rose of China	Book: Bolton; Lyrics: PGW; Music: Armand Vecsey	47	Lyric, N.Y.
1920	Sally	Book: Bolton; Lyrics: Clifford Grey (2 by PGW); Music: Jerome Kern	570	New Amsterdam, N.Y.
1921	Sally	Book: Bolton; Lyrics: Clifford Grey (2 by PGW); Music: Jerome Kern	383	Winter Garden, London
1921	The Golden Moth	Book: Fred Thompson & PGW; Lyrics: PGW; Music: Ivor Novello	281	Adelphi, London
1922	The Cabaret Girl	Book: George Grossmith & PGW; Lyrics: Grossmith & PGW; Music: Jerome Kern	361	Winter Garden, London
1923	The Beauty Prize	Book: Grossmith & PGW; Lyrics: Grossmith & PGW; Music: Jerome Kern	213	Winter Garden, London

Date	Play	Details	Number of Performances	Place
1924	Sitting Pretty	Book: Bolton & PGW; Lyrics: PGW; Music: Jerome Kern	95	Fulton, N.Y.
1926	Hearts and Diamonds	Book: Marischka & Granichstaden, adapted PGW & Wylie; Lyrics: Graham John; Music: Granichstaden & Darewski	46	Strand, London
1926	The Play's the Thing	Book: Molnar, adapted PGW	326	Henry Miller's, N.Y.
1926	Oh, Kay!	Book: Bolton & PGW; Lyrics: Ira Gershwin; Music: George Gershwin	256	Imperial, N.Y.
1927	The Nightingale (based on Jenny Lind)	Book: Bolton; Lyrics: PGW; Music: Armand Vecsey	96	Jolson, N.Y.
1927	Her Cardboard Lover	Book: Wyngate & PGW (from the French by Jacques Duval)	152	Empire, N.Y.
1927	Good Morning, Bill	Book: PGW (based on Fodor)	146	Duke of York's, London
1928	Rosalie	Book: McGuire & Bolton; Lyrics: Ira Gershwin & PGW; Music: George Gershwin & Sigmund Romberg	335	New Amsterdam, N.Y.
1928	The Play's the Thing	Book: Molnar, adapted PGW	?	St. James's, London
1928	The Three Musketeers	Book: McGuire; Lyrics: PGW & Clifford Grey; Music: Rudolf Friml	319	Lyric, N.Y.

Date	Play	Details	Number of Performances	Place
1928	A Damsel in Distress	Book: Ian Hay & PGW	234	New, London
1929	Baa Baa Black Sheep	Book: Ian Hay & PGW	115	New, London
1929	Candlelight	Book: PGW, adapted from S. Geyer	128	Empire, N.Y.
1930	The Three Musketeers	Book: McGuire; Lyrics: PGW & Clifford Grey; Music: Rudolf Friml	240	Drury Lane, London
1930	Leave It to Psmith	Book: Ian Hay & PGW	156	Shaftesbury, London
1934	Who's Who	Book: Bolton & PGW	19	Duke of York's, London
1934	Good Morning, Bill	Book: PGW	78	Daly's, London
1935	The Inside Stand	Book: PGW	50	Saville, London
1948	The Play's the Thing	Molnar, adapted PGW	244	Booth, N.Y.
1948	Don't Listen, Ladies	Book: Bolton & PGW (from Sacha Guitzy)	219	St. James's, London
1960	Oh, Kay!	Book: Bolton & PGW; Lyrics: Ira Gershwin; Music: George Gershwin	89	East 74th Street, N.Y.

Appendix B

The address of the Public Orator, Oxford University, June 1939

Dr. Cyril Bailey, the Public Orator:

Ecce auctor magicus, quo non expertior alter
delectae animos hominum risusque movere.
Namque novas scaenae personas intulit et res
Ridiculas cuique adiunxit. Cui non bene notus
dives opum iuvenis, comisque animique benigni,
nec quod vult fecisse capax, nisi fidus Achates
ipse doli fabricator adest vestisque decentis
arbiter? Aut comes ille loquax et ventre rotundo
cui patruusque neposque agnatorum et domus omnis
miranda in vita—sic narrat—fata obierunt?
Nobilis est etiam Clarens, fundique paterni
et suis eximiae dominues, Psmintheusque "relicta
cui fac cuncta," Augustus item qui novit amores
ranicularum, aliusque alio sub sidere natus.
Non vitia autem hominum naso suspendit adunco
sed tenera pietate notat, peccataque ridet.
Hoc quoque, lingua etsi repleat plebeia chartas,
non incomposito patitur pede currere verba,
concinnus, lepidus, puri sermonis amator.

Quid multa? Quem novere omnes, testimonio non eget. Praesento vobis festivun caput—Petroniumne dicam an Terentium nostrum?—Pelham Grenville Wodehouse, Societatis Regiae Litterarum sodalem, ut admittatur honoris causa ad gradum Doctoris in litteris.

Vice-Chancellor George Gordon, President of Magdalen:

Vir lepidisissime, facetissime, venustissime, iocosissime, ridibundissime, te cum turba tua Leporum, Facetiarum, Venustatum, Iocorum, Risuum, ego auctoritate mea et totius Universitatis admitto ad gradum Doctoris in Litteris honoris causa.

Appendix C

The manuscript version attached to the Cussen Report of
Wodehouse's last four broadcasts from Germany

TALK 2

I broke off my Odyssey of the internees of Le Touquet last week, if you
remember, with our little band of pilgrims entering Loos Prison. Owing to
having led a blameless life since infancy, I had never seen the interior of a
calaboose before, and directly I set eyes on the official in the front office, I
regretted that I was doing so now. There are moments, as we pass through
life, when we gaze into a stranger's face and say to ourselves "I have met a
friend." This was not one of those occasions. There is probably nobody in the
world less elfin than a French prison official, and the one now twirling a
Grover Whalen moustache at me looked like something out of a film about
Devil's Island.

Still, an author never quite gives up hope, and I think there was just a faint
idea at the back of my mind that mine host, on hearing my name, would start
to his feet with a cry of *"Quoi? Monsieur VODEHOUSE? Embrassez-moi,
maître!"* and offer me his bed for the night, adding that he had long been one
of my warmest admirers and would I give his little daughter my autograph.

Nothing like that happened. He just twirled the moustache again, entered
my name in a large book,—or rather, he put down "Widhorse," the silly son
of a bachelor—and motioned to the bashi-bazouks to lead me to my cell. Or,
as it turned out, the communal cell of myself, Algy of Algy's Bar, and Mr.
Cartmell, our courteous and popular piano-tuner. For in those piping times of
war—I don't know how it is on ordinary occasions—Loos Prison was bedding
out its guests three to the room.

It was now getting on for ten o'clock at night, and it was this, I discovered
later, that saved us a lot of unpleasantness. Round about the hour of ten, the
French prison official tends to slacken up a bit. He likes to get into something
loose and relax over a good book, and this makes him go through the motions
of housing a batch of prisoners quickly and perfunctorily. When I got out into

the exercise yard next morning and met some of the men who had been in the place for a week I found that they, on arrival, had been stood with their faces to the wall, stripped to the BVD's, deprived of all their belongings, and generally made to feel like so many imprisoned pieces of cheese. All they did to us was take away our knives and money and leave us.

Cells in French prisons are built for privacy. Where in the gaols of America there are bars, here you have only a wall with an iron-studded door in it. You go in, and this door is slammed and locked behind you, and you find yourself in a snug little apartment measuring about twelve feet by eight. At the far end is a window and under it a bed. Against the opposite wall to the bed there stands a small table and—chained to it—a chair of the type designed for the use of Singer's Midgets. In the corner by the door is a faucet with a basin beneath it, and beyond this what Chic Sale would call a "family one-holer." The only pictures on the walls, which are of whitewashed stone, are those drawn from time to time by French convicts—boldly executed pencil sketches very much in the vein which you would expect from French convicts.

Cartmell being the senior member of our trio, we gave him the bed, and Algy and I turned in on the floor. It was the first time I had tried dossing on a thin mattress on a granite floor, but we Wodehouses are tough stuff, and it was not long before the tired eyelids closed in sleep. My last waking thought, I remember, was that, while this was a hell of a thing to have happened to a respectable old gentleman in his declining years, it was all pretty darned interesting and that I could hardly wait to see what the morrow would bring forth.

What the morrow brought forth, at seven sharp, was a rattling of keys and the opening of a small panel in the door, through which were thrust three tin mugs containing a thin and lukewarm soup and three loaves of bread, a dark sepia in color. This, one gathered, was breakfast, and the problem arose of how to play our part in the festivities. The soup was all right. One could manage that. You just took a swallow, and then another swallow—to see if it had really tasted as bad as it had seemed to the first time, and before you knew where you were, it had gone. But how, not having knives, we were to deal with the bread presented a greater test to our ingenuity. Biting bits off it was not a practical proposition for my companions, whose teeth were not of the best: and it was no good hammering it on the edge of the table, because it simple splintered the woodwork. But there is always a way of getting around life's little difficulties, if you give your mind to it. I became the breadbiter to the community, and I think I gave satisfaction. At any rate, I got the stuff apart.

At eight-thirty, the key rattled again, and we were let out for air, recreation and exercise. That is to say, we were taken into an enclosure with high brick walls, partially open to the sky, and allowed to stand there for half an hour.

There was nothing much we could do except stand, for the enclosure—constructed, apparently, by an architect who had seen the Black Hole of Calcutta and admired it—was about twelve yards long, six yards wide at the broad end, tapering off to two yards wide at the narrow end, and we had to share it with the occupants of other cells. No chance, I mean, of getting up an informal football game or a cross-country run or anything like that.

Having stood for thirty minutes, we returned to our cells, greatly refreshed, and remained there for the next twenty-three-and-a-half hours. At twelve, we got some soup, and at five some more soup. Different kinds of soup, of course. Into the twelve o'clock ration a cabbage had been dipped—hastily, by a cook who didn't like getting his hands wet—and in the other there was a bean, actually, floating about, visible to the naked eye.

Next day, the key rattled in the lock at seven, and we got soup, and at eight-thirty our scamper in the great open spaces, followed by soup at twelve and more soup at five. The day after that, the key rattled in the lock at seven, and we . . . But you get the idea. What you would call a healthy, regular life, giving a man plenty of leisure for reading the Complete Works of William Shakespeare—as, if you remember, I had resolved to do.

Apart from Shakespeare, who is unquestionably a writer who takes you away from it all, what made existence tolerable was the window. I had always understood that prison cells had small windows of ground glass, placed high up near the ceiling, but ours was a spacious affair of about five feet by four, and you could open it wide and even, by standing on the bed, get a glimpse from it of a vegetable garden and fields beyond. And the air that came through it was invaluable in keeping our cell smell within reasonable bounds.

The cell smell is a great feature of all French prisons. Ours in Number Forty-Four at Loos was one of those fine, broad-shouldered, young smells which stand with both feet on the ground and look the world in the eye. We became very fond and proud of it, championing it hotly against other prisoners who claimed that theirs had more authority and bouquet, and when the first German officer to enter our little sanctum rocked back on his heels and staggered out backwards, we took it as almost a personal compliment. It was like hearing a tribute paid to an old friend.

Nevertheless, in spite of the interest of hobnobbing with our smell, we found time hung a little heavy on our hands. I was all right. I had my Complete Works of William Shakespeare. But Algy had no drinks to mix, and Cartmell no pianos to tune. And a piano-tuner suddenly deprived of pianos is like a tiger whose medical adviser has put it on a vegetarian diet. Cartmell used to talk to us of pianos he had tuned in the past, and sometimes he would speak easily and well of pianos he hoped to tune in the future, but it was not the same. You could see that what the man wanted was a piano *now*. Either that, or something to take his mind off the thing.

It was on the fourth morning, accordingly, that we addressed a petition to the German Kommandant, pointing out that, as we were civil internees, not convicts, there was surely no need for all this "Ballad of Reading Gaol" stuff, and asking if it would not be possible to inject a little more variety into our lives.

This appeal to Caesar worked like magic. Apparently the Kommandant had not had a notion that we were being treated as we were—the French had thought it up all by themselves—and he exploded like a bomb. We could hear distant reverberations of his wrath echoing along the corridors, and presently there came the old, familiar rattle of keys, and pallid warders opened the doors and informed us that from now on we were at liberty to roam about the prison at will.

Everything is relative—as somebody once said—probably Shakespeare in his Complete Works—and I cannot remember when I have felt such a glorious sense of freedom as when I strolled out of my cell, leaving the door open behind me, and started to saunter up and down outside.

And, even if it shows a vindictive spirit, I must confess that the pleasure was increased by the sight of the horror and anguish on the faces of the prison personnel. If there is one man who is a stickler for tradition and etiquette, for what is done and what is not done, it is the French prison warder, and here were tradition and etiquette being chucked straight into the ash-can, and nothing to be done about it. I suppose their feelings were rather what those of a golf professional would be, if he had to submit to seeing people dancing on his putting greens in high-heeled shoes.

In the end, we got quite sorry for the poor chaps, and relented to the extent of allowing them to lock us in for the night. It was pathetic to see how they brightened up at this concession. It paved the way to an understanding, and before we left the place we had come to be on quite friendly terms. One of them actually unbent to the extent of showing us the condemned cell—much as the host at a country house takes his guest round the stables.

Our great topic of conversation, as we strolled about the corridors, was, of course, where we were going from here, and when. For we could not believe that Loos Prison was anything but a temporary resting place. And we were right. A week after we had arrived, we were told to line up in the corridor, and presently the Kommandant appeared and informed us that, after our papers had been examined, we were to pack and be ready to leave.

Men of sixty and over, he added, would be released and sent home, so these lucky stiffs went and stood to one side in a row, looking like a beauty chorus. On the strength of being fifty-eight and three quarters, I attempted to join them, but was headed back. Fifty-eight and three quarters was good, I was given to understand, but not good enough.

I did not brood about this much, however, for it had just occurred to me that, having left my passport behind, I might quite easily have to stay on after the others had gone wherever they were going. Fortunately, I had twelve stout fellows from Le Touquet to testify to my identity and respectability, and they all lined up beside me and did their stuff. The Kommandant was plainly staggered by this cloud of witnesses, and in the end I just got under the wire.

This was on the Saturday evening, and far into the night the place buzzed with speculation. I don't know who first started the rumour that we were going to the barracks at Liège, but he turned out to the be quite right. That was where we were headed for, and at eleven o'clock next morning we were given our mid-day soup and hustled out and dumped into vans and driven to the station.

One would have supposed from the atmosphere of breathless bustle that the train was scheduled to pull out at about eleven-thirty, but this was not the case. Our Kommandant was a careful man. I think he must once have missed an important train, and it preyed on his mind. At any rate, he got us there at eleven-forty a.m. and the journey actually started at eight o'clock in the evening. I can picture the interview between him and the sergeant when the latter returned. "Did those boys make that train?" . . . "Yes, sir—by eight hours and twenty minutes." . . . "Whew! Close thing. Mustn't run it so fine another time."

As a matter of fact, all through my period of internment I noticed this tendency on the part of the Germans to start our little expeditions off with a whopp and a rush and then sort of lose interest. It reminded me of Hollywood. When you are engaged to work at Hollywood, you get a cable saying that it is absolutely vital that you be there by ten o'clock on the morning of June the first. Ten-five will be too late, and as for getting there on June the second, that means ruin to the industry. So you rush about and leap into aeroplanes, and at ten o'clock on June the first you are at the studio, being told that you cannot see your employer now, as he has gone to Palm Springs. Nothing happens after this till October the twentieth, when you are given an assignment and told that every moment is precious.

It is the same with the Germans in this matter of making train. They like to leave a margin.

Summing up my experience as a gaol-bird, I would say that a prison is all right for a visit, but I wouldn't live there, if you gave me the place. On my part, at any rate, there was no moaning at the bar when I left Loos. I was glad to go. The last I saw of the old Alma Mater was the warder closing the door of the van and standing back with the French equivalent of "Right away." He said "*Au revoir*" to me—which I thought a little tactless.

TALK 3

The instalment of my serial narrative entitled "How To Be An Internee And Like It" ended, you may remember, with our bank of pilgrims catching the train from Lille by the skin of our teeth—that is to say, with a bare eight hours and twenty minutes to spare. The next thing that happened was the journey to Liège.

One drawback to being an internee is that, when you move from spot to spot, you have to do it in company with eight hundred other men. This precludes anything in the nature of travel de luxe. We made the twenty-four-hour trip in a train consisting of those "Quarante Hommes, Huit Chevaux" things—in other words, cattle trucks. I had sometimes seen them on sidings on French railroads in times of peace, and had wondered what it would be like to be one of the Quarante Hommes. I now found out, and the answer is that it is pretty darned awful. Eight horses might manage to make themselves fairly comfortable in one of these cross-country loose-boxes, but forty men are cramped. Every time I stretched my legs, I kicked a human soul. This would not have mattered so much, but every time the human souls stretched *their* legs, they kicked *me*. The only pleasant recollection I have of that journey is the time when we were let out for ten minutes on the banks of the Meuse.

Arriving at Liège, and climbing the hill to the barracks, we found an atmosphere of unpreparedness. Germany at that time was like the old woman who lived in a shoe. She had so many adopted children that she didn't know what to do with them. As regards our little lot, I had a feeling that she did not really want us, but didn't like to throw us away.

The arrangements for our reception at Liège seemed incomplete. It was as if one had got to a party much too early. Here, for instance, were eight hundred men who were going to live mostly on soup—and though the authorities knew where to lay their hands on some soup all right, nothing had been provided to put it in.

And eight hundred internees can't just go to the cauldron and lap. For one thing, they would burn their tongues, and for another the quick swallowers would get more than their fair share. The situation was one that called for quick thinking, and it was due to our own resourcefulness that the problem was solved. At the back of the barrack yard there was an enormous rubbish heap, into which Belgian soldiers through the ages had been dumping old mess tins, old cans, cups with bits chipped off them, bottles, kettles, and containers for motor oil. We dug these out, gave them a wash and brush up, and there we were. I had the good fortune to secure one of the motor oil containers. It added to the taste of the soup just that little something that the others hadn't got.

Liège bore the same resemblance to a regular prison camp, like the one we were eventually to settle down in at Tost, which a rough scenario does to a finished novel. There was a sort of rudimentary organization—that is to say, we were divided into dormitories, each with a Room Warden—but when I think of Tost, with its Camp Captain, Camp Adjutants, Camp Committees and so on, Liège seems very primitive. It was also extraordinarily dirty, as are most places which have recently been occupied by Belgian soliders. A Belgian solider doesn't consider home is home, unless he can write his name in the alluvial deposits on the floor.

We spent a week at Liège, and, looking back, I can hardly believe that our stay there lasted only a mere seven days. This is probably due to the fact that there was practically nothing to do but stand around. We shared the barracks with a number of French military prisoners, and as we were not allowed to mix with them, we had to confine ourselves to a smallish section of the barrack yard. There was not room to do anything much except stand, so we stood. I totted up one day the amount of standing I had done between reveille and lights out—including parades and queuing up for meals—and it amounted to nearly six hours. The only time we were not standing was when we were lying on our beds in the afternoon. For we had beds at Liège, which was about the only improvement on the dear old prison we had left.

Parades took place at eight in the morning and eight in the evening, and as far as they were concerned I did not object to having to stand each time for fifty minutes or so, for they provided solid entertainment for the thoughtful mind. You might think that fifty minutes was a long time for eight hundred men to get themselves counted, but you would have understood, if you had seen us in action. I don't know why it was, but we could never get the knack of parading. We meant well, but we just didn't seem able to click.

The proceedings would start with the Sergeant telling us to form fives. This order having beeen passed along the line by the linguists who understood German, we would nod intelligently and form fours, then threes, then sixes. And when eventually, just in time to save the Sergeant from having a nervous breakdown, we managed to get into fives, was this the end? No, sir. It was not an end, but a beginning. What happened then was that Old Bill in Row Forty-Two would catch sight of Old George in Row Twenty-Three and shuffle across to have a chat with him, a cigarette hanging from his lower lip.

Time marches on. Presently, Old Bill, having heard all Old George has to say about the European situation, decides to shuffle back—only to find that his place has been filled up, like a hole by the tide. This puzzles him for a moment, but he soon sees what to do. He forms up as the seventh man of a row, just behind Old Percy, who has been chatting with Old Fred and had just come back and lined up as Number Six.

A Corporal with sheep-dog blood in him now comes into the picture. He cuts Bill and Percy out of the flock and chivvies them around for a while, and after a good deal of shouting the ranks are apparently in order once more.

But is *this* the end? Again no. The Sergeant, the Corporal, and a French soldier interpreter now walk the length of the ranks, counting. They then step aside and go into a sort of football huddle. A long delay. Something is wrong. The word goes round that we are one short, and the missing man is believed to be Old Joe. We discuss this with growing interest. Has Old Joe escaped? Maybe the jailer's daughter smuggled him in a file in a meat pie.

No. Here comes Old Joe, sauntering along with a pipe in his mouth eyeing us in an indulgent sort of way, as who should say "Hullo, boys. Playing soldiers, eh? May *I* join in?" He is thoroughly cursed—in German by the Sergeant, in French by the interpreter, and in English by us—and takes his place in the parade.

As practically the whole of the personnel has left the ranks to cluster round and listen to the Sergeant talking to Old Joe, it is now necessary to count us again. This is done, and there is another conference. This time, in some mysterious way, we have become short, and a discouraged feeling grows among us. It looks as if we were losing ground.

A Priest now steps forward. He is a kind of liaison officer between us and the Germans. He asks "Have the six men who came from Ghent registered at the bureau?" But Lord Peter Wimsey is not going to solve the mystery as easily as that. Apparently they have, and there follows another huddle. Then all Room Wardens are invited to join the conference, and it is announced that we are to return to our dormitories, where the Room Wardens will check up their men and assemble them.

My dormitory—52B—goes to the length of getting a large sheet of cardboard and writing on it in chalk the words "Zwanzig Männer, Stimmt"— which our linguist assures us means "Twenty Men, All Present," and when the whistle blows again for the renewal of the parade, I hold this in front of me like a London sandwich-man.

It doesn't get a smile from Teacher, which is disappointing, but this is perhaps not to be wondered at, for he is very busy trying to count us again in our peculiar formation. For Old Bill has once more strolled off to Old George and has got into an argument with him about whether yesterday's coffee tasted more strongly of gasoline than today's. Bill thinks Yes, George isn't so sure.

They are chased back by the Corporal, now baying like a blood-hound, and there is another conference. We are now five short. The situation seems to be at a deadlock, with no hope of ever finding a formula, when some bright person—Monsieur Poirot, perhaps—says "How about the men in hospital?" These prove to be five in number, and we are dismissed. We have spent a pleasant and instructive fifty minutes, and learned much about our fellow men.

Much the same thing happens when we line up at seven a.m. for breakfast, and at eleven-thirty and seven p.m. for lunch and supper—except that here we are in movement, and so can express ourselves better. For if we are a little weak on keeping the ranks when standing still, we go all haywire when walking, and not many steps are required to turn us into something like a mob charging out of a burning building.

Meals are served from large cauldrons outside the cookhouse door at the far end of the barrack yard, and the Corporal, not with very much hope in his voice, for he has seen us in action before, tells us to form fours. We do so, and for a while it looks as if the thing were really going to be a success this time. Then it suddenly occurs to Old Bill, Old George, Old Joe and Old Percy, together with perhaps a hundred and twenty of their fellow internees, that by leaving their places at the tail of the procession and running around and joining the front row, they will gèt theirs quicker. They immediately proceed to do this, and are at once followed by about eighty other rapid thinkers, who have divined their thought-processes and have come to the conclusion that the idea is a good one. Twenty minutes later, a white-haired Corporal with deep furrows in his forehead has restored the formation into fours, and we start again.

On a good morning—I mean a morning when Old Bill and his associates were in their best form—it would take three quarters of an hour for the last in line to reach the cookhouse, and one used to wonder what it would be like on a rainy day.

Fortunately, the rainy day never came. The weather was still fine when, a week from our arrival, we were loaded into vans and driven to the station, our destination being the Citadel of Huy, about twenty-five miles away—another Belgian army center.

If somebody were to ask me whose quarters I would prefer to take over, those of French convicts or Belgian soliders, I would find it hard to say. French convicts draw pictures on the walls of their cells which bring the blush of shame to the cheek of modesty, but they are fairly tidy in their habits, whereas Belgian soldiers, as I have mentioned before, make lots of work for their successors. Without wishing to be indelicate, I may say that, until you have helped to clean out a Belgian soliders' latrine, you ain't seen nuttin'.

It was my stay at Liège, and subsequently at the Citadel of Huy, that gave me that wholesome loathing for Belgians which is the hall-mark of the discriminating man. If I never see anything Belgian again in this world, it will be all right with me.

TALK 4

In putting these talks on How To Be An Internee Without Previous Training, I find myself confronted by the difficulty of deciding what aspects of my daily life, when in custody, will have entertainment value for listeners.

When the war is over and I have my grandchildren as an audience, this problem, of course, will not arise. The unfortunate little blighters will get the whole thing, night after night, without cuts. But now I feel that a certain process of selection is necessary. A good deal that seems to an internee thrilling and important is so only to himself. Would it interest you, for instance, to hear that it took us four hours to do the twenty-five-mile journey from Liège to Huy, and that there were moments during the walk up the mountainside when the old boy thought he was going to expire? No, I thought not.

It is for this reason that I propose to pass fairly lightly over my five weeks' stay at Huy. Don't let that name confuse you, by the way. It is spelled *H-u-y*, and in any other country but Belgium would be pronounced Hoo-ey. So remember that, when I say Huy, I don't mean "we," I mean Huy.

The Citadel of Huy is one of those show-places they charge you two francs to go into in times of peace. I believe that it was actually built in the time of the Napoleonic wars, but its atmosphere is purely mediaeval. It looks down on the River Meuse from the summit of a mountain—the sort of mountain Gutzon Borglum would love to carve pictures on—and it is one of those places where once you're in you're in. Its walls are fourteen feet thick, and the corridors are lighted by bays, in which are narrow slits of windows. It is through these, if you are a married man with a wife living in Belgium, that you shout to her when she comes to visit you. She stands on the slope below, as high up as she can get, and shouts to *you*. Neither can see the other, and the whole thing is like something out of *Il Trovatore*.

The only place in the building from which it is possible to get a view of somebody down below is the window of what afterwards became the canteen room. Men would rush in there and fling themselves through the window and lie face down on the broad sill, shouting. It was startling till one got used to it, and one never quite lost the fear that they would lose their heads and jump. But this lying on sills was forbidden later, as were most things at Huy, where the slogan seemed to be "Go and see what the internees are doing, and tell them they mustn't." I remember an extra parade being called, so that we might be informed that stealing was forbidden. This hit us very hard.

These extra parades were a great feature of life at Huy, for our Kommandant seemed to have a passion for them.

Mind you, I can find excuses for him. If I had been in his place, I would have ordered extra parades myself. His headquarters were down in the town, and there was no road connecting the Citadel with the outer world—just a steep, winding path. So that, when he came to visit us, he had to walk. He was a fat, short-legged man in the middle sixties, and walking up steep, winding paths does something to fat, short-legged men who are not as young as they were. Duty called him now and then to march up the hill and to march down again, but nothing was going to make him like it.

I picture him starting out, full of loving kindness—all sweetness and light, as it were—and gradually becoming more and more soured as he plodded along. So that when he eventually came to journey's end with a crick in the back and the old dogs feeling as if they were about to burst like shrapnel, and saw us loafing around at our ease, the sight was too much for him and he just reached for his whistle and blew it for an extra parade.

Extra parades were also called two or three times a day by the Sergeant, when there was any announcement to be made. At Tost we had a notice board, on which camp orders were posted each day, but this ingenious system had not occurred to anyone at Huy. The only way they could think of establishing communication between the front office and the internees was to call a parade. Three whistles would blow, and we would assemble in the yard, and after a long interval devoted to getting into some sort of formation we would be informed that there was a parcel for Yakob—or that we must shave daily—or that we must not smoke on parade—or that we must not keep our hands in our pockets on parade—or that we might buy playing cards—(and next day that we might *not* buy playing cards)—or that boys must not cluster round the guardroom trying to scrounge food from the soldiers—or that there was a parcel for Yakob.

I remember once, in the days when I used to write musical comedies, a chorus girl complaining to me with some bitterness that, if a carpenter had to drive a nail into a flat, the management would be sure to call a chorus rehearsal to watch him do it, and I could now understand just how she had felt. I don't know anything that brings the grimness of life home to one more than hearing three whistles blow just as you are in the middle of a bath—and leaping into your clothes without drying—and lining up in the yard and waiting twenty minutes at attention—and then being informed that there is a parcel for Yakob.

The thing that embittered us about these parcels for Yakob was not that we had anything against Yakob personally, but that there was never a parcel for anyone else. He happened to have been interned right on the spot where all his friends and relatives lived, while the rest of us were far from home and had not yet been able to get in touch with our wives. It was that that made these first weeks of internment such a nightmare. Not receiving parcels was merely a side-issue. It would have been nice to have had some, but we could do without them. But we did wish that we could have got some information as to how our wives were getting on. It was only later, at Tost, that we began to receive letters and to be able to write them.

The few letters which did trickle in to Huy from time to time were regarded by the authorities with strong suspicion. After a parade had been called, for us to watch them given out, their recipients would be allowed a couple of minutes to read them—then they would have to hand them back to the Corporal, who tore them up. And when Yakob got one of his parcels, its contents would all be opened before he was permitted to take them away—from the first can of sardines to the last bit of chocolate. I believe this was due entirely to the smart alecks who, at the end of the last war, wrote books telling how clever they had been at escaping from German prison camps by means of codes sent by letter and compasses and so on enclosed in potted meat. They meant no harm, but they certainly made it tough for us.

Tough is the adjective I would use to describe the whole of those five weeks at Huy. The first novelty of internment had worn off, and we had become acutely alive to the fact that we were in the soup and likely to stay there for a considerable time. Also, tobacco was beginning to run short, and our stomachs had not yet adjusted themselves to a system of rationing, which, while quite good for a prison camp, was far from being what we had been accustomed to at home. We were hearty feeders who had suddenly been put on a diet, and our stomachs sat up on their hind legs and made quite a fuss about it.

Rations consisted of bread, near-coffee, jam or grease, and soup. Sometimes, instead of bread, we would get fifty small crackers apiece. When this happened, a group of men would usually club together, each contributing fifteen biscuits, which would be mashed up and mixed with jam and taken to the cookhouse to be baked into a cake. It was always a problem whether it was worth sacrificing fifteen crackers to this end. The cake was always wonderful, but one's portion just slid down one's throat and was gone. Whereas one could chew a cracker.

People began to experiment with foods. One man found a bush in the corner of the yard with berries on it, and ate those—a sound move, as it turned out, for they happened by a fluke not to be poisonous. Another man used to save some of his soup at mid-day, and jam, and eat the result cold in the evening. I myself got rather fond of wooden matches. You chew your match between the front teeth, then champ it up into a pulp and swallow. Shakespeare's Sonnets also make good eating, especially if you have a little cheese to go with them. And when the canteen started, we could generally get cheese.

Not much of it, of course. The way the canteen worked was that two men were allowed to go to the town with a guard and bring back as much as they could carry in a haversack apiece—the stuff being split eight hundred ways. It generally worked out at a piece of cheese about two and a half inches long and two wide per man.

When the tobacco gave out, most of us smoked tea or straw. Tea-smokers were unpopular with the rest of their dormitory, owing to the smell caused by their activities—a sort of sweet, sickly smell which wraps itself round the atmosphere and clings for hours. Tea-smoking has also the disadvantage that it leads to a mild form of fits. It was quite usual to see men, puffing away, suddenly pitch over sideways and have to be revived with first aid.

Another drawback to Huy was that it appeared to have been expecting us even less than Liège had done. You may remember my telling you last week that our arrival seemed to come upon Liège as a complete surprise, and that there was nothing provided in the way of vessels to sip our soup out of. What Huy was short on was bedding.

An internee does not demand much in the way of bedding—give him a wisp or two of straw and he is satisfied—but at Huy it looked for a while as if there would not even be straw. However, they eventually dug us out enough to form a thin covering on the floors, but that was as far as they were able to go. Of blankets there were enough for twenty men. I was not one of the twenty. I don't know why it is, but I never am one of the twenty men who get anything. For the first three weeks, all I had over me at night was a raincoat, and one of these days I am hoping to meet Admiral Byrd and compare notes with him.

Though I probably shan't let him get a word in edgeways. He will start off on some anecdote about the winter evenings at the South Pole, and I shall chip in and say "Juss a minute, Byrd, juss a minute. Let me describe to you my sensations at Huy from August 3, 1940, till the day my dressing-gown arrived. Don't talk to me about the South Pole—it's like someone telling Noah about a drizzle."

Well, now you see what I meant when I said just now that what seems important to an internee merely makes the general public yawn and switch off the radio. From the rockbound coast of Maine to the Everglades of Florida, I don't suppose there is a single soul who gives a hoot that, when I was at Huy, ice formed on my upper slopes and my little pink toes dropped off one by one with frost-bite. But, boy, wait till I meet my grandchildren!

However, as somebody once observed, it is always darkest before the dawn. And, as Methuselah said to the reporter who was interviewing him for the local sheet and had asked what it felt like to live to nine hundred—"The first five hundred years are hard, but after that it's pie." It was the same with us. The first seven weeks of our internment had been hard, but the pie was waiting just around the corner. There was, in short, a good time coming. On September the eighth, exactly five weeks from the day of our arrival, we were paraded and this time informed—not that Yakob had received a parcel, but that we were to pack our belongings and proceed once more to an unknown destination.

This proved to be the village of Tost in Upper Silesia.

TALK 5

I broke off last week with our eight hundred internees setting out for the village of Tost in Upper Silesia. I don't know how well acquainted my listeners are with central European geography, so I will mention that Upper Silesia is right at the end of Germany, and that Tost is right at the end of Upper Silesia—in fact, another yard or two from where we eventually fetched up, and we should have been in Poland.

We made the journey this time, not in cattle trucks but in a train divided into small compartments, eight men to the compartment, and it took us three days and three nights, during which we did not stir from our cosy little cubbyhole. On leaving Huy, we had been given half a loaf of bread apiece and half a sausage, and after we had been thirty-two hours on the train we got another half loaf and some soup. It was at night time that the trip became rather unpleasant. One had the choice between trying to sleep sitting upright, and leaning forward with one's elbows on one's knees, in which case one bumped one's head against that of the man opposite. I had never realised the full meaning of the expression "a hardheaded Yorkshireman" till my frontal bone kept colliding with that of Charlie Webb, who was born and raised in that county.

As a result of this, and not being able to wash for three days, I was not at my most dapper when we arrived at Tost Lunatic Asylum, which had been converted into a camp for our reception. But in spite of looking like something the carrion crow had brought in, I was far from being downhearted. I could see at a glance that this was going to be a great improvement on our previous resting places.

One thing that tended to raise the spirits was the discovery that Scabies had been left behind. This was the affectionate name we had given to one of our fellow internees at Huy. He was a public menace and had given me many an uneasy moment during the five weeks in which we had been in close contact. His trouble was that he had not only got lice but had contracted a particularly contagious form of skin disease, and in his lexicon there was no such word as *isolation.* He was a friendly, gregarious soul, who used to slink about like an alley cat, rubbing himself against people. One time, I found him helping to peel the potatoes. It was a relief to find that he was no longer in our midst.

That was one thing that cheered me up on arrival at Tost. Another was that it looked as if at last we were going to have elbow-room. An Associated Press man, who came down to interview me later, wrote in his piece that Tost Lunatic Asylum was no Blandings Castle. Well, it wasn't, of course, but still it was roomy. If you had had a cat, and had wished to swing it, you could have done so quite easily in our new surroundings.

This Upper Silesian loony-bin consisted of three buildings—one an enormous edifice of red brick, capable of housing about thirteen hundred; the other two smaller, but still quite spacious. We lived and slept in the first-named, and took our meals in one of the others, where the hospital was also situated. The third building, known as the White House, stood at the bottom of the park, beyond the barbed wire, and for the first month or two was used only as a sort of clearing-station for new arrivals. Later, it was thrown open and became the center of Tost life and thought—being the place where our musicians practised and gave their concerts, where church services were held on Sundays, and where—after I had been given a padded cell to myself for working purposes—I eventually wrote a novel.

The park was a genuine park, full of trees, and somebody who measured it found that it was exactly three hundred yards in circumference. After five weeks at Huy, it looked like the Yellowstone. A high wall ran along one side of it, but on the other you got a fine view of some picturesque old barbed wire and a farm yard. There was a path running across its center which, when our sailors had provided a ball by taking a nut and winding string round it, we used in the Summer as a cricket pitch.

The thing about Tost that particularly attracted me, that day of our arrival, was that it was evidently a going concern. Through the barbed wire, as we paraded in front of the White House, we could see human forms strolling about, and their presence meant that we had not got to start building our little nest from the bottom up, as had been the case at Liège and Huy. For the first time, we were in a real camp, and not a makeshift.

This was brought home to us still more clearly by the fact that the reception committee included several English-speaking interpreters. And when, after we had had our baggage examined and had been given a bath, a gentleman presented himself who said that he was the Camp Adjutant, we knew that this was the real thing.

It may be of interest to my listeners to hear how a genuine civil internment camp is run. You start off with a Kommandant, some Captains and Oberleutnants and a couple of hundred soldiers, and you put them in barracks outside the barbed wire. Pay no attention to these, for they do not enter into the internee's life, and you never see anything of them except for the few who come to relieve the sentries. The really important thing is the inner camp—that is to say, the part where, instead of being outside, looking in, you are inside, looking out.

This is presided over by a Lagerführer and four Corporals, one to each floor, who are known as Company Commanders—in our case, Pluto, Rosebud, Ginger and Donald Duck. Their job is to get you up in the morning, to see that the counting of the internees on parade is completed before the Lagerführer arrives to inspect, and to pop up unexpectedly at intervals and catch you smoking in the corridor during prohibited hours.

Co-operating with these is the little group of Internee Officers—the Camp Captain, the two Camp Adjutants, the Floor Wardens, and the Room Wardens. The Room Wardens ward the rooms, the Floor Wardens ward the floors, the Adjutants bustle about, trying to look busy, and the Camp Captain keeps in touch with the Lagerführer, going to see him in his office every Friday morning with hard-luck stories gleaned from the rabble—that is to say, me and the rest of the boys. If, for instance, the coffee is cold two days in succession, the proletariat tells the Camp Captain, who tells the Lagerführer, who tells the Kommandant.

There is also another inner camp official whom I forgot to mention—the Sonderführer. I suppose the best way to describe him is to say that he is the führer who sonders.

The great advantage of a real internment camp, like Tost, is that the internee is left to himself all through the day. I was speaking last week of the extra parades at Huy. In all my forty-two weeks at Tost, we had only three extra parades. The authorities seemed to take the view that all they wanted to know was that we were all present in the morning and also at night, so we were counted at seven-thirty a.m. and again an hour before lights-out. Except for that, we were left to ourselves.

Nor was there anything excessive in the way of discipline and formalities. We were expected to salute officers, when we met them—which we seldom did—and there was a camp order that ran "When internees are standing in groups, the first to see an officer must shout '*Achtung*' "—a pleasant variant on the old game of Beaver. "Whereat," the order continues, "all face officer at attention, with hands on seam of trousers"—the internees' trousers, of course— "and look at him, assuming an erect bearing." The only catch about this was that it gave too much scope to our humorists. A man can have a lot of quiet fun by shouting "*Achtung*" and watching his friends reach for the seams of their trousers and assume an erect bearing, when there is not an officer within miles.

One great improvement at Tost, from my viewpoint, was that men of fifty and over were not liable for fatigues—in other words, the dirty work. At Liège and Huy, there had been no age limit. We had all pitched in together, reverend elders and beardless boys alike—cleaning out latrines with one hand and peeling potatoes with the other, so to speak. At Tost, the old dodderers like myself lived the life of Riley. For us, the arduous side of life was limited to making one's bed, brushing the floor under and around it, and washing one's linen. Repairs to clothes and shoes were done in the tailor's and cobbler's shops.

Where there was man's work to be done, like hauling coal or shovelling snow, we just sat and looked on, swapping reminiscences of the Victorian Age, while our juniors snapped into it. I don't know anything that so braces one up on a cold winter morning, with an Upper Silesian blizzard doing its stuff, as to light one's pipe and look out of the window and watch a gang of younger men shovelling snow. It makes you realize what the men meant who said that Age has its pleasures as well as Youth.

There were certain fatigues which were warmly competed for, like acting as a server or a carrier for meals and working in the cookhouse. For these, you got double rations. But the only reward of the ordinary fatigue, like hauling coal, was the joy of labor. I suppose a really altruistic young man would have been all pepped up by the thought, after he had put in an hour or two hauling coal, that he had been promoting the happiness of the greatest number, but I never heard one of our toilers talk along these lines. It was more usual to hear them say that, next time their turn came along, they were ruddy well going to sprain an ankle and report sick.

One thing that made Tost so great an improvement on our other camps was the presence there of the internees from Holland. A good many of them were language teachers, lecturers and musicians, and we had a great organiser in Professor Doyle-Davidson of Breda University. This meant that we were no longer restricted for intellectual entertainment to standing about in groups or playing that old Army game known alternatively as "House" and "Ousey-Ousey," where you pay ten pfennigs for a paper with numbers on it and the banker draws numbers out of a hat and the first man to fill up his papers scoops the pool.

Lectures and concerts were arranged, and we also had three revues and a straight comedy—which would have been a bigger success even than it was, but for the fact of our leading lady getting two days' cells right in the middle of the run.

It was also possible for internees to learn French, German, Italian, Spanish, first-aid and shorthand, and also to get a thorough grounding in French and English literature. In fact, we were not so much internees as a student body. Towards the end of my stay, we had our own paper—a bright little sheet called *The Tost Times,* published twice a month.

It is a curious experience, being completely shut off from the outer world, as one is in an internment camp. One lives on potatoes and rumours. One of my friends used to keep a note-book, in which he would jot down all the rumours that spread through the corridors, and they made curious reading. To military prisoners, I believe, rumours are known for some reason as "Blue Pigeons." We used to call them bedtime stories. They never turned out true, but a rumour a day kept depression away, so they served their purpose. Certainly, whether owing to bedtime stories or simply the feeling that, if one was in, one was in and it was no use making heavy weather about it, the morale of the men at Tost was wonderful. I never met a more cheerful crowd, and I loved them like brothers.

With this talk, I bring to an end the story of my adventures as British Civilian Prisoner Number 796, and before concluding I should like once more to thank all the kind people in America who wrote me letters while I was in camp. Nobody who has not been in a prison camp can realize what letters, especially letters like those I received, mean to an internee.

Appendix D

Wodehouse's first broadcast from Germany, as published in *Encounter*

If anyone listening to me seems to detect in my remarks a slight goofiness, the matter, as Bertie Wooster would say, is susceptible of a ready explanation. I have just emerged from a forty-nine weeks' sojourn in a German prison camp for civil internees, what is technically known as an Ilag, and the old bean is not the bean it was.

An Ilag, by the way, must not be confused with an Oflag or a Stalag. An Oflag is where captured officers go. Stalags are reserved for N.C.O.'s and privates. The civil internee gets the Ilag. But whether you call the Lag an Off, a Sta or an I, it makes no difference. Slice it where you like, it is still a German prison camp.

Young men starting out in life have often asked me, "How can I become an internee?" Well, there are several ways. You can be a grocer at Douai or a farm labourer at Ambricourt or a coal miner at Lille. You can be one of the crew of a liner which has been sunk by enemy destroyers. You can be a War Graves gardener in the War Cemeteries of France. Or, like me, you can settle down in a villa at Le Touquet and get stuck there till the place is occupied. That is as simple a method as any. You buy the villa, and the Germans do the rest.

One's reactions on finding oneself suddenly surrounded by the armed strength of a hostile power are rather interesting. The first time you see a German soldier in your garden, your impulse is to jump ten feet straight up into the air, and you do so. But this feeling of embarrassment soon passes. A week later you find you are only jumping five feet. And in the end familiarity so breeds indifference that you are able to sustain without a tremor the spectacle of men in steel helmets riding round your lawn on bicycles and even the discovery that two or three of them have dropped in and are taking a bath in your bathroom. The motto of the German army in occupied territory is "What's yours is mine," and any nonsense about an Englishman's home being his castle is soon dispelled.

347

From the moment when the first German soldier appeared in Le Touquet, I had devoted considerable thought to the subject of internment. In the early days of the occupation it had seemed like Today's Safety Bet. Then, as the weeks went by and nothing happened, optimism began to steal back, for it seemed so obvious that if the German head men had any intention of cracking down, they would have done it long before this. And then, one lovely Sunday morning, the morning of June 21st, I went down to the Kommandatur in Paris Plage to report as usual, and as I reached it I saw one of our little company coming along. And instantly the old stomach did a double buck-and-wing and the heart started beating like a trap drum.

He was carrying a suitcase.

Well, there might, I suppose, have been a dozen reasons for a British resident of Paris Plage carrying a suitcase, but I was able to think of only one. What made the spectacle so immediately sinister was that this man ought not to have been there at all. For some reason which I cannot recall, I think because he was working on a job somewhere, he had been allowed to report an hour earlier than the rest of us and until today had not been present at our gatherings. It struck me instantly, as it would have struck Hercule Poirot, that he must have rolled up at eleven, been informed that the internment order had gone out and been sent home to pack his things and return to the tryst.

Algy, of Algy's Bar, came up and found me gulping.

"Lovely morning," said Algy. "The lark's on the wing, the snail's on the thorn, God's in His Heaven, all's right with the world, don't you think?"

"No, Algy," I replied hollowly, "I do not. Look at Harold."

"Coo! He's got a suitcase!"

"He's got a suitcase," I said. "I fear the worst."

A few moments later my apprehensions were fulfilled. Entering the Kommandatur, I found it in a state of bustle and excitement. I said, *"Es ist schönes Wetter,"* once or twice, trying to make the party go, but nobody took any notice. And presently the interpreter stepped forward and announced that the curse had come upon us and that we were for it.

It was a pretty nasty shock, even though I had been expecting it, and it is not too much to say that for an instant I shook from base to apex like a jelly in an earthquake. My emotions, I suppose, were very much those of the man in the dock when the Judge, reaching for the black cap, begins, "Well, prisoner at the bar, it's been nice knowing you. . . ." The room swam before my eyes. I seemed to be surrounded by German soldiers, all doing the shimmy.

It was the horrible finality of the thing which was so unnerving. The situation which had arisen was so obviously one that could not be handled by means of a telegram of regret at the last moment.

It might have consoled me a little had I been aware that though Fate had dealt me a shrewd buffet I was a good deal luckier than other victims of the drag-net. Why it should have been so I have never been able to understand, but an unusual leniency was shown to the British citizens of Paris Plage, who were picked up a week later than those in other spots along the coast. In Boulogne, for instance, the British residents had been living for nine days in the Petit Vitesse railway station, about the last place in the world, I gathered from their accounts when I met them, where one would wish to live for even nine hours.

We, for some reason, were allowed to go home and put a few things together. And as my home was three kilometres away and an early start desired, I was actually sent there in a car.

It took a little of the edge off the uplifted mood caused by this luxury to discover on arriving that the soldier who was escorting me expected me to make it snappy. My idea had been to have a cold shower and a change and then light a pipe and sit down and muse for a while, deciding in a calm and unhurried spirit what to take and what could be left behind. His seemed to be that five minutes was ample.

Eventually we compromised on ten.

I would like my biographers to make careful note of the fact that the very first thought that occurred to me was that here was my big chance to buckle down and read the Complete Works of William Shakespeare. Reading the Complete Works of William Shakespeare was a thing I had been meaning to do any time these last forty years, and about three years previously I had bought the Oxford edition for that purpose. But you know how it is. Just as you have got *Hamlet* and *Macbeth* under your belt, and are preparing to read the stuffing out of *Henry the Sixth, Parts One, Two, and Three*, something of Agatha Christie's catches your eye and you weaken.

I did not know what internment implied—it might be for years, or it might be a mere matter of weeks—but the whole situation seemed to point to the Complete Works of William Shakespeare, so in they went.

I am happy to say that I am now crammed with Shakespeare to the brim, so whatever else internment has done for me, I am, at any rate, that much ahead of the game.

I wonder what my listeners would have packed in my place, always remembering that there was an excitable German soldier with a bayonet behind me all the time, confusing my thought processes by shouting *"Schnell!"* It is extraordinary how that sort of thing puts you off. One of my fellow internees told me that in similar circumstances all he could think of to put in his valise was a sponge and a Latin Grammar.

I did better than that. I put in tobacco, pencils, scribbling pads, pipes, a pair of shoes, a razor, some soap, some drawers, a sweater, a couple of cardigans, six pairs of socks, Tennyson's poems, half a pound of tea, and, of course, the Complete Works of William Shakespeare. My wife donated a cold mutton chop and a slab of chocolate. She wanted to add a pound of butter, but I rejected this. There are practically no limits to what a pound of butter can do in warm weather in a small suitcase.

In the end, the only thing of importance I left behind was my passport, which was the thing I ought to have packed first. The internee is always being told to show his passport, and if he has not got one, the authorities tend to look squiggle-eyed. I had never really appreciated what class distinctions can be till I became an internee without a passport, thereby achieving a social position somewhere in between a wharf rat and the man the police have detained for questioning in connection with the smash-and-grab raid.

Having closed the suitcase and grabbed a raincoat and said goodbye to my wife, I was driven back to the Kommandatur, where, of course, I found that I could have taken an hour and a half over my packing and still been in time to be Queen of the May. It was not till nearly two o'clock that together with the rest of the gang, numbering twelve in all, I drove off in a motor omnibus for an unknown destination.

That is one of the drawbacks to travelling when you are an internee. Your destination always is unknown. A little more of the spirit of confidence and a frank pooling of information would do much to brighten the internee's lot. It is unsettling when you start out not to have the slightest idea whether you are going half-way across Europe or just to the next town.

Actually, we were headed for Loos, a suburb of Lille, a distance of about seventy miles. What with stopping at various points along the road to pick up other foundation members, the journey took seven hours.

An internee's enjoyment of the process of being taken for a ride depends very largely on the mental attitude of the sergeant in charge. Ours fortunately turned out to be in holiday mood. He sang a good deal, gave us cigarettes and let us get off and buy red wine at all stops, infusing into the expedition something of the pleasant atmosphere of a school treat.

One thing which helped to keep the pecker up during the journey was the fact that we all knew each other pretty intimately. Three of us were from the golf club: Arthur Grant, the pro, Jeff, the starter, and Max, the caddy-master. Algy of Algy's Bar in the rue St. Jean was there, and Alfred of Alfred's Bar in the rue de Paris. So were ex–Regimental Sergeant-Major Moore, and a couple of supplementary Moores, and the rest, like Jock Monaghan, the bank manager, and Charlie Webb and Bill Illidge, who ran garages, were all well-known Paris Plage figures.

So, what with the jolly society and the red wine, we were all in much more buoyant mood than might have been expected. But it would be exaggerating to say that we were absolutely rollicking. As the evening shadows began to fall and the effects of the red wine began to wear off, we gradually became conscious of a certain sinking feeling. It was borne in on us that we were very far from our snug homes and getting farther all the time, and we were not at all sure that we liked the shape of things to come.

What exactly was the shape of things to come nobody seemed to know. This was the first time we had been interned, and we had no data. By and large, there was a good deal of speculation on the point.

Algy, the human sunbeam, refused to be downhearted. He pictured a bright and attractive future. We should, he said, be housed in villas somewhere. . . .

Villas, Algy?

That's right. Villas.

With honeysuckle climbing over the porch?

Well, he was not quite sure about that. There might or might not be honeysuckle. It all depended. But they would put us in villas and we would be asked to give our parole, and after that we would be allowed to saunter as we pleased about the countryside. We might even get a bit of fishing.

The picture he drew cheered us up enormously, for a time. We felt that villas would be fine. We looked forward to the fishing. Those of us who were not fond of fishing said they would be quite all right just pottering about in the sunshine.

The reaction set in when we suddenly realised, after expanding like watered flowers, that Algy didn't know a thing about it and was almost certainly talking through the back of his neck. Why villas, we began to ask. If the Germans wanted to see us living in villas, why would they go to all the trouble of removing us from the villas we were in, and putting us in a lot of other villas?

After that we definitely sagged. Uneasiness took the place of optimism. And our spirits hit a new low when, having passed through Lille, we turned up a side lane and came to a halt outside a forbidding-looking building which was only too evidently the local hoose-gow or calaboose.

A man in the uniform of the French provincial police flung wide the gate, and we rolled through.

Appendix E

Works About P. G. Wodehouse*

BIBLIOGRAPHIES

Jasen, David A. *A Bibliography and Reader's Guide to the First Editions of P. G. Wodehouse.* Hamden, Conn: Archon Books, 1970.

Whitt, J. F. *The Strand Magazine, 1891–1950: A Selective Checklist Listing All Material Relating to Arthur Conan Doyle, All Stories by P. G. Wodehouse, and a Selection of Other Contributions.* London: J. F. Whitt, 1979.

FULL-LENGTH STUDIES

Cazalet-Keir, Thelma, ed. *Homage to P. G. Wodehouse.* London: Barrie and Jenkins, 1973.

Connolly, Joseph. *P. G. Wodehouse: An Illustrated Biography with Complete Bibliography and Collector's Guide.* London: Orbis, 1979.

Edwards, Owen Dudley. *P. G. Wodehouse: A Critical and Historical Essay.* London: Brian and O'Keefe, 1977.

French, R. B. D. *P. G. Wodehouse.* Edinburgh: Oliver and Boyd, 1966.

Green, Benny. *P. G. Wodehouse: A Literary Biography.* London: Pavillion Books, 1981.

Hall, Robert A., Jr. *The Comic Style of P. G. Wodehouse.* Hamden, Conn: Archon Books, 1974.

Jaggard, Geoffrey. *Blandings the Blest and the Blue Blood: A Companion to the Blandings Castle Saga of P. G. Wodehouse.* London: Macdonald, 1967.

Jasen, David A. *P. G. Wodehouse: A Portrait of a Master.* New York: Mason and Lipscomb, 1974. London: Garnstone Press, 1975.

*With grateful acknowledgements to the Pierpont Morgan Library P. G. Wodehouse Centenary Exhibition Catalogue.

Jasen, David A. *The Theatre of P. G. Wodehouse.* London: Batsford, 1979.

Morris, J. C. *Thank You, Wodehouse.* London: Weidenfeld & Nicolson, 1981.

Sproat, Iain, *Wodehouse at War.* London: Milner, 1981.

Usborne, Richard. *Dr. Sir Pelham Wodehouse—Old Boy: The Text of an Address Given by Richard Usborne at the Opening of the P. G. Wodehouse Corner in the Library of Dulwich College, 15 October 1977.* London: Heineman, 1978.

Usborne, Richard. *A Wodehouse Companion.* London: Elm Tree, 1981.

Usborne, Richard. *Wodehouse at Work to the End.* London: Barrie & Jenkins, 1976.

Voorhees, Richard J. *P. G. Wodehouse.* New York: Twayne Publishers, 1966.

Wind, Herbert Warren. *The World of P. G. Wodehouse.* New York: Praeger, 1972; London: Hutchinson, 1981.

CHAPTERS DEVOTED TO WODEHOUSE

Clarke, Gerald. "P. G. Wodehouse" in *Writers at Work: The Paris Review Interviews.* New York: Viking, 1981; London: Penguin, 1981.

Flannery, Harry W. *Assignment to Berlin.* London: Michael Joseph, 1942.

Hamilton, Cosmo. "P. G. Wodehouse: A Mere Humourous Person" in *People Worth Talking About.* London: Hutchinson, 1934.

Kingsmill, Hugh. "P. G. Wodehouse" in *The Progress of a Biographer.* London: Methuen, 1949.

Lancaster, Osbert. "Great Houses of Fiction Revisited: Blandings Castle" in *Scene Changes.* London: John Murray, 1978.

Medcalf, Stephen. "The Innocence of P. G. Wodehouse" in *The Modern English Novel: The Reader, the Writer and the Work.* Edited by Gabriel Josipovici. New York: Barnes & Noble, 1976.

Mikes, George. "P. G. Wodehouse" in *Eight Humorists.* London: Allan Wingate, 1954.

Muggeridge, Malcolm. *Tread Softly for You Tread on My Jokes.* London: Collins, 1966.

Nicholls, Beverley. "P. G. Wodehouse or a Few 'Plums' " in *Are They the Same at Home?* London: Jonathan Cape, 1927.

Sheed, Wilfrid. "P. G. Wodehouse: Leave It to Psmith" in *The Good Word and Other Words.* New York: Dutton, 1978; London: Sidgewick & Jackson, 1979.

Swinnerton, Frank. "Some Later Novelists: David Garnet, P. G. Wodehouse,

J. B. Priestley, A. P. Herbert" in *The Georgian Literary Scene*. London: Hutchinson, 1935.

Thompson, Anthony Hugh. "The P. G. Wodehouse Affair" in *Censorship in Public Libraries in the United Kingdom During the Twentieth Century*. Epping, Essex: Bowker, 1975.

Notes

PREFACE

1. Charles Graves, *And the Greeks* (London: Geoffrey Bles, 1930).
2. Herbert Warren Wind, *The New Yorker*, 15 May 1971.
3. Alistair Cooke, *The Guardian*, 13 October 1961.

INTRODUCTION

1. Bernard Levin, *The Times*, 18 February 1975.
2. Evelyn Waugh, *The Sunday Times Magazine*, 16 July 1961.
3. John Hayward, *The Saturday Book* (London: Hutchinson, 1941), pp. 372–89.
4. Alistair Cooke, *The Guardian*, 13 October 1961.
5. Levin, *op. cit.*
6. Frances Donaldson, *Evelyn Waugh: Portrait of a Country Neighbor* (London: Weidenfeld & Nicolson, 1967), p. 73.
7. P. G. Wodehouse, *Peforming Flea*, introduction and additional notes by William Townend (London: Herbert Jenkins, 1953), p. 26.
8. *Ibid.*, p. 28.
9. *Ibid.*, p. 87.
10. Ernest Newman, *From the World of Music* (London: Calder, 1956), p. 182.
11. Wodehouse, *op. cit.*, p. 131.
12. *Ibid.*, p. 21.
13. David Jasen, *P. G. Wodehouse: A Portrait of a Master* (London: Garnstone Press, 1975), p. 3.
14. Alistair Cooke, *The Guardian*, 13 October 1961.
15. Waugh, *op. cit.*
16. Rebecca West, *Black Lamb and Grey Falcon*, vol. 1 (London: Macmillan, 1942), p. 3.
17. P. G. Wodehouse, *Sunset at Blandings*, notes and appendices by Richard Usborne (London: Chatto & Windus, 1977), p. 112.

18. Evelyn Waugh, *The Diaries of Evelyn Waugh* (London: Weidenfeld & Nicolson, 1976), p. 663.

19. Anthony Powell, *Daily Telegraph,* 20 October 1961.

20. Wodehouse, *Sunset at Blandings, op. cit.,* p. 24.

21. Thelma Cazalet-Keir, ed., *Homage to P. G. Wodehouse* (London: Barrie & Jenkins, 1973), p. 82.

22. Levin, *op. cit.*

23. David Cecil in Cazalet-Keir, *op. cit.,* p. 38.

24. Philip Toynbee, *The Observer,* 29 October 1972.

25. Waugh, *The Sunday Times Magazine, op. cit.*

26. Wodehouse, *Performing Flea, op. cit.,* pp. 17, 64, 15.

27. Anthony Powell, *Messengers of Day* (London: Heinemann, 1978), p. 87.

28. P. G. Wodehouse, "Berlin Broadcasts," *Encounter,* October 1954, p. 19.

29. P. G. Wodehouse, *Over Seventy: An Autobiography with Digressions* (London: Herbert Jenkins, 1957), p. 39.

30. Owen Dudley Edwards, *P. G. Wodehouse* (London: Martin Brian & O'Keeffe, 1977), p. 7.

31. Anthony Hope, "The Dolly Dialogues," *Westminster Gazette* (1894), pp. 64–5.

32. Leonard Woolf, "Hunting the Highbrow," in *The Hogarth Essays* (London: Hogarth Press, 1927), p. 10.

33. *Ibid.,* p. 19.

34. Unpublished letter, 9 March 1959.

35. Woolf, *op. cit.,* p. 29.

36. P. G. Wodehouse, "Pots o' Money," *Strand,* c. 1911.

37. Levin, *op. cit.*

38. Ferdinand Mount, *Spectator,* 15 October 1977.

CHAPTER I

1. Anthony Powell, *Daily Telegraph,* 20 October 1961.

2. David Jasen, *P. G. Wodehouse: A Portrait of a Master* (London: Garnstone Press, 1975), p. 2.

3. Paul Henry Mussen *et al., Readings in Child Development and Personality,* quoted in Jonathan Gathorne-Hardy, *The Rise and Fall of the British Nanny* (Kent: Hodder & Stoughton, 1972), pp. 227–8.

4. Jasen, *op. cit.,* p. 9.

5. *Ibid.,* pp. 6–7.

6. *Ibid.,* p. 7.

7. *Ibid.,* p. 11.

8. *Ibid.,* p. 15.

9. *Ibid.,* p. 18.

10. *Ibid.*

11. *Ibid.*, p. 17.

12. Richard Usborne, *Wodehouse at Work to the End* (London: Barrie & Jenkins, 1976), p. 52.

13. Jasen, *op. cit.*, p. 18.

14. Usborne, *op. cit.*, pp. 52–3.

15. Gathorne-Hardy, *op. cit.*, p. 326.

CHAPTER 2

1. P. G. Wodehouse, *Over Seventy: An Autobiography with Digressions* (London: Herbert Jenkins, 1957), p. 27.

2. David Jasen, *P. G. Wodehouse: A Portrait of a Master* (London: Garnstone Press, 1975), p. 27.

3. P. G. Wodehouse and Herbert Westbrook, *The By the Way Book* (Globe Publishing Co., 1908), p. 32.

4. Jasen, *op. cit.*, p. 42.

5. *Punch*, 8 October 1902.

6. Angus Wilson, *The Strange Ride of Rudyard Kipling* (London: Secker & Warburg, 1977), p. 48.

7. *Ibid.*, p. 49.

CHAPTER 3

1. Stephen King-Hall, *My Naval Life* (London: Faber & Faber, 1952), p. 25.

2. Letter to the author from Mrs. Alistair MacLeod.

3. Evelyn Waugh, *The Sunday Times Magazine*, 16 July 1961.

4. P. G. Wodehouse and Herbert Westbrook, *Not George Washington* (London: Cassell & Co., 1907), p. 12.

5. *Ibid.*, p. 13.

6. *Ibid.*, p. 18.

7. P. G. Wodehouse, *Over Seventy: An Autobiography with Digressions* (London: Herbert Jenkins, 1957), p. 29.

8. R. Hammer, *Playboy's Illustrated History of Organized Crime* (Chicago: Playboy Press, 1975), pp. 16–17.

9. David Jasen, *P. G. Wodehouse: A Portrait of a Master* (London: Garnstone Press, 1975), p. 36.

CHAPTER 4

1. Ellaline Terris, *Just a Little Bit of String* (London: Hutchinson, 1955), p. 181.

2. Quoted in David Jasen, *P. G. Wodehouse: A Portrait of a Master* (London: Garnstone Press, 1975), p. 145.

CHAPTER 5

1. Richard Usborne, *Wodehouse at Work to the End* (London: Barrie & Jenkins, 1976), p. 162.

CHAPTER 6

1. P. G. Wodehouse, *Performing Flea*, introduction and additional notes by William Townend (London: Herbert Jenkins, 1953), p. 92.
2. *Ibid.*, pp. 156–7.
3. Evelyn Waugh, *The Sunday Times Magazine*, 16 July 1961.
4. R. B. D. French, *P. G. Wodehouse* (Edinburgh: Oliver & Boyd, 1966), p. 6.
5. David Jasen, *P. G. Wodehouse: A Portrait of a Master* (London: Garnstone Press, 1975), p. 56.
6. P. G. Wodehouse, *The World of Jeeves* (London: Herbert Jenkins, 1967), p. viii.
7. Letter to the author from Richard Usborne.
8. Richard Usborne, *Wodehouse at Work to the End* (London: Barrie & Jenkins, 1976), pp. 184–6.
9. Gerald Bordman, *American Musical Theatre: A Chronicle* (New York: Oxford University Press, 1978), pp. 318–20.
10. Quoted in Jasen, *op. cit.*, p. 75.
11. *Ibid.*, pp. 75–6.
12. *Ibid.*, pp. 68–9.

CHAPTER 7

1. Denis Mackail, *Life with Topsy* (London: Heinemann, 1942), p. 40.
2. *Ibid.*, p. 41.
3. *Ibid.*, pp. 53–4.
4. David Jasen, *P. G. Wodehouse: A Portrait of a Master* (London: Garnstone Press, 1975), p. 107.
5. P. G. Wodehouse, *Performing Flea*, introduction and additional notes by William Townend (London: Herbert Jenkins, 1953), p. 34.
6. *Ibid.*, p. 46.

CHAPTER 8

1. P. G. Wodehouse, *Performing Flea*, introduction and additional notes by William Townend (London: Herbert Jenkins, 1953), p. 53.
2. *Ibid.*, pp. 54–5.
3. *Ibid.*, p. 57.

CHAPTER 9

1. P. G. Wodehouse, *Over Seventy: An Autobiography with Digressions* (London: Herbert Jenkins, 1957), p. 107.

2. Paul R. Reynolds, *The Middle Man: The Adventures of a Literary Agent* (New York: Morrow, 1972), p. 108.

3. Alexander Woollcott, *While Rome Burns* (Arthur Barker, 1934), p. 91.

4. P. G. Wodehouse, *Performing Flea*, introduction and additional notes by William Townend (London: Herbert Jenkins, 1953), pp. 90–1.

5. David Jasen, *P. G. Wodehouse: A Portrait of a Master* (London: Garnstone Press, 1975), p. 153.

6. *Ibid.*, p. 155.

7. Wodehouse, *Performing Flea, op. cit.*, p. 96.

8. *Ibid.*, p. 99.

CHAPTER 11

1. Unpublished letter to William Townend.

2. P. G. Wodehouse, "Now That I've Turned Both Cheeks," unpublished manuscript.

3. Cussen Report, pp. 6–7.

4. *Ibid.*, p. 7.

5. Wodehouse, *op. cit.*

6. *Ibid.*

7. *Ibid.*

8. Cussen Report, pp. 8–9.

9. *Ibid.*, p. 9.

10. *Ibid.*

11. *Ibid.*, p. 10.

12. Harry W. Flannery, *Assignment to Berlin* (London: Michael Joseph, 1942), p. 118.

13. Wodehouse, *op. cit.*

14. Flannery, *op. cit.*, pp. 245–9.

15. Cussen Report, pp. 10–11.

16. George Orwell, "In Defence of P. G. Wodehouse," in *Critical Essays* (London: Secker & Warburg, 1946), p. 159.

17. Cussen Report, p. 10.

18. Richard Usborne, unpublished account.

CHAPTER 12

1. Compton Mackenzie, *My Life and Times, Octave 8, 1939–1946* (London: Chatto & Windus, 1969), p. 129. The version that appears in *Homage to Wodehouse* is different, but not significantly.

2. *Hansard Parliamentary Debates*, 5th series, vol. 373, 8–9 July 1941.

3. Charles Graves, *Off the Record* (London: Hutchinson, 1942), p. 193.

4. *Ibid.*, pp. 198–9.

5. *Hansard Parliamentary Debates*, 5th series, vol. 373, 16 July 1941.

CHAPTER 13

1. From the von Bodenhausen Papers, now in the collection of James Heineman.

2. Cussen Report, pp. 11–12.

3. Malcolm Muggeridge, *Chronicles of Wasted Time*, vol. 2 (London: Collins, 1973), p. 231.

CHAPTER 14

1. Malcolm Muggeridge, *Chronicles of Wasted Time*, vol. 2 (London: Collins, 1973), pp. 227–8.

2. *Ibid.*, p. 231.

3. Thelma Cazalet-Keir, ed., *Homage to P. G. Wodehouse* (London: Barrie & Jenkins, 1973), p. 96.

4. Muggeridge, *op. cit.*, p. 234.

5. *Ibid.*, p. 233.

6. *Hansard Parliamentary Debates*, 5th series, vol. 406, 6 December 1944.

7. *Ibid.*, 15 December 1944.

8. *Ibid.*, 21 December 1944.

9. P. G. Wodehouse, "Now That I've Turned Both Cheeks," unpublished manuscript.

CHAPTER 15

1. *Hansard Parliamentary Debates*, 5th series, 13 March 1946.

CHAPTER 16

1. David Jasen, *P. G. Wodehouse: A Portrait of a Master* (London: Garnstone Press, 1975), p. 205.

2. P. G. Wodehouse, *Performing Flea*, introduction and additional notes by William Townend (London: Herbert Jenkins, 1953), p. 217.

3. *Ibid.*

CHAPTER 18

1. P. G. Wodehouse, *Author! Author!* (New York: Simon & Schuster, 1962), p. 13.

CHAPTER 19

1. *Uncle Fred in the Springtime,* Chapter 10.
2. *The Heart of a Goof,* Dedication.
3. *Ibid.,* Chapter 1.
4. P. G. Wodehouse, *Over Seventy: An Autobiography with Digressions* (London: Herbert Jenkins, 1957), Chapter 5.

Index

A Note on the Type

The text of this book was set via computer-driven cathode-ray tube in a digitized version of Stempel Garamond. Produced in 1925 by the Stempel type foundry in Frankfurt, Germany, it is based on a typeface first cut by Claude Garamond (c. 1480–1561). The noted typographic scholar Beatrice Warde has determined that the typeface upon which Stempel based its design was one of the last types actually cut by Garamond.

All of Garamond's roman types follow the classical Renaissance style begun by Aldus Manutius, but they reflect Garamond's own incomparable skill as an engraver. Garamond gave his letters an elegance and beauty of form that led to their widespread use in his own day and has ensured their continued popularity.

Composed by Centennial Graphics, Inc., Ephrata, Pennsylvania.

Printed and bound by R. R. Donnelly & Sons, Co.
Harrisonburg, Virginia.